Miranda Revisited

THE CASE OF *DICKERSON* V. *U.S.* AND SUSPECT RIGHTS ADVISEMENTS IN THE UNITED STATES

FRANK SCHMALLEGER, PH.D.

Prentice
Hall

Upper Saddle River, New Jersey 07458

Publisher: Dave Garza
Senior Acquisitions Editor: Kim Davies
Managing Editor: Mary Carnis
Production Editor: Lori Dalberg
Interior Design and Formatting: Carlisle Communications
Production Liaison: Adele M. Kupchik
Director of Manufacturing and Production: Bruce Johnson
Manufacturing Buyer: Ed O'Dougherty
Creative Director: Marianne Frasco
Cover Design Coordinator: Miguel Ortiz
Editorial Assistant: Liberty Price
**Director of Marketing Communication
    and New Media:** Frank Mortimer, Jr.
Marketing Manager: Chris Ruel
Marketing Assistant: Joe Toohey
Marketing Coordinator: Adam Kloza
Printer/Binder: Banta, Harrisonburg, VA
Cover Design: Joe Sengotta
Cover Printer: Banta, Harrisonburg, VA

Prentice-Hall International (UK) Limited, *London*
Prentice-Hall of Australia Pty. Limited, *Sydney*
Prentice-Hall Canada Inc., *Toronto*
Prentice-Hall Hispanoamericana, S.A., *Mexico*
Prentice-Hall of India Private Limited, *New Delhi*
Prentice-Hall of Japan, Inc., *Tokyo*
Prentice-Hall Singapore Pte. Ltd.
Editora Prentice-Hall do Brasil, Ltda., *Rio de Janeiro*

10 9 8 7 6 5 4 3 2 1
ISBN 0-13-091103-8

This book is dedicated to American police officers. As Mr. Justice Clark wrote in his 1966 dissenting *Miranda* opinion: "The police agencies – all the way from municipal and state forces to the federal bureaus – are responsible for law enforcement and public safety in this country. I am proud of their efforts. . ."

TABLE OF CONTENTS

ACKNOWLEDGMENTS

The author gratefully acknowledges Professor Paul G. Cassell of the University of Utah College of Law, and Carter G. Phillips, counsel for petitioner Charles Dickerson, for the time they spent helping me understand cogent legal principles and court opinions relevant to the materials found in this book. Thanks, also, to Lori Dalberg at Carlisle Publishers Services, and to Adele Kupchik, Kim Davies, Mary Carnis, Marianne Frasco, Frank Mortimer, and others at Prentice Hall who helped make this book a reality.

ABOUT THE AUTHOR

Frank Schmalleger, Ph.D., is Director of the Justice Research Association, a private consulting firm and "think-tank" focusing on issues of crime and justice. The Justice Research Association, which is based in Hilton Head Island, South Carolina, serves the needs of the nation's civil and criminal-justice planners and administrators through workshops, conferences, and grant-writing and program evaluation support. It can be reached on the Web at http://cjcentral.com/jra). Dr. Schmalleger is also founder and co-director of the Criminal Justice Distance Learning Consortium (http://cjcentral.com/cjdlc).

Dr. Schmalleger holds degrees from the University of Notre Dame and Ohio State University, having earned both a master's (1970) and doctorate in sociology (1974) from Ohio State University with a special emphasis in criminology. From 1976 to 1994 he taught criminal justice courses at The University of North Carolina at Pembroke. For the last 16 of those years he chaired the university's Department of Sociology, Social Work, and Criminal Justice. As an adjunct professor with Webster University in St. Louis, Missouri, Schmalleger helped develop the university's graduate program in security administration and loss prevention. He taught courses in that curriculum for more than a decade. Schmalleger has also taught in the New School for Social Research's on-line graduate program, helping to build the world's first electronic classrooms in support of distance learning through computer telecommunications. An avid web developer, Schmalleger is also the creator of a number of award winning World Wide Web sites, including some which support this textbook (http://www.prenhall.com/schmalleger; http://cjtoday.com; and http://talkjustice.com/cybrary.asp).

Frank Schmalleger is the author of numerous articles and many books, including the widely used *Criminal Justice Today* (Prentice Hall, 2001), *Corrections in the Twenty-First Century* (Glencoe/McGraw-Hill, 2001); *Criminology Today* (Prentice Hall, 1999); *Criminal Justice: A Brief Introduction* (Prentice Hall, 2001); *Criminal Law Today* (Prentice Hall, 1999); *Crime and the Justice System in America: An Encyclopedia* (Greenwood Publishing Group, 1997); *Trial of the Century: People of the State of California vs. Orenthal James Simpson* (Prentice Hall, 1996); *Computers in Criminal Justice* (Wyndham Hall Press, 1991); *Career Paths: A Guide to Jobs in Federal Law Enforcement* (Regents/Prentice Hall, 1994); *Criminal Justice Ethics* (Greenwood Press, 1991); *Finding Criminal Justice in the Library* (Wyndham Hall Press, 1991); *Ethics in Criminal Justice* (Wyndham Hall Press, 1990); *A History of Corrections* (Foundations Press of Notre Dame, 1983); and *The Social Basis of Criminal Justice* (University Press of America, 1981).

Schmalleger is also founding editor of the journal *The Justice Professional.* He served as editor for the Prentice Hall series *Criminal Justice in the Twenty-first Century* and as Imprint Advisor for Greenwood Publishing Group's criminal justice reference series.

NOTE TO READERS

Note to readers: As should be the case when reprinting legal papers, the documents in this book are true to their originals. Hence, typographical errors have *not* been corrected where they existed in the original.

SECTION
I

𝔍𝔫𝔱𝔯𝔬𝔡𝔲𝔠𝔱𝔦𝔬𝔫

In 1963, following reports that a young woman had been kidnapped and raped in the desert outside of Phoenix, Arizona, a suspect named Ernesto Miranda was arrested and immediately taken to the city's police station. Miranda was a 23-year-old ninth-grade dropout, and a drifter with a criminal record. Within a short time, the victim, an 18-year-old girl, identified Miranda as the perpetrator, and officers brought him into an interrogation room for questioning. At the end of two hours of questioning by two detectives Miranda confessed to the crimes, and signed a confession. At the top of the handwritten confession was a typed paragraph stating that the confession had been made voluntarily, without threats or promises of immunity, and with "full knowledge of my legal rights, understanding [that] any statement I make may be used against me."

Although Miranda was convicted of kidnapping and rape, the U.S. Supreme Court, led at the time by Chief Justice Earl Warren, overturned Miranda's conviction upon appeal. That 1966 case, which was decided by a narrow 5-4 majority, came to be known as *Miranda* v. *Arizona* (384 U.S. 436, 1966). The majority opinion held that "the defendant's confession was inadmissible because he was not in any way [informed] of his right to council nor was his privilege against self-incrimination effectively protected in any other manner." At the time, the ruling seemed strange to many since there was little reason, prior to the *Miranda* decision, to think that police officers were required to provide legal advice to criminal defendants in their custody.

Nonetheless, the *Miranda* ruling quickly became one of the most significant building blocks of our present-day system of criminal justice. Under *Miranda,* suspects who are subject to questioning must be told of their right to remain silent and of their right to an attorney, before questioning can begin.

Following the *Miranda* decision, many in the U.S. Congress thought that the Supreme Court had gone too far in helping criminal suspects avoid prosecution by placing the requirements for a rights advisement on police officers. Lawmakers feared that the *Miranda* decision would allow guilty parties to go free on "technicalities," and that those so freed might endanger the lives and well-being of innocent citizens.

In 1968, in direct response to the Court's *Miranda* ruling, Congress passed legislation (18 U.S.C. 3501) intended to allow the use of confessions obtained from suspects in criminal cases—even if the requirements of a *Miranda*-style rights advisement were not met—as long as those confessions were made voluntarily. The 1968 law, however, went unenforced, and remained largely unnoticed for three decades. Some believed that Congress did not have the authority to contravene *Miranda.* Moreover, presidential administrations—especially those of the 1990s—supported the spirit of the Court's 1966 *Miranda* ruling, neglecting to enforce the federal statute even when it might have allowed the in-court use of otherwise inadmissible confessions of criminal activity.

In April, 1999, however, in the case of *United States* v. *Dickerson* (166 F.3d 667, 4ᵗʰ Cir. 1999), the Fourth U.S. Circuit Court of Appeals ruled that the law passed by Congress in 1968 was valid, and that it should permit, at least in federal criminal cases, the in-court use of voluntary confessions taken in violation of *Miranda* requirements. This finding by the Fourth U.S. Circuit Court of Appeals was unacceptable to the Clinton Administration and to Attorney General Janet Reno who argued before the U.S. Supreme Court that it should be overturned.

The Justice Department urged the Court not to overrule it's 1966 *Miranda* decision, partially on the grounds that doing so would undermine the public's confidence in the American criminal justice system.

A more crucial issue, from the legal standpoint, however, was whether the 1968 federal law was constitutional. The Justice Department claimed that it was not, and said that *Miranda* protections are essentially enshrined within the Fifth Amendment to the U.S. Constitution. Therefore, it argued, they cannot be overruled by Congressional action. Moreover, said Justice Department briefs filed in the matter, *Miranda* rules must in fact be constitutionally based since the Supreme Court has repeatedly enforced them in cases arising in state courts—something that it can do only if state laws or state criminal procedures contravene the U.S. Constitution.

Not everyone, of course, agreed with the position taken by the Justice Department. A day after the Clinton administration filed its brief in support of *Miranda*, Senator Strom Thurmond of South Carolina denounced the action from the floor of the Senate saying that "the Justice Department has deliberately chosen to side with defense attorneys over prosecutors and law enforcement." "This is a serious error," said Thurmond. "The department should not make arguments in the courts on behalf of criminals."(1)

The Supreme Court's final decision on the issue came on June 26, 2000. In a 7-to-2 vote, the Court upheld *Miranda,* declaring that the 1966 case established a "constitutional rule." Moreover, said the Court, 18 U.S.C. 3501 was itself unconstitutional since it contravened guarantees inherent in the Bill of Rights. Although the majority opinion was not seen as a ringing endorsement of *Miranda,* Chief Justice William H. Rehnquist, the opinion's author, noted: "Whether or not we agree with *Miranda's* reasoning and its resulting rule...the principles of *stare decisis* weigh heavily against overruling it now."

In a stinging rebuttal, however, dissenting Justices Antonin Scalia and Clarence Thomas accused the Court's majority of playing intellectually dishonest "word games," and of misusing their authority by effectively creating an "extraconstitutional Constitution, binding on Congress and the states."

The dissenting opinion noted that even Justice Rehnquist, in a 1974 decision (*Michigan* v. *Tucker*) had said that the "procedural safeguards" adopted in *Miranda* "were not themselves rights protected by the Constitution..."

A footnote on Ernesto Miranda: Although Miranda's original conviction was overturned, he was retried on the same charges. His signed confession was not used in court since it had been ruled inadmissible. Still, he was convicted again—this time based on the testimony of a former girlfriend who testified that he had told her about the kidnapping and rape. Miranda was sent to prison, but was paroled in 1972. Two years later he was stabbed to death in a bar. No one has ever been charged with his murder.

ENDNOTE

1. See "Justice Department Urges Court Not to Overrule Miranda," *Criminal Justice Newsletter,* Volume 30, Number 12 (June 15, 1999), p. 2.

SECTION II

Supreme Court of the United States

MIRANDA V. ARIZONA

384 U.S. 436

CERTIORARI TO THE SUPREME COURT OF ARIZONA.
No. 759.
Argued February 28 - March 1, 1966.
Decided June 13, 1966. *

---

* Together with No. 760, *Vignera* v. *New York*, on certiorari to the Court of Appeals of New York and No. 761, *Westover* v. *United States*, on certiorari to the United States Court of Appeals for the Ninth Circuit, both argued February 28 - March 1, 1966; and No. 584, *California* v. *Stewart*, on certiorari to the Supreme Court of California, argued February 28 - March 2, 1966.

SYLLABUS

In each of these cases the defendant while in police custody was questioned by police officers, detectives, or a prosecuting attorney in a room in which he was cut off from the outside world. None of the defendants was given a full and effective warning of his rights at the outset of the interrogation process. In all four cases the questioning elicited oral admissions, and in three of them signed statements as well, which were admitted at their trials. All defendants were convicted and all convictions, except in No. 584, were affirmed on appeal.

Held:

    1. The prosecution may not use statements, whether exculpatory or inculpatory, stemming from questioning initiated by law enforcement officers after a person has been taken into custody or otherwise deprived of his freedom of action in any significant way, unless it demonstrates the use of procedural safeguards effective to secure the Fifth Amendment's privilege against self-incrimination. Pp. 444-491.

    (a) The atmosphere and environment of incommunicado interrogation as it exists today is inherently intimidating and works to undermine the privilege against self-incrimination. Unless adequate preventive measures are taken to dispel the compulsion inherent in custodial surroundings,

3

no statement obtained from the defendant can truly be the product of his free choice. Pp. 445-458.

(b) The privilege against self-incrimination, which has had a long and expansive historical development, is the essential mainstay of our adversary system and guarantees to the individual the "right to remain silent unless he chooses to speak in the unfettered exercise of his own will," during a period of custodial interrogation as well as in the courts or during the course of other official investigations. Pp. 458-465.

(c) The decision in *Escobedo* v. *Illinois*, 378 U.S. 478 , stressed the need for protective devices to make the process of police interrogation conform to the dictates of the privilege. Pp. 465-466.

(d) In the absence of other effective measures the following procedures to safeguard the Fifth Amendment privilege must be observed: The person in custody must, prior to interrogation, be clearly informed that he has the right to remain silent, and that anything he says will be used against him in court; he must be clearly informed that he has the right to consult with a lawyer and to have the lawyer with him during interrogation, and that, if he is indigent, a lawyer will be appointed to represent him. Pp. 467-473.

(e) If the individual indicates, prior to or during questioning, that he wishes to remain silent, the interrogation must cease; if he states that he wants an attorney, the questioning must cease until an attorney is present. Pp. 473-474.

(f) Where an interrogation is conducted without the presence of an attorney and a statement is taken, a heavy burden rests on the Government to demonstrate that the defendant knowingly and intelligently waived his right to counsel. P. 475.

(g) Where the individual answers some questions during in-custody interrogation he has not waived his privilege and may invoke his right to remain silent thereafter. Pp. 475-476.

(h) The warnings required and the waiver needed are, in the absence of a fully effective equivalent, prerequisites to the admissibility of any statement, inculpatory or exculpatory, made by a defendant. Pp. 476-477.

2. The limitations on the interrogation process required for the protection of the individual's constitutional rights should not cause an undue interference with a proper system of law enforcement, as demonstrated by the procedures of the FBI and the safeguards afforded in other jurisdictions. Pp. 479-491.

3. In each of these cases the statements were obtained under circumstances that did not meet constitutional standards for protection of the privilege against self-incrimination. Pp. 491-499.

98 Ariz. 18, 401 P.2d 721; 15 N. Y. 2d 970, 207 N. E. 2d 527; 16 N. Y. 2d 614, 209 N. E. 2d 110; 342 F.2d 684, reversed; 62 Cal. 2d 571, 400 P.2d 97, affirmed.

John J. Flynn argued the cause for petitioner in No. 759. With him on the brief was John P. Frank. Victor M. Earle III argued the cause and filed a brief for petitioner in No. 760. F. Conger Fawcett argued the cause and filed a brief for petitioner in No. 761. Gordon Ringer, Deputy Attorney General of California, argued the cause for petitioner in No. 584. With him on the briefs were Thomas C. Lynch, Attorney General, and William E. James, Assistant Attorney General.

Gary K. Nelson, Assistant Attorney General of Arizona, argued the cause for respondent in No. 759. With him on the brief was Darrell F. Smith, Attorney General. William I. Siegel argued the cause for respondent in No. 760. With him on the brief was Aaron E. Koota. Solicitor General Marshall argued the cause for the United States in No. 761. With him on the brief were Assistant Attorney General Vinson, Ralph S. Spritzer, Nathan Lewin, Beatrice Rosenberg and Ronald L. Gainer. William A. Norris, by appointment of the Court, 382 U.S. 952 , argued the cause and filed a brief for respondent in No. 584.

Telford Taylor, by special leave of Court, argued the cause for the State of New York, as amicus curiae, in all cases. With him on the brief were Louis J. Lefkowitz, Attorney General of New York, Samuel A. Hirshowitz, First Assistant Attorney General, and Barry Mahoney and George D. Zuckerman, Assistant Attorneys General, joined by the Attorneys General for their respective States and jurisdictions as follows: Richmond M. Flowers of Alabama, Darrell F. Smith of Arizona, Bruce Bennett of Arkansas, Duke W. Dunbar of Colorado, David P. Buckson of Delaware, Earl Faircloth of Florida, Arthur K. Bolton of Georgia, Allan G. Shepard of Idaho, William G. Clark of Illinois, Robert C. Londerholm of Kansas, Robert Matthews of Kentucky, Jack P. F. Gremillion of Louisiana, Richard J. Dubord of Maine, Thomas B. Finan of Maryland, Norman H. Anderson of Missouri, Forrest H. Anderson of Montana, Clarence A. H. Meyer of Nebraska, T. Wade Bruton of North Carolina, Helgi Johanneson of North Dakota, Robert Y. Thornton of Oregon, Walter E. Alessandroni of Pennsylvania, J. Joseph Nugent of Rhode Island, Daniel R. McLeod of South Carolina, Waggoner Carr of Texas, Robert Y. Button of Virginia, John J. O'Connell of Washington, C. Donald Robertson of West Virginia, John F. Raper of Wyoming, Rafael Hernandez Colon of Puerto Rico and Francisco Corneiro of the Virgin Islands.

Duane R. Nedrud, by special leave of Court, argued the cause for the National District Attorneys Association, as amicus curiae, urging affirmance in Nos. 759 and 760, and reversal in No. 584. With him on the brief was Marguerite D. Oberto.

Anthony G. Amsterdam, Paul J. Mishkin, Raymond L. Bradley, Peter Hearn and Melvin L. Wulf filed a brief for the American Civil Liberties Union, as amicus curiae, in all cases.

MR. CHIEF JUSTICE WARREN delivered the opinion of the Court.

The cases before us raise questions which go to the roots of our concepts of American criminal jurisprudence: the restraints society must observe consistent with the Federal Constitution in prosecuting individuals for crime. More specifically, we deal with the admissibility of statements obtained from an individual who is subjected to custodial police interrogation and the necessity for procedures which assure that the individual is accorded his privilege under the Fifth Amendment to the Constitution not to be compelled to incriminate himself.

We dealt with certain phases of this problem recently in *Escobedo* v. *Illinois,* 378 U.S. 478 (1964). There, as in the four cases before us, law enforcement officials took the defendant into custody and interrogated him in a police station for the purpose of obtaining a confession. The police did not effectively advise him of his right to remain silent or of his right to consult with his attorney. Rather, they confronted him with an alleged accomplice who accused him of having perpetrated a murder. When the defendant denied the accusation and said "I didn't shoot Manuel, you did it," they handcuffed him and took him to an interrogation room. There, while handcuffed and standing, he was questioned for four hours until he confessed. During this interrogation, the police denied his request to speak to his attorney, and they prevented his retained attorney, who had come to the police station, from consulting with him. At his trial, the State, over his objection, introduced the confession against him. We held that the statements thus made were constitutionally inadmissible.

This case has been the subject of judicial interpretation and spirited legal debate since it was decided two years ago. Both state and federal courts, in assessing its implications, have arrived at varying conclusions. [footnote 1] A wealth of scholarly

[1]Compare *United States* v. *Childress*, 347 F.2d 448 (C. A. 7th Cir. 1965), with *Collins* v. *Beto*, 348 F.2d 823 (C. A. 5th Cir. 1965). Compare *People* v. *Dorado*, 62 Cal. 2d 338, 398 P.2d 361, 42 Cal. Rptr. 169 (1964) with *People* v. *Hartgraves*, 31 Ill. 2d 375, 202 N. E. 2d 33 (1964).

material has been written tracing its ramifications and underpinnings. [footnote 2] Police and prosecutor have speculated on its range and desirability. [footnote 3] We granted certiorari in these cases, 382 U.S. 924, 925 , 937, in order further to explore some facets of the problems, thus exposed, of applying the privilege against self-incrimination to in-custody interrogation, and to give concrete constitutional guidelines for law enforcement agencies and courts to follow.

We start here, as we did in Escobedo, with the premise that our holding is not an innovation in our jurisprudence, but is an application of principles long recognized and applied in other settings. We have undertaken a thorough re-examination of the Escobedo decision and the principles it announced, and we reaffirm it. That case was but an explication of basic rights that are enshrined in our Constitution - that "No person . . . shall be compelled in any criminal case to be a witness against himself," and that "the accused shall . . . have the Assistance of Counsel" - rights which were put in jeopardy in that case through official overbearing. These precious rights were fixed in our Constitution only after centuries of persecution and struggle. And in the words of Chief Justice Marshall, they were secured "for ages to come, and . . . designed to approach immortality as nearly as human institutions can approach it," *Cohens* v. *Virginia*, 6 Wheat. 264, 387 (1821).

Over 70 years ago, our predecessors on this Court eloquently stated:

- "The maxim *nemo tenetur seipsum accusare* had its origin in a protest against the inquisitorial and manifestly unjust methods of interrogating accused persons, which [have] long obtained in the continental system, and, until the expulsion of the Stuarts from the British throne in 1688, and the erection of additional barriers for the protection of the people against the exercise of arbitrary power, [were] not uncommon even in England. While the admissions or confessions of the prisoner, when voluntarily and freely made, have always ranked high in the scale of incriminating evidence, if an accused person be asked to explain his apparent connection with a crime under investigation, the ease with which the questions put to him may assume an inquisitorial character, the temptation to press the witness unduly, to browbeat him if he be timid or reluctant, to push him into a corner, and to entrap him into fatal contradictions, which is so painfully evident in many of the earlier state trials, notably in those of Sir Nicholas Throckmorton, and Udal, the Puritan

[2]See, e. g., Enker & Elsen, Counsel for the Suspect: *Massiah* v. *United States* and *Escobedo* v. *Illinois,* 49 Minn. L. Rev. 47 (1964); Herman, The Supreme Court and Restrictions on Police Interrogation, 25 Ohio St. L. J. 449 (1964); Kamisar, Equal Justice in the Gatehouses and Mansions of American Criminal Procedure, in Criminal Justice in Our Time 1 (1965); *Dowling, Escobedo* and Beyond: The Need for a Fourteenth Amendment Code of Criminal Procedure, 56 J. Crim. L., C. & P. S. 143, 156 (1965).

The complex problems also prompted discussions by jurists. Compare Bazelon, Law, Morality, and Civil Liberties, 12 U. C. L. A. L. Rev. 13 (1964), with Friendly, The Bill of Rights as a Code of Criminal Procedure, 53 Calif. L. Rev. 929 (1965).

[3]For example, the Los Angeles Police Chief stated that "If the police are required . . . to . . . establish that the defendant was apprised of his constitutional guarantees of silence and legal counsel prior to the uttering of any admission or confession, and that he intelligently waived these guarantees . . . a whole Pandora's box is opened as to under what circumstances . . . can a defendant intelligently waive these rights. . . . Allegations that modern criminal investigation can compensate for the lack of a confession or admission in every criminal case is totally absurd!" Parker, 40 L. A. Bar Bull. 603, 607, 642 (1965). His prosecutorial counterpart, District Attorney Younger, stated that "[I]t begins to appear that many of these seemingly restrictive decisions are going to contribute directly to a more effective, efficient and professional level of law enforcement." L. A. Times, Oct. 2, 1965, p. 1. The former Police Commissioner of New York, Michael J. Murphy, stated of *Escobedo*: "What the Court is doing is akin to requiring one boxer to fight by Marquis of Queensbury rules while permitting the other to butt, gouge and bite." N. Y. Times, May 14, 1965, p. 39. The former United States Attorney for the District of Columbia, David C. Acheson, who is presently Special Assistant to the Secretary of the Treasury (for Enforcement), and directly in charge of the Secret Service and the Bureau of Narcotics, observed that "Prosecution procedure has, at most, only the most remote causal connection with crime. Changes in court decisions and prosecution procedure would have about the same effect on the crime rate as an aspirin would have on a tumor of the brain." Quoted in Herman, supra, n. 2, at 500, n. 270. Other views on the subject in general are collected in Weisberg, Police Interrogation of Arrested Persons: A Skeptical View, 52 J. Crim. L., C. & P. S. 21 (1961).

minister, made the system so odious as to give rise to a demand for its total abolition. The change in the English criminal procedure in that particular seems to be founded upon no statute and no judicial opinion, but upon a general and silent acquiescence of the courts in a popular demand. But, however adopted, it has become firmly embedded in English, as well as in American jurisprudence. So deeply did the iniquities of the ancient system impress themselves upon the minds of the American colonists that the States, with one accord, made a denial of the right to question an accused person a part of their fundamental law, so that a maxim, which in England was a mere rule of evidence, became clothed in this country with the impregnability of a constitutional enactment." *Brown* v. *Walker*, 161 U.S. 591, 596 -597 (1896).

In stating the obligation of the judiciary to apply these constitutional rights, this Court declared in *Weems* v. *United States,* 217 U.S. 349, 373 (1910):

- ". . . our contemplation cannot be only of what has been but of what may be. Under any other rule a constitution would indeed be as easy of application as it would be deficient in efficacy and power. Its general principles would have little value and be converted by precedent into impotent and lifeless formulas. Rights declared in words might be lost in reality. And this has been recognized. The meaning and vitality of the Constitution have developed against narrow and restrictive construction."

This was the spirit in which we delineated, in meaningful language, the manner in which the constitutional rights of the individual could be enforced against overzealous police practices. It was necessary in *Escobedo,* as here, to insure that what was proclaimed in the Constitution had not become but a "form of words," *Silverthorne Lumber Co.* v. *United States,* 251 U.S. 385, 392 (1920), in the hands of government officials. And it is in this spirit, consistent with our role as judges, that we adhere to the principles of *Escobedo* today.

Our holding will be spelled out with some specificity in the pages which follow but briefly stated it is this: the prosecution may not use statements, whether exculpatory or inculpatory, stemming from custodial interrogation of the defendant unless it demonstrates the use of procedural safeguards effective to secure the privilege against self-incrimination. By custodial interrogation, we mean questioning initiated by law enforcement officers after a person has been taken into custody or otherwise deprived of his freedom of action in any significant way. [footnote 4] As for the procedural safeguards to be employed, unless other fully effective means are devised to inform accused persons of their right of silence and to assure a continuous opportunity to exercise it, the following measures are required. Prior to any questioning, the person must be warned that he has a right to remain silent, that any statement he does make may be used as evidence against him, and that he has a right to the presence of an attorney, either retained or appointed. The defendant may waive effectuation of these rights, provided the waiver is made voluntarily, knowingly and intelligently. If, however, he indicates in any manner and at any stage of the process that he wishes to consult with an attorney before speaking there can be no questioning. Likewise, if the individual is alone and indicates in any manner that he does not wish to be interrogated, the police may not question him. The mere fact that he may have answered some questions or volunteered some statements on his own does not deprive him of the right to refrain from answering any further inquiries until he has consulted with an attorney and thereafter consents to be questioned.

---

[4]This is what we meant in *Escobedo* when we spoke of an investigation which had focused on an accused.

I.

The constitutional issue we decide in each of these cases is the admissibility of statements obtained from a defendant questioned while in custody or otherwise deprived of his freedom of action in any significant way. In each, the defendant was questioned by police officers, detectives, or a prosecuting attorney in a room in which he was cut off from the outside world. In none of these cases was the defendant given a full and effective warning of his rights at the outset of the interrogation process. In all the cases, the questioning elicited oral admissions, and in three of them, signed statements as well which were admitted at their trials. They all thus share salient features - incommunicado interrogation of individuals in a police-dominated atmosphere, resulting in self-incriminating statements without full warnings of constitutional rights.

An understanding of the nature and setting of this in-custody interrogation is essential to our decisions today. The difficulty in depicting what transpires at such interrogations stems from the fact that in this country they have largely taken place incommunicado. From extensive factual studies undertaken in the early 1930's, including the famous Wickersham Report to Congress by a Presidential Commission, it is clear that police violence and the "third degree" flourished at that time. [footnote 5] In a series of cases decided by this Court long after these studies, the police resorted to physical brutality - beating, hanging, whipping - and to sustained and protracted questioning incommunicado in order to extort confessions. [footnote 6] The Commission on Civil Rights in 1961 found much evidence to indicate that "some policemen still resort to physical force to obtain confessions," 1961 Comm'n on Civil Rights Rep., Justice, pt. 5, 17. The use of physical brutality and violence is not, unfortunately, relegated to the past or to any part of the country. Only recently in Kings County, New York, the police brutally beat, kicked and placed lighted cigarette butts on the back of a potential witness under interrogation for the purpose of securing a statement incriminating a third party. *People* v. *Portelli,* 15 N. Y. 2d 235, 205 N. E. 2d 857, 257 N. Y. S. 2d 931 (1965). [footnote 7]

The examples given above are undoubtedly the exception now, but they are sufficiently widespread to be the object of concern. Unless a proper limitation upon custodial interrogation is achieved - such as these decisions will advance - there can be no assurance that practices of this nature will be eradicated in the foreseeable future.

---

[5]See, for example, IV National Commission on Law Observance and Enforcement, Report on Lawlessness in Law Enforcement (1931) [Wickersham Report]; Booth, Confessions, and Methods Employed in Procuring Them, 4 So. Calif. L. Rev. 83 (1930); Kauper, Judicial Examination of the Accused - A Remedy for the Third Degree, 30 Mich. L. Rev. 1224 (1932). It is significant that instances of third-degree treatment of prisoners almost invariably took place during the period between arrest and preliminary examination. Wickersham Report, at 169; Hall, The Law of Arrest in Relation to Contemporary Social Problems, 3 U. Chi. L. Rev. 345, 357 (1936). See also Foote, Law and Police Practice: Safeguards in the Law of Arrest, 52 Nw. U. L. Rev. 16 (1957).

[6]*Brown* v. *Mississippi*, 297 U.S. 278 (1936); *Chambers* v. *Florida*, 309 U.S. 227 (1940); *Canty* v. *Alabama,* 309 U.S. 629 (1940); *White* v. *Texas,* 310 U.S. 530 (1940); *Vernon* v. *Alabama,* 313 U.S. 547 (1941); *Ward* v. *Texas,* 316 U.S. 547 (1942); *Ashcraft* v. *Tennessee,* 322 U.S. 143 (1944); *Malinski* v. *New York,* 324 U.S. 401 (1945); *Leyra* v. *Denno,* 347 U.S. 556 (1954). See also *Williams* v. *United States,* 341 U.S. 97 (1951).

[7]In addition, see *People* v. *Wakat,* 415 Ill. 610, 114 N. E. 2d 706 (1953); *Wakat* v. *Harlib,* 253 F.2d 59 (C. A. 7th Cir. 1958) (defendant suffering from broken bones, multiple bruises and injuries sufficiently serious to require eight months' medical treatment after being manhandled by five policemen); *Kier* v. *State,* 213 Md. 556, 132 A. 2d 494 (1957) (police doctor told accused, who was strapped to a chair completely nude, that he proposed to take hair and skin scrapings from anything that looked like blood or sperm from various parts of his body); *Bruner* v. *People,* 113 Colo. 194, 156 P.2d 111 (1945) (defendant held in custody over two months, deprived of food for 15 hours, forced to submit to a lie detector test when he wanted to go to the toilet); *People* v. *Matlock,* 51 Cal. 2d 682, 336 P.2d 505 (1959) (defendant questioned incessantly over an evening's time, made to lie on cold board and to answer questions whenever it appeared he was getting sleepy). Other cases are documented in American Civil Liberties Union, Illinois Division, Secret Detention by the Chicago Police (1959); Potts, The Preliminary Examination and "The Third Degree," 2 Baylor L. Rev. 131 (1950); Sterling, Police Interrogation and the Psychology of Confession, 14 J. Pub. L. 25 (1965).

The conclusion of the Wickersham Commission Report, made over 30 years ago, is still pertinent:

- "To the contention that the third degree is necessary to get the facts, the reporters aptly reply in the language of the present Lord Chancellor of England (Lord Sankey): 'It is not admissible to do a great right by doing a little wrong. . . . It is not sufficient to do justice by obtaining a proper result by irregular or improper means.' Not only does the use of the third degree involve a flagrant violation of law by the officers of the law, but it involves also the dangers of false confessions, and it tends to make police and prosecutors less zealous in the search for objective evidence. As the New York prosecutor quoted in the report said, 'It is a short cut and makes the police lazy and unenterprising.' Or, as another official quoted remarked: 'If you use your fists, you are not so likely to use your wits.' We agree with the conclusion expressed in the report, that 'The third degree brutalizes the police, hardens the prisoner against society, and lowers the esteem in which the administration of justice is held by the public.' " IV National Commission on Law Observance and Enforcement, Report on Lawlessness in Law Enforcement 5 (1931).

Again we stress that the modern practice of in-custody interrogation is psychologically rather than physically oriented. As we have stated before, "Since *Chambers* v. *Florida,* 309 U.S. 227, this Court has recognized that coercion can be mental as well as physical, and that the blood of the accused is not the only hallmark of an unconstitutional inquisition." *Blackburn* v. *Alabama,* 361 U.S. 199, 206 (1960). Interrogation still takes place in privacy. Privacy results in secrecy and this in turn results in a gap in our knowledge as to what in fact goes on in the interrogation rooms. A valuable source of information about present police practices, however, may be found in various police manuals and texts which document procedures employed with success in the past, and which recommend various other effective tactics. [footnote 8] These texts are used by law enforcement agencies themselves as guides [footnote 9] It should be noted that these texts professedly present the most enlightened and effective means presently used to obtain statements through custodial interrogation. By considering these texts and other data, it is possible to describe procedures observed and noted around the country.

The officers are told by the manuals that the "principal psychological factor contributing to a successful interrogation is privacy - being alone with the person under interrogation." [footnote 10] The efficacy of this tactic has been explained as follows:

- "If at all practicable, the interrogation should take place in the investigator's office or at least in a room of his own choice. The subject should be deprived of every psychological advantage. In his own home he may be

---

[8]The manuals quoted in the text following are the most recent and representative of the texts currently available. Material of the same nature appears in Kidd, Police Interrogation (1940); Mulbar, Interrogation (1951); Dienstein, Technics for the Crime Investigator 97-115 (1952). Studies concerning the observed practices of the police appear in LaFave, Arrest: The Decision To Take a Suspect Into Custody 244-437, 490-521 (1965); LaFave, Detention for Investigation by the Police: An Analysis of Current Practices, 1962 Wash. U. L. Q. 331; Barrett, Police Practices and the Law - From Arrest to Release or Charge, 50 Calif. L. Rev. 11 (1962); Sterling, supra, n. 7, at 47-65.

[9]The methods described in Inbau & Reid, Criminal Interrogation and Confessions (1962), are a revision and enlargement of material presented in three prior editions of a predecessor text, Lie Detection and Criminal Interrogation (3d ed. 1953). The authors and their associates are officers of the Chicago Police Scientific Crime Detection Laboratory and have had extensive experience in writing, lecturing and speaking to law enforcement authorities over a 20-year period. They say that the techniques portrayed in their manuals reflect their experiences and are the most effective psychological stratagems to employ during interrogations. Similarly, the techniques described in O'Hara, Fundamentals of Criminal Investigation (1956), were gleaned from long service as observer, lecturer in police science, and work as a federal criminal investigator. All these texts have had rather extensive use among law enforcement agencies and among students of police science, with total sales and circulation of over 44,000.

[10]Inbau & Reid, Criminal Interrogation and Confessions (1962), at 1.

confident, indignant, or recalcitrant. He is more keenly aware of his rights and more reluctant to tell of his indiscretions or criminal behavior within the walls of his home. Moreover his family and other friends are nearby, their presence lending moral support. In his own office, the investigator possesses all the advantages. The atmosphere suggests the invincibility of the forces of the law." [footnote 11]

To highlight the isolation and unfamiliar surroundings, the manuals instruct the police to display an air of confidence in the suspect's guilt and from outward appearance to maintain only an interest in confirming certain details. The guilt of the subject is to be posited as a fact. The interrogator should direct his comments toward the reasons why the subject committed the act, rather than court failure by asking the subject whether he did it. Like other men, perhaps the subject has had a bad family life, had an unhappy childhood, had too much to drink, had an unrequited desire for women. The officers are instructed to minimize the moral seriousness of the offense, [footnote 12] to cast blame on the victim or on society. [footnote 13] These tactics are designed to put the subject in a psychological state where his story is but an elaboration of what the police purport to know already - that he is guilty. Explanations to the contrary are dismissed and discouraged.

The texts thus stress that the major qualities an interrogator should possess are patience and perseverance. One writer describes the efficacy of these characteristics in this manner:

- "In the preceding paragraphs emphasis has been placed on kindness and stratagems. The investigator will, however, encounter many situations where the sheer weight of his personality will be the deciding factor. Where emotional appeals and tricks are employed to no avail, he must rely on an oppressive atmosphere of dogged persistence. He must interrogate steadily and without relent, leaving the subject no prospect of surcease. He must dominate his subject and overwhelm him with his inexorable will to obtain the truth. He should interrogate for a spell of several hours pausing only for the subject's necessities in acknowledgment of the need to avoid a charge of duress that can be technically substantiated. In a serious case, the interrogation may continue for days, with the required intervals for food and sleep, but with no respite from the atmosphere of domination. It is possible in this way to induce the subject to talk without resorting to duress or coercion. The method should be used only when the guilt of the subject appears highly probable." [footnote 14]

The manuals suggest that the suspect be offered legal excuses for his actions in order to obtain an initial admission of guilt. Where there is a suspected revenge-killing, for example, the interrogator may say:

- "Joe, you probably didn't go out looking for this fellow with the purpose of shooting him. My guess is, however, that you expected something from him and that's why you carried a gun - for your own protection. You knew him for what he was, no good. Then when you met him he probably started using foul, abusive language and he gave some indication that he was about to pull

---

[11]O'Hara, supra, at 99.

[12]Inbau & Reid, supra, at 34-43, 87. For example, in *Leyra v. Denno*, 347 U.S. 556 (1954), the interrogator-psychiatrist told the accused, "We do sometimes things that are not right, but in a fit of temper or anger we sometimes do things we aren't really responsible for," id., at 562, and again, "We know that morally you were just in anger. Morally, you are not to be condemned," id., at 582.

[13]Inbau & Reid, supra, at 43-55.

[14]O'Hara, supra, at 112.

a gun on you, and that's when you had to act to save your own life. That's about it, isn't it, Joe?" [footnote 15]

Having then obtained the admission of shooting, the interrogator is advised to refer to circumstantial evidence which negates the self-defense explanation. This should enable him to secure the entire story. One text notes that "Even if he fails to do so, the inconsistency between the subject's original denial of the shooting and his present admission of at least doing the shooting will serve to deprive him of a self-defense 'out' at the time of trial." [footnote 16]

When the techniques described above prove unavailing, the texts recommend they be alternated with a show of some hostility. One ploy often used has been termed the "friendly-unfriendly" or the "Mutt and Jeff" act:

- ". . . In this technique, two agents are employed. Mutt, the relentless investigator, who knows the subject is guilty and is not going to waste any time. He's sent a dozen men away for this crime and he's going to send the subject away for the full term. Jeff, on the other hand, is obviously a kindhearted man. He has a family himself. He has a brother who was involved in a little scrape like this. He disapproves of Mutt and his tactics and will arrange to get him off the case if the subject will cooperate. He can't hold Mutt off for very long. The subject would be wise to make a quick decision. The technique is applied by having both investigators present while Mutt acts out his role. Jeff may stand by quietly and demur at some of Mutt's tactics. When Jeff makes his plea for cooperation, Mutt is not present in the room." [footnote 17]

The interrogators sometimes are instructed to induce a confession out of trickery. The technique here is quite effective in crimes which require identification or which run in series. In the identification situation, the interrogator may take a break in his questioning to place the subject among a group of men in a line-up. "The witness or complainant (previously coached, if necessary) studies the line-up and confidently points out the subject as the guilty party." [footnote 18] Then the questioning resumes "as though there were now no doubt about the guilt of the subject." A variation on this technique is called the "reverse line-up":

- "The accused is placed in a line-up, but this time he is identified by several fictitious witnesses or victims who associated him with different offenses. It is expected that the subject will become desperate and confess to the offense under investigation in order to escape from the false accusations." [footnote 19]

The manuals also contain instructions for police on how to handle the individual who refuses to discuss the matter entirely, or who asks for an attorney or relatives. The examiner is to concede him the right to remain silent. "This usually has a very undermining effect. First of all, he is disappointed in his expectation of an unfavorable reaction on the part of the interrogator. Secondly, a concession of this right to remain silent impresses the subject with the apparent fairness of his interrogator."

---

[15]Inbau & Reid, supra, at 40.

[16]Ibid.

[17]O'Hara, supra, at 104, Inbau & Reid, supra, at 58-59. See *Spano* v. *New York,* 360 U.S. 315 (1959). A variant on the technique of creating hostility is one of engendering fear. This is perhaps best described by the prosecuting attorney in *Malinski* v. *New York,* 324 U.S. 401, 407 (1945): "Why this talk about being undressed? Of course, they had a right to undress him to look for bullet scars, and keep the clothes off him. That was quite proper police procedure. That is some more psychology - let him sit around with a blanket on him, humiliate him there for a while; let him sit in the corner, let him think he is going to get a shellacking."

[18]O'Hara, supra, at 105-106.

[19]Id., at 106.

[footnote 20] After this psychological conditioning, however, the officer is told to point out the incriminating significance of the suspect's refusal to talk:

- "Joe, you have a right to remain silent. That's your privilege and I'm the last person in the world who'll try to take it away from you. If that's the way you want to leave this, O. K. But let me ask you this. Suppose you were in my shoes and I were in yours and you called me in to ask me about this and I told you, 'I don't want to answer any of your questions.' You'd think I had something to hide, and you'd probably be right in thinking that. That's exactly what I'll have to think about you, and so will everybody else. So let's sit here and talk this whole thing over." [footnote 21]

Few will persist in their initial refusal to talk, it is said, if this monologue is employed correctly.

In the event that the subject wishes to speak to a relative or an attorney, the following advice is tendered:

- "[T]he interrogator should respond by suggesting that the subject first tell the truth to the interrogator himself rather than get anyone else involved in the matter. If the request is for an attorney, the interrogator may suggest that the subject save himself or his family the expense of any such professional service, particularly if he is innocent of the offense under investigation. The interrogator may also add, 'Joe, I'm only looking for the truth, and if you're telling the truth, that's it. You can handle this by yourself.' " [footnote 22]

From these representative samples of interrogation techniques, the setting prescribed by the manuals and observed in practice becomes clear. In essence, it is this: To be alone with the subject is essential to prevent distraction and to deprive him of any outside support. The aura of confidence in his guilt undermines his will to resist. He merely confirms the preconceived story the police seek to have him describe. Patience and persistence, at times relentless questioning, are employed. To obtain a confession, the interrogator must "patiently maneuver himself or his quarry into a position from which the desired objective may be attained." [footnote 23] When normal procedures fail to produce the needed result, the police may resort to deceptive stratagems such as giving false legal advice. It is important to keep the subject off balance, for example, by trading on his insecurity about himself or his surroundings. The police then persuade, trick, or cajole him out of exercising his constitutional rights.

Even without employing brutality, the "third degree" or the specific stratagems described above, the very fact of custodial interrogation exacts a heavy toll on individual liberty and trades on the weakness of individuals. [footnote 24] This fact may be illustrated simply by referring to three confession cases decided by this Court in the Term immediately preceding our Escobedo decision. In *Townsend* v. *Sain,* 372 U.S. 293 (1963), the defendant was a 19-year-old heroin addict, described as a "near mental defective," id., at 307-310. The defendant in *Lynumn* v. *Illinois,* 372 U.S. 528 (1963), was a woman who confessed to the arresting officer after being importuned

---

[20]Inbau & Reid, supra, at 111.

[21]Ibid.

[22]Inbau & Reid, supra, at 112.

[23]Inbau & Reid, Lie Detection and Criminal Interrogation 185 (3d ed. 1953).

[24]Interrogation procedures may even give rise to a false confession. The most recent conspicuous example occurred in New York, in 1964, when a Negro of limited intelligence confessed to two brutal murders and a rape which he had not committed. When this was discovered, the prosecutor was reported as saying: "Call it what you want - brain-washing, hypnosis, fright. They made him give an untrue confession. The only thing I don't believe is that Whitmore was beaten." N. Y. Times, Jan. 28, 1965, p. 1, col. 5. In two other instances, similar events had occurred. N. Y. Times, Oct. 20, 1964, p. 22, col. 1; N. Y. Times, Aug. 25, 1965, p. 1, col. 1. In general, see Borchard, Convicting the Innocent (1932); Frank & Frank, Not Guilty (1957).

to "cooperate" in order to prevent her children from being taken by relief authorities. This Court as in those cases reversed the conviction of a defendant in *Haynes* v. *Washington,* 373 U.S. 503 (1963), whose persistent request during his interrogation was to phone his wife or attorney. [footnote 25] In other settings, these individuals might have exercised their constitutional rights. In the incommunicado police-dominated atmosphere, they succumbed.

In the cases before us today, given this background, we concern ourselves primarily with this interrogation atmosphere and the evils it can bring. In No. 759, *Miranda* v. *Arizona,* the police arrested the defendant and took him to a special interrogation room where they secured a confession. In No. 760, *Vignera* v. *New York,* the defendant made oral admissions to the police after interrogation in the afternoon, and then signed an inculpatory statement upon being questioned by an assistant district attorney later the same evening. In No. 761, *Westover* v. *United States,* the defendant was handed over to the Federal Bureau of Investigation by local authorities after they had detained and interrogated him for a lengthy period, both at night and the following morning. After some two hours of questioning, the federal officers had obtained signed statements from the defendant. Lastly, in No. 584, *California* v. *Stewart,* the local police held the defendant five days in the station and interrogated him on nine separate occasions before they secured his inculpatory statement.

In these cases, we might not find the defendants' statements to have been involuntary in traditional terms. Our concern for adequate safeguards to protect precious Fifth Amendment rights is, of course, not lessened in the slightest. In each of the cases, the defendant was thrust into an unfamiliar atmosphere and run through menacing police interrogation procedures. The potentiality for compulsion is forcefully apparent, for example, in *Miranda,* where the indigent Mexican defendant was a seriously disturbed individual with pronounced sexual fantasies, and in Stewart, in which the defendant was an indigent Los Angeles Negro who had dropped out of school in the sixth grade. To be sure, the records do not evince overt physical coercion or patent psychological ploys. The fact remains that in none of these cases did the officers undertake to afford appropriate safeguards at the outset of the interrogation to insure that the statements were truly the product of free choice.

It is obvious that such an interrogation environment is created for no purpose other than to subjugate the individual to the will of his examiner. This atmosphere carries its own badge of intimidation. To be sure, this is not physical intimidation, but it is equally destructive of human dignity. [footnote 26] The current practice of incommunicado interrogation is at odds with one of our Nation's most cherished principles - that the individual may not be compelled to incriminate himself. Unless adequate protective devices are employed to dispel the compulsion inherent in custodial surroundings, no statement obtained from the defendant can truly be the product of his free choice.

---

[25]In the fourth confession case decided by the Court in the 1962 Term, *Fay* v. *Noia,* 372 U.S. 391 (1963), our disposition made it unnecessary to delve at length into the facts. The facts of the defendant's case there, however, paralleled those of his co-defendants, whose confessions were found to have resulted from continuous and coercive interrogation for 27 hours, with denial of requests for friends or attorney. See *United States* v. *Murphy,* 222 F.2d 698 (C. A. 2d Cir. 1955) (Frank, J.); *People* v. *Bonino,* 1 N. Y. 2d 752, 135 N. E. 2d 51 (1956).

[26]The absurdity of denying that a confession obtained under these circumstances is compelled is aptly portrayed by an example in Professor Sutherland's recent article, Crime and Confession, 79 Harv. L. Rev. 21, 37 (1965):

- "Suppose a well-to-do testatrix says she intends to will her property to Elizabeth. John and James want her to bequeath it to them instead. They capture the testatrix, put her in a carefully designed room, out of touch with everyone but themselves and their convenient 'witnesses,' keep her secluded there for hours while they make insistent demands, weary her with contradictions of her assertions that she wants to leave her money to Elizabeth, and finally induce her to execute the will in their favor. Assume that John and James are deeply and correctly convinced that Elizabeth is unworthy and will make base use of the property if she gets her hands on it, whereas John and James have the noblest and most righteous intentions. Would any judge of probate accept the will so procured as the 'voluntary' act of the testatrix?"

From the foregoing, we can readily perceive an intimate connection between the privilege against self-incrimination and police custodial questioning. It is fitting to turn to history and precedent underlying the Self-Incrimination Clause to determine its applicability in this situation.

II.

We sometimes forget how long it has taken to establish the privilege against self-incrimination, the sources from which it came and the fervor with which it was defended. Its roots go back into ancient times. [footnote 27] Perhaps the critical historical event shedding light on its origins and evolution was the trial of one John Lilburn, a vocal anti-Stuart Leveller, who was made to take the Star Chamber Oath in 1637. The oath would have bound him to answer to all questions posed to him on any subject. The Trial of John Lilburn and John Wharton, 3 How. St. Tr. 1315 (1637). He resisted the oath and declaimed the proceedings, stating:

- "Another fundamental right I then contended for, was, that no man's conscience ought to be racked by oaths imposed, to answer to questions concerning himself in matters criminal, or pretended to be so." Haller & Davies, The Leveller Tracts 1647-1653, p. 454 (1944).

On account of the Lilburn Trial, Parliament abolished the inquisitorial Court of Star Chamber and went further in giving him generous reparation. The lofty principles to which Lilburn had appealed during his trial gained popular acceptance in England. [footnote 28] These sentiments worked their way over to the Colonies and were implanted after great struggle into the Bill of Rights. [footnote 29] Those who framed our Constitution and the Bill of Rights were ever aware of subtle encroachments on individual liberty. They knew that "illegitimate and unconstitutional practices get their first footing . . . by silent approaches and slight deviations from legal modes of procedure." *Boyd* v. *United States,* 116 U.S. 616, 635 (1886). The privilege was elevated to constitutional status and has always been "as broad as the mischief against which it seeks to guard." *Counselman* v. *Hitchcock,* 142 U.S. 547, 562 (1892). We cannot depart from this noble heritage.

Thus we may view the historical development of the privilege as one which groped for the proper scope of governmental power over the citizen. As a "noble principle often transcends its origins," the privilege has come rightfully to be recognized in part as an individual's substantive right, a "right to a private enclave where he may lead a private life. That right is the hallmark of our democracy." *United States* v. *Grunewald,* 233 F.2d 556, 579, 581-582 (Frank, J., dissenting), rev'd, 353 U.S. 391 (1957). We have recently noted that the privilege against self-incrimination - the essential mainstay of our adversary system - is founded on a complex of values, *Murphy* v. *Waterfront Comm'n,* 378 U.S. 52, 55 -57, n. 5 (1964); *Tehan* v. *Shott,* 382 U.S. 406, 414 -415, n. 12 (1966). All these policies point to one overriding thought: the constitutional foundation underlying the privilege is the respect a government - state or federal - must accord to the dignity and integrity of its citizens. To maintain a "fair

---

[27]Thirteenth century commentators found an analogue to the privilege grounded in the Bible. "To sum up the matter, the principle that no man is to be declared guilty on his own admission is a divine decree." Maimonides, Mishneh Torah (Code of Jewish Law), Book of Judges, Laws of the Sanhedrin, c. 18, 6, III Yale Judaica Series 52-53. See also Lamm, The Fifth Amendment and Its Equivalent in the Halakhah, 5 Judaism 53 (Winter 1956).

[28]See Morgan, The Privilege Against Self-Incrimination, 34 Minn. L. Rev. 1, 9-11 (1949); 8 Wigmore, Evidence 289-295 (*McNaughton* rev. 1961). See also Lowell, The Judicial Use of Torture, Parts I and II, 11 Harv. L. Rev. 220, 290 (1897).

[29]See Pittman, The Colonial and Constitutional History of the Privilege Against Self-Incrimination in America, 21 Va. L. Rev. 763 (1935); *Ullmann* v. *United States,* 350 U.S. 422, 445 -449 (1956) (DOUGLAS, J., dissenting).

state-individual balance," to require the government "to shoulder the entire load," 8 Wigmore, Evidence 317 (*McNaughton* rev. 1961), to respect the inviolability of the human personality, our accusatory system of criminal justice demands that the government seeking to punish an individual produce the evidence against him by its own independent labors, rather than by the cruel, simple expedient of compelling it from his own mouth. *Chambers* v. *Florida,* 309 U.S. 227, 235 -238 (1940). In sum, the privilege is fulfilled only when the person is guaranteed the right "to remain silent unless he chooses to speak in the unfettered exercise of his own will." *Malloy* v. *Hogan,* 378 U.S. 1, 8 (1964).

The question in these cases is whether the privilege is fully applicable during a period of custodial interrogation. In this Court, the privilege has consistently been accorded a liberal construction. *Albertson* v. *SACB,* 382 U.S. 70, 81 (1965); *Hoffman* v. *United States,* 341 U.S. 479, 486 (1951); *Arndstein* v. *McCarthy,* 254 U.S. 71, 72 - 73 (1920); *Counselman* v. *Hitchock,* 142 U.S. 547, 562 (1892). We are satisfied that all the principles embodied in the privilege apply to informal compulsion exerted by law-enforcement officers during in-custody questioning. An individual swept from familiar surroundings into police custody, surrounded by antagonistic forces, and subjected to the techniques of persuasion described above cannot be otherwise than under compulsion to speak. As a practical matter, the compulsion to speak in the isolated setting of the police station may well be greater than in courts or other official investigations, where there are often impartial observers to guard against intimidation or trickery. [footnote 30]

This question, in fact, could have been taken as settled in federal courts almost 70 years ago, when, in *Bram* v. *United States,* 168 U.S. 532, 542 (1897), this Court held:

- "In criminal trials, in the courts of the United States, wherever a question arises whether a confession is incompetent because not voluntary, the issue is controlled by that portion of the Fifth Amendment . . . commanding that no person 'shall be compelled in any criminal case to be a witness against himself.' "

In *Bram,* the Court reviewed the British and American history and case law and set down the Fifth Amendment standard for compulsion which we implement today:

- "Much of the confusion which has resulted from the effort to deduce from the adjudged cases what would be a sufficient quantum of proof to show that a confession was or was not voluntary, has arisen from a misconception of the subject to which the proof must address itself. The rule is not that in order to render a statement admissible the proof must be adequate to establish that the particular communications contained in a statement were voluntarily made, but it must be sufficient to establish that the making of the statement was voluntary; that is to say, that from the causes, which the law treats as legally sufficient to engender in the mind of the accused hope or fear in respect to the crime charged, the accused was not involuntarily impelled to make a statement, when but for the improper influences he would have remained silent. . . ." 168 U.S., at 549. And see, id., at 542.

The Court has adhered to this reasoning. In 1924, Mr. Justice Brandeis wrote for a unanimous Court in reversing a conviction resting on a compelled confession, *Wan* v. *United States,* 266 U.S. 1. He stated:

- "In the federal courts, the requisite of voluntariness is not satisfied by establishing merely that the confession was not induced by a promise or a threat. A confession is voluntary in law if, and only if, it was, in fact, voluntarily made. A confession may have been given voluntarily, although it was made

---

[30]Compare *Brown* v. *Walker, 161 U.S. 591* (1896); *Quinn* v. *United States, 349 U.S. 155* (1955).

to police officers, while in custody, and in answer to an examination conducted by them. But a confession obtained by compulsion must be excluded whatever may have been the character of the compulsion, and whether the compulsion was applied in a judicial proceeding or otherwise. *Bram* v. *United States,* 168 U.S. 532." 266 U.S., at 14 -15.

In addition to the expansive historical development of the privilege and the sound policies which have nurtured its evolution, judicial precedent thus clearly establishes its application to incommunicado interrogation. In fact, the Government concedes this point as well established in No. 761, *Westover* v. *United States,* stating: "We have no doubt . . . that it is possible for a suspect's Fifth Amendment right to be violated during in-custody questioning by a law-enforcement officer." [footnote 31]

Because of the adoption by Congress of Rule 5 (a) of the Federal Rules of Criminal Procedure, and this Court's effectuation of that Rule in *McNabb* v. *United States,* 318 U.S. 332 (1943), and *Mallory* v. *United States,* 354 U.S. 449 (1957), we have had little occasion in the past quarter century to reach the constitutional issues in dealing with federal interrogations. These supervisory rules, requiring production of an arrested person before a commissioner "without unnecessary delay" and excluding evidence obtained in default of that statutory obligation, were nonetheless responsive to the same considerations of Fifth Amendment policy that unavoidably face us now as to the States. In *McNabb,* 318 U.S., at 343 -344, and in *Mallory,* 354 U.S., at 455 -456, we recognized both the dangers of interrogation and the appropriateness of prophylaxis stemming from the very fact of interrogation itself. [footnote 32]

Our decision in *Malloy* v. *Hogan,* 378 U.S. 1 (1964), necessitates an examination of the scope of the privilege in state cases as well. In *Malloy,* we squarely held the privilege applicable to the States, and held that the substantive standards underlying the privilege applied with full force to state court proceedings. There, as in *Murphy* v. *Waterfront Comm'n,* 378 U.S. 52 (1964), and *Griffin* v. *California,* 380 U.S. 609 (1965), we applied the existing Fifth Amendment standards to the case before us. Aside from the holding itself, the reasoning in *Malloy* made clear what had already become apparent - that the substantive and procedural safeguards surrounding admissibility of confessions in state cases had become exceedingly exacting, reflecting all the policies embedded in the privilege, 378 U.S., at 7 -8. [footnote 33] The voluntariness doctrine in the state cases, as *Malloy* indicates, encompasses all interrogation practices which are likely to exert such pressure upon an individual as to disable him from making a free and rational choice. [footnote 34] The implications of

---

[31]Brief for the United States, p. 28. To the same effect, see Brief for the United States, pp. 40-49, n. 44, *Anderson* v. *United States,* 318 U.S. 350 (1943); Brief for the United States, pp. 17-18, *McNabb* v. *United States,* 318 U.S. 332 (1943).

[32]Our decision today does not indicate in any manner, of course, that these rules can be disregarded. When federal officials arrest an individual, they must as always comply with the dictates of the congressional legislation and cases thereunder. See generally, Hogan & Snee, The McNabb-Mallory Rule: Its Rise, Rationale and Rescue, 47 Geo. L. J. 1 (1958).

[33]The decisions of this Court have guaranteed the same procedural protection for the defendant whether his confession was used in a federal or state court. It is now axiomatic that the defendant's constitutional rights have been violated if his conviction is based, in whole or in part, on an involuntary confession, regardless of its truth or falsity. *Rogers* v. *Richmond,* 365 U.S. 534, 544 (1961); *Wan* v. *United States,* 266 U.S. 1 (1924). This is so even if there is ample evidence aside from the confession to support the conviction, e. g., *Malinski* v. *New York,* 324 U.S. 401, 404 (1945); *Bram* v. *United States,* 168 U.S. 532, 540 -542 (1897). Both state and federal courts now adhere to trial procedures which seek to assure a reliable and clear-cut determination of the voluntariness of the confession offered at trial, *Jackson* v. *Denno,* 378 U.S. 368 (1964); *United States* v. *Carignan,* 342 U.S. 36, 38 (1951); see also *Wilson* v. *United States,* 162 U.S. 613, 624 (1896). Appellate review is exacting, see *Haynes* v. *Washington,* 373 U.S. 503 (1963); *Blackburn* v. *Alabama,* 361 U.S. 199 (1960). Whether his conviction was in a federal or state court, the defendant may secure a post-conviction hearing based on the alleged involuntary character of his confession, provided he meets the procedural requirements, *Fay* v. *Noia,* 372 U.S. 391 (1963); *Townsend* v. *Sain,* 372 U.S. 293 (1963). In addition, see *Murphy* v. *Waterfront Comm'n,* 378 U.S. 52 (1964).

[34]See *Lisenba* v. *California,* 314 U.S. 219, 241 (1941); *Ashcraft* v. *Tennessee,* 322 U.S. 143 (1944); *Malinski* v. *New York,* 324 U.S. 401 (1945); *Spano* v. *New York,* 360 U.S. 315 (1959); *Lynumn* v. *Illinois,* 372 U.S. 528 (1963); *Haynes* v. *Washington,* 373 U.S. 503 (1963).

this proposition were elaborated in our decision in *Escobedo* v. *Illinois,* 378 U.S. 478, decided one week after *Malloy* applied the privilege to the States.

Our holding there stressed the fact that the police had not advised the defendant of his constitutional privilege to remain silent at the outset of the interrogation, and we drew attention to that fact at several points in the decision, 378 U.S., at 483, 485, 491. This was no isolated factor, but an essential ingredient in our decision. The entire thrust of police interrogation there, as in all the cases today, was to put the defendant in such an emotional state as to impair his capacity for rational judgment. The abdication of the constitutional privilege - the choice on his part to speak to the police - was not made knowingly or competently because of the failure to apprise him of his rights; the compelling atmosphere of the in-custody interrogation, and not an independent decision on his part, caused the defendant to speak.

A different phase of the *Escobedo* decision was significant in its attention to the absence of counsel during the questioning. There, as in the cases today, we sought a protective device to dispel the compelling atmosphere of the interrogation. In *Escobedo,* however, the police did not relieve the defendant of the anxieties which they had created in the interrogation rooms. Rather, they denied his request for the assistance of counsel, 378 U.S., at 481, 488, 491. [footnote 35] This heightened his dilemma, and made his later statements the product of this compulsion. Cf. *Haynes* v. *Washington,* 373 U.S. 503, 514 (1963). The denial of the defendant's request for his attorney thus undermined his ability to exercise the privilege - to remain silent if he chose or to speak without any intimidation, blatant or subtle. The presence of counsel, in all the cases before us today, would be the adequate protective device necessary to make the process of police interrogation conform to the dictates of the privilege. His presence would insure that statements made in the government-established atmosphere are not the product of compulsion.

It was in this manner that Escobedo explicated another facet of the pre-trial privilege, noted in many of the Court's prior decisions: the protection of rights at trial. [footnote 36] That counsel is present when statements are taken from an individual during interrogation obviously enhances the integrity of the fact-finding processes in court. The presence of an attorney, and the warnings delivered to the individual, enable the defendant under otherwise compelling circumstances to tell his story without fear, effectively, and in a way that eliminates the evils in the interrogation process. Without the protections flowing from adequate warnings and the rights of counsel, "all the careful safeguards erected around the giving of testimony, whether by an accused or any other witness, would become empty formalities in a procedure where the most compelling possible evidence of guilt, a confession, would have already been obtained at the unsupervised pleasure of the police." *Mapp* v. *Ohio,* 367 U.S. 643, 685 (1961) (HARLAN, J., dissenting). Cf. *Pointer* v. *Texas,* 380 U.S. 400 (1965).

III.

Today, then, there can be no doubt that the Fifth Amendment privilege is available outside of criminal court proceedings and serves to protect persons in all settings in which their freedom of action is curtailed in any significant way from being compelled to incriminate themselves. We have concluded that without proper safeguards the process of in-custody interrogation of persons suspected or accused of crime contains

---

[35]The police also prevented the attorney from consulting with his client. Independent of any other constitutional proscription, this action constitutes a violation of the Sixth Amendment right to the assistance of counsel and excludes any statement obtained in its wake. See *People* v. *Donovan,* 13 N. Y. 2d 148, 193 N. E. 2d 628, 243 N. Y. S. 2d 841 (1963) (Fuld, J.).

[36]In re Groban, 352 U.S. 330, 340 -352 (1957) (BLACK, J., dissenting); Note, 73 Yale L. J. 1000, 1048-1051 (1964); Comment, 31 U. Chi. L. Rev. 313, 320 (1964) and authorities cited.

inherently compelling pressures which work to undermine the individual's will to resist and to compel him to speak where he would not otherwise do so freely. In order to combat these pressures and to permit a full opportunity to exercise the privilege against self-incrimination, the accused must be adequately and effectively apprised of his rights and the exercise of those rights must be fully honored.

It is impossible for us to foresee the potential alternatives for protecting the privilege which might be devised by Congress or the States in the exercise of their creative rule-making capacities. Therefore we cannot say that the Constitution necessarily requires adherence to any particular solution for the inherent compulsions of the interrogation process as it is presently conducted. Our decision in no way creates a constitutional straitjacket which will handicap sound efforts at reform, nor is it intended to have this effect. We encourage Congress and the States to continue their laudable search for increasingly effective ways of protecting the rights of the individual while promoting efficient enforcement of our criminal laws. However, unless we are shown other procedures which are at least as effective in apprising accused persons of their right of silence and in assuring a continuous opportunity to exercise it, the following safeguards must be observed.

At the outset, if a person in custody is to be subjected to interrogation, he must first be informed in clear and unequivocal terms that he has the right to remain silent. For those unaware of the privilege, the warning is needed simply to make them aware of it - the threshold requirement for an intelligent decision as to its exercise. More important, such a warning is an absolute prerequisite in overcoming the inherent pressures of the interrogation atmosphere. It is not just the subnormal or woefully ignorant who succumb to an interrogator's imprecations, whether implied or expressly stated, that the interrogation will continue until a confession is obtained or that silence in the face of accusation is itself damning and will bode ill when presented to a jury. [footnote 37] Further, the warning will show the individual that his interrogators are prepared to recognize his privilege should he choose to exercise it.

The Fifth Amendment privilege is so fundamental to our system of constitutional rule and the expedient of giving an adequate warning as to the availability of the privilege so simple, we will not pause to inquire in individual cases whether the defendant was aware of his rights without a warning being given. Assessments of the knowledge the defendant possessed, based on information as to his age, education, intelligence, or prior contact with authorities, can never be more than speculation; [footnote 38] a warning is a clearcut fact. More important, whatever the background of the person interrogated, a warning at the time of the interrogation is indispensable to overcome its pressures and to insure that the individual knows he is free to exercise the privilege at that point in time.

The warning of the right to remain silent must be accompanied by the explanation that anything said can and will be used against the individual in court. This warning is needed in order to make him aware not only of the privilege, but also of the consequences of forgoing it. It is only through an awareness of these conse-

---

[37]See p. 454, supra. Lord Devlin has commented:

- "It is probable that even today, when there is much less ignorance about these matters than formerly, there is still a general belief that you must answer all questions put to you by a policeman, or at least that it will be the worse for you if you do not." Devlin, The Criminal Prosecution in England 32 (1958).

In accord with our decision today, it is impermissible to penalize an individual for exercising his Fifth Amendment privilege when he is under police custodial interrogation. The prosecution may not, therefore, use at trial the fact that he stood mute or claimed his privilege in the face of accusation. Cf. *Griffin* v. *California*, 380 U.S. 609 (1965); *Malloy* v. *Hogan*, 378 U.S. 1, 8 (1964); Comment, 31 U. Chi. L. Rev. 556 (1964); Developments in the Law - Confessions, 79 Harv. L. Rev. 935, 1041-1044 (1966). See also *Bram* v. *United States*, 168 U.S. 532, 562 (1897).

[38]Cf. *Betts* v. *Brady*, 316 U.S. 455 (1942), and the recurrent inquiry into special circumstances it necessitated. See generally, Kamisar, *Betts* v. *Brady* Twenty Years Later: The Right to Counsel and Due Process Values, 61 Mich. L. Rev. 219 (1962).

quences that there can be any assurance of real understanding and intelligent exercise of the privilege. Moreover, this warning may serve to make the individual more acutely aware that he is faced with a phase of the adversary system - that he is not in the presence of persons acting solely in his interest.

The circumstances surrounding in-custody interrogation can operate very quickly to overbear the will of one merely made aware of his privilege by his interrogators. Therefore, the right to have counsel present at the interrogation is indispensable to the protection of the Fifth Amendment privilege under the system we delineate today. Our aim is to assure that the individual's right to choose between silence and speech remains unfettered throughout the interrogation process. A once-stated warning, delivered by those who will conduct the interrogation, cannot itself suffice to that end among those who most require knowledge of their rights. A mere warning given by the interrogators is not alone sufficient to accomplish that end. Prosecutors themselves claim that the admonishment of the right to remain silent without more "will benefit only the recidivist and the professional." Brief for the National District Attorneys Association as amicus curiae, p. 14. Even preliminary advice given to the accused by his own attorney can be swiftly overcome by the secret interrogation process. Cf. *Escobedo* v. *Illinois,* 378 U.S. 478, 485, n. 5. Thus, the need for counsel to protect the Fifth Amendment privilege comprehends not merely a right to consult with counsel prior to questioning, but also to have counsel present during any questioning if the defendant so desires.

The presence of counsel at the interrogation may serve several significant subsidiary functions as well. If the accused decides to talk to his interrogators, the assistance of counsel can mitigate the dangers of untrustworthiness. With a lawyer present the likelihood that the police will practice coercion is reduced, and if coercion is nevertheless exercised the lawyer can testify to it in court. The presence of a lawyer can also help to guarantee that the accused gives a fully accurate statement to the police and that the statement is rightly reported by the prosecution at trial. See *Crooker* v. *California,* 357 U.S. 433, 443 -448 (1958) (DOUGLAS, J., dissenting).

An individual need not make a pre-interrogation request for a lawyer. While such request affirmatively secures his right to have one, his failure to ask for a lawyer does not constitute a waiver. No effective waiver of the right to counsel during interrogation can be recognized unless specifically made after the warnings we here delineate have been given. The accused who does not know his rights and therefore does not make a request may be the person who most needs counsel. As the California Supreme Court has aptly put it:

- "Finally, we must recognize that the imposition of the requirement for the request would discriminate against the defendant who does not know his rights. The defendant who does not ask for counsel is the very defendant who most needs counsel. We cannot penalize a defendant who, not understanding his constitutional rights, does not make the formal request and by such failure demonstrates his helplessness. To require the request would be to favor the defendant whose sophistication or status had fortuitously prompted him to make it." *People* v. *Dorado,* 62 Cal. 2d 338, 351, 398 P.2d 361, 369-370, 42 Cal. Rptr. 169, 177-178 (1965) (Tobriner, J.).

In *Carnley* v. *Cochran,* 369 U.S. 506, 513 (1962), we stated: "[I]t is settled that where the assistance of counsel is a constitutional requisite, the right to be furnished counsel does not depend on a request." This proposition applies with equal force in the context of providing counsel to protect an accused's Fifth Amendment privilege in the face of interrogation. [footnote 39] Although the role of counsel at trial differs

---

[39]See Herman, The Supreme Court and Restrictions on Police Interrogation, 25 Ohio St. L. J. 449, 480 (1964).

from the role during interrogation, the differences are not relevant to the question whether a request is a prerequisite.

Accordingly we hold that an individual held for interrogation must be clearly informed that he has the right to consult with a lawyer and to have the lawyer with him during interrogation under the system for protecting the privilege we delineate today. As with the warnings of the right to remain silent and that anything stated can be used in evidence against him, this warning is an absolute prerequisite to interrogation. No amount of circumstantial evidence that the person may have been aware of this right will suffice to stand in its stead: Only through such a warning is there ascertainable assurance that the accused was aware of this right.

If an individual indicates that he wishes the assistance of counsel before any interrogation occurs, the authorities cannot rationally ignore or deny his request on the basis that the individual does not have or cannot afford a retained attorney. The financial ability of the individual has no relationship to the scope of the rights involved here. The privilege against self-incrimination secured by the Constitution applies to all individuals. The need for counsel in order to protect the privilege exists for the indigent as well as the affluent. In fact, were we to limit these constitutional rights to those who can retain an attorney, our decisions today would be of little significance. The cases before us as well as the vast majority of confession cases with which we have dealt in the past involve those unable to retain counsel. [footnote 40] While authorities are not required to relieve the accused of his poverty, they have the obligation not to take advantage of indigence in the administration of justice. [footnote 41] Denial of counsel to the indigent at the time of interrogation while allowing an attorney to those who can afford one would be no more supportable by reason or logic than the similar situation at trial and on appeal struck down in *Gideon* v. *Wainwright,* 372 U.S. 335 (1963), and *Douglas* v. *California,* 372 U.S. 353 (1963).

In order fully to apprise a person interrogated of the extent of his rights under this system then, it is necessary to warn him not only that he has the right to consult with an attorney, but also that if he is indigent a lawyer will be appointed to represent him. Without this additional warning, the admonition of the right to consult with counsel would often be understood as meaning only that he can consult with a lawyer if he has one or has the funds to obtain one. The warning of a right to counsel would be hollow if not couched in terms that would convey to the indigent - the person most often subjected to interrogation - the knowledge that he too has a right to have counsel present. [footnote 42] As with the warnings of the right to remain silent and of the general right to counsel, only by effective and express explanation to the indigent of this right can there be assurance that he was truly in a position to exercise it. [footnote 43]

---

[40]Estimates of 50-90% indigency among felony defendants have been reported. Pollock, Equal Justice in Practice, 45 Minn. L. Rev. 737, 738-739 (1961); Birzon, Kasanof & Forma, The Right to Counsel and the Indigent Accused in Courts of Criminal Jurisdiction in New York State, 14 Buffalo L. Rev. 428, 433 (1965).

[41]See Kamisar, Equal Justice in the Gatehouses and Mansions of American Criminal Procedure, in Criminal Justice in Our Time 1, 64-81 (1965). As was stated in the Report of the Attorney General's Committee on Poverty and the Administration of Federal Criminal Justice 9 (1963):

- "When government chooses to exert its powers in the criminal area, its obligation is surely no less than that of taking reasonable measures to eliminate those factors that are irrelevant to just administration of the law but which, nevertheless, may occasionally affect determinations of the accused's liability or penalty. While government may not be required to relieve the accused of his poverty, it may properly be required to minimize the influence of poverty on its administration of justice."

[42]Cf. United States ex rel. *Brown* v. *Fay,* 242 F. Supp. 273, 277 (D.C. S. D. N. Y. 1965); *People* v. *Witenski,* 15 N. Y. 2d 392, 207 N. E. 2d 358, 259 N. Y. S. 2d 413 (1965).

[43]While a warning that the indigent may have counsel appointed need not be given to the person who is known to have an attorney or is known to have ample funds to secure one, the expedient of giving a warning is too simple and the rights involved too important to engage in ex post facto inquiries into financial ability when there is any doubt at all on that score.

Once warnings have been given, the subsequent procedure is clear. If the individual indicates in any manner, at any time prior to or during questioning, that he wishes to remain silent, the interrogation must cease. [footnote 44] At this point he has shown that he intends to exercise his Fifth Amendment privilege; any statement taken after the person invokes his privilege cannot be other than the product of compulsion, subtle or otherwise. Without the right to cut off questioning, the setting of in-custody interrogation operates on the individual to overcome free choice in producing a statement after the privilege has been once invoked. If the individual states that he wants an attorney, the interrogation must cease until an attorney is present. At that time, the individual must have an opportunity to confer with the attorney and to have him present during any subsequent questioning. If the individual cannot obtain an attorney and he indicates that he wants one before speaking to police, they must respect his decision to remain silent.

This does not mean, as some have suggested, that each police station must have a "station house lawyer" present at all times to advise prisoners. It does mean, however, that if police propose to interrogate a person they must make known to him that he is entitled to a lawyer and that if he cannot afford one, a lawyer will be provided for him prior to any interrogation. If authorities conclude that they will not provide counsel during a reasonable period of time in which investigation in the field is carried out, they may refrain from doing so without violating the person's Fifth Amendment privilege so long as they do not question him during that time.

If the interrogation continues without the presence of an attorney and a statement is taken, a heavy burden rests on the government to demonstrate that the defendant knowingly and intelligently waived his privilege against self-incrimination and his right to retained or appointed counsel. *Escobedo* v. *Illinois,* 378 U.S. 478, 490, n. 14. This Court has always set high standards of proof for the waiver of constitutional rights, *Johnson* v. *Zerbst,* 304 U.S. 458 (1938), and we re-assert these standards as applied to in-custody interrogation. Since the State is responsible for establishing the isolated circumstances under which the interrogation takes place and has the only means of making available corroborated evidence of warnings given during incommunicado interrogation, the burden is rightly on its shoulders.

An express statement that the individual is willing to make a statement and does not want an attorney followed closely by a statement could constitute a waiver. But a valid waiver will not be presumed simply from the silence of the accused after warnings are given or simply from the fact that a confession was in fact eventually obtained. A statement we made in *Carnley* v. *Cochran,* 369 U.S. 506, 516 (1962), is applicable here:

- "Presuming waiver from a silent record is impermissible. The record must show, or there must be an allegation and evidence which show, that an accused was offered counsel but intelligently and understandingly rejected the offer. Anything less is not waiver."

See also *Glasser* v. *United States,* 315 U.S. 60 (1942). Moreover, where in-custody interrogation is involved, there is no room for the contention that the privilege is waived if the individual answers some questions or gives some information on his own prior to invoking his right to remain silent when interrogated. [footnote 45]

---

[44]If an individual indicates his desire to remain silent, but has an attorney present, there may be some circumstances in which further questioning would be permissible. In the absence of evidence of overbearing, statements then made in the presence of counsel might be free of the compelling influence of the interrogation process and might fairly be construed as a waiver of the privilege for purposes of these statements.

[45]Although this Court held in *Rogers* v. *United States, 340 U.S. 367* (1951), over strong dissent, that a witness before a grand jury may not in certain circumstances decide to answer some questions and then refuse to answer others, that decision has no application to the interrogation situation we deal with today. No legislative or judicial fact-finding authority is involved here, nor is there a possibility that the individual might make self-serving statements of which he could make use at trial while refusing to answer incriminating statements.

Whatever the testimony of the authorities as to waiver of rights by an accused, the fact of lengthy interrogation or incommunicado incarceration before a statement is made is strong evidence that the accused did not validly waive his rights. In these circumstances the fact that the individual eventually made a statement is consistent with the conclusion that the compelling influence of the interrogation finally forced him to do so. It is inconsistent with any notion of a voluntary relinquishment of the privilege. Moreover, any evidence that the accused was threatened, tricked, or cajoled into a waiver will, of course, show that the defendant did not voluntarily waive his privilege. The requirement of warnings and waiver of rights is a fundamental right with respect to the Fifth Amendment privilege and not simply a preliminary ritual to existing methods of interrogation.

The warnings required and the waiver necessary in accordance with our opinion today are, in the absence of a fully effective equivalent, prerequisites to the admissibility of any statement made by a defendant. No distinction can be drawn between statements which are direct confessions and statements which amount to "admissions" of part or all of an offense. The privilege against self-incrimination protects the individual from being compelled to incriminate himself in any manner; it does not distinguish degrees of incrimination. Similarly, for precisely the same reason, no distinction may be drawn between inculpatory statements and statements alleged to be merely "exculpatory." If a statement made were in fact truly exculpatory it would, of course, never be used by the prosecution. In fact, statements merely intended to be exculpatory by the defendant are often used to impeach his testimony at trial or to demonstrate untruths in the statement given under interrogation and thus to prove guilt by implication. These statements are incriminating in any meaningful sense of the word and may not be used without the full warnings and effective waiver required for any other statement. In *Escobedo* itself, the defendant fully intended his accusation of another as the slayer to be exculpatory as to himself.

The principles announced today deal with the protection which must be given to the privilege against self-incrimination when the individual is first subjected to police interrogation while in custody at the station or otherwise deprived of his freedom of action in any significant way. It is at this point that our adversary system of criminal proceedings commences, distinguishing itself at the outset from the inquisitorial system recognized in some countries. Under the system of warnings we delineate today or under any other system which may be devised and found effective, the safeguards to be erected about the privilege must come into play at this point.

Our decision is not intended to hamper the traditional function of police officers in investigating crime. See *Escobedo* v. *Illinois,* 378 U.S. 478, 492. When an individual is in custody on probable cause, the police may, of course, seek out evidence in the field to be used at trial against him. Such investigation may include inquiry of persons not under restraint. General on-the-scene questioning as to facts surrounding a crime or other general questioning of citizens in the fact-finding process is not affected by our holding. It is an act of responsible citizenship for individuals to give whatever information they may have to aid in law enforcement. In such situations the compelling atmosphere inherent in the process of in-custody interrogation is not necessarily present. [footnote 46]

In dealing with statements obtained through interrogation, we do not purport to find all confessions inadmissible. Confessions remain a proper element in law enforcement. Any statement given freely and voluntarily without any compelling in-

---

[46]The distinction and its significance has been aptly described in the opinion of a Scottish court:

- "In former times such questioning, if undertaken, would be conducted by police officers visiting the house or place of business of the suspect and there questioning him, probably in the presence of a relation or friend. However convenient the modern practice may be, it must normally create a situation very unfavorable to the suspect." *Chalmers* v. *H. M. Advocate*, 1954. Sess. Cas. 66, 78 (J. C.).

fluences is, of course, admissible in evidence. The fundamental import of the privilege while an individual is in custody is not whether he is allowed to talk to the police without the benefit of warnings and counsel, but whether he can be interrogated. There is no requirement that police stop a person who enters a police station and states that he wishes to confess to a crime, [footnote 47] or a person who calls the police to offer a confession or any other statement he desires to make. Volunteered statements of any kind are not barred by the Fifth Amendment and their admissibility is not affected by our holding today.

To summarize, we hold that when an individual is taken into custody or otherwise deprived of his freedom by the authorities in any significant way and is subjected to questioning, the privilege against self-incrimination is jeopardized. Procedural safeguards must be employed to protect the privilege, and unless other fully effective means are adopted to notify the person of his right of silence and to assure that the exercise of the right will be scrupulously honored, the following measures are required. He must be warned prior to any questioning that he has the right to remain silent, that anything he says can be used against him in a court of law, that he has the right to the presence of an attorney, and that if he cannot afford an attorney one will be appointed for him prior to any questioning if he so desires. Opportunity to exercise these rights must be afforded to him throughout the interrogation. After such warnings have been given, and such opportunity afforded him, the individual may knowingly and intelligently waive these rights and agree to answer questions or make a statement. But unless and until such warnings and waiver are demonstrated by the prosecution at trial, no evidence obtained as a result of interrogation can be used against him. [footnote 48]

IV.

A recurrent argument made in these cases is that society's need for interrogation outweighs the privilege. This argument is not unfamiliar to this Court. See, e. g., *Chambers* v. *Florida,* 309 U.S. 227, 240 -241 (1940). The whole thrust of our foregoing discussion demonstrates that the Constitution has prescribed the rights of the individual when confronted with the power of government when it provided in the Fifth Amendment that an individual cannot be compelled to be a witness against himself. That right cannot be abridged. As Mr. Justice Brandeis once observed:

- "Decency, security and liberty alike demand that government officials shall be subjected to the same rules of conduct that are commands to the citizen. In a government of laws, existence of the government will be imperilled if it fails to observe the law scrupulously. Our Government is the potent, the omnipresent teacher. For good or for ill, it teaches the whole people by its example. Crime is contagious. If the Government becomes a lawbreaker, it breeds contempt for law; it invites every man to become a law unto himself; it invites anarchy. To declare that in the administration of the criminal law the end justifies the means . . . would bring terrible retribution. Against that pernicious doctrine this Court should resolutely set its face." *Olmstead* v. *United States,* 277 U.S. 438, 485 (1928) (dissenting opinion). [footnote 49]

---

[47]See *People* v. *Dorado,* 62 Cal. 2d 338, 354, 398 P.2d 361, 371, 42 Cal. Rptr. 169, 179 (1965).

[48]In accordance with our holdings today and in *Escobedo* v. *Illinois,* 378 U.S. 478, 492, *Crooker* v. *California,* 357 U.S. 433 (1958) and *Cicenia* v. *Lagay,* 357 U.S. 504 (1958) are not to be followed.

[49]In quoting the above from the dissenting opinion of Mr. Justice Brandeis we, of course, do not intend to pass on the constitutional questions involved in the *Olmstead* case.

In this connection, one of our country's distinguished jurists has pointed out: "The quality of a nation's civilization can be largely measured by the methods it uses in the enforcement of its criminal law." [footnote 50]

If the individual desires to exercise his privilege, he has the right to do so. This is not for the authorities to decide. An attorney may advise his client not to talk to police until he has had an opportunity to investigate the case, or he may wish to be present with his client during any police questioning. In doing so an attorney is merely exercising the good professional judgment he has been taught. This is not cause for considering the attorney a menace to law enforcement. He is merely carrying out what he is sworn to do under his oath - to protect to the extent of his ability the rights of his client. In fulfilling this responsibility the attorney plays a vital role in the administration of criminal justice under our Constitution.

In announcing these principles, we are not unmindful of the burdens which law enforcement officials must bear, often under trying circumstances. We also fully recognize the obligation of all citizens to aid in enforcing the criminal laws. This Court, while protecting individual rights, has always given ample latitude to law enforcement agencies in the legitimate exercise of their duties. The limits we have placed on the interrogation process should not constitute an undue interference with a proper system of law enforcement. As we have noted, our decision does not in any way preclude police from carrying out their traditional investigatory functions. Although confessions may play an important role in some convictions, the cases before us present graphic examples of the overstatement of the "need" for confessions. In each case authorities conducted interrogations ranging up to five days in duration despite the presence, through standard investigating practices, of considerable evidence against each defendant. [footnote 51] Further examples are chronicled in our prior cases. See, e. g., *Haynes* v. *Washington,* 373 U.S. 503, 518 - 519 (1963); *Rogers* v. *Richmond,* 365 U.S. 534, 541 (1961); *Malinski* v. *New York,* 324 U.S. 401, 402 (1945). [footnote 52]

It is also urged that an unfettered right to detention for interrogation should be allowed because it will often redound to the benefit of the person questioned. When police inquiry determines that there is no reason to believe that the person has committed any crime, it is said, he will be released without need for further formal procedures. The person who has committed no offense, however, will be better able to clear himself after warnings with counsel present than without. It can be assumed that in such circumstances a lawyer would advise his client to talk freely to police in order to clear himself.

Custodial interrogation, by contrast, does not necessarily afford the innocent an opportunity to clear themselves. A serious consequence of the present practice of the interrogation alleged to be beneficial for the innocent is that many arrests "for investigation" subject large numbers of innocent persons to detention and interrogation. In one of the cases before us, No. 584, *California* v. *Stewart,* police held four persons, who were in the defendant's house at the time of the arrest, in jail for five days until defendant confessed. At that time they were finally released. Police stated that there was "no evidence to connect them with any crime." Available statistics on the extent

---

[50]Schaefer, Federalism and State Criminal Procedure, 70 Harv. L. Rev. 1, 26 (1956).

[51]Miranda, Vignera, and Westover were identified by eyewitnesses. Marked bills from the bank robbed were found in Westover's car. Articles stolen from the victim as well as from several other robbery victims were found in Stewart's home at the outset of the investigation.

[52]Dealing as we do here with constitutional standards in relation to statements made, the existence of independent corroborating evidence produced at trial is, of course, irrelevant to our decisions. *Haynes* v. *Washington,* 373 U.S. 503, 518 -519 (1963); *Lynumn* v. *Illinois,* 372 U.S. 528, 537 -538 (1963); *Rogers* v. *Richmond,* 365 U.S. 534, 541 (1961); *Blackburn* v. *Alabama,* 361 U.S. 199, 206 (1960).

of this practice where it is condoned indicate that these four are far from alone in being subjected to arrest, prolonged detention, and interrogation without the requisite probable cause. [footnote 53]

Over the years the Federal Bureau of Investigation has compiled an exemplary record of effective law enforcement while advising any suspect or arrested person, at the outset of an interview, that he is not required to make a statement, that any statement may be used against him in court, that the individual may obtain the services of an attorney of his own choice and, more recently, that he has a right to free counsel if he is unable to pay. [footnote 54] A letter received from the Solicitor General in response to a question from the Bench makes it clear that the present pattern of warnings and respect for the rights of the individual followed as a practice by the FBI is consistent with the procedure which we delineate today. It states:

- "At the oral argument of the above cause, Mr. Justice Fortas asked whether I could provide certain information as to the practices followed by the Federal Bureau of Investigation. I have directed these questions to the attention of the Director of the Federal Bureau of Investigation and am submitting herewith a statement of the questions and of the answers which we have received.

- " '(1) When an individual is interviewed by agents of the Bureau, what warning is given to him?

- " 'The standard warning long given by Special Agents of the FBI to both suspects and persons under arrest is that the person has a right to say nothing and a right to counsel, and that any statement he does make may be used against him in court. Examples of this warning are to be found in the *Westover* case at 342 F.2d 684 (1965), and *Jackson* v. *U.S.,* 337 F.2d 136 (1964), cert. den. 380 U.S. 935 .

- " 'After passage of the Criminal Justice Act of 1964, which provides free counsel for Federal defendants unable to pay, we added to our instructions to Special Agents the requirement that any person who is under arrest for an offense under FBI jurisdiction, or whose arrest is contemplated following the interview, must also be advised of his right to free counsel if he is unable to pay, and the fact that such counsel will be assigned by the Judge. At the same time, we broadened the right to counsel warning to read counsel of his own choice, or anyone else with whom he might wish to speak.

- " '(2) When is the warning given?

---

[53]See, e. g., Report and Recommendations of the [District of Columbia] Commissioners' Committee on Police Arrests for Investigation (1962); American Civil Liberties Union, Secret Detention by the Chicago Police (1959). An extreme example of this practice occurred in the District of Columbia in 1958. Seeking three "stocky" young Negroes who had robbed a restaurant, police rounded up 90 persons of that general description. Sixty-three were held overnight before being released for lack of evidence. A man not among the 90 arrested was ultimately charged with the crime. Washington Daily News, January 21, 1958, p. 5, col. 1; Hearings before a Subcommittee of the Senate Judiciary Committee on H. R. 11477, S. 2970, S. 3325, and S. 3355, 85th Cong., 2d Sess. (July 1958), pp. 40, 78.

[54]In 1952, J. Edgar Hoover, Director of the Federal Bureau of Investigation, stated:

- "Law enforcement, however, in defeating the criminal, must maintain inviolate the historic liberties of the individual. To turn back the criminal, yet, by so doing, destroy the dignity of the individual, would be a hollow victory.

- "We can have the Constitution, the best laws in the land, and the most honest reviews by courts - but unless the law enforcement profession is steeped in the democratic tradition, maintains the highest in ethics, and makes its work a career of honor, civil liberties will continually - and without end - be violated. . . . The best protection of civil liberties is an alert, intelligent and honest law enforcement agency. There can be no alternative.

- ". . . Special Agents are taught that any suspect or arrested person, at the outset of an interview, must be advised that he is not required to make a statement and that any statement given can be used against him in court. Moreover, the individual must be informed that, if he desires, he may obtain the services of an attorney of his own choice."

Hoover, Civil Liberties and Law Enforcement: The Role of the FBI, 37 Iowa L. Rev. 175, 177-182 (1952).

- " 'The FBI warning is given to a suspect at the very outset of the interview, as shown in the *Westover* case, cited above. The warning may be given to a person arrested as soon as practicable after the arrest, as shown in the *Jackson* case, also cited above, and in *U.S.* v. *Konigsberg,* 336 F.2d 844 (1964), cert. den. 379 U.S. 933, but in any event it must precede the interview with the person for a confession or admission of his own guilt.

- " '(3) What is the Bureau's practice in the event that (a) the individual requests counsel and (b) counsel appears?

- " 'When the person who has been warned of his right to counsel decides that he wishes to consult with counsel before making a statement, the interview is terminated at that point, *Shultz* v. *U.S.,* 351 F.2d 287 (1965). It may be continued, however, as to all matters other than the person's own guilt or innocence. If he is indecisive in his request for counsel, there may be some question on whether he did or did not waive counsel. Situations of this kind must necessarily be left to the judgment of the interviewing Agent. For example, in *Hiram* v. *U.S.,* 354 F.2d 4 (1965), the Agent's conclusion that the person arrested had waived his right to counsel was upheld by the courts.

- " 'A person being interviewed and desiring to consult counsel by telephone must be permitted to do so, as shown in *Caldwell* v. *U.S.,* 351 F.2d 459 (1965). When counsel appears in person, he is permitted to confer with his client in private.

- " '(4) What is the Bureau's practice if the individual requests counsel, but cannot afford to retain an attorney?

- " 'If any person being interviewed after warning of counsel decides that he wishes to consult with counsel before proceeding further the interview is terminated, as shown above. FBI Agents do not pass judgment on the ability of the person to pay for counsel. They do, however, advise those who have been arrested for an offense under FBI jurisdiction, or whose arrest is contemplated following the interview, of a right to free counsel if they are unable to pay, and the availability of such counsel from the Judge.' " [footnote 55]

The practice of the FBI can readily be emulated by state and local enforcement agencies. The argument that the FBI deals with different crimes than are dealt with by state authorities does not mitigate the significance of the FBI experience. [footnote 56]

The experience in some other countries also suggests that the danger to law enforcement in curbs on interrogation is overplayed. The English procedure since 1912 under the Judges' Rules is significant. As recently strengthened, the Rules require that a cautionary warning be given an accused by a police officer as soon as he has evidence that affords reasonable grounds for suspicion; they also require that any

---

[55]We agree that the interviewing agent must exercise his judgment in determining whether the individual waives his right to counsel. Because of the constitutional basis of the right, however, the standard for waiver is necessarily high. And, of course, the ultimate responsibility for resolving this constitutional question lies with the courts.

[56]Among the crimes within the enforcement jurisdiction of the FBI are kidnapping, 18 U.S.C. 1201 (1964 ed.), white slavery, 18 U.S.C. 2421-2423 (1964 ed.), bank robbery, 18 U.S.C. 2113 (1964 ed.), interstate transportation and sale of stolen property, 18 U.S.C. 2311-2317 (1964 ed.), all manner of conspiracies, 18 U.S.C. 371 (1964 ed.), and violations of civil rights, 18 U.S.C. 241-242 (1964 ed.). See also 18 U.S.C. 1114 (1964 ed.) (murder of officer or employee of the United States).

statement made be given by the accused without questioning by police. [footnote 57] The right of the individual to consult with an attorney during this period is expressly recognized. [footnote 58]

The safeguards present under Scottish law may be even greater than in England. Scottish judicial decisions bar use in evidence of most confessions obtained through police interrogation. [footnote 59] In India, confessions made to police not in the presence of a magistrate have been excluded by rule of evidence since 1872, at a time when it operated under British law. [footnote 60] Identical provisions appear in the Evidence Ordinance of Ceylon, enacted in 1895. [footnote 61] Similarly, in our country the Uni-

---

[57] 1964. Crim. L. Rev., at 166-170. These Rules provide in part:

- "II. As soon as a police officer has evidence which would afford reasonable grounds for suspecting that a person has committed an offence, he shall caution that person or cause him to be cautioned before putting to him any questions, or further questions, relating to that offence.

- "The caution shall be in the following terms:

- "'You are not obliged to say anything unless you wish to do so but what you say may be put into writing and given in evidence.'

- "When after being cautioned a person is being questioned, or elects to make a statement, a record shall be kept of the time and place at which any such questioning or statement began and ended and of the persons present.

- "III. . . .

- "(b) It is only in exceptional cases that questions relating to the offence should be put to the accused person after he has been charged or informed that he may be prosecuted....

- "IV. All written statements made after caution shall be taken in the following manner:

- "(a) If a person says that he wants to make a statement he shall be told that it is intended to make a written record of what he says.

- "He shall always be asked whether he wishes to write down himself what he wants to say; if he says that he cannot write or that he would like someone to write it for him, a police officer may offer to write the statement for him. . . .

- "(b) Any person writing his own statement shall be allowed to do so without any prompting as distinct from indicating to him what matters are material....

- "(d) Whenever a police officer writes the statement, he shall take down the exact words spoken by the person making the statement, without putting any questions other than such as may be needed to make the statement coherent, intelligible and relevant to the material matters: he shall not prompt him."

The prior Rules appear in Devlin, The Criminal Prosecution in England 137-141 (1958).

Despite suggestions of some laxity in enforcement of the Rules and despite the fact some discretion as to admissibility is invested in the trial judge, the Rules are a significant influence in the English criminal law enforcement system. See, e. g., 1964. Crim. L. Rev., at 182; and articles collected in 1960. Crim. L. Rev., at 298-356.

[58] The introduction to the Judges' Rules states in part:

- "These Rules do not affect the principles. . . . .

- "(c) That every person at any stage of an investigation should be able to communicate and to consult privately with a solicitor. This is so even if he is in custody provided that in such a case no unreasonable delay or hindrance is caused to the processes of investigation or the administration of justice by his doing so . . . ." 1964. Crim. L. Rev., at 166-167.

[59] As stated by the Lord Justice General in *Chalmers v. H. M. Advocate,* 1954. Sess. Cas. 66, 78 (J. C.):

- "The theory of our law is that at the stage of initial investigation the police may question anyone with a view to acquiring information which may lead to the detection of the criminal; but that, when the stage has been reached at which suspicion, or more than suspicion, has in their view centred upon some one person as the likely perpetrator of the crime, further interrogation of that person becomes very dangerous, and, if carried too far, e. g., to the point of extracting a confession by what amounts to cross-examination, the evidence of that confession will almost certainly be excluded. Once the accused has been apprehended and charged he has the statutory right to a private interview with a solicitor and to be brought before a magistrate with all convenient speed so that he may, if so advised, emit a declaration in presence of his solicitor under conditions which safeguard him against prejudice."

[60] "No confession made to a police officer shall be proved as against a person accused of any offence." Indian Evidence Act 25.

- "No confession made by any person whilst he is in the custody of a police officer unless it be made in the immediate presence of a Magistrate, shall be proved as against such person." Indian Evidence Act 26. See 1 Ramaswami & Rajagopalan, Law of Evidence in India 553-569 (1962). To avoid any continuing effect of police pressure or inducement, the Indian Supreme Court has invalidated a confession made shortly after police brought a suspect before a magistrate, suggesting: "[I]t would, we think, be reasonable to insist upon giving an accused person at least 24 hours to decide whether or not he should make a confession." *Sarwan Singh* v. *State of Punjab,* 44 All India Rep. 1957, Sup. Ct. 637, 644.

[61] I Legislative Enactments of Ceylon 211 (1958).

form Code of Military Justice has long provided that no suspect may be interrogated without first being warned of his right not to make a statement and that any statement he makes may be used against him. [footnote 62] Denial of the right to consult counsel during interrogation has also been proscribed by military tribunals. [footnote 63] There appears to have been no marked detrimental effect on criminal law enforcement in these jurisdictions as a result of these rules. Conditions of law enforcement in our country are sufficiently similar to permit reference to this experience as assurance that lawlessness will not result from warning an individual of his rights or allowing him to exercise them. Moreover, it is consistent with our legal system that we give at least as much protection to these rights as is given in the jurisdictions described. We deal in our country with rights grounded in a specific requirement of the Fifth Amendment of the Constitution, whereas other jurisdictions arrived at their conclusions on the basis of principles of justice not so specifically defined. [footnote 64]

It is also urged upon us that we withhold decision on this issue until state legislative bodies and advisory groups have had an opportunity to deal with these problems by rule making. [footnote 65] We have already pointed out that the Constitution does not require any specific code of procedures for protecting the privilege against self-incrimination during custodial interrogation. Congress and the States are free to develop their own safeguards for the privilege, so long as they are fully as effective as those described above in informing accused persons of their right of silence and in affording a continuous opportunity to exercise it. In any event, however, the issues presented are of constitutional dimensions and must be determined by the courts. The admissibility of a statement in the face of a claim that it was obtained in violation of the defendant's constitutional rights is an issue the resolution of which has long since been undertaken by this Court. See *Hopt* v. *Utah,* 110 U.S. 574 (1884). Judicial solutions to problems of constitutional dimension have evolved decade by decade. As courts have been presented with the need to enforce constitutional rights, they have found means of doing so. That was our responsibility when *Escobedo* was before us and it is our responsibility today. Where rights secured by the Constitution are involved, there can be no rule making or legislation which would abrogate them.

V.

Because of the nature of the problem and because of its recurrent significance in numerous cases, we have to this point discussed the relationship of the Fifth Amendment privilege to police interrogation without specific concentration on the facts of the cases before us. We turn now to these facts to consider the application to these cases of the constitutional principles discussed above. In each instance, we have concluded that statements were obtained from the defendant under circumstances that did not meet constitutional standards for protection of the privilege.

No. 759. *Miranda* v. *Arizona.*

On March 13, 1963, petitioner, Ernesto Miranda, was arrested at his home and taken in custody to a Phoenix police station. He was there identified by the complaining witness. The police then took him to "Interrogation Room No. 2" of the detective bureau. There he was questioned by two police officers. The officers admit-

---

[62]10 U.S.C. 831 (b) (1964 ed.).

[63]*United States* v. *Rose,* 24 CMR 251 (1957); *United States* v. *Gunnels,* 23 CMR 354 (1957).

[64]Although no constitution existed at the time confessions were excluded by rule of evidence in 1872, India now has a written constitution which includes the provision that "No person accused of any offence shall be compelled to be a witness against himself." Constitution of India, Article 20 (3). See Tope, The Constitution of India 63-67 (1960).

[65]Brief for United States in No. 761, *Westover* v. *United States,* pp. 44-47; Brief for the State of New York as amicus curiae, pp. 35-39. See also Brief for the National District Attorneys Association as amicus curiae, pp. 23-26.

ted at trial that Miranda was not advised that he had a right to have an attorney present. [footnote 66] Two hours later, the officers emerged from the interrogation room with a written confession signed by Miranda. At the top of the statement was a typed paragraph stating that the confession was made voluntarily, without threats or promises of immunity and "with full knowledge of my legal rights, understanding any statement I make may be used against me." [footnote 67]

At his trial before a jury, the written confession was admitted into evidence over the objection of defense counsel, and the officers testified to the prior oral confession made by Miranda during the interrogation. Miranda was found guilty of kidnapping and rape. He was sentenced to 20 to 30 years' imprisonment on each count, the sentences to run concurrently. On appeal, the Supreme Court of Arizona held that Miranda's constitutional rights were not violated in obtaining the confession and affirmed the conviction. 98 Ariz. 18, 401 P.2d 721. In reaching its decision, the court emphasized heavily the fact that Miranda did not specifically request counsel.

We reverse. From the testimony of the officers and by the admission of respondent, it is clear that Miranda was not in any way apprised of his right to consult with an attorney and to have one present during the interrogation, nor was his right not to be compelled to incriminate himself effectively protected in any other manner. Without these warnings the statements were inadmissible. The mere fact that he signed a statement which contained a typed-in clause stating that he had "full knowledge" of his "legal rights" does not approach the knowing and intelligent waiver required to relinquish constitutional rights. Cf. *Haynes* v. *Washington,* 373 U.S. 503, 512-513 (1963); *Haley* v. *Ohio,* 332 U.S. 596, 601 (1948) (opinion of MR. JUSTICE DOUGLAS).

No. 760. *Vignera* v. *New York.*

Petitioner, Michael Vignera, was picked up by New York police on October 14, 1960, in connection with the robbery three days earlier of a Brooklyn dress shop. They took him to the 17th Detective Squad headquarters in Manhattan. Sometime thereafter he was taken to the 66th Detective Squad. There a detective questioned Vignera with respect to the robbery. Vignera orally admitted the robbery to the detective. The detective was asked on cross-examination at trial by defense counsel whether Vignera was warned of his right to counsel before being interrogated. The prosecution objected to the question and the trial judge sustained the objection. Thus, the defense was precluded from making any showing that warnings had not been given. While at the 66th Detective Squad, Vignera was identified by the store owner and a saleslady as the man who robbed the dress shop. At about 3 p. m. he was formally arrested. The police then transported him to still another station, the 70th Precinct in Brooklyn, "for detention." At 11 p. m. Vignera was questioned by an assistant district attorney in the presence of a hearing reporter who transcribed the questions and Vignera's answers. This verbatim account of these proceedings contains no statement of any warnings given by the assistant district attorney. At Vignera's trial on a charge of first degree robbery, the detective testified as to the oral confession. The transcription of the statement taken was also introduced in evidence. At the conclusion of the testimony, the trial judge charged the jury in part as follows:

- "The law doesn't say that the confession is void or invalidated because the police officer didn't advise the defendant as to his rights. Did you hear what I said? I am telling you what the law of the State of New York is."

---

[66]Miranda was also convicted in a separate trial on an unrelated robbery charge not presented here for review. A statement introduced at that trial was obtained from Miranda during the same interrogation which resulted in the confession involved here. At the robbery trial, one officer testified that during the interrogation he did not tell Miranda that anything he said would be held against him or that he could consult with an attorney. The other officer stated that they had both told Miranda that anything he said would be used against him and that he was not required by law to tell them anything.

[67]One of the officers testified that he read this paragraph to Miranda. Apparently, however, he did not do so until after Miranda had confessed orally.

Vignera was found guilty of first degree robbery. He was subsequently adjudged a third-felony offender and sentenced to 30 to 60 years' imprisonment. [footnote 68] The conviction was affirmed without opinion by the Appellate Division, Second Department, 21 App. Div. 2d 752, 252 N. Y. S. 2d 19, and by the Court of Appeals, also without opinion, 15 N. Y. 2d 970, 207 N. E. 2d 527, 259 N. Y. S. 2d 857, remittitur amended, 16 N. Y. 2d 614, 209 N. E. 2d 110, 261 N. Y. S. 2d 65. In argument to the Court of Appeals, the State contended that Vignera had no constitutional right to be advised of his right to counsel or his privilege against self-incrimination.

We reverse. The foregoing indicates that Vignera was not warned of any of his rights before the questioning by the detective and by the assistant district attorney. No other steps were taken to protect these rights. Thus he was not effectively apprised of his Fifth Amendment privilege or of his right to have counsel present and his statements are inadmissible.

No. 761. *Westover* v. *United States.*

At approximately 9:45 p. m. on March 20, 1963, petitioner, Carl Calvin Westover, was arrested by local police in Kansas City as a suspect in two Kansas City robberies. A report was also received from the FBI that he was wanted on a felony charge in California. The local authorities took him to a police station and placed him in a line-up on the local charges, and at about 11:45 p. m. he was booked. Kansas City police interrogated Westover [384 U.S. 436, 495] on the night of his arrest. He denied any knowledge of criminal activities. The next day local officers interrogated him again throughout the morning. Shortly before noon they informed the FBI that they were through interrogating Westover and that the FBI could proceed to interrogate him. There is nothing in the record to indicate that Westover was ever given any warning as to his rights by local police. At noon, three special agents of the FBI continued the interrogation in a private interview room of the Kansas City Police Department, this time with respect to the robbery of a savings and loan association and a bank in Sacramento, California. After two or two and one-half hours, Westover signed separate confessions to each of these two robberies which had been prepared by one of the agents during the interrogation. At trial one of the agents testified, and a paragraph on each of the statements states, that the agents advised Westover that he did not have to make a statement, that any statement he made could be used against him, and that he had the right to see an attorney.

Westover was tried by a jury in federal court and convicted of the California robberies. His statements were introduced at trial. He was sentenced to 15 years' imprisonment on each count, the sentences to run consecutively. On appeal, the conviction was affirmed by the Court of Appeals for the Ninth Circuit. 342 F.2d 684.

We reverse. On the facts of this case we cannot find that Westover knowingly and intelligently waived his right to remain silent and his right to consult with counsel prior to the time he made the statement. [footnote 69] At the time the FBI agents began questioning Westover, he had been in custody for over 14 hours and had been interrogated at length during that period. The FBI interrogation began immediately upon the conclusion of the interrogation by Kansas City police and was conducted in local police headquarters. Although the two law enforcement authorities are legally distinct and the crimes for which they interrogated Westover were different,

---

[68]Vignera thereafter successfully attacked the validity of one of the prior convictions, *Vignera* v. *Wilkins,* Civ. 9901 (D.C. W. D. N. Y. Dec. 31, 1961) (unreported), but was then resentenced as a second-felony offender to the same term of imprisonment as the original sentence. R. 31-33.

[69]The failure of defense counsel to object to the introduction of the confession at trial, noted by the Court of Appeals and emphasized by the Solicitor General, does not preclude our consideration of the issue. Since the trial was held prior to our decision in *Escobedo* and, of course, prior to our decision today making the objection available, the failure to object at trial does not constitute a waiver of the claim. See, e. g., *United States ex rel. Angelet* v. *Fay,* 333 F.2d 12, 16 (C. A. 2d Cir. 1964), aff'd, 381 U.S. 654 (1965). Cf. *Ziffrin, Inc.* v. *United States,* 318 U.S. 73, 78 (1943).

the impact on him was that of a continuous period of questioning. There is no evidence of any warning given prior to the FBI interrogation nor is there any evidence of an articulated waiver of rights after the FBI commenced its interrogation. The record simply shows that the defendant did in fact confess a short time after being turned over to the FBI following interrogation by local police. Despite the fact that the FBI agents gave warnings at the outset of their interview, from Westover's point of view the warnings came at the end of the interrogation process. In these circumstances an intelligent waiver of constitutional rights cannot be assumed.

We do not suggest that law enforcement authorities are precluded from questioning any individual who has been held for a period of time by other authorities and interrogated by them without appropriate warnings. A different case would be presented if an accused were taken into custody by the second authority, removed both in time and place from his original surroundings, and then adequately advised of his rights and given an opportunity to exercise them. But here the FBI interrogation was conducted immediately following the state interrogation in the same police station - in the same compelling surroundings. Thus, in obtaining a confession from Westover [384 U.S. 436, 497] the federal authorities were the beneficiaries of the pressure applied by the local in-custody interrogation. In these circumstances the giving of warnings alone was not sufficient to protect the privilege.

No. 584. *California* v. *Stewart.*

In the course of investigating a series of purse-snatch robberies in which one of the victims had died of injuries inflicted by her assailant, respondent, Roy Allen Stewart, was pointed out to Los Angeles police as the endorser of dividend checks taken in one of the robberies. At about 7:15 p. m., January 31, 1963, police officers went to Stewart's house and arrested him. One of the officers asked Stewart if they could search the house, to which he replied, "Go ahead." The search turned up various items taken from the five robbery victims. At the time of Stewart's arrest, police also arrested Stewart's wife and three other persons who were visiting him. These four were jailed along with Stewart and were interrogated. Stewart was taken to the University Station of the Los Angeles Police Department where he was placed in a cell. During the next five days, police interrogated Stewart on nine different occasions. Except during the first interrogation session, when he was confronted with an accusing witness, Stewart was isolated with his interrogators.

During the ninth interrogation session, Stewart admitted that he had robbed the deceased and stated that he had not meant to hurt her. Police then brought Stewart before a magistrate for the first time. Since there was no evidence to connect them with any crime, the police then released the other four persons arrested with him.

Nothing in the record specifically indicates whether Stewart was or was not advised of his right to remain silent or his right to counsel. In a number of instances, however, the interrogating officers were asked to recount everything that was said during the interrogations. None indicated that Stewart was ever advised of his rights.

Stewart was charged with kidnapping to commit robbery, rape, and murder. At his trial, transcripts of the first interrogation and the confession at the last interrogation were introduced in evidence. The jury found Stewart guilty of robbery and first degree murder and fixed the penalty as death. On appeal, the Supreme Court of California reversed. 62 Cal. 2d 571, 400 P.2d 97, 43 Cal. Rptr. 201. It held that under this Court's decision in Escobedo, Stewart should have been advised of his right to remain silent and of his right to counsel and that it would not presume in the face of a silent record that the police advised Stewart of his rights. [footnote 70]

---

[70]Because of this disposition of the case, the California Supreme Court did not reach the claims that the confession was coerced by police threats to hold his ailing wife in custody until he confessed, that there was no hearing as required by *Jackson* v. *Denno,* 378 U.S. 368 (1964), and that the trial judge gave an instruction condemned by the California Supreme Court's decision in *People* v. *Morse,* 60 Cal. 2d 631, 388 P.2d 33, 36 Cal. Rptr. 201 (1964).

We affirm. [footnote 71] In dealing with custodial interrogation, we will not presume that a defendant has been effectively apprised of his rights and that his privilege against self-incrimination has been adequately safeguarded on a record that does not show that any warnings have been given or that any effective alternative has been employed. Nor can a knowing and intelligent waiver of these rights be assumed on a silent record. Furthermore, Stewart's steadfast denial of the alleged offenses through eight of the nine interrogations over a period of five days is subject to no other construction than that he was compelled by persistent interrogation to forgo his Fifth Amendment privilege.

Therefore, in accordance with the foregoing, the judgments of the Supreme Court of Arizona in No. 759, of the New York Court of Appeals in No. 760, and of the Court of Appeals for the Ninth Circuit in No. 761 are reversed. The judgment of the Supreme Court of California in No. 584 is affirmed.

- It is so ordered.

MR. JUSTICE CLARK, dissenting in Nos. 759, 760, and 761, and concurring in the result in No. 584.

It is with regret that I find it necessary to write in these cases. However, I am unable to join the majority because its opinion goes too far on too little, while my dissenting brethren do not go quite far enough. Nor can I join in the Court's criticism of the present practices of police and investigatory agencies as to custodial interrogation. The materials it refers to as "police manuals" [footnote 1] are, as I read them, merely writings in this field by professors and some police officers. Not one is shown by the record here to be the official manual of any police department, much less in universal use in crime detection. Moreover, the examples of police brutality mentioned by the Court [footnote 2] are rare exceptions to the thousands of cases that appear every year in the law reports. The police agencies - all the way from municipal and state forces to the federal bureaus - are responsible for law enforcement and public safety in this country. I am proud of their efforts, which in my view are not fairly characterized by the Court's opinion.

I.

The ipse dixit of the majority has no support in our cases. Indeed, the Court admits that "we might not find the defendants' statements [here] to have been involuntary in traditional terms." Ante, p. 457. In short, the Court has added more to the requirements that the accused is entitled to consult with his lawyer and that he must be given the traditional warning that he may remain silent and that anything that he says may be used against him. Escobedo v. Illinois, 378 U.S. 478, 490-491 (1964). Now, the Court fashions a constitutional rule that the police may engage in no custodial interrogation without additionally advising the accused that he has a right under the Fifth Amendment to the presence of counsel during interrogation and that, if he is without funds, counsel will be furnished him. When at any point during an interrogation the accused seeks affirmatively or impliedly to invoke his rights to silence or counsel, in-

---

[71] After certiorari was granted in this case, respondent moved to dismiss on the ground that there was no final judgment from which the State could appeal since the judgment below directed that he be retried. In the event respondent was successful in obtaining an acquittal on retrial, however, under California law the State would have no appeal. Satisfied that in these circumstances the decision below constituted a final judgment under 28 U.S.C. 1257 (3) (1964 ed.), we denied the motion. 383 U.S. 903.

[1] E. G., Inbau & Reid, Criminal Interrogation and Confessions (1962); O'Hara, Fundamentals of Criminal Investigation (1956); Dienstein, Technics for the Crime Investigator (1952); Mulbar, Interrogation (1951); Kidd, Police Interrogation (1940).

[2] As developed by my Brother HARLAN, post, pp. 506-514, such cases, with the exception of the long-discredited decision in Bram v. United States, 168 U.S. 532 (1897), were adequately treated in terms of due process.

terrogation must be forgone or postponed. The Court further holds that failure to follow the new procedures requires inexorably the exclusion of any statement by the accused, as well as the fruits thereof. Such a strict constitutional specific inserted at the nerve center of crime detection may well kill the patient. [footnote 3] Since there is at this time a paucity of information and an almost total lack of empirical knowledge on the practical operation of requirements truly comparable to those announced by the majority, I would be more restrained lest we go too far too fast.

II.

Custodial interrogation has long been recognized as "undoubtedly an essential tool in effective law enforcement." *Haynes* v. *Washington,* 373 U.S. 503, 515 (1963). Recognition of this fact should put us on guard against the promulgation of doctrinaire rules. Especially is this true where the Court finds that "the Constitution has prescribed" its holding and where the light of our past cases, from *Hopt* v. *Utah,* 110 U.S. 574, (1884), down to *Haynes* v. *Washington,* supra, is to the contrary. Indeed, even in *Escobedo* the Court never hinted that an affirmative "waiver" was a prerequisite to questioning; that the burden of proof as to waiver was on the prosecution; that the presence of counsel - absent a waiver - during interrogation was required; that a waiver can be withdrawn at the will of the accused; that counsel must be furnished during an accusatory stage to those unable to pay; nor that admissions and exculpatory statements are "confessions." To require all those things at one gulp should cause the Court to choke over more cases than *Crooker* v. *California,* 357 U.S. 433 (1958), and *Cicenia* v. *Lagay,* 357 U.S. 504 (1958), which it expressly overrules today.

The rule prior to today - as Mr. Justice Goldberg, the author of the Court's opinion in Escobedo, stated it in *Haynes* v. *Washington* - depended upon "a totality of circumstances evidencing an involuntary . . . admission of guilt." 373 U.S., at 514. And he concluded:

- "Of course, detection and solution of crime is, at best, a difficult and arduous task requiring determination and persistence on the part of all responsible officers charged with the duty of law enforcement. And, certainly, we do not mean to suggest that all interrogation of witnesses and suspects is impermissible. Such questioning is undoubtedly an essential tool in effective law enforcement. The line between proper and permissible police conduct and techniques and methods offensive to due process is, at best, a difficult one to draw, particularly in cases such as this where it is necessary to make fine judgments as to the effect of psychologically coercive pressures and inducements on the mind and will of an accused. . . . We are here impelled to the conclusion, from all of the facts presented, that the bounds of due process have been exceeded." Id., at 514-515.

---

[3]The Court points to England, Scotland, Ceylon and India as having equally rigid rules. As my Brother HARLAN points out, post, pp. 521-523, the Court is mistaken in this regard, for it overlooks counterbalancing prosecutorial advantages. Moreover, the requirements of the Federal Bureau of Investigation do not appear from the Solicitor General's letter, ante, pp. 484-486, to be as strict as those imposed today in at least two respects: (1) The offer of counsel is articulated only as "a right to counsel"; nothing is said about a right to have counsel present at the custodial interrogation. (See also the examples cited by the Solicitor General, *Westover* v. *United States,* 342 F.2d 684, 685 (1965) ("right to consult counsel"); *Jackson* v. *United States,* 337 F.2d 136, 138 (1964) (accused "entitled to an attorney").) Indeed, the practice is that whenever the suspect "decides that he wishes to consult with counsel before making a statement, the interview is terminated at that point . . . . When counsel appears in person, he is permitted to confer with his client in private." This clearly indicates that the FBI does not warn that counsel may be present during custodial interrogation. (2) The Solicitor General's letter states: "[T]hose who have been arrested for an offense under FBI jurisdiction, or whose arrest is contemplated following the interview, [are advised] of a right to free counsel if they are unable to pay, and the availability of such counsel from the Judge." So phrased, this warning does not indicate that the agent will secure counsel. Rather, the statement may well be interpreted by the suspect to mean that the burden is placed upon himself and that he may have counsel appointed only when brought before the judge or at trial - but not at custodial interrogation. As I view the FBI practice, it is not as broad as the one laid down today by the Court.

III.

I would continue to follow that rule. Under the "totality of circumstances" rule of which my Brother Goldberg spoke in Haynes, I would consider in each case whether the police officer prior to custodial interrogation added the warning that the suspect might have counsel present at the interrogation and, further, that a court would appoint one at his request if he was too poor to employ counsel. In the absence of warnings, the burden would be on the State to prove that counsel was knowingly and intelligently waived or that in the totality of the circumstances, including the failure to give the necessary warnings, the confession was clearly voluntary.

Rather than employing the arbitrary Fifth Amendment rule [footnote 4] which the Court lays down I would follow the more pliable dictates of the Due Process Clauses of the Fifth and Fourteenth Amendments which we are accustomed to administering and which we know from our cases are effective instruments in protecting persons in police custody. In this way we would not be acting in the dark nor in one full sweep changing the traditional rules of custodial interrogation which this Court has for so long recognized as a justifiable and proper tool in balancing individual rights against the rights of society. It will be soon enough to go further when we are able to appraise with somewhat better accuracy the effect of such a holding.

I would affirm the convictions in *Miranda* v. *Arizona*, No. 759; *Vignera* v. *New York*, No. 760; and *Westover* v. *United States*, No. 761. In each of those cases I find from the circumstances no warrant for reversal. In *California* v. *Stewart*, No. 584, I would dismiss the writ of certiorari for want of a final judgment, 28 U.S.C. 1257 (3) (1964 ed.); but if the merits are to be reached I would affirm on the ground that the State failed to fulfill its burden, in the absence of a showing that appropriate warnings were given, of proving a waiver or a totality of circumstances showing voluntariness. Should there be a retrial, I would leave the State free to attempt to prove these elements.

MR. JUSTICE HARLAN, whom MR. JUSTICE STEWART and MR. JUSTICE WHITE join, dissenting.

I believe the decision of the Court represents poor constitutional law and entails harmful consequences for the country at large. How serious these consequences may prove to be only time can tell. But the basic flaws in the Court's justification seem to me readily apparent now once all sides of the problem are considered.

- I. INTRODUCTION.

At the outset, it is well to note exactly what is required by the Court's new constitutional code of rules for confessions. The foremost requirement, upon which later admissibility of a confession depends, is that a fourfold warning be given to a person in custody before he is questioned, namely, that he has a right to remain silent, that anything he says may be used against him, that he has a right to have present an attorney during the questioning, and that if indigent he has a right to a lawyer without charge. To forgo these rights, some affirmative statement of rejection is seemingly required, and threats, tricks, or cajolings to obtain this waiver are forbidden. If before or during questioning the suspect seeks to invoke his right to remain silent, interrogation must be forgone or cease; a request for counsel brings about the same result until a lawyer is procured. Finally, there are a miscellany of minor directives, for example, the burden of proof of waiver is on the State, admissions and exculpatory

---

[4]In my view there is "no significant support" in our cases for the holding of the Court today that the Fifth Amendment privilege, in effect, forbids custodial interrogation. For a discussion of this point see the dissenting opinion of my Brother WHITE, post, pp. 526-531.

statements are treated just like confessions, withdrawal of a waiver is always permitted, and so forth. [footnote 1]

While the fine points of this scheme are far less clear than the Court admits, the tenor is quite apparent. The new rules are not designed to guard against police brutality or other unmistakably banned forms of coercion. Those who use third-degree tactics and deny them in court are equally able and destined to lie as skillfully about warnings and waivers. Rather, the thrust of the new rules is to negate all pressures, to reinforce the nervous or ignorant suspect, and ultimately to discourage any confession at all. The aim in short is toward "voluntariness" in a utopian sense, or to view it from a different angle, voluntariness with a vengeance.

To incorporate this notion into the Constitution requires a strained reading of history and precedent and a disregard of the very pragmatic concerns that alone may on occasion justify such strains. I believe that reasoned examination will show that the Due Process Clauses provide an adequate tool for coping with confessions and that, even if the Fifth Amendment privilege against self-incrimination be invoked, its precedents taken as a whole do not sustain the present rules. Viewed as a choice based on pure policy, these new rules prove to be a highly debatable, if not one-sided, appraisal of the competing interests, imposed over widespread objection, at the very time when judicial restraint is most called for by the circumstances.

• II. CONSTITUTIONAL PREMISES.

It is most fitting to begin an inquiry into the constitutional precedents by surveying the limits on confessions the Court has evolved under the Due Process Clause of the Fourteenth Amendment. This is so because these cases show that there exists a workable and effective means of dealing with confessions in a judicial manner; because the cases are the baseline from which the Court now departs and so serve to measure the actual as opposed to the professed distance it travels; and because examination of them helps reveal how the Court has coasted into its present position.

The earliest confession cases in this Court emerged from federal prosecutions and were settled on a nonconstitutional basis, the Court adopting the common-law rule that the absence of inducements, promises, and threats made a confession voluntary and admissible. *Hopt* v. *Utah*, 110 U.S. 574; *Pierce* v. *United States*, 160 U.S. 355. While a later case said the Fifth Amendment privilege controlled admissibility, this proposition was not itself developed in subsequent decisions. [footnote 2] The Court did, however, heighten the test of admissibility in federal trials to one of voluntariness "in fact," *Wan* v. *United States*, 266 U.S. 1, 14 (quoted, ante, p. 462), and then by and large left federal judges to apply the same standards the Court began to derive in a string of state court cases.

This new line of decisions, testing admissibility by the Due Process Clause, began in 1936 with *Brown* v. *Mississippi*, 297 U.S. 278, and must now embrace somewhat more than 30 full opinions of the Court. [footnote 3] While the voluntariness rubric was repeated in many instances, e. g., *Lyons* v. *Oklahoma*, 322 U.S. 596, the Court never pinned it down to a single meaning but on the contrary infused it with

---

[1]My discussion in this opinion is directed to the main questions decided by the Court and necessary to its decision; in ignoring some of the collateral points, I do not mean to imply agreement.

[2]The case was *Bram* v. *United States,* 168 U.S. 532 (quoted, ante, p. 461). Its historical premises were afterwards disproved by Wigmore, who concluded "that no assertions could be more unfounded." 3 Wigmore, Evidence 823, at 250, n. 5 (3d ed. 1940). The Court in *United States* v. *Carignan,* 342 U.S. 36, 41, declined to choose between *Bram* and *Wigmore,* and *Stein* v. *New York,* 346 U.S. 156, 191, n. 35, cast further doubt on *Bram.* There are, however, several Court opinions which assume in dicta the relevance of the Fifth Amendment privilege to confessions. *Burdeau* v. *McDowell,* 256 U.S. 465, 475; see *Shotwell Mfg. Co.* v. *United States,* 371 U.S. 341, 347. On *Bram* and the federal confession cases generally, see Developments in the Law - Confessions, 79 Harv. L. Rev. 935, 959-961 (1966).

[3]Comment, 31 U. Chi. L. Rev. 313 & n. 1 (1964), states that by the 1963 Term 33 state coerced-confession cases had been decided by this Court, apart from per curiams. *Spano* v. *New York,* 360 U.S. 315, 321, n. 2, collects 28 cases.

a number of different values. To travel quickly over the main themes, there was an initial emphasis on reliability, e. g., *Ward* v. *Texas,* 316 U.S. 547, supplemented by concern over the legality and fairness of the police practices, e. g., *Ashcraft* v. *Tennessee,* 322 U.S. 143, in an "accusatorial" system of law enforcement, *Watts* v. *Indiana,* 338 U.S. 49, 54, and eventually by close attention to the individual's state of mind and capacity for effective choice, e. g., *Gallegos* v. *Colorado,* 370 U.S. 49. The outcome was a continuing re-evaluation on the facts of each case of how much pressure on the suspect was permissible. [footnote 4]

Among the criteria often taken into account were threats or imminent danger, e. g., *Payne* v. *Arkansas,* 356 U.S. 560, physical deprivations such as lack of sleep or food, e. g., *Reck* v. *Pate,* 367 U.S. 433, repeated or extended interrogation, e. g., *Chambers* v. *Florida,* 309 U.S. 227, limits on access to counsel or friends, *Crooker* v. *California,* 357 U.S. 433; *Cicenia* v. *Lagay,* 357 U.S. 504, length and illegality of detention under state law, e. g., *Haynes* v. *Washington,* 373 U.S. 503, and individual weakness or incapacities, *Lynumn* v. *Illinois,* 372 U.S. 528. Apart from direct physical coercion, however, no single default or fixed combination of defaults guaranteed exclusion, and synopses of the cases would serve little use because the overall gauge has been steadily changing, usually in the direction of restricting admissibility. But to mark just what point had been reached before the Court jumped the rails in *Escobedo* v. *Illinois,* 378 U.S. 478, it is worth capsulizing the then-recent case of *Haynes* v. *Washington,* 373 U.S. 503. There, Haynes had been held some 16 or more hours in violation of state law before signing the disputed confession, had received no warnings of any kind, and despite requests had been refused access to his wife or to counsel, the police indicating that access would be allowed after a confession. Emphasizing especially this last inducement and rejecting some contrary indicia of voluntariness, the Court in a 5-to-4 decision held the confession inadmissible.

There are several relevant lessons to be drawn from this constitutional history. The first is that with over 25 years of precedent the Court has developed an elaborate, sophisticated, and sensitive approach to admissibility of confessions. It is "judicial" in its treatment of one case at a time, see *Culombe* v. *Connecticut,* 367 U.S. 568, 635 (concurring opinion of THE CHIEF JUSTICE), flexible in its ability to respond to the endless mutations of fact presented, and ever more familiar to the lower courts. Of course, strict certainty is not obtained in this developing process, but this is often so with constitutional principles, and disagreement is usually confined to that borderland of close cases where it matters least.

The second point is that in practice and from time to time in principle, the Court has given ample recognition to society's interest in suspect questioning as an instrument of law enforcement. Cases countenancing quite significant pressures can be cited without difficulty, [footnote 5] and the lower courts may often have been yet more tolerant. Of course the limitations imposed today were rejected by necessary implication in case after case, the right to warnings having been explicitly rebuffed in this Court many years ago. *Powers* v. *United States,* 223 U.S. 303; *Wilson* v. *United States,* 162 U.S. 613. As recently as *Haynes* v. *Washington,* 373 U.S. 503, 515, the Court openly acknowledged that questioning of witnesses and suspects "is undoubtedly an essential tool in effective law enforcement." Accord, *Crooker* v. *California,* 357 U.S. 433, 441.

---

[4]Bator & Vorenberg, Arrest, Detention, Interrogation and the Right to Counsel, 66 Col. L. Rev. 62, 73 (1966): "In fact, the concept of involuntariness seems to be used by the courts as a shorthand to refer to practices which are repellent to civilized standards of decency or which, under the circumstances, are thought to apply a degree of pressure to an individual which unfairly impairs his capacity to make a rational choice." See Herman, The Supreme Court and Restrictions on Police Interrogation, 25 Ohio St. L. J. 449, 452-458 (1964); Developments, supra, n. 2, at 964-984.

[5]See the cases synopsized in Herman, supra, n. 4, at 456, nn. 36-39. One not too distant example is *Stroble* v. *California,* 343 U.S. 181, in which the suspect was kicked and threatened after his arrest, questioned a little later for two hours, and isolated from a lawyer trying to see him; the resulting confession was held admissible.

Finally, the cases disclose that the language in many of the opinions overstates the actual course of decision. It has been said, for example, that an admissible confession must be made by the suspect "in the unfettered exercise of his own will," *Malloy* v. *Hogan,* 378 U.S. 1, 8, and that "a prisoner is not 'to be made the deluded instrument of his own conviction,'" *Culombe* v. *Connecticut,* 367 U.S. 568, 581 (Frankfurter, J., announcing the Court's judgment and an opinion). Though often repeated, such principles are rarely observed in full measure. Even the word "voluntary" may be deemed somewhat misleading, especially when one considers many of the confessions that have been brought under its umbrella. See, e. g., supra, n. 5. The tendency to overstate may be laid in part to the flagrant facts often before the Court; but in any event one must recognize how it has tempered attitudes and lent some color of authority to the approach now taken by the Court.

I turn now to the Court's asserted reliance on the Fifth Amendment, an approach which I frankly regard as a trompe l'oeil. The Court's opinion in my view reveals no adequate basis for extending the Fifth Amendment's privilege against self-incrimination to the police station. Far more important, it fails to show that the Court's new rules are well supported, let alone compelled, by Fifth Amendment precedents. Instead, the new rules actually derive from quotation and analogy drawn from precedents under the Sixth Amendment, which should properly have no bearing on police interrogation.

The Court's opening contention, that the Fifth Amendment governs police station confessions, is perhaps not an impermissible extension of the law but it has little to commend itself in the present circumstances. Historically, the privilege against self-incrimination did not bear at all on the use of extra-legal confessions, for which distinct standards evolved; indeed, "the history of the two principles is wide apart, differing by one hundred years in origin, and derived through separate lines of precedents . . . ." 8 Wigmore, Evidence 2266, at 401 (McNaughton rev. 1961). Practice under the two doctrines has also differed in a number of important respects. [footnote 6] Even those who would readily enlarge the privilege must concede some linguistic difficulties since the Fifth Amendment in terms proscribes only compelling any person "in any criminal case to be a witness against himself." Cf. Kamisar, Equal Justice in the Gatehouses and Mansions of American Criminal Procedure, in Criminal Justice in Our Time 1, 25-26 (1965).

Though weighty, I do not say these points and similar ones are conclusive, for, as the Court reiterates, the privilege embodies basic principles always capable of expansion. [footnote 7] Certainly the privilege does represent a protective concern for the accused and an emphasis upon accusatorial rather than inquisitorial values in law enforcement, although this is similarly true of other limitations such as the grand jury requirement and the reasonable doubt standard. Accusatorial values, however, have openly been absorbed into the due process standard governing confessions; this indeed is why at present "the kinship of the two rules [governing confessions and self-incrimination] is too apparent for denial." McCormick, Evidence 155 (1954). Since extension of the general principle has already occurred, to insist that the privilege applies as such serves only to carry over inapposite historical details and engaging rhetoric and to obscure the policy choices to be made in regulating confessions.

Having decided that the Fifth Amendment privilege does apply in the police station, the Court reveals that the privilege imposes more exacting restrictions than

---

[6]Among the examples given in 8 Wigmore, Evidence 2266, at 401 (McNaughton rev. 1961), are these: the privilege applies to any witness, civil or criminal, but the confession rule protects only criminal defendants; the privilege deals only with compulsion, while the confession rule may exclude statements obtained by trick or promise; and where the privilege has been nullified - as by the English Bankruptcy Act - the confession rule may still operate.

[7]Additionally, there are precedents and even historical arguments that can be arrayed in favor of bringing extra-legal questioning within the privilege. See generally Maguire, Evidence of Guilt 2.03, at 15-16 (1959).

does the Fourteenth Amendment's voluntariness test. [footnote 8] It then emerges from a discussion of *Escobedo* that the Fifth Amendment requires for an admissible confession that it be given by one distinctly aware of his right not to speak and shielded from "the compelling atmosphere" of interrogation. See ante, pp. 465-466. From these key premises, the Court finally develops the safeguards of warning, counsel, and so forth. I do not believe these premises are sustained by precedents under the Fifth Amendment. [footnote 9]

The more important premise is that pressure on the suspect must be eliminated though it be only the subtle influence of the atmosphere and surroundings. The Fifth Amendment, however, has never been thought to forbid all pressure to incriminate one's self in the situations covered by it. On the contrary, it has been held that failure to incriminate one's self can result in denial of removal of one's case from state to federal court, *Maryland v. Soper,* 270 U.S. 9; in refusal of a military commission, *Orloff* v. *Willoughby,* 345 U.S. 83; in denial of a discharge in bankruptcy, *Kaufman v. Hurwitz,* 176 F.2d 210; and in numerous other adverse consequences. See 8 *Wigmore,* Evidence 2272, at 441-444, n. 18 (*McNaughton* rev. 1961); *Maguire,* Evidence of Guilt 2.062 (1959). This is not to say that short of jail or torture any sanction is permissible in any case; policy and history alike may impose sharp limits. See, e.g., *Griffin* v. *California,* 380 U.S. 609. However, the Court's unspoken assumption that any pressure violates the privilege is not supported by the precedents and it has failed to show why the Fifth Amendment prohibits that relatively mild pressure the Due Process Clause permits.

The Court appears similarly wrong in thinking that precise knowledge of one's rights is a settled prerequisite under the Fifth Amendment to the loss of its protections. A number of lower federal court cases have held that grand jury witnesses need not always be warned of their privilege, e. g., *United States* v. *Scully,* 225 F.2d 113, 116, and *Wigmore* states this to be the better rule for trial witnesses. See 8 Wigmore, Evidence 2269 (McNaughton rev. 1961). Cf. *Henry* v. *Mississippi,* 379 U.S. 443, 451-452 (waiver of constitutional rights by counsel despite defendant's ignorance held allowable). No Fifth Amendment precedent is cited for the Court's contrary view. There might of course be reasons apart from Fifth Amendment precedent for requiring warning or any other safeguard on questioning but that is a different matter entirely. See infra, pp. 516-517.

A closing word must be said about the Assistance of Counsel Clause of the Sixth Amendment, which is never expressly relied on by the Court but whose judicial precedents turn out to be linchpins of the confession rules announced today. To support its requirement of a knowing and intelligent waiver, the Court cites *Johnson* v. *Zerbst,* 304 U.S. 458, ante, p. 475; appointment of counsel for the indigent suspect is tied to *Gideon* v. *Wainwright,* 372 U.S. 335, and *Douglas* v. *California,* 372 U.S. 353, ante, p. 473; the silent-record doctrine is borrowed from *Carnley* v. *Cochran,* 369 U.S. 506, ante, p. 475, as is the right to an express offer of counsel, ante, p. 471. All these cases imparting glosses to the Sixth Amendment concerned counsel at trial or on appeal. While the Court finds no pertinent difference between judicial proceedings and

---

[8]This, of course, is implicit in the Court's introductory announcement that "[o]ur decision in *Malloy* v. *Hogan,* 378 U.S. 1 (1964) [extending the Fifth Amendment privilege to the States] necessitates an examination of the scope of the privilege in state cases as well." Ante, p. 463. It is also inconsistent with *Malloy* itself, in which extension of the Fifth Amendment to the States rested in part on the view that the Due Process Clause restriction on state confessions has in recent years been "the same standard" as that imposed in federal prosecutions assertedly by the Fifth Amendment. 378 U.S., at 7.

[9]I lay aside *Escobedo* itself; it contains no reasoning or even general conclusions addressed to the Fifth Amendment and indeed its citation in this regard seems surprising in view of *Escobedo's* primary reliance on the Sixth Amendment.

police interrogation, I believe the differences are so vast as to disqualify wholly the Sixth Amendment precedents as suitable analogies in the present cases. [footnote 10]

The only attempt in this Court to carry the right to counsel into the station house occurred in *Escobedo,* the Court repeating several times that that stage was no less "critical" than trial itself. See 378 U.S., 485-488. This is hardly persuasive when we consider that a grand jury inquiry, the filing of a certiorari petition, and certainly the purchase of narcotics by an undercover agent from a prospective defendant may all be equally "critical" yet provision of counsel and advice on that score have never been thought compelled by the Constitution in such cases. The sound reason why this right is so freely extended for a criminal trial is the severe injustice risked by confronting an untrained defendant with a range of technical points of law, evidence, and tactics familiar to the prosecutor but not to himself. This danger shrinks markedly in the police station where indeed the lawyer in fulfilling his professional responsibilities of necessity may become an obstacle to truthfinding. See infra, n. 12. The Court's summary citation of the Sixth Amendment cases here seems to me best described as "the domino method of constitutional adjudication . . . wherein every explanatory statement in a previous opinion is made the basis for extension to a wholly different situation." Friendly, supra, n. 10, at 950.

• III. POLICY CONSIDERATIONS.

Examined as an expression of public policy, the Court's new regime proves so dubious that there can be no due compensation for its weakness in constitutional law. The foregoing discussion has shown, I think, how mistaken is the Court in implying that the Constitution has struck the balance in favor of the approach the Court takes. Ante, p. 479. Rather, precedent reveals that the Fourteenth Amendment in practice has been construed to strike a different balance, that the Fifth Amendment gives the Court little solid support in this context, and that the Sixth Amendment should have no bearing at all. Legal history has been stretched before to satisfy deep needs of society. In this instance, however, the Court has not and cannot make the powerful showing that its new rules are plainly desirable in the context of our society, something which is surely demanded before those rules are engrafted onto the Constitution and imposed on every State and county in the land.

Without at all subscribing to the generally black picture of police conduct painted by the Court, I think it must be frankly recognized at the outset that police questioning allowable under due process precedents may inherently entail some pressure on the suspect and may seek advantage in his ignorance or weaknesses. The atmosphere and questioning techniques, proper and fair though they be, can in themselves exert a tug on the suspect to confess, and in this light "[t]o speak of any confessions of crime made after arrest as being 'voluntary' or 'uncoerced' is somewhat inaccurate, although traditional. A confession is wholly and incontestably voluntary only if a guilty person gives himself up to the law and becomes his own accuser." *Ashcraft* v. *Tennessee,* 322 U.S. 143, 161 (Jackson, J., dissenting). Until today, the role of the Constitution has been only to sift out undue pressure, not to assure spontaneous confessions. [footnote 11]

The Court's new rules aim to offset these minor pressures and disadvantages intrinsic to any kind of police interrogation. The rules do not serve due process interests in preventing blatant coercion since, as I noted earlier, they do nothing to contain the policeman who is prepared to lie from the start. The rules work for reliability in

---

[10]Since the Court conspicuously does not assert that the Sixth Amendment itself warrants its new police-interrogation rules, there is no reason now to draw out the extremely powerful historical and precedential evidence that the Amendment will bear no such meaning. See generally Friendly, The Bill of Rights as a Code of Criminal Procedure, 53 Calif. L. Rev. 929, 943-948 (1965).

[11]See supra, n. 4, and text. Of course, the use of terms like voluntariness involves questions of law and terminology quite as much as questions of fact. See *Collins* v. *Beto,* 348 F.2d 823, 832 (concurring opinion); Bator & Vorenberg, supra, n. 4, at 72-73.

confessions almost only in the Pickwickian sense that they can prevent some from being given at all. [footnote 12] In short, the benefit of this new regime is simply to lessen or wipe out the inherent compulsion and inequalities to which the Court devotes some nine pages of description. Ante, pp. 448-456.

What the Court largely ignores is that its rules impair, if they will not eventually serve wholly to frustrate, an instrument of law enforcement that has long and quite reasonably been thought worth the price paid for it. [footnote 13] There can be little doubt that the Court's new code would markedly decrease the number of confessions. To warn the suspect that he may remain silent and remind him that his confession may be used in court are minor obstructions. To require also an express waiver by the suspect and an end to questioning whenever he demurs must heavily handicap questioning. And to suggest or provide counsel for the suspect simply invites the end of the interrogation. See, supra, n. 12.

How much harm this decision will inflict on law enforcement cannot fairly be predicted with accuracy. Evidence on the role of confessions is notoriously incomplete, see Developments, supra, n. 2, at 941-944, and little is added by the Court's reference to the FBI experience and the resources believed wasted in interrogation. See infra, n. 19, and text. We do know that some crimes cannot be solved without confessions, that ample expert testimony attests to their importance in crime control, [footnote 14] and that the Court is taking a real risk with society's welfare in imposing its new regime on the country. The social costs of crime are too great to call the new rules anything but a hazardous experimentation.

While passing over the costs and risks of its experiment, the Court portrays the evils of normal police questioning in terms which I think are exaggerated. Albeit stringently confined by the due process standards interrogation is no doubt often inconvenient and unpleasant for the suspect. However, it is no less so for a man to be arrested and jailed, to have his house searched, or to stand trial in court, yet all this may properly happen to the most innocent given probable cause, a warrant, or an indictment. Society has always paid a stiff price for law and order, and peaceful interrogation is not one of the dark moments of the law.

This brief statement of the competing considerations seems to me ample proof that the Court's preference is highly debatable at best and therefore not to be read into the Constitution. However, it may make the analysis more graphic to consider the actual facts of one of the four cases reversed by the Court. *Miranda* v. *Arizona* serves best, being neither the hardest nor easiest of the four under the Court's standards. [footnote 15]

On March 3, 1963, an 18-year-old girl was kidnapped and forcibly raped near Phoenix, Arizona. Ten days later, on the morning of March 13, petitioner Miranda was arrested and taken to the police station. At this time Miranda was 23 years old, indigent, and educated to the extent of completing half the ninth grade. He had "an emotional illness" of the schizophrenic type, according to the doctor who eventually

---

[12]The Court's vision of a lawyer "mitigat[ing] the dangers of untrustworthiness" (ante, p. 470) by witnessing coercion and assisting accuracy in the confession is largely a fancy; for if counsel arrives, there is rarely going to be a police station confession. *Watts* v. *Indiana*, 338 U.S. 49, 59 (separate opinion of Jackson, J.): "[A]ny lawyer worth his salt will tell the suspect in no uncertain terms to make no statement to police under any circumstances." See Enker & Elsen, Counsel for the Suspect, 49 Minn. L. Rev. 47, 66-68 (1964).

[13]This need is, of course, what makes so misleading the Court's comparison of a probate judge readily setting aside as involuntary the will of an old lady badgered and beleaguered by the new heirs. Ante, pp. 457-458, n. 26. With wills, there is no public interest save in a totally free choice; with confessions, the solution of crime is a countervailing gain, however the balance is resolved.

[14]See, e. g., the voluminous citations to congressional committee testimony and other sources collected in *Culombe* v. *Connecticut*, 367 U.S. 568, 578-579 (Frankfurter, J., announcing the Court's judgment and an opinion).

[15]In Westover, a seasoned criminal was practically given the Court's full complement of warnings and did not heed them. The *Stewart* case, on the other hand, involves long detention and successive questioning. In *Vignera*, the facts are complicated and the record somewhat incomplete.

examined him; the doctor's report also stated that Miranda was "alert and oriented as to time, place, and person," intelligent within normal limits, competent to stand trial, and sane within the legal definition. At the police station, the victim picked Miranda out of a lineup, and two officers then took him into a separate room to interrogate him, starting about 11:30 a. m. Though at first denying his guilt, within a short time Miranda gave a detailed oral confession and then wrote out in his own hand and signed a brief statement admitting and describing the crime. All this was accomplished in two hours or less without any force, threats or promises and - I will assume this though the record is uncertain, ante, 491-492 and nn. 66-67 - without any effective warnings at all.

Miranda's oral and written confessions are now held inadmissible under the Court's new rules. One is entitled to feel astonished that the Constitution can be read to produce this result. These confessions were obtained during brief, daytime questioning conducted by two officers and unmarked by any of the traditional indicia of coercion. They assured a conviction for a brutal and unsettling crime, for which the police had and quite possibly could obtain little evidence other than the victim's identifications, evidence which is frequently unreliable. There was, in sum, a legitimate purpose, no perceptible unfairness, and certainly little risk of injustice in the interrogation. Yet the resulting confessions, and the responsible course of police practice they represent, are to be sacrificed to the Court's own finespun conception of fairness which I seriously doubt is shared by many thinking citizens in this country. [footnote 16]

The tenor of judicial opinion also falls well short of supporting the Court's new approach. Although *Escobedo* has widely been interpreted as an open invitation to lower courts to rewrite the law of confessions, a significant heavy majority of the state and federal decisions in point have sought quite narrow interpretations. [footnote 17] Of the courts that have accepted the invitation, it is hard to know how many have felt compelled by their best guess as to this Court's likely construction; but none of the state decisions saw fit to rely on the state privilege against self-incrimination, and no decision at all has gone as far as this Court goes today. [footnote 18]

It is also instructive to compare the attitude in this case of those responsible for law enforcement with the official views that existed when the Court undertook three major revisions of prosecutorial practice prior to this case, *Johnson* v. *Zerbst,* 304 U.S. 458, *Mapp* v. *Ohio,* 367 U.S. 643, and *Gideon* v. *Wainwright,* 372 U.S. 335. In *Johnson,* which established that appointed counsel must be offered the indigent in federal criminal trials, the Federal Government all but conceded the basic issue, which had in fact been recently fixed as Department of Justice policy. See Beaney, Right to Counsel 29-30, 36-42 (1955). In *Mapp,* which imposed the exclusionary rule on the States for Fourth Amendment violations, more than half of the States had themselves already adopted some such rule. See 367 U.S., at 651. In *Gideon,* which extended

---

[16]"[J]ustice, though due to the accused, is due to the accuser also. The concept of fairness must not be strained till it is narrowed to a filament. We are to keep the balance true." *Snyder* v. *Massachusetts,* 291 U.S. 97, 122 (Cardozo, J.).

[17]A narrow reading is given in: *United States* v. *Robinson,* 354 F.2d 109 (C. A. 2d Cir.); *Davis* v. *North Carolina,* 339 F.2d 770 (C. A. 4th Cir.); *Edwards* v. *Holman,* 342 F.2d 679 (C. A. 5th Cir.); *United States ex rel. Townsend* v. *Ogilvie,* 334 F.2d 837 (C. A. 7th Cir.); *People* v. *Hartgraves,* 31 Ill. 2d 375, 202 N. E. 2d 33; *State* v. *Fox,* ___ Iowa ___, 131 N. W. 2d 684; *Rowe* v. *Commonwealth,* 394 S. W. 2d 751 (Ky.); *Parker* v. *Warden,* 236 Md. 236, 203 A. 2d 418; *State* v. *Howard,* 383 S. W. 2d 701 (Mo.); *Bean* v. *State,* ___ Nev. ___, 398 P.2d 251; *State* v. *Hodgson,* 44 N. J. 151, 207 A. 2d 542; *People* v. *Gunner,* 15 N. Y. 2d 226, 205 N. E. 2d 852; *Commonwealth ex rel. Linde* v. *Maroney,* 416 Pa. 331, 206 A. 2d 288; *Browne* v. *State,* 24 Wis. 2d 491, 131 N. W. 2d 169.

An ample reading is given in: *United States ex rel. Russo* v. *New Jersey,* 351 F.2d 429 (C. A. 3d Cir.); *Wright* v. *Dickson,* 336 F.2d 878 (C. A. 9th Cir.); *People* v. *Dorado,* 62 Cal. 2d 338, 398 P.2d 361; *State* v. *Dufour,* ___ R. I. ___, 206 A. 2d 82; *State* v. *Neely,* 239 Ore. 487, 395 P.2d 557, modified, 398 P.2d 482.

The cases in both categories are those readily available; there are certainly many others.

[18]For instance, compare the requirements of the catalytic case of *People* v. *Dorado,* 62 Cal. 2d 338, 398 P.2d 361, with those laid down today. See also Traynor, The Devils of Due Process in Criminal Detection, Detention, and Trial, 33 U. Chi. L. Rev. 657, 670.

Johnson v. *Zerbst* to the States, an amicus brief was filed by 22 States and Commonwealths urging that course; only two States besides that of the respondent came forward to protest. See 372 U.S., at 345. By contrast, in this case new restrictions on police questioning have been opposed by the United States and in an amicus brief signed by 27 States and Commonwealths, not including the three other States which are parties. No State in the country has urged this Court to impose the newly announced rules, nor has any State chosen to go nearly so far on its own.

The Court in closing its general discussion invokes the practice in federal and foreign jurisdictions as lending weight to its new curbs on confessions for all the States. A brief resume will suffice to show that none of these jurisdictions has struck so one-sided a balance as the Court does today. Heaviest reliance is placed on the FBI practice. Differing circumstances may make this comparison quite untrustworthy, [footnote 19] but in any event the FBI falls sensibly short of the Court's formalistic rules. For example, there is no indication that FBI agents must obtain an affirmative "waiver" before they pursue their questioning. Nor is it clear that one invoking his right to silence may not be prevailed upon to change his mind. And the warning as to appointed counsel apparently indicates only that one will be assigned by the judge when the suspect appears before him; the thrust of the Court's rules is to induce the suspect to obtain appointed counsel before continuing the interview. See ante, pp. 484-486. Apparently American military practice, briefly mentioned by the Court, has these same limits and is still less favorable to the suspect than the FBI warning, making no mention of appointed counsel. Developments, supra, n. 2, at 1084-1089.

The law of the foreign countries described by the Court also reflects a more moderate conception of the rights of the accused as against those of society when other data are considered. Concededly, the English experience is most relevant. In that country, a caution as to silence but not counsel has long been mandated by the "Judges' Rules," which also place other somewhat imprecise limits on police cross-examination of suspects. However, in the court's discretion confessions can be and apparently quite frequently are admitted in evidence despite disregard of the Judges' Rules, so long as they are found voluntary under the common-law test. Moreover, the check that exists on the use of pretrial statements is counterbalanced by the evident admissibility of fruits of an illegal confession and by the judge's often-used authority to comment adversely on the defendant's failure to testify. [footnote 20]

India, Ceylon, and Scotland are the other examples chosen by the Court. In India and Ceylon the general ban on police-adduced confessions cited by the Court is subject to a major exception: if evidence is uncovered by police questioning, it is fully admissible at trial along with the confession itself, so far as it relates to the evidence and is not blatantly coerced. See Developments, supra, n. 2, at 1106-1110; *Reg.* v. *Ramasamy* 1965. A. C. 1 (P. C.). Scotland's limits on interrogation do measure up to the Court's; however, restrained comment at trial on the defendant's failure to take the stand is allowed the judge, and in many other respects Scotch law redresses the prosecutor's disadvantage in ways not permitted in this country. [footnote 21] The Court ends its survey by imputing added strength to our privilege against self-incrimination since, by contrast to other countries, it is embodied in a written Constitution. Considering the liberties the Court has today taken with constitutional history and precedent, few will find this emphasis persuasive.

---

[19]The Court's obiter dictum notwithstanding, ante, p. 486, there is some basis for believing that the staple of FBI criminal work differs importantly from much crime within the ken of local police. The skill and resources of the FBI may also be unusual.

[20]For citations and discussion covering each of these points, see Developments, supra, n. 2, at 1091-1097, and Enker & Elsen, supra, n. 12, at 80 & n. 94.

[21]On comment, see Hardin, Other Answers: Search and Seizure, Coerced Confession, and Criminal Trial in Scotland, 113 U. Pa. L. Rev. 165, 181 and nn. 96-97 (1964). Other examples are less stringent search and seizure rules and no automatic exclusion for violation of them, id., at 167-169; guilt based on majority jury verdicts, id., at 185; and pre-trial discovery of evidence on both sides, id., at 175.

In closing this necessarily truncated discussion of policy considerations attending the new confession rules, some reference must be made to their ironic untimeliness. There is now in progress in this country a massive re-examination of criminal law enforcement procedures on a scale never before witnessed. Participants in this undertaking include a Special Committee of the American Bar Association, under the chairmanship of Chief Judge Lumbard of the Court of Appeals for the Second Circuit; a distinguished study group of the American Law Institute, headed by Professors Vorenberg and Bator of the Harvard Law School; and the President's Commission on Law Enforcement and Administration of Justice, under the leadership of the Attorney General of the United States. [footnote 22] Studies are also being conducted by the District of Columbia Crime Commission, the Georgetown Law Center, and by others equipped to do practical research. [footnote 23] There are also signs that legislatures in some of the States may be preparing to re-examine the problem before us. [footnote 24]

It is no secret that concern has been expressed lest long-range and lasting reforms be frustrated by this Court's too rapid departure from existing constitutional standards. Despite the Court's disclaimer, the practical effect of the decision made today must inevitably be to handicap seriously sound efforts at reform, not least by removing options necessary to a just compromise of competing interests. Of course legislative reform is rarely speedy or unanimous, though this Court has been more patient in the past. [footnote 25] But the legislative reforms when they come would have the vast advantage of empirical data and comprehensive study, they would allow experimentation and use of solutions not open to the courts, and they would restore the initiative in criminal law reform to those forums where it truly belongs.

- IV. CONCLUSIONS.

All four of the cases involved here present express claims that confessions were inadmissible, not because of coercion in the traditional due process sense, but solely because of lack of counsel or lack of warnings concerning counsel and silence. For the reasons stated in this opinion, I would adhere to the due process test and reject the new requirements inaugurated by the Court. On this premise my disposition of each of these cases can be stated briefly.

In two of the three cases coming from state courts, *Miranda* v. *Arizona* (No. 759) and *Vignera* v. *New York* (No. 760), the confessions were held admissible and no other errors worth comment are alleged by petitioners. I would affirm in these two cases. The other state case is *California* v. *Stewart* (No. 584), where the state supreme court held the confession inadmissible and reversed the conviction. In that case I would dismiss the writ of certiorari on the ground that no final judgment is before us, 28 U.S.C. 1257 (1964 ed.); putting aside the new trial open to the State in any event, the confession itself has not even been finally excluded since the California Supreme Court left the State free to show proof of a waiver. If the merits of the decision in *Stewart* be reached, then I believe it should be reversed and the case remanded so the state supreme court may pass on the other claims available to respondent.

---

[22]Of particular relevance is the ALI's drafting of a Model Code of Pre-Arraignment Procedure, now in its first tentative draft. While the ABA and National Commission studies have wider scope, the former is lending its advice to the ALI project and the executive director of the latter is one of the reporters for the Model Code.

[23]See Brief for the United States in *Westover*, p. 45. *The N. Y. Times*, June 3, 1966, p. 41 (late city ed.) reported that the Ford Foundation has awarded $1,100,000 for a five-year study of arrests and confessions in New York.

[24]The New York Assembly recently passed a bill to require certain warnings before an admissible confession is taken, though the rules are less strict than are the Court's. *N. Y. Times*, May 24, 1966, p. 35 (late city ed.).

[25]The Court waited 12 years after *Wolf* v. *Colorado*, 338 U.S. 25, declared privacy against improper state intrusions to be constitutionally safeguarded before it concluded in *Mapp* v. *Ohio*, 367 U.S. 643, that adequate state remedies had not been provided to protect this interest so the exclusionary rule was necessary.

In the federal case, *Westover* v. *United States* (No. 761), a number of issues are raised by petitioner apart from the one already dealt with in this dissent. None of these other claims appears to me tenable, nor in this context to warrant extended discussion. It is urged that the confession was also inadmissible because not voluntary even measured by due process standards and because federal-state cooperation brought the McNabb-Mallory rule into play under *Anderson* v. *United States, 318 U.S. 350.* However, the facts alleged fall well short of coercion in my view, and I believe the involvement of federal agents in petitioner's arrest and detention by the State too slight to invoke Anderson. I agree with the Government that the admission of the evidence now protested by petitioner was at most harmless error, and two final contentions - one involving weight of the evidence and another improper prosecutor comment - seem to me without merit. I would therefore affirm Westover's conviction.

In conclusion: Nothing in the letter or the spirit of the Constitution or in the precedents squares with the heavy-handed and one-sided action that is so precipitously taken by the Court in the name of fulfilling its constitutional responsibilities. The foray which the Court makes today brings to mind the wise and farsighted words of Mr. Justice Jackson in *Douglas* v. *Jeannette,* 319 U.S. 157, 181 (separate opinion): "This Court is forever adding new stories to the temples of constitutional law, and the temples have a way of collapsing when one story too many is added."

MR. JUSTICE WHITE, with whom MR. JUSTICE HARLAN and MR. JUSTICE STEWART join, dissenting.

I.

The proposition that the privilege against self-incrimination forbids in-custody interrogation without the warnings specified in the majority opinion and without a clear waiver of counsel has no significant support in the history of the privilege or in the language of the Fifth Amendment. As for the English authorities and the common-law history, the privilege, firmly established in the second half of the seventeenth century, was never applied except to prohibit compelled judicial interrogations. The rule excluding coerced confessions matured about 100 years later, "[b]ut there is nothing in the reports to suggest that the theory has its roots in the privilege against self-incrimination. And so far as the cases reveal, the privilege, as such, seems to have been given effect only in judicial proceedings, including the preliminary examinations by authorized magistrates." Morgan, The Privilege Against Self-Incrimination, 34 Minn. L. Rev. 1, 18 (1949).

Our own constitutional provision provides that no person "shall be compelled in any criminal case to be a witness against himself." These words, when "[c]onsidered in the light to be shed by grammar and the dictionary . . . appear to signify simply that nobody shall be compelled to give oral testimony against himself in a criminal proceeding under way in which he is defendant." Corwin, The Supreme Court's Construction of the Self-Incrimination Clause, 29 Mich. L. Rev. 1, 2. And there is very little in the surrounding circumstances of the adoption of the Fifth Amendment or in the provisions of the then existing state constitutions or in state practice which would give the constitutional provision any broader meaning. Mayers, The Federal Witness' Privilege Against Self-Incrimination: Constitutional or Common-Law? 4 American Journal of Legal History 107 (1960). Such a construction, however, was considerably narrower than the privilege at common law, and when eventually faced with the issues, the Court extended the constitutional privilege to the compulsory production of books and papers, to the ordinary witness before the grand jury and to witnesses generally. *Boyd* v. *United States,* 116 U.S. 616, and *Counselman* v. *Hitchcock,* 142 U.S. 547. Both rules had solid support in common-law history, if not in the history of our own constitutional provision.

A few years later the Fifth Amendment privilege was similarly extended to encompass the then well-established rule against coerced confessions: "In criminal trials, in the courts of the United States, wherever a question arises whether a confession is incompetent because not voluntary, the issue is controlled by that portion of the Fifth Amendment to the Constitution of the United States, commanding that no person 'shall be compelled in any criminal case to be a witness against himself.' " *Bram* v. *United States,* 168 U.S. 532, 542. Although this view has found approval in other cases, *Burdeau* v. *McDowell,* 256 U.S. 465, 475; *Powers* v. *United States,* 223 U.S. 303, 313; *Shotwell* v. *United States,* 371 U.S. 341, 347, it has also been questioned, see *Brown* v. *Mississippi,* 297 U.S. 278, 285; *United States* v. *Carignan,* 342 U.S. 36, 41; *Stein* v. *New York,* 346 U.S. 156, 191, n. 35, and finds scant support in either the English or American authorities, see generally *Regina* v. *Scott, Dears, & Bell* 47; 3 *Wigmore,* Evidence 823 (3d ed. 1940), at 249 ("a confession is not rejected because of any connection with the privilege against self-crimination"), and 250, n. 5 (particularly criticizing *Bram*); 8 Wigmore, Evidence 2266, at 400-401 (McNaughton rev. 1961). Whatever the source of the rule excluding coerced confessions, it is clear that prior to the application of the privilege itself to state courts, *Malloy* v. *Hogan,* 378 U.S. 1, the admissibility of a confession in a state criminal prosecution was tested by the same standards as were applied in federal prosecutions. Id., at 6-7, 10.

Bram, however, itself rejected the proposition which the Court now espouses. The question in *Bram* was whether a confession, obtained during custodial interrogation, had been compelled, and if such interrogation was to be deemed inherently vulnerable the Court's inquiry could have ended there. After examining the English and American authorities, however, the Court declared that:

- "In this court also it has been settled that the mere fact that the confession is made to a police officer, while the accused was under arrest in or out of prison, or was drawn out by his questions, does not necessarily render the confession involuntary, but, as one of the circumstances, such imprisonment or interrogation may be taken into account in determining whether or not the statements of the prisoner were voluntary." 168 U.S., at 558.

In this respect the Court was wholly consistent with prior and subsequent pronouncements in this Court.

Thus prior to *Bram* the Court, in *Hopt* v. *Utah,* 110 U.S. 574, 583-587, had upheld the admissibility of a confession made to police officers following arrest, the record being silent concerning what conversation had occurred between the officers and the defendant in the short period preceding the confession. Relying on *Hopt,* the Court ruled squarely on the issue in *Sparf and Hansen* v. *United States,* 156 U.S. 51, 55:

- "Counsel for the accused insist that there cannot be a voluntary statement, a free open confession, while a defendant is confined and in irons under an accusation of having committed a capital offence. We have not been referred to any authority in support of that position. It is true that the fact of a prisoner being in custody at the time he makes a confession is a circumstance not to be overlooked, because it bears upon the inquiry whether the confession was voluntarily made or was extorted by threats or violence or made under the influence of fear. But confinement or imprisonment is not in itself sufficient to justify the exclusion of a confession, if it appears to have been voluntary, and was not obtained by putting the prisoner in fear or by promises. Wharton's Cr. Ev. 9th ed. 661, 663, and authorities cited."

Accord, *Pierce* v. *United States,* 160 U.S. 355, 357.

And in *Wilson* v. *United States,* 162 U.S. 613, 623, the Court had considered the significance of custodial interrogation without any antecedent warnings regarding the right to remain silent or the right to counsel. There the defendant had answered questions posed by a Commissioner, who had failed to advise him of his rights, and his answers were held admissible over his claim of involuntariness. "The fact that [a defendant] is in custody and manacled does not necessarily render his statement involuntary, nor is that necessarily the effect of popular excitement shortly preceding. . . . And it is laid down that it is not essential to the admissibility of a confession that it should appear that the person was warned that what he said would be used against him, but on the contrary, if the confession was voluntary, it is sufficient though it appear that he was not so warned."

Since *Bram*, the admissibility of statements made during custodial interrogation has been frequently reiterated. *Powers* v. *United States*, 223 U.S. 303, cited Wilson approvingly and held admissible as voluntary statements the accused's testimony at a preliminary hearing even though he was not warned that what he said might be used against him. Without any discussion of the presence or absence of warnings, presumably because such discussion was deemed unnecessary, numerous other cases have declared that "[t]he mere fact that a confession was made while in the custody of the police does not render it inadmissible," *McNabb* v. *United States*, 318 U.S. 332, 346; accord, *United States* v. *Mitchell*, 322 U.S. 65, despite its having been elicited by police examination, *Wan* v. *United States*, 266 U.S. 1, 14; *United States* v. *Carignan*, 342 U.S. 36, 39. Likewise, in *Crooker* v. *California*, 357 U.S. 433, 437, the Court said that "the bare fact of police 'detention and police examination in private of one in official state custody' does not render involuntary a confession by the one so detained." And finally, in *Cicenia* v. *Lagay*, 357 U.S. 504, a confession obtained by police interrogation after arrest was held voluntary even though the authorities refused to permit the defendant to consult with his attorney. See generally *Culombe* v. *Connecticut*, 367 U.S. 568, 587-602 (opinion of Frankfurter, J.); 3 Wigmore, Evidence 851, at 313 (3d ed. 1940); see also Joy, Admissibility of Confessions 38, 46 (1842).

Only a tiny minority of our judges who have dealt with the question, including today's majority, have considered in-custody interrogation, without more, to be a violation of the Fifth Amendment. And this Court, as every member knows, has left standing literally thousands of criminal convictions that rested at least in part on confessions taken in the course of interrogation by the police after arrest.

II.

That the Court's holding today is neither compelled nor even strongly suggested by the language of the Fifth Amendment, is at odds with American and English legal history, and involves a departure from a long line of precedent does not prove either that the Court has exceeded its powers or that the Court is wrong or unwise in its present reinterpretation of the Fifth Amendment. It does, however, underscore the obvious - that the Court has not discovered or found the law in making today's decision, nor has it derived it from some irrefutable sources; what it has done is to make new law and new public policy in much the same way that it has in the course of interpreting other great clauses of the Constitution. [footnote 1] This is what the Court historically has done. Indeed, it is what it must do and will continue to do until and unless there is some fundamental change in the constitutional distribution of governmental powers.

But if the Court is here and now to announce new and fundamental policy to govern certain aspects of our affairs, it is wholly legitimate to examine the mode of this or any other constitutional decision in this Court and to inquire into the advisa-

---

[1]Of course the Court does not deny that it is departing from prior precedent; it expressly overrules *Crooker and Cicenia*, ante, at 479, n. 48, and it acknowledges that in the instant "cases we might not find the defendants' statements to have been involuntary in traditional terms," ante, at 457.

bility of its end product in terms of the long-range interest of the country. At the very least the Court's text and reasoning should withstand analysis and be a fair exposition of the constitutional provision which its opinion interprets. Decisions like these cannot rest alone on syllogism, metaphysics or some ill-defined notions of natural justice, although each will perhaps play its part. In proceeding to such constructions as it now announces, the Court should also duly consider all the factors and interests bearing upon the cases, at least insofar as the relevant materials are available; and if the necessary considerations are not treated in the record or obtainable from some other reliable source, the Court should not proceed to formulate fundamental policies based on speculation alone.

III.

First, we may inquire what are the textual and factual bases of this new fundamental rule. To reach the result announced on the grounds it does, the Court must stay within the confines of the Fifth Amendment, which forbids self-incrimination only if compelled. Hence the core of the Court's opinion is that because of the "compulsion inherent in custodial surroundings, no statement obtained from [a] defendant [in custody] can truly be the product of his free choice," ante, at 458, absent the use of adequate protective devices as described by the Court. However, the Court does not point to any sudden inrush of new knowledge requiring the rejection of 70 years' experience. Nor does it assert that its novel conclusion reflects a changing consensus among state courts, see *Mapp* v. *Ohio,* 367 U.S. 643, or that a succession of cases had steadily eroded the old rule and proved it unworkable, see *Gideon* v. *Wainwright,* 372 U.S. 335. Rather than asserting new knowledge, the Court concedes that it cannot truly know what occurs during custodial questioning, because of the innate secrecy of such proceedings. It extrapolates a picture of what it conceives to be the norm from police investigatorial manuals, published in 1959 and 1962 or earlier, without any attempt to allow for adjustments in police practices that may have occurred in the wake of more recent decisions of state appellate tribunals or this Court. But even if the relentless application of the described procedures could lead to involuntary confessions, it most assuredly does not follow that each and every case will disclose this kind of interrogation or this kind of consequence. [footnote 2] Insofar as appears from the Court's opinion, it has not examined a single transcript of any police interrogation, let alone the interrogation that took place in any one of these cases which it decides today. Judged by any of the standards for empirical investigation utilized in the social sciences the factual basis for the Court's premise is patently inadequate.

Although in the Court's view in-custody interrogation is inherently coercive, the Court says that the spontaneous product of the coercion of arrest and detention is still to be deemed voluntary. An accused, arrested on probable cause, may blurt out a confession which will be admissible despite the fact that he is alone and in custody, without any showing that he had any notion of his right to remain silent or of the consequences of his admission. Yet, under the Court's rule, if the police ask him a single question such as "Do you have anything to say?" or "Did you kill your wife?" his response, if there is one, has somehow been compelled, even if the accused has been clearly warned of his right to remain silent. Common sense informs us to the con-

---

[2]In fact, the type of sustained interrogation described by the Court appears to be the exception rather than the rule. A survey of 399 cases in one city found that in almost half of the cases the interrogation lasted less than 30 minutes. Barrett, Police Practices and the Law - From Arrest to Release or Charge, 50 Calif. L. Rev. 11, 41-45 (1962). Questioning tends to be confused and sporadic and is usually concentrated on confrontations with witnesses or new items of evidence, as these are obtained by officers conducting the investigation. See generally LaFave, Arrest: The Decision to Take a Suspect into Custody 386 (1965); ALI, A Model Code of Pre-Arraignment Procedure, Commentary 5.01, at 170, n. 4 (Tent. Draft No. 1, 1966).

trary. While one may say that the response was "involuntary" in the sense the question provoked or was the occasion for the response and thus the defendant was induced to speak out when he might have remained silent if not arrested and not questioned, it is patently unsound to say the response is compelled.

Today's result would not follow even if it were agreed that to some extent custodial interrogation is inherently coercive. See *Ashcraft* v. *Tennessee,* 322 U.S. 143, 161 (Jackson, J., dissenting). The test has been whether the totality of circumstances deprived the defendant of a "free choice to admit, to deny, or to refuse to answer," *Lisenba* v. *California,* 314 U.S. 219, 241, and whether physical or psychological coercion was of such a degree that "the defendant's will was overborne at the time he confessed," *Haynes* v. *Washington,* 373 U.S. 503, 513; *Lynumn* v. *Illinois,* 372 U.S. 528, 534. The duration and nature of incommunicado custody, the presence or absence of advice concerning the defendant's constitutional rights, and the granting or refusal of requests to communicate with lawyers, relatives, or friends have all been rightly regarded as important data bearing on the basic inquiry. See, e. g., *Ashcraft* v. *Tennessee,* 322 U.S. 143; *Haynes* v. *Washington,* 373 U.S. 503. [footnote 3] But it has never been suggested, until today, that such questioning was so coercive and accused persons so lacking in hardihood that the very first response to the very first question following the commencement of custody must be conclusively presumed to be the product of an overborne will.

If the rule announced today were truly based on a conclusion that all confessions resulting from custodial interrogation are coerced, then it would simply have no rational foundation. Compare *Tot* v. *United States,* 319 U.S. 463, 466; *United States* v. *Romano,* 382 U.S. 136. A fortiori that would be true of the extension of the rule to exculpatory statements, which the Court effects after a brief discussion of why, in the Court's view, they must be deemed incriminatory but without any discussion of why they must be deemed coerced. See *Wilson* v. *United States,* 162 U.S. 613, 624. Even if one were to postulate that the Court's concern is not that all confessions induced by police interrogation are coerced but rather that some such confessions are coerced and present judicial procedures are believed to be inadequate to identify the confessions that are coerced and those that are not, it would still not be essential to impose the rule that the Court has now fashioned. Transcripts or observers could be required, specific time limits, tailored to fit the cause, could be imposed, or other devices could be utilized to reduce the chances that otherwise indiscernible coercion will produce an inadmissible confession.

On the other hand, even if one assumed that there was an adequate factual basis for the conclusion that all confessions obtained during in-custody interrogation are the product of compulsion, the rule propounded by the Court would still be irrational, for, apparently, it is only if the accused is also warned of his right to counsel and waives both that right and the right against self-incrimination that the inherent compulsiveness of interrogation disappears. But if the defendant may not answer without a warning a question such as "Where were you last night?" without having his answer be a compelled one, how can the Court ever accept his negative answer to the question of whether he wants to consult his retained counsel or counsel whom the court will appoint? And why if counsel is present and the accused nevertheless confesses, or counsel tells the accused to tell the truth, and that is what the accused

---

[3] By contrast, the Court indicates that in applying this new rule it "will not pause to inquire in individual cases whether the defendant was aware of his rights without a warning being given." Ante, at 468. The reason given is that assessment of the knowledge of the defendant based on information as to age, education, intelligence, or prior contact with authorities can never be more than speculation, while a warning is a clear-cut fact. But the officers' claim that they gave the requisite warnings may be disputed, and facts respecting the defendant's prior experience may be undisputed and be of such a nature as to virtually preclude any doubt that the defendant knew of his rights. See *United States* v. *Bolden,* 355 F.2d 453 (C. A. 7th Cir. 1965), petition for cert. pending No. 1146, O. T. 1965 (Secret Service agent); *People* v. *Du Bont,* 235 Cal. App. 2d 844, 45 Cal. Rptr. 717, pet. for cert. pending No. 1053, Misc., O. T. 1965 (former police officer).

does, is the situation any less coercive insofar as the accused is concerned? The Court apparently realizes its dilemma of foreclosing questioning without the necessary warnings but at the same time permitting the accused, sitting in the same chair in front of the same policemen, to waive his right to consult an attorney. It expects, however, that the accused will not often waive the right; and if it is claimed that he has, the State faces a severe, if not impossible burden of proof.

All of this makes very little sense in terms of the compulsion which the Fifth Amendment proscribes. That amendment deals with compelling the accused himself. It is his free will that is involved. Confessions and incriminating admissions, as such, are not forbidden evidence; only those which are compelled are banned. I doubt that the Court observes these distinctions today. By considering any answers to any interrogation to be compelled regardless of the content and course of examination and by escalating the requirements to prove waiver, the Court not only prevents the use of compelled confessions but for all practical purposes forbids interrogation except in the presence of counsel. That is, instead of confining itself to protection of the right against compelled self-incrimination the Court has created a limited Fifth Amendment right to counsel - or, as the Court expresses it, a "need for counsel to protect the Fifth Amendment privilege . . . ." Ante, at 470. The focus then is not on the will of the accused but on the will of counsel and how much influence he can have on the accused. Obviously there is no warrant in the Fifth Amendment for thus installing counsel as the arbiter of the privilege.

In sum, for all the Court's expounding on the menacing atmosphere of police interrogation procedures, it has failed to supply any foundation for the conclusions it draws or the measures it adopts.

IV.

Criticism of the Court's opinion, however, cannot stop with a demonstration that the factual and textual bases for the rule it propounds are, at best, less than compelling. Equally relevant is an assessment of the rule's consequences measured against community values. The Court's duty to assess the consequences of its action is not satisfied by the utterance of the truth that a value of our system of criminal justice is "to respect the inviolability of the human personality" and to require government to produce the evidence against the accused by its own independent labors. Ante, at 460. More than the human dignity of the accused is involved; the human personality of others in the society must also be preserved. Thus the values reflected by the privilege are not the sole desideratum; society's interest in the general security is of equal weight.

The obvious underpinning of the Court's decision is a deep-seated distrust of all confessions. As the Court declares that the accused may not be interrogated without counsel present, absent a waiver of the right to counsel, and as the Court all but admonishes the lawyer to advise the accused to remain silent, the result adds up to a judicial judgment that evidence from the accused should not be used against him in any way, whether compelled or not. This is the not so subtle overtone of the opinion - that it is inherently wrong for the police to gather evidence from the accused himself. And this is precisely the nub of this dissent. I see nothing wrong or immoral, and certainly nothing unconstitutional, in the police's asking a suspect whom they have reasonable cause to arrest whether or not he killed his wife or in confronting him with the evidence on which the arrest was based, at least where he has been plainly advised that he may remain completely silent, see *Escobedo* v. *Illinois,* 378 U.S. 478, 499 (dissenting opinion). Until today, "the admissions or confessions of the prisoner, when voluntarily and freely made, have always ranked high in the scale of incriminating evidence." *Brown* v. *Walker,* 161 U.S. 591, 596 ; see also *Hopt* v. *Utah,* 110 U.S. 574, 584-585. Particularly when corroborated, as where the police have confirmed the accused's disclosure of the

hiding place of implements or fruits of the crime, such confessions have the highest reliability and significantly contribute to the certitude with which we may believe the accused is guilty. Moreover, it is by no means certain that the process of confessing is in-
jurious to the accused. To the contrary it may provide psychological relief and enhance
the prospects for rehabilitation.

This is not to say that the value of respect for the inviolability of the accused's
individual personality should be accorded no weight or that all confessions should
be indiscriminately admitted. This Court has long read the Constitution to proscribe
compelled confessions, a salutary rule from which there should be no retreat. But I
see no sound basis, factual or otherwise, and the Court gives none, for concluding
that the present rule against the receipt of coerced confessions is inadequate for the
task of sorting out inadmissible evidence and must be replaced by the per se rule
which is now imposed. Even if the new concept can be said to have advantages of
some sort over the present law, they are far outweighed by its likely undesirable impact on other very relevant and important interests.

The most basic function of any government is to provide for the security of the
individual and of his property. *Lanzetta* v. *New Jersey,* 306 U.S. 451, 455. These ends
of society are served by the criminal laws which for the most part are aimed at the
prevention of crime. Without the reasonably effective performance of the task of preventing private violence and retaliation, it is idle to talk about human dignity and
civilized values.

The modes by which the criminal laws serve the interest in general security are
many. First the murderer who has taken the life of another is removed from the
streets, deprived of his liberty and thereby prevented from repeating his offense. In
view of the statistics on recidivism in this country [footnote 4] and of the number of
instances in which apprehension occurs only after repeated offenses, no one can sensibly claim that this aspect of the criminal law does not prevent crime or contribute
significantly to the personal security of the ordinary citizen.

Secondly, the swift and sure apprehension of those who refuse to respect the
personal security and dignity of their neighbor unquestionably has its impact on others who might be similarly tempted. That the criminal law is wholly or partly inef-
fective with a segment of the population or with many of those who have been apprehended and convicted is a very faulty basis for concluding that it is not effective
with respect to the great bulk of our citizens or for thinking that without the crimi-

---

[4]Precise statistics on the extent of recidivism are unavailable, in part because not all crimes are solved and in part because criminal
records of convictions in different jurisdictions are not brought together by a central data collection agency. Beginning in 1963, however, the Federal Bureau of Investigation began collating data on "Careers in Crime," which it publishes in its Uniform Crime Reports. Of 92,869 offenders processed in 1963 and 1964, 76% had a prior arrest record on some charge. Over a period of 10 years the
group had accumulated 434,000 charges. FBI, Uniform Crime Reports - 1964, 27-28. In 1963 and 1964 between 23% and 25% of all
offenders sentenced in 88 federal district courts (excluding the District Court for the District of Columbia) whose criminal records
were reported had previously been sentenced to a term of imprisonment of 13 months or more. Approximately an additional 40%
had a prior record less than prison (juvenile record, probation record, etc.). Administrative Office of the United States Courts, Federal Offenders in the United States District Courts: 1964, x, 36 (hereinafter cited as Federal Offenders: 1964); Administrative Office
of the United States Courts, Federal Offenders in the United States District Courts: 1963, 25-27 (hereinafter cited as Federal Offenders: 1963). During the same two years in the District Court for the District of Columbia between 28% and 35% of those sentenced
had prior prison records and from 37% to 40% had a prior record less than prison. Federal Offenders: 1964, xii, 64, 66; Administrative Office of the United States Courts, Federal Offenders in the United States District Court for the District of Columbia: 1963, 8,
10 (hereinafter cited as District of Columbia Offenders: 1963).

A similar picture is obtained if one looks at the subsequent records of those released from confinement. In 1964, 12.3% of persons
on federal probation had their probation revoked because of the commission of major violations (defined as one in which the pro-
bationer has been committed to imprisonment for a period of 90 days or more, been placed on probation for over one year on a new
offense, or has absconded with felony charges outstanding). Twenty-three and two-tenths percent of parolees and 16.9% of those
who had been mandatorily released after service of a portion of their sentence likewise committed major violations. Reports of the
Proceedings of the Judicial Conference of the United States and Annual Report of the Director of the Administrative Office of the
United States Courts: 1965, 138. See also Mandel et al., Recidivism Studied and Defined, 56 J. Crim. L., C. & P. S. 59 (1965) (within
five years of release 62.33% of sample had committed offenses placing them in recidivist category).

nal laws, or in the absence of their enforcement, there would be no increase in crime. Arguments of this nature are not borne out by any kind of reliable evidence that I have seen to this date.

Thirdly, the law concerns itself with those whom it has confined. The hope and aim of modern penology, fortunately, is as soon as possible to return the convict to society a better and more law-abiding man than when he left. Sometimes there is success, sometimes failure. But at least the effort is made, and it should be made to the very maximum extent of our present and future capabilities.

The rule announced today will measurably weaken the ability of the criminal law to perform these tasks. It is a deliberate calculus to prevent interrogations, to reduce the incidence of confessions and pleas of guilty and to increase the number of trials. [footnote 5] Criminal trials, no matter how efficient the police are, are not sure bets for the prosecution, nor should they be if the evidence is not forthcoming. Under the present law, the prosecution fails to prove its case in about 30% of the criminal cases actually tried in the federal courts. See Federal Offenders: 1964, supra, note 4, at 6 (Table 4), 59 (Table 1); Federal Offenders: 1963, supra, note 4, at 5 (Table 3); District of Columbia Offenders: 1963, supra, note 4, at 2 (Table 1). But it is something else again to remove from the ordinary criminal case all those confessions which heretofore have been held to be free and voluntary acts of the accused and to thus establish a new constitutional barrier to the ascertainment of truth by the judicial process. There is, in my view, every reason to believe that a good many criminal defendants who otherwise would have been convicted on what this Court has previously thought to be the most satisfactory kind of evidence will now, under this new version of the Fifth Amendment, either not be tried at all or will be acquitted if the State's evidence, minus the confession, is put to the test of litigation.

I have no desire whatsoever to share the responsibility for any such impact on the present criminal process.

In some unknown number of cases the Court's rule will return a killer, a rapist or other criminal to the streets and to the environment which produced him, to repeat his crime whenever it pleases him. As a consequence, there will not be a gain, but a loss, in human dignity. The real concern is not the unfortunate consequences of this new decision on the criminal law as an abstract, disembodied series of authoritative proscriptions, but the impact on those who rely on the public authority for protection and who without it can only engage in violent self-help with guns, knives, and the help of their neighbors similarly inclined. There is, of course, a saving factor: the next victims are uncertain, unnamed, and unrepresented in this case.

Nor can this decision do other than have a corrosive effect on the criminal law as an effective device to prevent crime. A major component in its effectiveness in this regard is its swift and sure enforcement. The easier it is to get away with rape and murder, the less the deterrent effect on those who are inclined to attempt it. This is still good common sense. If it were not, we should posthaste liquidate the whole law enforcement establishment as a useless, misguided effort to control human conduct.

---

[5]Eighty-eight federal district courts (excluding the District Court for the District of Columbia) disposed of the cases of 33,381 criminal defendants in 1964. Only 12.5% of those cases were actually tried. Of the remaining cases, 89.9% were terminated by convictions upon pleas of guilty and 10.1% were dismissed. Stated differently, approximately 90% of all convictions resulted from guilty pleas. Federal Offenders: 1964, supra, note 4, 3-6. In the District Court for the District of Columbia a higher percentage, 27%, went to trial, and the defendant pleaded guilty in approximately 78% of the cases terminated prior to trial. Id., at 58-59. No reliable statistics are available concerning the percentage of cases in which guilty pleas are induced because of the existence of a confession or of physical evidence unearthed as a result of a confession. Undoubtedly the number of such cases is substantial.

Perhaps of equal significance is the number of instances of known crimes which are not solved. In 1964, only 388,946, or 23.9% of 1,626,574 serious known offenses were cleared. The clearance rate ranged from 89.8% for homicides to 18.7% for larceny. FBI, Uniform Crime Reports - 1964, 20-22, 101. Those who would replace interrogation as an investigatorial tool by modern scientific investigation techniques significantly overestimate the effectiveness of present procedures, even when interrogation is included.

And what about the accused who has confessed or would confess in response to simple, noncoercive questioning and whose guilt could not otherwise be proved? Is it so clear that release is the best thing for him in every case? Has it so unquestionably been resolved that in each and every case it would be better for him not to confess and to return to his environment with no attempt whatsoever to help him? I think not. It may well be that in many cases it will be no less than a callous disregard for his own welfare as well as for the interests of his next victim.

There is another aspect to the effect of the Court's rule on the person whom the police have arrested on probable cause. The fact is that he may not be guilty at all and may be able to extricate himself quickly and simply if he were told the circumstances of his arrest and were asked to explain. This effort, and his release, must now await the hiring of a lawyer or his appointment by the court, consultation with counsel and then a session with the police or the prosecutor. Similarly, where probable cause exists to arrest several suspects, as where the body of the victim is discovered in a house having several residents, compare *Johnson v. State,* 238 Md. 140, 207 A. 2d 643 (1965), cert. denied, 382 U.S. 1013, it will often be true that a suspect may be cleared only through the results of interrogation of other suspects. Here too the release of the innocent may be delayed by the Court's rule.

Much of the trouble with the Court's new rule is that it will operate indiscriminately in all criminal cases, regardless of the severity of the crime or the circumstances involved. It applies to every defendant, whether the professional criminal or one committing a crime of momentary passion who is not part and parcel of organized crime. It will slow down the investigation and the apprehension of confederates in those cases where time is of the essence, such as kidnapping, see *Brinegar v. United States,* 338 U.S. 160, 183 (Jackson, J., dissenting); *People v. Modesto,* 62 Cal. 2d 436, 446, 398 P.2d 753, 759 (1965), those involving the national security, see *United States v. Drummond,* 354 F.2d 132, 147 (C. A. 2d Cir. 1965) (en banc) (espionage case), pet. for cert. pending, No. 1203, Misc., O. T. 1965; cf. *Gessner v. United States,* 354 F.2d 726, 730, n. 10 (C. A. 10th Cir. 1965) (upholding, in espionage case, trial ruling that Government need not submit classified portions of interrogation transcript), and some of those involving organized crime. In the latter context the lawyer who arrives may also be the lawyer for the defendant's colleagues and can be relied upon to insure that no breach of the organization's security takes place even though the accused may feel that the best thing he can do is to cooperate.

At the same time, the Court's per se approach may not be justified on the ground that it provides a "bright line" permitting the authorities to judge in advance whether interrogation may safely be pursued without jeopardizing the admissibility of any information obtained as a consequence. Nor can it be claimed that judicial time and effort, assuming that is a relevant consideration, will be conserved because of the ease of application of the new rule. Today's decision leaves open such questions as whether the accused was in custody, whether his statements were spontaneous or the product of interrogation, whether the accused has effectively waived his rights, and whether nontestimonial evidence introduced at trial is the fruit of statements made during a prohibited interrogation, all of which are certain to prove productive of uncertainty during investigation and litigation during prosecution. For all these reasons, if further restrictions on police interrogation are desirable at this time, a more flexible approach makes much more sense than the Court's constitutional straitjacket which forecloses more discriminating treatment by legislative or rule-making pronouncements.

Applying the traditional standards to the cases before the Court, I would hold these confessions voluntary. I would therefore affirm in Nos. 759, 760, and 761, and reverse in No. 584.

SECTION
III

The Fifth Amendment to the United States Constitution

The Miranda decision was based upon the Fifth Amendment to the U.S. Constitution. That Amendment reads as follows:

No person shall be held to answer for a capital, or otherwise infamous crime, unless on a presentment or indictment of a Grand Jury, except in cases arising in the land or naval forces, or in the Militia, when in actual service in time of War or public danger; nor shall any person be subject for the same offence to be twice put in jeopardy of life or limb; nor shall be compelled in any criminal case to be a witness against himself, nor be deprived of life, liberty, or property, without due process of law; nor shall private property be taken for public use, without just compensation.

SECTION
IV

18 U.S.C. 3501

TITLE 18 - CRIMES AND CRIMINAL PROCEDURE
PART II - CRIMINAL PROCEDURE
CHAPTER 223 - WITNESSES AND EVIDENCE

Sec. 3501. Admissibility of confessions

- (a) In any criminal prosecution brought by the United States or by the District of Columbia, a confession, as defined in subsection (e) hereof, shall be admissible in evidence if it is voluntarily given. Before such confession is received in evidence, the trial judge shall, out of the presence of the jury, determine any issue as to voluntariness. If the trial judge determines that the confession was voluntarily made it shall be admitted in evidence and the trial judge shall permit the jury to hear relevant evidence on the issue of voluntariness and shall instruct the jury to give such weight to the confession as the jury feels it deserves under all the circumstances.

- (b) The trial judge in determining the issue of voluntariness shall take into consideration all the circumstances surrounding the giving of the confession, including (1) the time elapsing between arrest and arraignment of the defendant making the confession, if it was made after arrest and before arraignment, (2) whether such defendant knew the nature of the offense with which he was charged or of which he was suspected at the time of making the confession,

  - (3) whether or not such defendant was advised or knew that he was not required to make any statement and that any such statement could be used against him, (4) whether or not such defendant had been advised prior to questioning of his right to the assistance of counsel; and (5) whether or not such defendant was without the assistance of counsel when questioned and when giving such confession.

    The presence or absence of any of the above-mentioned factors to be taken into consideration by the judge need not be conclusive on the issue of voluntariness of the confession.

- (c) In any criminal prosecution by the United States or by the District of Columbia, a confession made or given by a person who is a defendant therein, while such person was under arrest or other detention in the custody of any law-enforcement officer or law-enforcement agency, shall not be inadmissible solely because of delay in bringing such person before a magistrate or other officer empowered to commit persons charged with offenses against the laws of the United States or of the District of Columbia if such confession is found by the trial judge to have been made voluntarily and if the weight to be given the confession is left to the jury and if such confession was made or given by such person within six hours immediately following his arrest or other detention: Provided, That the time limitation contained in this subsection shall not apply in any case in which the delay in bringing such person before such magistrate or other officer beyond such six-hour period is found by the trial judge to be reasonable considering the means of transportation and the distance to be traveled to the nearest available such magistrate or other officer.

- (d) Nothing contained in this section shall bar the admission in evidence of any confession made or given voluntarily by any person to any other person without interrogation by anyone, or at any time at which the person who made or gave such confession was not under arrest or other detention.

- (e) As used in this section, the term "confession" means any confession of guilt of any criminal offense or any self-incriminating statement made or given orally or in writing.

SECTION
V

United States b. Dickerson,

UNITED STATES COURT OF APPEALS FOR THE FOURTH CIRCUIT
NO. 97-4750
February 8, 1999

UNITED STATES OF AMERICA, PLAINTIFF-APPELLANT,
v.
CHARLES THOMAS DICKERSON, DEFENDANT-APPELLEE. WASHINGTON LEGAL FOUNDATION; SAFE STREETS COALITION, AMICI CURIAE.

Appeal from the United States District Court for the Eastern District of Virginia, at Alexandria. James C. Cacheris, Senior District Judge. (CR-97-159-A)

Counsel Argued: Vincent L. Gambale, Assistant United States Attorney, Alexandria, Virginia, for Appellant. Paul George Cassell, College of Law, University of Utah, Salt Lake City, Utah, for Amici Curiae. James Warren Hundley, Briglia & Hundley, Fairfax, Virginia, for Appellee. on Brief: Helen F. Fahey, United States Attorney, William G. Otis, Senior Litigation Counsel, Justin W. Williams, Assistant United States Attorney/Chief, Criminal Division, Robert A. Spencer, Assistant United States Attorney, Alexandria, Virginia, for Appellant. Daniel J. Popeo, Paul D. Kamenar, Washington Legal Foundation, Washington, D.C., for Amici Curiae.

Before Williams and Michael, Circuit Judges, and Kiser, Senior United States District Judge for the Western District of Virginia, sitting by designation.

The opinion of the court was delivered by: Williams, Circuit Judge

Published: February 8, 1999

Argued: January 30, 1998

Reversed and remanded by published opinion. Judge Williams wrote the opinion, in which Senior Judge Kiser joined. Judge Michael wrote an opinion Concurring in part and Dissenting in part.

OPINION

In response to the Supreme Court's decision in *Miranda* v. *Arizona,* 384 U.S. 436 (1966), the Congress of the United States enacted 18 U.S.C.A. § 3501 (West 1985), with the clear intent of restoring voluntariness as the test for admitting confessions in federal court. Although duly enacted by the United States Congress and signed into law by the President of the United States, the United States Department of Justice has steadfastly refused to enforce the provision. In fact, after initially "taking the Fifth" on the statute's constitutionality, the Department of Justice has now asserted, without explanation, that the provision is unconstitutional. With the issue squarely presented, we hold that Congress, pursuant to its power to establish the rules of evidence and procedure in the federal courts, acted well within its authority in enacting § 3501. As a consequence, § 3501, rather than *Miranda,* governs the admissibility of confessions in federal court. Accordingly, the district court erred in suppressing Dickerson's voluntary confession on the grounds that it was obtained in technical violation of *Miranda.*

I.

On January 27, 1997, Charles T. Dickerson confessed to robbing a series of banks in Maryland and Virginia. Dickerson was subsequently indicted by a federal grand jury on one count of conspiracy to commit bank robbery in violation of 18 U.S.C.A.§ 371 (West Supp. 1998), three counts of bank robbery in violation of 18 U.S.C.A. § 2113(a) & (d) (West Supp. 1998), and three counts of using a firearm during and in relation to a crime of violence in violation of 18 U.S.C.A. § 924(c)(1) (West Supp. 1998). Shortly thereafter, Dickerson moved to suppress his confession. Although the district court specifically found that Dickerson's confession was voluntary for purposes of the Fifth Amendment, it nevertheless suppressed the confession because it was obtained in technical violation of *Miranda.*[footnote 1]

In ruling on the admissibility of Dickerson's confession, the district court failed to consider § 3501, which provides, in pertinent part, that "a confession . . . shall be admissible in evidence if it is voluntarily given." 18 U.S.C.A. § 3501(a). Based upon the statutory language, it is evident that Congress enacted § 3501 with the express purpose of legislatively overruling Miranda and restoring voluntariness as the test for admitting confessions in federal court. Thus, if Congress possessed the authority to enact § 3501, Dickerson's voluntary confession is admissible as substantive evidence in the Government's casein-chief.

Congress enacted § 3501 as a part of the Omnibus Crime Control Act of 1968, just two years after the Supreme Court decided Miranda. Although the Supreme Court has referred to § 3501 as "the statute governing the admissibility of confessions in federal prosecutions," *United States* v. *Alvarez-Sanchez,* 511 U.S. 350, 351 (1994), the Court has never considered whether the statute overruled Miranda, see *Davis* v. *United States,* 512 U.S. 452, 457 n.* (1994). Indeed, although several lower courts have found that § 3501, rather than Miranda, governs the admissibility of confessions in federal court, see *United States* v. *Crocker,* 510 F.2d 1129, 1137 (10th Cir. 1975); *United States* v. *Rivas-Lopez,* 988 F. Supp. 1424, 1430-36 (D. Utah 1997), no Administration since the provision's enactment has pressed the point, see Davis, 512 U.S. at 463-64 (Scalia, J., Concurring) (noting that "the provision has been studiously avoided by every Administration . . . since its enactment more than 25 years ago"); see also U.S. Dep't of Justice, Report to Attorney General on Law of Pre-Trial Interrogation 72-73 (1986) (discussing "[t]he abortive implementation of § 3501" after its passage in 1968). In fact, after initially declining to take a position on the applicability of § 3501, see Davis, 512 U.S. at 457 n.*, the current Administration has now asserted, without explanation, that the provision is unconstitutional, see Letter from Janet Reno, Attorney General, to Congress (Sept. 10, 1997).

---

[1]The district court also suppressed the physical evidence obtained during the search of Dickerson's apartment because the warrant was not sufficiently particular in describing the items to be seized. Finding that the warrant was sufficiently particular in describing the items to be seized, see post part IV.A, or, in the alternative, that the officers executing the warrant acted in good faith, see post part IV.B, we reverse that ruling also.

Recently, Justice Scalia expressed his concern with the Department of Justice's failure to enforce § 3501. See Davis, 512 U.S. at 465 (Scalia, J., Concurring). In addition to "caus[ing] the federal judiciary to confront a host of 'Miranda' issues that might be entirely irrelevant under federal law," id., Justice Scalia noted that the Department of Justice's failure to invoke the provision "may have produced—during an era of intense national concern about the problem of run-away crime—the acquittal and the non-prosecution of many dangerous felons," id. This is just such a case. Dickerson voluntarily confessed to participating in a series of armed bank robberies. Without his confession it is possible, if not probable, that he will be acquitted. Despite that fact, the Department of Justice, elevating politics over law, prohibited the U.S. Attorney's Office from arguing that Dickerson's confession is admissible under the mandate of § 3501.

Fortunately, we are a court of law and not politics. Thus, the Department of Justice cannot prevent us from deciding this case under the governing law simply by refusing to argue it. See *United States Nat'l Bank of Or.* v. *Independent Ins. Agents of America, Inc.*, 508 U.S. 439, 445-48 (1993). Here, the district court has suppressed a confession that, on its face, is admissible under the mandate of § 3501, i.e., the confession was voluntary under the Due Process Clause, but obtained in technical violation of *Miranda.* Thus, the question of whether § 3501 governs the admissibility of confessions in federal court is squarely before us today.

Determining whether Congress possesses the authority to enact § 3501 is relatively straightforward. Congress has the power to overrule judicially created rules of evidence and procedure that are not required by the Constitution. See *Carlisle* v. *United States,* 517 U.S. 416, 426 (1996); *Palermo* v. *United States,* 360 U.S. 343, 345-48 (1959). Thus, whether Congress has the authority to enact § 3501 turns on whether the rule set forth by the Supreme Court in *Miranda* is required by the Constitution. Clearly it is not. At no point did the Supreme Court in *Miranda* refer to the warnings as constitutional rights. Indeed, the Court acknowledged that the Constitution did not require the warnings, 384 U.S. at 467, disclaimed any intent to create a "constitutional straitjacket," id., referred to the warnings as "procedural safeguards," id. at 444, and invited Congress and the States "to develop their own safeguards for [protecting] the privilege," id. at 490. Since deciding *Miranda,* the Supreme Court has consistently referred to the *Miranda* warnings as "prophylactic," *New York* v. *Quarles,* 467 U.S. 649, 654 (1984), and "not themselves rights protected by the Constitution," *Michigan* v. *Tucker,* 417 U.S. 433, 444 (1974). We have little difficulty concluding, therefore, that § 3501, enacted at the invitation of the Supreme Court and pursuant to Congress's unquestioned power to establish the rules of procedure and evidence in the federal courts, is constitutional. As a consequence, we hold that the admissibility of confessions in federal court is governed by § 3501, rather than the judicially created rule of *Miranda.*

II.

Because of the unique posture of this case, i.e., an interlocutory appeal from the denial of a motion to reopen a suppression hearing, and the significant legal questions raised therein, we have set forth the factual background and the procedural history in painstaking detail. Although rather lengthy, we believe that it is helpful in understanding the important legal issues that must be addressed.

On January 24, 1997, an individual using a silver semi-automatic handgun and carrying a black leather bag robbed the First Virginia Bank in Old Town, Alexandria, Virginia, of approximately $876. An eyewitness saw the robber exit the bank, run down the street, and get into a white Oldsmobile Ciera with District of Columbia license plate number D5286. Within seconds, the robber exited the car, placed something in the trunk, and then re-entered the car on the passenger side. The car then drove away.

The subsequent investigation into the bank robbery revealed that the getaway car was registered to Charles T. Dickerson of Tacoma Park, Maryland. On January 27, 1997, approximately ten FBI agents and an Alexandria police detective (the agents) traveled to Dickerson's Tacoma Park address. Upon arrival, the agents noticed a white Oldsmobile Ciera with D.C. license plate number D5286 parked on the street in front of Dickerson's apartment. Special Agent Christopher Lawlor knocked on Dickerson's door and identified himself. After some delay, Dickerson opened the door. Special Agent Lawlor informed Dickerson that the agents were investigating a bank robbery.

Although the parties dispute whether the agents had consent to enter Dickerson's apartment, there is no dispute that several agents did, in fact, do so. After a short conversation, Special Agent Lawlor asked Dickerson if he would accompany them to the FBI Field Office in Washington, D.C. Dickerson agreed,[footnote 2] but requested that he be allowed to retrieve his coat from his bedroom. As Dickerson picked up his coat, Special Agent Lawlor noticed a large amount of cash on the bed. After placing the money in his coat pocket, Dickerson told the agents that it was gambling proceeds from Atlantic City. After denying the agents' request to search his apartment, Dickerson rode with the agents to the FBI Field Office. Dickerson was not formally placed under arrest and was not handcuffed. Several agents, including Agent Lawrence Wenko, remained in the vicinity of Dickerson's apartment.

At the FBI Field Office, Dickerson was interviewed by Special Agent Lawlor and Detective Thomas Durkin of the Alexandria Police Department. Dickerson denied any involvement in the robbery, but admitted that he had driven to Old Town on the morning in question to look at a restaurant. While in the vicinity of the First Virginia Bank, Dickerson claims that he ran into an old friend named Terrance, who asked for a ride to Suitland, Maryland. Dickerson agreed, and drove Terrance to Suitland, where he dropped Terrance off near a liquor store.

Special Agent Lawlor left the interview room and called United States Magistrate Judge James E. Kenkel to obtain a warrant to search Dickerson's apartment. Based upon the tape-recorded conversation between Special Agent Lawlor and Judge Kenkel, it is undisputed that Special Agent Lawlor described the circumstances of the robbery, including that the robber used a handgun, carried a bag, requested unmarked bills, and left the scene in a car registered to Dickerson. In addition, Special Agent Lawlor noted that Dickerson had over $550 in cash when picked up, had just that day paid his landlord $1350 to cover back rent, and had admitted that he was near the bank at the time of the robbery. Finally, Special Agent Lawlor explained that he was seeking a telephonic warrant because Dickerson was not under arrest and could easily go home and destroy any evidence of the bank robbery.

Based upon Special Agent Lawlor's sworn statement, Judge Kenkel stated that he was convinced "that there is probable cause to believe at that residence there may be . . . evidence of . . . the bank robbery in question." (J.A. at 69.) In the section of the warrant used to identify the property to be seized, Special Agent Lawlor wrote: "Evidence of the crime of bank robbery." (J.A. at 66.) In the section of the warrant used to identify the time issued, Special Agent Lawlor wrote: "8:50 p.m."[footnote 3] (J.A. at 66.) Special Agent Lawlor then called Agent Wenko, who had remained in the vicinity of Dickerson's apartment, to inform him that a warrant had been issued authorizing the agents to search Dickerson's apartment for evidence of the First Virginia

---

[2]Dickerson testified at the suppression hearing that he did not feel he had a choice about whether to accompany the agents to the field office.

[3]Because the warrant was obtained over the telephone, Judge Kenkel was not able to sign the warrant personally. Instead, Judge Kenkel instructed Special Agent Lawlor to sign the Judge's name, followed by a slash and Special Agent Lawlor's name, on the line used to identify the name of the judicial officer authorizing the warrant.

Bank robbery. Immediately after being notified about the warrant, Agent Wenko and a team of agents proceeded to search Dickerson's apartment.

After returning to the interview room, Special Agent Lawlor told Dickerson that agents were about to search his apartment. At some point thereafter, Dickerson informed Special Agent Lawlor and Detective Durkin that he wished to make a statement. In his statement, Dickerson admitted to being the getaway driver in a series of bank robberies. Dickerson then identified Jimmy Rochester as the actual bank robber. Of particular importance to this case, Dickerson told the agents that on January 24, 1997, the pair drove to Old Town, Alexandria. Dickerson admitted that he stopped the car near the First Virginia Bank, that Rochester got out of the car, that Rochester returned a short while later and placed something in the trunk, that Rochester got back in the car, and that the pair drove away. Dickerson also told the agents that Rochester gave him a silver handgun[footnote 4] and some dye-stained money that Rochester feared the police might find in his apartment. Following these statements, Dickerson was placed under arrest.

As a result of Dickerson's confession, Rochester was apprehended by the police and placed under arrest. At that time, Rochester admitted to robbing eleven banks in Georgia, three banks in Virginia (including the First Virginia Bank in Old Town, Alexandria), four banks in Maryland, and an armored car in Maryland. Of particular importance here, Rochester stated that Dickerson was his getaway driver in each of the Maryland and Virginia bank robberies.

The search of Dickerson's apartment produced a silver .45 caliber handgun, dye-stained money, a bait bill from another robbery, ammunition, masks, and latex gloves. The agents also found a small quantity of drugs in plain view. A subsequent warrant-authorized search of Dickerson's Oldsmobile Ciera produced a black leather bag and solvent used to clean dye-stained money.

Based upon his confession, Rochester's statements, and the aforementioned physical evidence discovered during the searches of his apartment and car, Dickerson was indicted by a federal grand jury on one count of conspiracy to commit bank robbery in violation of 18 U.S.C.A. § 371 (West Supp. 1998), on three counts of bank robbery in violation of 18 U.S.C.A. § 2113(a) and (d) (West Supp. 1998), and on three counts of using a firearm during and in relation to a crime of violence in violation of 18 U.S.C.A. § 924(c)(1) (West Supp. 1998). On May 19, 1997, Dickerson filed a motion to suppress (1) the statements he made at the FBI Field Office; (2) the evidence found as a result of his statements; (3) the physical evidence obtained during the search of his apartment; and (4) the physical evidence obtained during the search of his car. The Government submitted a brief in opposition to the motion to suppress. Several days later, the Government supplemented its brief in opposition. A hearing on the motion to suppress was held in the United States District Court for the Eastern District of Virginia on May 30, 1997.

At the suppression hearing, the Government relied exclusively upon the testimony of Special Agent Lawlor. Among other things, Special Agent Lawlor testified that Dickerson was read (and waived) his rights under Miranda prior to his confession. Of particular importance here, Special Agent Lawlor testified that Dickerson confessed "shortly after" he obtained the warrant to search Dickerson's apartment. In contrast, Dickerson testified that he confessed prior to being read (and waiving) his Miranda rights and about thirty minutes after being informed about the warrant to search his apartment. The advice of-rights form indicates that Dickerson waived his Miranda rights at 9:41 p.m. (J.A. at 72.) After the hearing, the district court asked the parties to submit supplemental briefs in support of their respective positions. The Government filed a supplemental memorandum on June 3, 1997.

---

[4]Dickerson told Special Agent Lawlor and Detective Durkin that he had the handgun in question in his hand when the agents knocked on the door of his apartment.

On July 1, 1997, the district court issued an Order and Memorandum Opinion. The district court, among other things, suppressed Dickerson's statement implicating himself and Rochester in the First Virginia Bank robbery, finding that it was made while he was in police custody,[footnote 5] in response to police interrogation, and without the necessary *Miranda* warnings. In so holding, the district court found that Dickerson's in-court testimony was more credible than that of Special Agent Lawlor. This finding rested, in part, upon the fact that Special Agent Lawlor's testimony— that he read Dickerson his Miranda warnings "shortly after" obtaining the warrant— was contradicted by the warrant (issued at "8:50 p.m.") and the advice-of rights form (executed at "9:41 p.m."). Because the documentary evidence undermined Special Agent Lawlor's credibility [footnote 6] (and supported Dickerson's testimony, i.e., he was read his *Miranda* rights about thirty minutes after being told about the warrant), the district court found that "Dickerson was not advised of his *Miranda* rights until after he had completed his statement to the government." (J.A. at 98.)

Although the district court suppressed the statement obtained in violation of *Miranda,* it nevertheless denied Dickerson's motion to suppress the evidence found as a result thereof, e.g., the statement made by Rochester identifying Dickerson as the getaway driver. The district court, relying upon this Court's decision in *United States* v. *Elie,* 111 F.3d 1135 (4th Cir. 1997), noted that evidence found as a result of a statement made in violation of *Miranda* may only be suppressed if the statement was involuntary within the meaning of the Due Process Clause of the Fifth Amendment. Because Dickerson's statement was voluntary under the Fifth Amendment, the district court concluded that the evidence found as a result thereof was admissible at trial.

The district court did, however, suppress the physical evidence discovered during the search of Dickerson's apartment on January 27, 1997. The district court concluded that the warrant was insufficiently particular in describing the items to be seized. Moreover, the district court concluded that the good-faith exception to the exclusionary rule was inapplicable because the agents "[e]xecuting the [w]arrant [a]cted

---

[5]The Government does not challenge on appeal the district court's finding that Dickerson was in police custody for *Miranda* purposes when he was initially brought to the FBI Field Office.

[6]The documentary evidence, which clearly contradicted Special Agent Lawlor's testimony, was not the only reason the district court gave for finding that Special Agent Lawlor's testimony lacked credibility. First, Special Agent Lawlor testified that when he knocked on Dickerson's door he did not have his gun drawn and "didn't expect one way or the other" whether his colleagues would have their guns drawn. The district court found it "simply not credible for a well-trained Special Agent of the FBI to assert that" he did not expect his colleagues to have their weapons drawn when confronting a suspect in an armed bank robbery. (J.A. at 95 n.7.) Second, Special Agent Lawlor told Judge Kenkel that a telephonic warrant was necessary because Dickerson was not under arrest and could easily go home and destroy any evidence of the bank robbery. The district court concluded that "[i]t strains credibility to believe that the FBI would simply release" Dickerson. (J.A. at 90 n.3.) Third, Special Agent Lawlor testified that Judge Kenkel instructed him to write "evidence of the crime of bank robbery" in the section of the warrant used to identify the property to be seized. The district court found "nothing in the transcript of the telephonic application for the warrant to support" this testimony. (J.A. at 84 n.1.) Although the district court is uniquely suited for assessing witness credibility, see *United States* v. *Oregon State Med. Soc'y,* 343 U.S. 326, 339 (1952), the aforementioned credibility determinations were, as the district court acknowledged, not based on the cadence, tone, or inflection of Special Agent Lawlor's voice. Nor, for that matter, were they based on any other factor that would be difficult to evaluate on appeal. Instead, they were based on the content of his testimony. As a result, we are as uniquely suited for assessing these particular findings as the district court. We cannot say that Special Agent Lawlor's explanation for seeking a telephonic warrant strains credibility. Although the agents had probable cause to arrest Dickerson, there is no requirement that the police arrest a suspect the very moment that probable cause is established. Indeed, there are legitimate law enforcement reasons not to do so. See, e.g., *United States* v. *Lovasco,* 431 U.S. 783, 791 (1977) (noting that there are legitimate reasons not to arrest a suspect the moment probable cause is established); *United States* v. *Jones,* 18 F.3d 1145, 1155 (4th Cir. 1994) (recognizing that need to delay arrests even after probable cause is established). As such, we do not believe, as the district court seemingly suggests, that a telephonic warrant was improperly obtained in this case, see Fed. R. Crim. p. 41(c)(2) (authorizing telephonic warrants), or that Special Agent Lawlor was untruthful when he testified that the agents did not intend to arrest Dickerson without additional evidence. We also cannot say that "nothing" in the transcript of the telephonic application supports Special Agent Lawlor's testimony that Judge Kenkel instructed him to write "evidence of the crime of bank robbery" in the section of the warrant used to identify the property to be seized. An examination of the transcript reveals that Judge Kenkel instructed Special Agent Lawlor on what to write in virtually every section of the warrant. Although Judge Kenkel did not specifically tell Special Agent Lawlor what to write in the section in question, he did state that there was probable cause to search Dickerson's apartment for "evidence of . . . the bank robbery in question." (J.A. at 69.)

in [b]ad [f]aith" by relying upon a warrant that was so facially deficient. (J.A. at 91.) Finally, the district court denied Dickerson's motion to suppress the evidence discovered in the trunk of his car. The district court found that the warrant to search Dickerson's car, unlike the warrant to search his apartment, was sufficiently particular in describing the items to be seized.[footnote 7] Moreover, the district court found that the search of the car was supported by the eyewitness accounts of the bank robbery.

On July 15, 1997, the Government filed a motion asking the district court to reconsider its Order suppressing the statements made by Dickerson at the FBI Field Office and the physical evidence found during the search of Dickerson's apartment. The Government's motion included affidavits from Detective Durkin and Agent Wenko, and a statement written by Dickerson while at the FBI Field Office. In addition, the Government argued that because Dickerson's statements were voluntary, they were nonetheless admissible under the mandate of 18 U.S.C.A. § 3501 (West 1985).

Detective Durkin, who was in the interview room with Dickerson at all times, stated in his affidavit that "Dickerson was read his Miranda rights before he made th[e] statements" implicating himself and Rochester in the First Virginia Bank robbery. (J.A. at 121.) Detective Durkin explained that after Special Agent Lawlor returned to the interview room to announce that they were going to search Dickerson's apartment, Special Agent Lawlor immediately departed. According to Detective Durkin, it was not until Special Agent Lawlor returned some time later that they read Dickerson his Miranda warnings. In fact, Detective Durkin testified that when Dickerson was read his Miranda rights he still denied any involvement in the bank robbery. According to Detective Durkin, it was not until Dickerson was told that agents had found a bait bill from a bank robbery in his apartment that he decided to confess.

Attached to Detective Durkin's affidavit was a hand-written statement that Dickerson made while at the FBI Field Office in which he stated that he "was read [his] rights at 7:30 [p.m.]"[footnote 8] (J.A. at 123.) In addition, Dickerson wrote in the statement that he knew "nothing [about] the bank robbery" in question. (J.A. at 123.) Thus, according to his own hand-written note, Dickerson was read his Miranda warnings prior to implicating himself and Rochester in the First Virginia Bank robbery.[footnote 9] Finally, Agent Wenko's affidavit contradicted, among other things, the district court's finding that the agents who executed the search of Dickerson's apartment acted in bad faith. Agent Wenko, who was the lead agent during the search of Dickerson's apartment, stated that he was familiar with the specifics of the bank robbery in question and knew what specific evidence to look for. In addition, Agent Wenko stated that he had been investigating bank robberies for seven years and was very familiar with the type of evidence customarily associated with bank robberies, e.g., guns, money, bait bills, dye-stained money and clothes, disguises, carrying bags, and gloves.

---

[7]An affidavit attached to the warrant identified the following items: a. A black leather backpack, and its contents; b. Currency; c. Clothing and disguises; d. Items stained by dye from explosive dye-packs; e. Firearms, ammunition, and pellet guns; f. Money or cash straps; g. Demand notes; h. Carrying bags; i. Photographs, in particular, photographs of co-conspirators; j. Address books, Rolodexes, or other documents containing names of co-conspirators; and k. Evidence of the Disposition of cash obtained in bank or armed robberies. (J.A. at 85-86.)

[8]Although 7:30 p.m. does not correspond with the time that either Detective Durkin or Special Agent Lawlor gave for when Dickerson was read his Miranda rights, Detective Durkin explained in his affidavit that when Dickerson wrote 7:30 p.m., he "specifically recall[ed] thinking that Dickerson had no idea what time it was." (J.A. at 121.) In any event, the hand-written statement does correspond with the sequence of events that is so crucial to this appeal. Specifically, the statement corroborates the agents' position that Dickerson was read his Miranda warnings prior to his confession.

[9]Dickerson's hand-written statement reads, in pertinent part, as follows: I was read my rights at 7:30 [b]ut I was here at 5:30. I talked to the two Detectives . . . [for] two and a half hours and then was asked to take a polygraph test. I declined because after two hours I had knowledge of the bank robbery. I told them I know nothing of the bank robbery that happened Friday. Befor[e] today I didn't have any knowle[dge] of the bank robbery. (J.A. at 123.)

On August 4, 1997, the district court denied the Government's motion for reconsideration. See *United States* v. *Dickerson*, 971 F. Supp. 1023 (E.D. Va. 1997). Noting that no provision in the Federal Rules of Criminal Procedure governed motions for reconsideration, the district court used the standard set forth in Rule 59(e) of the Federal Rules of Civil Procedure as its guide. See id. at 1024. In so doing, the district court rejected the Government's motion for reconsideration upon the ground that the Government failed to establish that "the evidence . . . was unavailable at the time of the hearing." Id. This interlocutory appeal followed.

III.

Before determining whether Congress possesses the authority to enact § 3501, we must first consider whether the district court erred in refusing to entertain the Government's motion for reconsideration.[footnote 10]

Although a case of first impression in this Court, our sister circuits review a district court's refusal to reopen a suppression hearing for abuse of discretion. See, e.g., *United States* v. *Hassan*, 83 F.3d 693, 696 (5th Cir. 1996); *United States* v. *Roberts*, 978 F.2d 17, 20 (1st Cir. 1992); *United States* v. *Buffington*, 815 F.2d 1292, 1298 (9th Cir. 1987). We adopt that standard here.

Under an abuse of discretion standard, a reviewing court may not substitute its judgment for that of the district court. See, e.g., *United States* v. *Mason*, 52 F.3d 1286, 1289 (4th Cir. 1995). Indeed, an appeals court may uphold the exercise of a district court's discretion even where it might have ruled differently on the matter in the first instance. Instead, our task is simply to determine whether the district court's exercise of discretion was arbitrary or capricious in light of the governing law and the facts. See, e.g., id.

---

[10]Dickerson contends that federal law does not grant the Government the right to appeal an order denying reconsideration of a suppression ruling. It is well established that the Government cannot appeal an adverse ruling in a criminal prosecution without statutory authority. See *United States* v. *Martin Linen Supply Co.*, 430 U.S. 564, 568 (1977); *United States* v. *Sanges*, 144 U.S. 310, 312 (1892). Such authority, the Government maintains, is contained in 18 U.S.C.A. § 3731 (West Supp. 1998). See *United States* v. *Scott*, 437 U.S. 82, 84-85 (1978) (discussing the enactment of § 3731 to provide government appeals in criminal cases). Section 3731 provides, in pertinent part, as follows: An appeal by the United States shall lie to a court of appeals from a decision or order of a district court suppressing or excluding evidence. The appeal in all such cases shall be taken within thirty days after the decision, judgment or order has been rendered and shall be diligently prosecuted. The provisions of this section shall be liberally construed to effectuate its purposes. 18 U.S.C.A. § 3731. Although § 3731 authorizes the Government to appeal orders suppressing evidence, Dickerson contends that it does not expressly authorize the Government to appeal a decision denying reconsideration of a suppression ruling. The issue, not heretofore decided by this Court, is whether § 3731, which provides that it should be liberally construed to effectuate its purposes, can be so construed as to authorize this appeal. We conclude, for the reasons that follow, that it can. In *United States* v. *Ibarra*, 502 U.S. 1 (1991) (per curiam), the defendant was indicted for possession of cocaine with intent to distribute. See id. at 2. The district court, however, ordered that certain evidence be suppressed. See *United States* v. *Ibarra*, 725 F. Supp. 1195, 1202 (D. Wyo. 1989). The Government filed a motion for reconsideration, which was denied. See *United States* v. *Ibarra*, 731 F. Supp. 1037, 1041 (D. Wyo. 1990). On appeal, the Tenth Circuit dismissed the Government's appeal as untimely. See *United States* v. *Ibarra*, 920 F.2d 702, 707 (10th Cir. 1990) (holding that appeal must be filed within thirty days of a district court's suppression ruling). On petition for certiorari, the Supreme Court held that the thirty-day period in which the Government was required to file its appeal under § 3731 began to run on the date that the district court denied the Government's motion for reconsideration, not on the date of the district court's original suppression order. See Ibarra, 502 U.S. at 6-7. In so holding, the Supreme Court necessarily concluded that § 3731 authorizes the Government to appeal a decision denying reconsideration of a suppression ruling. Our Conclusion that we have jurisdiction to hear this appeal is also buttressed by the knowledge that, in enacting § 3731, "Congress intended to remove all statutory barriers to Government appeals and to allow appeals whenever the Constitution would permit." *United States* v. *Wilson*, 420 U.S. 332, 337 (1975); see also *Arizona* v. *Manypenny*, 451 U.S. 232, 247 & n.24, 249 (1981) (noting that Government appeals are permitted to the extent that they are not prohibited by the Constitution). Dickerson does not contend that the instant appeal is constitutionally prohibited. Thus, Dickerson's suggestion that we lack jurisdiction to hear this appeal is without merit. Accord *United States* v. *Hassan*, 83 F.3d 693, 697 (5th Cir. 1996) (holding that " 'an appeal from a denial of a motion to reconsider necessarily raises the underlying [suppression] judgment for review' " (quoting *United States* v. *Herrold*, 962 F.2d 1131, 1136 (3d Cir. 1992)); *United States* v. *Roberts*, 978 F.2d 17, 18 (1st Cir. 1992) (entertaining Government's appeal from the denial of a motion to reconsider a suppression ruling).

In its motion for reconsideration, the U.S. Attorney's Office asked the district court to reverse its suppression rulings on two grounds. First, the Government presented the district court with additional evidence that corroborated Special Agent Lawlor's testimony concerning when Dickerson was read his *Miranda* warnings. Second, the Government argued that even if Dickerson's confession was elicited in technical violation of *Miranda,* it was nevertheless admissible under 18 U.S.C.A. § 3501 (West 1985). We address each ground in turn.

A.

Relying upon Rule 59(e) of the Federal Rules of Civil Procedure, the district court rejected the Government's motion for reconsideration because the Government failed to establish that "the evidence . . . was unavailable at the time of the hearing." *United States* v. *Dickerson,* 971 F. Supp. 1023, 1024 (E.D. Va. 1997). The Government actually conceded, as it does on appeal, that the evidence forming the basis for its motion was available at the time of the suppression hearing. The Government explains, however, that the evidence was not introduced because (1) it never believed that the district court would find Dickerson more believable than Special Agent Lawlor; and (2) it did not want to burden the district court with cumulative evidence.

As an initial matter, although Rule 59(e) of the Federal Rules of Civil Procedure requires a showing that the evidence supporting a motion for reconsideration was not available at the time of the initial hearing, see *Hutchinson* v. *Staton,* 994 F.2d 1076, 1081 (4th Cir. 1993), the Federal Rules of Civil Procedure are not binding in criminal proceedings. As a result, that evidence was available to the movant prior to the suppression hearing does not, as a matter of law, defeat a motion for reconsideration in a criminal case. See, e.g., *United States* v. *Regilio,* 669 F.2d 1169, 1177 (7th Cir. 1981) (recognizing that "society's interest in admitting all relevant evidence militates strongly in favor of permitting reconsideration").

We also recognize, however, that the district court has a strong interest in controlling its docket and avoiding piecemeal litigation. Thus, when the evidence forming the basis for a party's motion for reconsideration was in the movant's possession at the time of the initial hearing, as was the case here, the movant must provide a legitimate reason for failing to introduce that evidence prior to the district court's ruling on the motion to suppress before we will determine that a district court abused its discretion in refusing to reconsider its suppression ruling.[footnote 11] Before considering the Government's reasons for failing to introduce the evidence in question, however, we note that it was given numerous opportunities to introduce the evidence prior to the district court's ruling on the suppression motion. Dickerson's motion to suppress was filed on May 19, 1997. On May 23, 1997, the Government filed a response to Dickerson's motion to suppress. Four days later, the Government supplemented its response. A hearing on the motion was held on May 30, 1997. Finally, at the district court's request, the Government was given yet another opportunity to file an additional supplemental memorandum in support of its position on June 3, 1997. At none of these junctures did the Government introduce the two affidavits and the statement.

---

[11]We note that granting a new trial on the basis of evidence available at the time of the trial is strictly prohibited. See, e.g., *United States* v. *Bales,* 813 F.2d 1289, 1295 (4th Cir. 1987) (noting that under Fed. R. Crim. P. 33 "the evidence must be, in fact, newly discovered, i.e., discovered since the trial"); *United States* v. *Singh,* 54 F.3d 1182, 1190 (4th Cir. 1995) (same). Of course, Rule 33 of the Federal Rules of Criminal Procedure, which governs new trial motions, does not apply to motions for reconsideration of evidentiary rulings prior to trial. As such, granting a motion for reconsideration on the basis of evidence available to the movant at the time of the suppression hearing is not strictly prohibited.

In light of the ample opportunities the Government had to introduce the evidence in question prior to the district court's ruling on the motion to suppress, its articulated reasons for failing to do so ring hollow. First, the Government contends that it never believed that the district court would find Dickerson more credible than Special Agent Lawlor. Even if this explanation was tenable prior to the suppression hearing, Special Agent Lawlor's testimony on the primary issue in dispute, i.e., whether Dickerson was read his *Miranda* warnings prior to his confession, was completely undermined by the Government's own documentary evidence, which supported Dickerson's version of events. After the hearing, therefore, the Government should have been firmly disabused of any misconceptions concerning whom the district court would find more credible. Because the Government was given the opportunity to file a supplemental memorandum after the hearing, the Government's failure to introduce the affidavits of Detective Durkin and Agent Wenko and the statement written by Dickerson cannot be explained by its first justification.

Next, the Government contends that it did not want to burden the district court with cumulative evidence. What the Government means by cumulative evidence is not entirely clear. Because every additional piece of evidence offered is, by definition, cumulative, cumulative evidence is not bad per se. Indeed, under the Federal Rules of Evidence it is the "needless presentation of cumulative evidence" that is to be avoided.[footnote 12] Fed. R. Evid. 403. With that understanding, the Government's argument necessarily assumes that Special Agent Lawlor's testimony should have been sufficient and that any additional evidence would, in fact, be needlessly cumulative. For the reasons stated above, however, the Government should have known after the hearing that additional evidence was not needlessly cumulative, but absolutely necessary.[footnote 13]

In any event, why the Government would consider the statement written by Dickerson—in which he admits that he was read his *Miranda* warnings prior to implicating himself in a series of bank robberies—to be needlessly cumulative on the pivotal question of whether he was read his Miranda warnings prior to implicating himself in a series of bank robberies is difficult to understand. Evidence that is so probative that it would likely change the mind of the factfinder is not needlessly cumulative. Cf. 22 Charles Alan Wright & Kenneth W. Graham, Jr., Federal Practice and Procedure § 5220, at 306 (1978) (noting similar principle under Rule 403). In sum, because the district court gave the Government the opportunity to introduce the affidavits of Detective Durkin and Agent Wenko and Dickerson's hand-written statement after the suppression hearing, we conclude that the Government's failure to do so cannot adequately be explained by its proffered reasons. Accordingly, we cannot say that the district court abused its discretion in denying the Government's motion for reconsideration based upon its refusal to consider evidence that was in the Government's possession at the time of the initial hearing.

---

[12]We do not mean to imply that the Federal Rules of Evidence are binding at a suppression hearing; they are not. See Fed. R. Evid. 104(a) (providing that the rules of evidence are not binding at a preliminary proceeding). We refer to Rule 403 only because it casts some light on the phrase "cumulative evidence."

[13]In its motion for reconsideration, the Government confessed that "this [was] one of those deals where they [throw] the case at [the Assistant United States Attorney] at 4:00 on the day before [the hearing]." *United States* v. *Dickerson,* 971 F. Supp. 1023, 1025 n.2 (E.D. Va. 1997) (final alteration in original). Similarly, during the hearing on the motion to reconsider the Government acknowledged "that the Assistant United States Attorney had very little time to prepare [Special] Agent Lawlor." Id. at 1024. Had the Government simply compared Special Agent Lawlor's recollection of events against its documentary evidence prior to the suppression hearing, it would have discovered the need to introduce additional evidence. While we respect the Government's candidness on this point, it raises further questions relating to the proffered reasons for failing to present the additional affidavits and statement earlier. For example, if the Government failed to prepare and present its case properly, we wonder how it could have known that additional evidence would be needlessly cumulative.

B.

Because "[a] district court by definition abuses its discretion when it makes an error of law," *Koon* v. *United States,* 116 S. Ct. 2035, 2047 (1996), we must address the Government's second proffered ground for reconsideration of the suppression ruling, namely whether § 3501, rather than *Miranda,* governs the admissibility of Dickerson's confession.

1.

Whether § 3501 or *Miranda* governs the admissibility of Dickerson's confession ultimately turns on the answers to two questions. Does § 3501 purport to supersede the rule set forth by the Supreme Court in *Miranda?* If it does, does Congress possess the authority legislatively to overrule *Miranda?* Prior to addressing these questions, however, we feel compelled to respond to the Dissent's assertion that the question of § 3501's applicability is not properly before us.

Although raised by the Government in its motion for reconsideration, the applicability of § 3501 was not briefed by the Government on appeal.[footnote 14] We note, however, that this was no simple oversight. The United States Department of Justice took the unusual step of actually prohibiting the U.S. Attorney's Office from briefing the issue. To be sure, this was not an isolated incident. Over the last several years, the Department of Justice has not only failed to invoke § 3501, it has affirmatively impeded its enforcement.

For example, in *Davis* v. *United States,* 512 U.S. 452 (1994), which involved the defendant's attempt to suppress an incriminating statement made after an ambiguous request for counsel, the Department of Justice expressly declined to take a position on the applicability of § 3501. See *id.* at 457 n.*. As a result, the majority opinion declined to consider the issue. See *id.* (declining to reach issue because "we are reluctant to do so when the issue is one of first impression involving the interpretation of a federal statute on which the Department of Justice expressly declines to take a position"). Justice Scalia, in a Concurring opinion, chided the Department of Justice for its failure to invoke § 3501:

"The United States' repeated refusal to invoke § 3501, combined with the courts' traditional (albeit merely prudential) refusal to consider arguments not

---

[14]Pursuant to Local Rule 27(c), the clerk's office granted the unopposed motion of the Washington Legal Foundation and the Safe Streets Coalition (amici) to file a brief in this case. In light of the Government's unwillingness to defend the constitutionality of § 3501, amici also sought leave to share five minutes of the Government's allotted oral argument time. Under the Federal Rules of Appellate Procedure, "[a] motion of an amicus curiae to participate in oral argument will be granted only for extraordinary reasons." Fed. R. App. P. 29. Because the Department of Justice's refusal to defend the constitutionality of an Act of Congress is an extraordinary event, we granted amici's motion to share oral argument time with the Government. Indeed, federal courts have frequently appointed amici to participate in oral argument where neither side will defend an important position. See, e.g., *Bousley* v. *United States,* 118 S. Ct. 1604, 1609 (1998) (inviting private party to file an amicus brief and to participate in oral argument when Government declined to defend ruling in its favor); *Bob Jones Univ.* v. *United States,* 461 U.S. 574, 585 n.9, 599 n.24 (1983) (same); *McKinney* v. *Indiana Michigan Power Co.,* 113 F.3d 770, 772 n.2 (7th Cir. 1996) (appointing amicus "so that [the court] might have the benefit of an adversary presentation of the issues raised by the appeal"); *United States* v. *Chagra,* 701 F.2d 354, 366 (5th Cir. 1983) (appointing amicus "to ensure that this appeal continues to be presented in an adversary context"). Amici urged this Court, both in its brief and during oral argument, to consider the admissibility of Dickerson's confession under the mandate of § 3501. Although we had the benefit of amici's briefing, the Dissent criticizes our application of § 3501 "without the benefit of any briefing in opposition." Post at 47. Although we would have preferred to have had such briefing, the Department of Justice, as we note in greater detail above, actually prohibited the U.S. Attorney's Office from briefing § 3501 in this case. Cf. Letter from John C. Keeney, Acting Assistant Attorney General, to all United States Attorneys and all Criminal Division Section Chiefs (Nov. 6, 1997) (forbidding "federal prosecutors [from] rely[ing] on the voluntariness provision of Section 3501"). Moreover, when pressed at oral argument, counsel for the United States informed the Court that he had been prohibited by his superiors at the Department of Justice from discussing § 3501. Because it is our duty to apply the governing law to every case or controversy before us, it was unfortunately necessary to proceed without any briefing from the Department of Justice.

raised, has caused the federal judiciary to confront a host of "Miranda" issues that might be entirely irrelevant under federal law. Worse still, it may have produced—during an era of intense national concern about the problem of run-away crime—the acquittal and the non-prosecution of many dangerous felons, enabling them to continue their depredations upon our citizens. There is no excuse for this." Id. at 465 (citations omitted).

Justice Scalia further questioned whether the Department of Justice's failure to invoke § 3501 was "consistent with the Executive's obligation to 'take Care that the Laws be faithfully executed.' " Id. (quoting U.S. Const. Art. II, § 3).

Over the past few years, career federal prosecutors have tried to invoke § 3501 in this Court only to be overruled by the Department of Justice.[footnote 15] In March of 1997, for example, the U.S. Attorney's Office in Alexandria, Virginia, appealed the suppression of a statement that the district court found was obtained in technical violation of *Miranda.* See *United States* v. *Sullivan,* 138 F.3d 126 (4th Cir. 1998). In its brief, the U.S. Attorney's Office urged this Court to reverse the district court on the basis of § 3501. The Department of Justice, however, ordered the U.S. Attorney's Office to withdraw its brief. In its place, a brief without any reference to § 3501 was filed. As a result, the Washington Legal Foundation and United States Senators Jeff Sessions, Jon Kyl, John Ashcroft, and Strom Thurmond filed an amicus brief urging this Court to consider the admissibility of Sullivan's confession under § 3501. Because we ultimately concluded that Sullivan was not in custody for *Miranda* purposes when the incriminating statements were made, we had no occasion to address the applicability of § 3501. See id. at 134 n.

In June of 1997, this Court issued an opinion upholding the suppression of a confession obtained in technical violation of *Miranda.* See *United States* v. *Leong,* 116 F.3d 1474 (4th Cir. 1997) (unpublished). Although the United States did not seek rehearing, the Washington Legal Foundation and the Safe Streets Coalition moved this Court for leave to proceed as amici curiae. In their motion, the putative amici took the Government to task for failing to assert the applicability of § 3501. As a result, we ordered the Department of Justice to address the effect of § 3501 on the admissibility of Leong's confession. In response, Attorney General Janet Reno, although purporting to follow the advice of her career prosecutors in other matters, notified Congress that the Department of Justice would not defend the constitutionality of § 3501, see 2 U.S.C.A. § 288k(b) (West 1997) (requiring the Department of Justice to notify the United States Congress whenever it will not defend the constitutionality of a federal statute), and filed with this Court a brief to the same effect.[footnote 16]

Against this background, the Government's failure to raise the applicability of § 3501 on appeal in this case does not come as a surprise. Of even greater importance, neither does it prevent us from considering the applicability of § 3501 on appeal.

---

[15]Justice's refusal to invoke § 3501 has not been limited to this Circuit. In *Cheely* v. *United States,* 21 F.3d 914 (9th Cir. 1994), the Ninth Circuit suppressed an incriminating statement that was obtained in technical violation of Edwards. Id. at 923. Although the Government did not petition for rehearing, the Ninth Circuit sua sponte asked the parties whether the case merited rehearing en banc. See *Cheely* v. *United States,* 92-30257 (9th Cir. May 25, 1994) (unpublished order). Curiously, Justice filed a memorandum opposing further review. One week later, the Supreme Court in *Davis* v. *United States,* 512 U.S. 452 (1994), would bring § 3501 to the attention of the legal community. In response, a career federal prosecutor sent a letter to the Ninth Circuit apprising them of the Court's decision in Davis. Later that same day, Solicitor General Drew Days withdrew the earlier letter and replaced it with a letter that downplayed the relevance of Davis to the issues at hand. Notwithstanding the letter from the Solicitor General, the Ninth Circuit "called for supplemental briefing from the parties as to the effect Davis might have on our Conclusion" to suppress the statements in question. *Cheely* v. *United States,* 36 F.3d 1439, 1448 (9th Cir. 1994). Although Justice filed a supplemental brief, it nevertheless failed to even argue the applicability of § 3501. Upon reconsideration, the Ninth Circuit still suppressed the statement. See id.

[16]The Department of Justice has taken the position that unless the Supreme Court overrules *Miranda,* "the United States is not free to urge the lower courts" to "rely on Section 3501." See Letter from John C. Keeney, Acting Assistant Attorney General, to all United States Attorneys and all Criminal Division Section Chiefs (Nov. 6, 1997) (noting that "[t]he Department has not yet decided whether it would ask the Supreme Court in an appropriate case to overrule or modify Miranda").

Even where the parties abdicate their responsibility to call relevant authority to this Court's attention, cf. Va. Code Prof. Resp. 7-20, they cannot prevent us from deciding the case under the governing law simply by refusing to argue it, see *United States Nat'l Bank of Or.* v. *Independent Ins. Agents of America, Inc.,* 508 U.S. 439, 445-48 (1993).[footnote 17] Indeed, it is now well established that "the proper administration of the criminal law cannot be left merely to the stipulation of parties." *Young* v. *United States,* 315 U.S. 257, 259 (1942). The Dissent contends that "we are faced with essentially the same situation that the Supreme Court confronted in *Davis* when it refused to take up § 3501." Post at 49. We disagree. Although the Supreme Court declined sua sponte to consider the applicability of § 3501 in *Davis,* 512 U.S. at 457 n., that decision was influenced by prudential concerns not present here, id. at 465 (Scalia, J., Concurring) (noting that the Court's decision not to consider the applicability of § 3501 was influenced by prudential concerns, rather than by statutory constraints on the Supreme Court's jurisdiction). As a general matter, "a court should avoid deciding a constitutional question when it can dispose of a case on another basis." *Jimenez* v. *BP Oil, Inc.,* 853 F.2d 268, 270 (4th Cir. 1988) (citing *Ashwander* v. *Tennessee Valley Auth.,* 297 U.S. 288, 346 (1936) (Brandeis, J., Concurring)). Having determined that the defendant's ambiguous reference to an attorney during a custodial interrogation was not a request for counsel for purposes of *Edwards* v. *Arizona,* 451 U.S. 477, 484-85 (1981), see *Davis,* 512 U.S. at 459, the Court had no reason to consider whether the defendant's confession was also admissible under the mandate of § 3501, especially because the Department of Justice had expressly declined to take a position on the provision's constitutionality, see id. at 457 n. Dickerson's confession, in contrast, was obtained in violation of *Miranda.* Thus, unlike the situation in *Davis,* we cannot avoid deciding the constitutional question associated with § 3501. Moreover, and again unlike the situation in *Davis,* the Department of Justice has now taken the position that § 3501 is unconstitutional. See Letter from Janet Reno, Attorney General, to Congress (Sept. 10, 1997) (notifying Congress that the Department of Justice will not defend the constitutionality of the statute). As a result, the specific prudential concerns that animated the Supreme Court's decision not to consider the applicability of § 3501 in Davis are simply not present here.

Furthermore, the primary reason for the Supreme Court's general reluctance to consider arguments not raised is not applicable to inferior federal courts such as this one. The Supreme Court "sits as a court of review." *Duignan* v. *United States,* 274 U.S. 195, 200 (1927). Thus, it generally will not consider issues "not pressed or passed upon below." Id.; see also *Pennsylvania Dep't of Corrections* v. *Yeskey,* 118 S. Ct. 1952, 1956 (1998) (declining to address issue that was not presented to either the District Court or the Court of Appeals); *Adickes* v. *S.H. Kress & Co.,* 398 U.S. 144, 147 n.2 (1970) ("Where issues are neither raised before nor considered by the Court of Appeals, this Court will not ordinarily consider them."). In contrast, "[t]he matter of what questions may be taken up and resolved for the first time on appeal is one left primarily to the discretion of the courts of appeals, to be exercised on the facts of individual cases." *Singleton* v. *Wulff,* 428 U.S. 106, 121 (1976); see also *United States Nat'l Bank of Or.,* 508 U.S. at 445-48 (stating that it was proper for the Court of Appeals to consider whether the controlling statute had been repealed despite the parties' failure to raise the issue).

---

[17]The Dissent argues, and we do not dispute, that "the only issues not raised by the parties that we are required to consider are those of subject matter jurisdiction and justiciability." Post at 48 (emphasis added). That observation, however, is of no real import. First, as we note above, this Court may, in its discretion, consider issues not raised below. See post at 25-26. Second, and more importantly, we are not considering an issue that was not raised by the parties. The issue on appeal is the district court's suppression ruling. Without question, we are free to address ourselves to any legal theory that would bear on the issue under appeal. See *Shafer* v. *Preston Memorial Hosp. Corp.,* 107 F.3d 274, 275 n.1 (4th Cir. 1997) ("We have consistently recognized that we may [decide a case] on different grounds than those employed by the district court."); *Jackson* v. *Kimel,* 992 F.2d 1318, 1322 (4th Cir. 1993) (same). Thus, because the Government has appealed the district court's suppression ruling, we are free to consider the applicability of § 3501.

Because the Department of Justice will not defend the constitutionality of § 3501—and no criminal defendant will press the issue—the question of whether that statute, rather than *Miranda,* governs the admission of confessions in federal court will most likely not be answered until a Court of Appeals exercises its discretion to consider the issue. Here, the district court has suppressed a confession that, on its face, is admissible under the mandate of § 3501, i.e., the confession was voluntary under the Due Process Clause, but obtained in technical violation of Miranda. As a result, we are required to consider the issue now. Cf. *Davis,* 512 U.S. at 464 (Scalia, J., Concurring) (noting that the "time will have arrived" to consider the applicability of § 3501 the next time "a case that comes within the terms of th[e] statute is . . . presented to us"); see also Eric D. Miller, comment, Should Courts Consider 18 U.S.C. § 3501 Sua Sponte?, 65 U. Chi. L. Rev. 1029 (1998) (answering question in the affirmative).

A.

Having determined that the issue is properly before the panel, we must first determine whether § 3501 purports to supersede the rule set forth by the Supreme Court in Miranda. To do so, a brief history of the rules governing the admissibility of confessions before and after *Miranda* is in order. See generally Development in the Law -Confessions, 79 Harv. L. Rev. 935 (1966) [hereinafter Developments].

"At early common law, confessions were admissible at trial without restrictions." Id. at 954; see also McCormick's Handbook on the Law of Evidence § 147, at 313 (1972) (Edward W. Cleary, ed., West 2d ed. 1972) (citing 3 Wigmore, Evidence § 818 (3d ed. 1940)). In the latter part of the eighteenth century, however, courts began to recognize that certain confessions were not trustworthy. See, e.g., *The King* v. *Rudd,* 168 Eng. Rep. 160 (K.B. 1783) (holding that "no credit ought to be given" to "a confession forced from the mind by the flattery of hope, or by the torture of fear"). Although several tests were developed to determine whether a confession was trustworthy, a confession was generally thought to be reliable only if made voluntarily. See, e.g., *Regina* v. *Garner,* 169 Eng. Rep. 267 (Ct. Crim. App. 1848); *Regina* v. *Baldry,* 169 Eng. Rep. 568 (Ct. Crim. App. 1852).

In *Hopt* v. *Utah,* 110 U.S. 574 (1884), the Supreme Court specifically adopted the common law rule that a confession was reliable, and therefore admissible, if it was made voluntarily. Id. at 584-85 (holding that a confession was voluntary if not induced by threat or promise) (citing *Regina* v. *Baldry,* 169 Eng. Rep. 568 (Ct. Crim. App. 1852)); see also *Pierce* v. *United States,* 160 U.S. 355, 357 (1896) (same). In subsequent cases, the Supreme Court applied the common law test of voluntariness to confessions. See Developments, supra, at 959. In so doing, the Court rejected the argument that a confession was involuntary simply because the suspect was in custody. See *Sparf* v. *United States,* 156 U.S. 51, 55 (1895). Similarly, in *Wilson* v. *United States,* 162 U.S. 613 (1896), the Supreme Court specifically held that the failure to warn a suspect of his right to remain silent and of his right to counsel did not render a confession involuntary. Id. at 624.

In *Bram* v. *United States,* 168 U.S. 532 (1897), the Supreme Court asserted, for the first time, a constitutional basis for its requirement that a confession be made voluntarily. Id. at 542 (stating that whether a confession is voluntary "is controlled by that portion of the fifth amendment . . . commanding that no person 'shall be compelled in any criminal case to be a witness against himself' " (quoting U.S. Const. amend. V.)). According to the Court, the Fifth Amendment privilege against self-incrimination "was but a crystallization" of the common law rule that only voluntary confessions are admissible as evidence. Id. Although the Supreme Court—prior to *Miranda* -would eventually place less reliance upon the approach taken in *Bram,* see, e.g., *United States* v. *Carignan,* 342 U.S. 36, 41 (1951) (expressing doubt about "[w]hether involuntary confessions are excluded from federal criminal trials on the ground of a violation of the Fifth Amendment's protection against self-incrimination, or from a rule that forced confessions are untrustworthy" (footnote omitted)), the Supreme Court in *Brown v. Mississippi,* 297 U.S. 278 (1936), invoked another constitutional basis for its requirement that a confession be made voluntarily: the Due Process Clause. Id. at 285-86. Thereafter, a confession was admissible only if voluntary within the meaning of the Due Process Clause. See, e.g., *Haynes v. Washington,* 373 U.S. 503 (1963); *Ashcraft v. Tennessee,* 322 U.S. 143, 154 (1944); *Chambers v. Florida,* 309 U.S. 227 (1940).

Thus, prior to *Miranda,* the rule governing the admissibility of confessions in federal court—if not the rule's justification—remained the same for nearly 180 years: confessions were admissible at trial if made voluntarily. See, e.g., *Davis v. United States,* 512 U.S. 452, 464 (1994) (Scalia, J., Concurring) (noting that prior to Miranda, "voluntariness vel non was the touchstone of admissibility of confessions"); *Miranda v. Arizona,* 384 U.S. 436, 506-07 (1966) (Harlan, J., Dissenting) (noting that voluntariness has been the test for admitting confessions since the earliest days of the Republic). Indeed, in *Lisenba v. California,* 314 U.S. 219 (1941), the Supreme Court specifically referred to "voluntariness" as the federal test for determining the admissibility of confessions. Id. at 236.

Such was the stage in 1966 when the Supreme Court decided *Miranda v. Arizona,* 384 U.S. 436 (1966). In *Miranda,* the Supreme Court announced a new analytical approach to the admissibility of confessions. Specifically, the Court rejected a case-by-case determination of whether a confession was voluntary. Instead, the Court held that any statement stemming from the custodial interrogation of a suspect would be presumed involuntary, and therefore inadmissible, unless the police first provided the suspect with four warnings.[footnote 18] Although the Court relied upon its prior decision in *Bram v. United States,* 168 U.S. 532 (1897) (holding that voluntariness is required by the Fifth Amendment), for support, *Miranda,* 384 U.S. at 461-62, the Court acknowledged that the Constitution requires no "particular solution for the inherent compulsions of the interrogation process," id. at 467, and left open the opportunity for the States and Congress to "develop their own safeguards for the privilege, so long as they are fully as effective as [the four warnings] in informing accused persons of their right of silence and in affording a continuous opportunity to exercise it," id. at 490. The Court held that until that time, the warning "safeguards must be observed." Id. at 467.

Congress enacted § 3501 just two years after the Supreme Court decided *Miranda.* When interpreting an act of Congress, "our inquiry begins with an examination of the language used in the statute." *Faircloth v. Lundy Packing Co.,* 91 F.3d 648, 653 (4th Cir. 1996) (citing *Stiltner v. Beretta U.S.A. Corp.,* 74 F.3d 1473, 1482 (4th Cir.), cert. denied, 117 S. Ct. 54 (1996)), cert. denied, 117 S. Ct. 738 (1997). Section 3501 provides as follows:

(a) In any criminal prosecution brought by the United States or by the District of Columbia, a confession, as defined in subsection (e) hereof, shall be admissible in evidence if it is voluntarily given. Before such confession is received in evidence, the trial Judge shall, out of the presence of the jury, determine any issue as to voluntariness. If the trial Judge determines that the confession was voluntarily made it shall be admitted in evidence and the trial Judge shall permit the jury to hear relevant evidence on the issue of voluntariness and shall instruct the jury to give such weight to the confession as the jury feels it deserves under all the circumstances.

---

[18]The four warnings are: (1) that the suspect has the right to remain silent; (2) that any statements he makes can be used against him; (3) that he has the right to the presence of an attorney during questioning; and (4) that an attorney will be appointed for him if he cannot afford one. See *Miranda v. Arizona,* 384 U.S. 436, 444 (1966).

(b) The trial Judge in determining the issue of voluntariness shall take into consideration all the circumstances surrounding the giving of the confession, including (1) the time elapsing between arrest and arraignment of the defendant making the confession, if it was made after arrest and before arraignment, (2) whether such defendant knew the nature of the offense with which he was charged or of which he was suspected at the time of making the confession, (3) whether or not such defendant was advised or knew that he was not required to make any statement and that any such statement could be used against him, (4) whether or not such defendant had been advised prior to questioning of his right to the assistance of counsel; and (5) whether or not such defendant was without the assistance of counsel when questioned and when giving such confession.

The presence or absence of any of the above-mentioned factors to be taken into consideration by the Judge need not be conclusive on the issue of voluntariness of the confession.

(c) In any criminal prosecution by the United States or by the District of Columbia, a confession made or given by a person who is a defendant therein, while such person was under arrest or other detention in the custody of any law enforcement officer or law-enforcement agency, shall not be inadmissible solely because of delay in bringing such person before a magistrate or other officer empowered to commit persons charged with offenses against the laws of the United States or of the District of Columbia if such confession is found by the trial Judge to have been made voluntarily and if the weight to be given the confession is left to the jury and if such confession was made or given by such person within six hours immediately following his arrest or other detention: Provided, That the time limitation contained in this subsection shall not apply in any case in which the delay in bringing such person before such magistrate or other officer beyond such six-hour period is found by the trial Judge to be reasonable considering the means of transportation and the distance to be traveled to the nearest available such magistrate or other officer.

(d) Nothing contained in this section shall bar the admission in evidence of any confession made or given voluntarily by any person to any other person without interrogation by anyone, or at any time at which the person who made or gave such confession was not under arrest or other detention.

(e) As used in this section, the term "confession" means any confession of guilt of any criminal offense or any self incriminating statement made or given orally or in writing. 18 U.S.C.A. § 3501. The above-quoted statutory language is plain. Congress has provided that "a confession . . . shall be admissible in evidence if it is voluntarily given." 18 U.S.C.A.§ 3501(a). Based upon the statutory language, it is perfectly clear that Congress enacted § 3501 with the express purpose of legislatively overruling Miranda and restoring voluntariness as the test for admitting confessions in federal court. See, e.g., Stephen A. Saltzburg & Daniel J. Capra, American Criminal Procedure 545 (5th ed. 1996) (noting that "the intent of Congress was to 'overrule' Miranda in favor of a return to the 'voluntariness' standard").

That Congress wished to return to a case-by-case determination of whether a confession was voluntarily given is undeniable. See S. Rep. No. 90-1097 (1968), reprinted in 1968 U.S.C.C.A.N. 2112. Although certainly not dispositive, it is worth noting that the Senate Report accompanying § 3501 specifically stated that "[t]he intent of the bill is to reverse the holding of Miranda v. Arizona, 384 U.S. 436 (1966)." Id. at 2141. Indeed, although acknowledging that "[t]he bill would also set aside the holdings of such cases as McNabb v. United States, 318 U.S. 332 (1943), and Mallory v. United States, 354 U.S. 449 (1957)," id., the Report stated that Miranda "is the case to which the bill is directly addressed," id. Senate opponents likewise recognized that § 3501, by making voluntariness the sole criterion for the admissibility of confessions, was meant to repeal the irrebuttable presumption created by Miranda. See id. at 2210-11 (noting that § 3501 was "squarely in conflict with the Supreme Court's decision in Miranda v. Arizona").

Similarly, both proponents and opponents of § 3501 in the House of Representatives noted that the statute was meant to overrule the irrebuttable presumption created by Miranda. See, e.g., 114 Cong. Rec. 16,066 (1968) (statement of Rep. Celler); id. at 16,074 (statement of Rep. Corman); id. at 16,278 (statement of Rep. Poff); id. at 16,279 (statement of Rep. Taylor); id. at 16,296 (statement of Rep. Randall); id. at 16,297-98 (statement of Rep. Pollock).

Although Congress enacted § 3501 with the express purpose of restoring voluntariness as the test for admitting confessions in federal court, it is important to note that Congress did not completely abandon the central holding of *Miranda,* i.e. , the four warnings are important safeguards in protecting the Fifth Amendment privilege against self-incrimination. Indeed, § 3501 specifically lists the *Miranda* warnings as factors that a district court should consider when determining whether a confession was voluntarily given. See 18 U.S.C.A. § 3501(b). Congress simply provided that the failure to administer the warnings to a suspect would no longer create an irrebuttable presumption that a subsequent confession was involuntarily given. See id. (providing that the *Miranda* warnings are not dispositive on the issue of voluntariness).

B.

Based on the statutory language alone, it is clear that Congress enacted § 3501 with the express purpose of returning to the pre-*Miranda* case-by-case determination of whether a confession was voluntary. We now turn to our next inquiry: Does Congress possess the authority to supersede the irrebuttable presumption created in *Miranda* that any unwarned statement to the police is involuntary, and therefore inadmissible?

Interestingly, much of the scholarly literature on *Miranda* deals not with whether Congress has the legislative authority to overrule the presumption created in *Miranda,* but whether it should. *Miranda's* opponents, like Professor Paul Cassell, contend that thousands of violent criminals escape Justice each year as a direct result of *Miranda.* See, e.g., Paul G. Cassell & Richard Fowles, Handcuffing the Cops? A Thirty-Year Perspective on *Miranda's* Harmful Effects on Law Enforcement, 50 Stan. L. Rev. 1055 (1998); Paul G. Cassell, All Benefits, No Costs: The Grand Illusion of Miranda's Defenders, 90 Nw. U. L. Rev. 1084 (1996); Paul G. Cassell, *Miranda's* Social Costs: An Empirical Reassessment, 90 Nw. U. L. Rev. 387 (1996). In contrast, its proponents, like Professor Stephen Schulhofer, argue that *Miranda* has had little impact on law enforcement's ability to obtain confessions. See, e.g., Stephen J. Schulhofer, *Miranda's* Practical Effect: Substantial Benefits and Vanishingly Small Social Costs, 90 Nw. U. L. Rev. 500 (1996); Stephen J. Schulhofer, Reconsidering *Miranda,* 54 U. Chi. L. Rev. 435 (1987). This debate, however, is one we need not enter. Whether Congress should overrule *Miranda* tells us nothing about whether it could. More importantly, it is not our role to answer that question. It is the province of the judiciary to determine what the law is, not what it should be. See *Marbury* v. *Madison,* 5 U.S. (1 Cranch) 137 (1803).

In *City of Boerne* v. *Flores,* 117 S. Ct. 2157 (1997), the Court recently held that Congress does not possess the legislative authority to supersede a Supreme Court decision construing the Constitution. See id. at 2172 (refusing to enforce federal statute establishing more narrow test for violation of the Free Exercise Clause than prior test established by Supreme Court). On the other hand, Congress possesses the legislative authority to overrule judicially created rules of evidence and procedure that are not required by the Constitution. See *Palermo* v. *United States*, 360 U.S. 343, 345-48 (1959) (upholding federal statute establishing more narrow disclosure of Jenks material than prior rule established by Supreme Court); see also *Carlisle* v. *United States,* 517 U.S. 416, 426 (1996) (noting that the federal courts may formulate rules of evidence and procedure so long as they do not conflict with an Act of Congress); *Vance* v. *Terrazas,* 444 U.S. 252, 265 (1980) (upholding statute altering the evidentiary standard for expatriation proceedings established by the Supreme Court because prior standard created by the Court was not required by "the Constitution"). In fact, the power of the Supreme Court to prescribe non-constitutional "rules of procedure and evidence for the federal courts exists only in the absence of a relevant Act of Congress." *Palermo,* 360 U.S. at 353 n.11 (citing *Funk* v. *United States,* 290 U.S. 371, 382 (1933), and *Gordon* v. *United States,* 344 U.S. 414, 418 (1953)).

Whether Congress has the authority to enact § 3501, therefore, turns on whether the rule set forth by the Supreme Court in *Miranda* is required by the Constitution. If it is, Congress lacked the authority to enact § 3501, and *Miranda* continues to control the admissibility of confessions in federal court. See *City of Boerne,* 117 S. Ct. at 2172. If it is not required by the Constitution, then Congress possesses the authority to supersede *Miranda* legislatively, and § 3501 controls the admissibility of confessions in federal court. See *Palermo,* 360 U.S. at 353 n.11.

Using the same analysis, several federal courts have found that § 3501 superseded the rule set forth in *McNabb* v. *United States,* 318 U.S. 332 (1943), and *Mallory* v. *United States,* 354 U.S. 449 (1957). See *United States* v. *Pugh,* 25 F.3d 669, 675 (8th Cir. 1994) (holding that § 3501 superseded the *McNabb/Mallory* rule); *United States* v. *Christopher,* 956 F.2d 536, 538-39 (6th Cir. 1991) (noting that § 3501, rather than *McNabb/Mallory,* governs the admissibility of confessions in federal court). In particular, the Eighth and Sixth Circuits first ascertained whether the rule set forth by the Supreme Court in *McNabb* and *Mallory* was required by the Constitution. See *Pugh,* 25 F.3d at 675; *Christopher,* 956 F.2d at 538-39. In *McNabb,* the Supreme Court exercised its supervisory power over the federal courts to exclude all incriminating statements, including voluntary confessions, obtained during an unreasonable delay between a defendant's arrest and initial appearance. See 318 U.S. at 343-44. In *Mallory* the Supreme Court affirmed the holding of *McNabb* under Rule 5(a) of the Federal Rules of Criminal Procedure. See 354 U.S. at 455-56. Finding that the rule set forth in McNabb and Mallory was not required by the Constitution, the Eighth and Sixth Circuits had little difficulty concluding that Congress possessed the legislative authority to overrule both cases. See *Pugh,* 25 F.3d at 675; *Christopher,* 956 F.2d at 538-39.[footnote 19]

We begin our analysis then, with the Supreme Court's decision in *Miranda.* Several passages in Chief Justice Warren's opinion for the Court suggest that the warnings safeguard rights guaranteed by the Constitution. See, e.g., *Miranda,* 384 U.S. at 490 (noting that the privilege against self-incrimination is guaranteed by the Constitution). Surprisingly, the sixty-page opinion does not specifically state the basis for its holding that a statement obtained from a suspect without the warnings would be presumed involuntary. The Court strongly suggested, however, that the basis for the rule was identical to that set forth in *McNabb* and *Mallory.* See id. at 463. In particular, just as the "supervisory" rule set forth in *McNabb* and *Mallory* permitted the Court to avoid the constitutional issues associated with federal interrogations, see id., the rule set forth in *Miranda* would allow the Court to avoid the constitutional issues associated with state interrogations, see id.

Although the Court failed to specifically state the basis for its holding in *Miranda,* it did specifically state what the basis was not. At no point does the Court

---

[19]Interestingly, although this Court has not addressed the effect of § 3501 on either Miranda or McNabb /Mallory, we have repeatedly cited the provision when making voluntariness determinations without ever suggesting that any part of the section is unconstitutional. See, e.g., *United States* v. *Braxton,* 112 F.3d 777, 784 & n.* (4th Cir.) (en banc), cert. denied, 118 S. Ct. 192 (1997); *United States* v. *Wilson,* 895 F.2d 168, 172-73 (4th Cir. 1990); *United States* v. *Pelton,* 835 F.2d 1067, 1074 (4th Cir. 1987); *United States* v. *Peoples,* 748 F.2d 934, 936 (4th Cir. 1984); *United States* v. *Gonzales,* 736 F.2d 981, 983 (4th Cir. 1984); *United States* v. *Dodier,* 630 F.2d 232, 236 (4th Cir. 1980); *United States* v. *Sauls,* 520 F.2d 568, 569 (4th Cir. 1975); *United States* v. *Johnson,* 495 F.2d 378, 382 (4th Cir. 1974). Indeed, in *United States* v. *Van Metre,* 150 F.3d 339 (4th Cir. 1998), we recently held that a fifty-five hour delay between the defendant's arrest and arraignment did not render the defendant's confession inadmissible, without citing either McNabb or Mallory, because under the mandate of § 3501 such delay "is only one factor to be considered when determining the admissibility of a confession." Id. at 348-49.

refer to the warnings as constitutional rights. Indeed, the Court acknowledged that the Constitution did not require the warnings, id. at 467, disclaimed any intent to create a "constitutional straightjacket," id., repeatedly referred to the warnings as "procedural safeguards," id. at 444, and invited Congress and the States "to develop their own safeguards for [protecting] the privilege," id. at 490.

Since deciding *Miranda,* the Supreme Court consistently (and repeatedly) has referred to the warnings as "prophylactic," *New York* v. *Quarles,* 467 U.S. 649, 654 (1984), and "not themselves rights protected by the Constitution," *Michigan* v. *Tucker,* 417 U.S. 433, 444 (1974); see also *Davis* v. *United States,* 512 U.S. 452, 457-58 (1994) (referring to *Miranda* warnings as "a series of recommended procedural safeguards" (internal quotation marks omitted)); *Withrow* v. *Williams,* 507 U.S. 680, 690-91 (1993) (acknowledging that *"Miranda's* safeguards are not constitutional in character"); *Duckworth* v. *Eagan,* 492 U.S. 195, 203 (1989) (noting that the *Miranda* warnings are not required by the Constitution); *Connecticut* v. *Barrett,* 479 U.S. 523, 528 (1987) (noting that "the *Miranda* Court adopted prophylactic rules designed to insulate the exercise of Fifth Amendment rights"); *Oregon* v. *Elstad,* 470 U.S. 298, 306 (1985) (noting that the *Miranda* exclusionary rule "may be triggered even in the absence of a Fifth Amendment violation"); *Edwards* v. *Arizona,* 451 U.S. 477, 492 (1981) (Powell, J., Concurring) (noting that the Court in *Miranda* "imposed a general prophylactic rule that is not manifestly required by anything in the text of the Constitution").

One of the first opinions construing *Miranda* was *Harris* v. *New York,* 401 U.S. 222 (1971). In Harris, the defendant, charged with selling heroin, made several statements to the police prior to receiving his *Miranda* warnings. See id. at 223-24. At trial, the defendant took the stand in his own defense. See id. at 223. During cross examination, he was asked whether he had previously made any statements to the police that contradicted his direct testimony. See id. Although not admissible as substantive evidence, the Court held, per Chief Justice Burger, that the statements in question could be admitted for purposes of impeaching his credibility because, although obtained in technical violation of *Miranda,* the statements were made voluntarily. See id. at 224-25; cf. *Mincey* v. *Arizona,* 437 U.S. 385, 401-02 (1978) (holding that involuntary statements, as opposed to statements made in technical violation of *Miranda,* could not even be admitted for impeachment purposes).

In Tucker, the Supreme Court was asked to apply the "tainted fruits" doctrine from *Wong Sun* v. *United States,* 371 U.S. 471 (1963), to the testimony of a witness whose identity was discovered as the result of a statement obtained from the defendant in violation of *Miranda.* See 417 U.S. at 436-37. In declining to extend the "tainted fruits" doctrine to the facts in *Tucker,* the Court noted that the unwarned questioning did not abridge the defendant's Fifth Amendment privilege, "but departed only from the prophylactic standards later laid down by this court in *Miranda* to safeguard that privilege." 417 U.S. at 445-46. Because the defendant's constitutional rights were not infringed, the Court in *Tucker* determined that the "fruit of the poisonous tree" doctrine did not apply. Id. at 445-46 & n.19.

In *Quarles,* the Supreme Court was asked by the State of New York to recognize an emergency exception to *Miranda.* See 467 U.S. at 649. In that case, a young woman told two police officers that she had just been raped, that her assailant had just entered a nearby store, and that he was carrying a gun. After entering the store the officers quickly spotted the defendant. After a short chase, the defendant was caught and searched. Because he was wearing an empty shoulder holster, the arresting officer asked him, prior to reading him his *Miranda* warnings, where the gun was located. See id. at 651-52. The defendant nodded in the direction of some empty cartons and stated, "the gun is over there." Id. at 652. Although obtained in technical violation of *Miranda,* the Government sought to introduce the defendant's statement in its case-in-chief. In recognizing an emergency exception to *Miranda,* the Supreme Court relied exclusively upon the fact that a violation of *Miranda* was not necessarily a violation of the Constitution. See id.

at 654 (stating that "[t]he prophylactic *Miranda* warnings . . . are 'not themselves rights protected by the Constitution' " (quoting Tucker, 417 U.S. at 444)); see also Saltzburg & Capra, supra, at 555-56 ("[I]f the *Miranda* safeguards were constitutionally required, then presumably any confession obtained in violation of them would have to be excluded—even if the officer was faced with a situation where giving the safeguards may have posed a threat to public safety.").

When presented with another opportunity to extend the *Wong Sun* "tainted fruits" doctrine, the Supreme Court in *Oregon* v. *Elstad,* 470 U.S. 298 (1985), once again declined the invitation to do so. In *Elstad,* two officers went to the defendant's home with a warrant for his arrest. See id. at 300. After executing the warrant, the officers questioned the defendant about his role in the burglary of a neighbor's house. See id. at 301. As a result of the interrogation, the defendant confessed to the burglary. See id. The defendant was then escorted to the police station where the officers advised him for the first time of his *Miranda* rights. After waiving his rights, the defendant once again confessed to the burglary. See id. Later, the defendant sought to suppress his second confession as the "fruit of the poisonous tree," arguing that it was obtained only as the result of his first confession that was made in violation of *Miranda.* See id. at 302. The *Elstad* majority, however, held that the "tainted fruits" doctrine did not apply to the second confession for the same reasons the doctrine did not apply in Tucker. See id. at 308. Specifically, the Court held that "[s]ince there was no actual infringement of the suspect's constitutional rights, the case was not controlled by the doctrine expressed in *Wong Sun* that fruits of a constitutional violation must be suppressed." Id. (emphasis added).

Of particular importance here, the Court in *Elstad* made the following observation about *Miranda:* The *Miranda* exclusionary rule, however, serves the Fifth Amendment and sweeps more broadly than the Fifth Amendment itself. It may be triggered even in the absence of a Fifth Amendment violation. The Fifth Amendment prohibits use by the prosecution in its case in chief only of compelled testimony. Failure to administer *Miranda* warnings creates a presumption of compulsion. Consequently, unwarned statements that are otherwise voluntary within the meaning of the Fifth Amendment must nevertheless be excluded from evidence under *Miranda.* Thus, in the individual case, *Miranda's* preventive medicine provides a remedy even to the defendant who has suffered no identifiable constitutional harm.

"But the *Miranda* presumption, though irrebuttable for purposes of the prosecution's case in chief, does not require that the statements and their fruits be discarded as inherently tainted. Despite the fact that patently voluntary statements taken in violation of *Miranda* must be excluded from the prosecution's case, the presumption of coercion does not bar their use for impeachment purposes on cross-examination." Id. at 306-07 (internal footnotes and citations omitted).

In light of the foregoing cases, it is certainly "well established that the failure to deliver *Miranda* warnings is not itself a constitutional violation." *United States* v. *Elie,* 111 F.3d 1135, 1142 (4th Cir. 1997) (citing Supreme Court cases); see also *Correll* v. *Thompson,* 63 F.3d 1279, 1290 (4th Cir. 1995) (holding that "a technical violation of *Miranda* [is not necessarily] a Fifth Amendment violation"). As a consequence, the irrebuttable presumption created by the Court in *Miranda*—that a confession obtained without the warnings is presumed involuntary—is a fortiori not required by the Constitution.[footnote 20] Accordingly, Congress necessarily possesses the legislative authority to supersede the conclusive presumption created by

---

[20]Conclusive presumptions are "designed to avoid the costs of excessive inquiry where a per se rule will achieve the correct result in almost all cases." *Coleman* v. *Thompson,* 501 U.S. 722, 737 (1991). As the Supreme Court has explained in another context: "Per se rules . . . require the Court to make broad generalizations. . . . Cases that do not fit the generalization may arise, but a per se rule reflects the judgment that such cases are not sufficiently common or important to justify the time and expense necessary to identify them." *Continental T.V., Inc.* v. *GTE Sylvania Inc.,* 433 U.S. 36, 50 n.16 (1977). It is apparent, therefore, that conclusive presumptions, like the one contained in Miranda, are dictated by convenience, not the Constitution.

Miranda pursuant to its authority to prescribe the rules of procedure and evidence in the federal courts. See *Carlisle* v. *United States,* 517 U.S. 416, 426 (1996); *Vance* v. *Terrazas,* 444 U.S. 252, 265 (1980); *Palermo* v. *United States,* 360 U.S. 343, 345-48 (1959); cf. Alfredo Garcia, Is *Miranda* Dead, Was It Overruled, Or Is It Irrelevant?, 10 St. Thomas L. Rev. 461, 461-65, 479 (1998) (concluding that § 3501 "overruled *Miranda*" but arguing that *Miranda* was already dead).[footnote 21]

It is worth recalling that Congress not only acted in response to the Court's invitation, see *Miranda,* 384 U.S. at 490 (inviting Congress and the States "to develop their own safeguards for [protecting] the privilege"), but that the Court in *Miranda* had acted in the absence of a relevant Act of Congress. It is well established that the Court's power to prescribe non-constitutional "rules of procedure and evidence for the federal courts exists only in the absence of a relevant Act of Congress." *Palermo,* 360 U.S. at 353 n.11. Thus, just as the Court was free to create an irrebuttable presumption that statements obtained without certain procedural safeguards are involuntary, Congress was free to overrule that judicially created rule.

To be sure, the *Miranda* warnings were meant to safeguard the Fifth Amendment privilege against self-incrimination. Indeed, under § 3501 any statement obtained in violation of the privilege must be suppressed. Thus, we cannot say that Congress's decision to eliminate the irrebuttable presumption created by *Miranda* lessens the protections afforded by the privilege. Indeed, the Court has recognized that *Miranda's* irrebuttable presumption goes beyond what is required to protect the privilege. As a result, even "patently voluntary statements . . . must be excluded." Elstad, 470 U.S. at 307. In enacting § 3501, Congress simply recognized the need to offset the harmful effects created by *Miranda's* irrebuttable presumption. [footnote 22] Cf. *Sandstrom* v. *Montana,* 442 U.S. 510, 523 (1979) (recognizing the harmful effects created by the use

---

[21]The Dissent does not dispute that the applicability of § 3501 turns on whether *Miranda* is a constitutional rule. Even more telling, after considering the merits, the Dissent is unable to conclude that *Miranda's* conclusive presumption is, in fact, required by the Constitution. In the end, the Dissent poses only the following rhetorical question: "If *Miranda* is not a constitutional rule, why does the Supreme Court continue to apply it in prosecutions arising in state courts." Post at 50. As noted above, the Supreme Court has stated in unmistakable terms that the rule set forth in *Miranda* is not required by the Constitution. See ante at 35-38. In fact, in one of the Supreme Court's most recent applications of *Miranda* to a state court prosecution the Supreme Court specifically stated that "*Miranda's* safeguards are not constitutional in character." *Withrow* v. *Williams,* 507 U.S. 680, 690-91 (1993). Thus, although the Dissent raises an interesting academic question, the answer to why the Supreme Court applies Miranda in prosecutions arising in state courts has no bearing on our Conclusion that *Miranda's* conclusive presumption is not required by the Constitution.

[22]In addition to recognizing the harmful effects created by *Miranda's* irrebuttable presumption, Congress concluded that the Court's justification for the conclusive presumption—that custodial interrogations were inherently coercive and intimidating—was simply incorrect as an empirical matter. See S. Rep. No. 90-1097 (1968), reprinted in 1968 U.S.C.C.A.N. 2112. During the subcommittee hearings, Senator Arlen Specter, then the district attorney of the City of Philadelphia, pointed out that the so-called third-degree methods deplored by the Supreme Court and cited as a basis for their opinion in *Miranda* is not a correct portrayal of what actually goes on in police stations across the country. While there are isolated cases of police using coercive tactics, this is the exception rather than the rule. Id. at 2134. Similarly, the final committee report concluded that the basis for the conclusive presumption in *Miranda* was faulty. Id. at 2142 (noting that the "data supporting the [Court's] Conclusion of inherent coercion in custodial interrogation were drawn solely from police manuals and texts which may or may not have been followed"); id. at 2134 (noting that "while . . . coercive practices might have been approved 30 years ago, they have no place in modern police techniques"); id. (finding that "the Court overreacted to defense claims that police brutality is widespread"). In sum, Congress, utilizing its superior fact-finding ability, concluded that custodial interrogations were not inherently coercive. As Senator Sam Ervin noted at the time § 3501 was enacted: A decision of the Supreme Court, if it is based on a factual assumption which is incorrect, may be subject to Congress' power to legislate. The Supreme Court has no right to make . . . determinations based on unsound factual assumptions. I don't believe the great majority of law enforcement officers in the United States are such disreputable people that they have to have the criminals protected against them. Hearings on the Supreme Court Before the Subcomm. on Separation of Powers of the Senate Comm. on the Judiciary, 90th Cong. 25 (1968). Senator Ervin's observation concerning Congress's authority to overrule Supreme Court decisions, whether or not correct as a general matter, is certainly correct when applied to judicially created presumptions. See ante note 20. It is well established that a conclusive presumption "should not be applied . . . in situations where the generalization is incorrect as an empirical matter." *Coleman* v. *Thompson,* 501 U.S. 722, 737 (1991). In fact, "the justification for a conclusive presumption disappears when application of the presumption will not reach the correct result most of the time." Id. According to congressional findings, the basis for *Miranda's* conclusive presumption is incorrect as an empirical matter, and the presumption does not reach the correct result, i.e., suppressing only coerced confessions, most of the time that it is applied. As a result, Congress, pursuant to its authority to prescribe the rules of procedure and evidence in the federal courts, was justified in abandoning the conclusive presumption when it enacted § 3501.

of mandatory conclusive presumptions in criminal cases). No longer will criminals who have voluntarily confessed their crimes be released on mere technicalities.

Finally, lest there be any confusion on the matter, nothing in today's opinion provides those in law enforcement with an incentive to stop giving the now familiar *Miranda* warnings. As noted above, those warnings are among the factors a district court should consider when determining whether a confession was voluntarily given. See 18 U.S.C.A. § 3501(b). Indeed, federal courts rarely find confessions obtained in technical compliance with *Miranda* to be involuntary under the Fifth Amendment. Cf. Elie, 111 F.3d at 1143 (noting "that very few incriminating statements, custodial or otherwise, are held to be involuntary" (internal quotation marks omitted)). Thus, providing the four *Miranda* warnings is still the best way to guarantee a finding of voluntariness.

In the end, and after an exhaustive review of the relevant authority, we are convinced that § 3501—enacted at the invitation of the Supreme Court and pursuant to Congress's unquestioned power to establish the rules of procedure and evidence in the federal courts—is constitutional. We are reassured in our Conclusion by the fact that our Dissenting colleague, after examining all of the relevant authority at his disposal, has been unable to conclude differently. At best, the Dissent can but pose a rhetorical question concerning the constitutionality of § 3501. See ante note 21. Apparently, all of the relevant authority of which the Dissent is aware supports the Conclusion we reach today. As a consequence, we have no difficulty holding that the admissibility of confessions in federal court is governed by § 3501, rather than the judicially created rule of *Miranda.*

2.

Having concluded that § 3501, rather than *Miranda,* governs the admissibility of confessions in federal court, our next step ordinarily would be to remand the case for a determination of whether Dickerson's confession was voluntary. That is unnecessary in this case, however, because the district court has already made that finding.

Although the district court suppressed the statements obtained in violation of *Miranda,* it nevertheless denied Dickerson's motion to suppress the evidence found as a result thereof, e.g., the statement made by Rochester identifying Dickerson as the getaway driver. In making this determination, the district court stated that it was bound by this Court's decision in *United States* v. *Elie,* 111 F.3d 1135 (4th Cir. 1997). See *United States* v. *Dickerson,* 971 F. Supp. 1023, 1024 n.1 (E.D. Va. 1997). In *Elie,* we held that evidence found as a result of a statement made in violation of *Miranda* may only be suppressed if the statement was involuntary within the meaning of the Due Process Clause of the Fifth Amendment. Therefore, by declining to suppress the evidence found as a result of Dickerson's unwarned statements, the district court necessarily found that Dickerson's statements were voluntary under the Fifth Amendment. During oral argument, Dickerson's counsel contended that the district court erred in finding that the statements in question were voluntary for purposes of the Fifth Amendment. The district court's finding on this matter, however, is currently unreviewable. See, e.g., *United States* v. *Becker,* 23 F.3d 1537, 1539 (9th Cir. 1994) (noting that the denial of a motion to suppress is not an appealable final order).

IV.

On appeal, the Government also contends that the district court erred in suppressing the fruits of the warrant-authorized search of Dickerson's apartment. The district court concluded that the warrant was insufficiently particular in describing the items to be seized. Moreover, the district court concluded that the agents executing the warrant could not have acted in good-faith because the warrant was facially deficient. We address these two rulings in turn.

A.

The warrant in question was obtained by Special Agent Lawlor via the telephone pursuant to Rule 41(c)(2) of the Federal Rules of Criminal Procedure. In his sworn oral testimony to Judge Kenkel, Special Agent Lawlor described the circumstances of the bank robbery, including that the robber used a handgun, carried a bag, requested unmarked bills, and left the scene in a car registered to Dickerson. In the section of the warrant used to identify the property to be seized, Special Agent Lawlor wrote: "Evidence of the crime of bank robbery." Whether that description, coupled with the description contained in Special Agent Lawlor's oral testimony, is sufficiently particular to pass constitutional scrutiny is a legal issue subject to de novo review. See *United States* v. *Hyppolite,* 65 F.3d 1151, 1156 (4th Cir. 1995).

The Fourth Amendment provides that a search warrant must "particularly describ[e] the place to be searched, and the persons or things to be seized." U.S. Const. amend. IV. The Supreme Court has identified two important purposes underlying the particularity requirement: (1) preventing general searches, and (2) ensuring that the executing officer is able to distinguish between those items which are to be seized and those that are not. See *Marron* v. *United States,* 275 U.S. 192, 196 (1927).

The Government argues that the warrant neither authorized an improper general search nor left to the discretion of the agents executing the warrant what to seize. Specifically, the Government contends that the warrant directed the agents to search for evidence of a particular crime—bank robbery—that tends to generate quite distinctive evidence, e.g., guns, masks, bait money, dye-stained bills and clothes, carrying bags. The test for the necessary particularity of a search warrant is "a pragmatic one: The degree of specificity required when describing the goods to be seized may necessarily vary according to the circumstances and type of items involved." *United States* v. *Torch,* 609 F.2d 1088, 1090 (4th Cir. 1979) (internal quotation marks omitted).

Some courts uphold warrants that identify the items to be seized as "evidence of [specific crime]" only "where a more precise description was not possible in the circumstances." *United States* v. *George,* 975 F.2d 72, 76 (2d Cir. 1992) (citing cases). Here, the Government admits, as it must, that it could have been more precise, but argues that this Court has routinely upheld warrants directing the police to search for evidence of a particular crime. See Appellant's Br. at 36-37 (citing *United States* v. *Fawole,* 785 F.2d 1141, 1144 (4th Cir. 1986), and *United States* v. *Ladd,* 704 F.2d 134 (4th Cir. 1983)).

As the Government correctly notes, the law of this Circuit does allow some discretion to the officers executing a search warrant, so long as the warrant at least minimally "confines the executing officers' discretion by allowing them to seize only evidence of a particular crime." *Fawole,* 785 F.2d at 1144. For example, in *Ladd* we upheld a warrant directing the police to seize all property relating to "the smuggling, packing, distribution, and use of controlled substances," as satisfying fully the particularity requirement. 704 F.2d at 136. Indeed, the panel in *Ladd* specifically held that "[m]ore specificity is not required by the Constitution." Id. ; see also 2 Wayne R. LaFave, Search and Seizure § 4.6(d), at 567 & n.81 (3d ed. 1996) (noting that "[s]ometimes a warrant will not attempt to describe instrumentalities except by reference to the criminal conduct in which they have been used") (collecting cases). As explained by the Second Circuit in *George,* a warrant authorizing a search for evidence relating to "a broad criminal statute or general criminal activity" such as "wire fraud," "fraud," "conspiracy," or "tax evasion," is overbroad because it "provides no readily ascertainable guidelines for the executing officers as to what items to seize." 975 F.2d at 76. In contrast, a warrant authorizing a search for evidence relating to "a specific illegal activity," such as "narcotics," or "theft of fur coats" is sufficiently particular. Id. (citing cases). The warrant in the instant case limited the agents' search to evidence relating to the commission of a particular crime: bank robbery. Bank robbery is a specific illegal activity that, as the Government notes, generates quite distinctive evidence. Though certainly broad in its description, we cannot say that the warrant failed to provide that degree of specificity required by the precedent of this Court.

The search of Dickerson's apartment produced a silver .45 caliber handgun, dye-stained money, a bait bill from another robbery, ammunition, masks, and latex gloves.[footnote 23] Rather than conducting an impermissible fishing expedition, it is clear that the agents conducting the search only seized those items reasonably associated with the crime of bank robbery. Thus, it is evident that the warrant was sufficiently definite so that the agents executing it were able to identify the property sought with reasonable certainty. As a consequence, we conclude that "evidence of the crime of bank robbery" adequately distinguishes between those items which are to be seized and those which are not. See *Marron,* 275 U.S. at 196.

In sum, the nature of a bank robbery is such that the evidence thereof is reasonably subject to identification. Since "[t]he degree of specificity required when describing the goods to be seized . . . var[ies] according to the . . . type of items involved," *Torch,* 609 F.2d at 1090, we have little difficulty concluding that the warrant was sufficiently particular in describing the items to be seized.

B.

Moreover, even if we assume that the warrant was not sufficiently particular in describing the items to be seized, we nevertheless would conclude that the evidence obtained during the search of Dickerson's apartment was admissible pursuant to the good faith exception to the exclusionary rule. See *United States* v. *Leon,* 468 U.S. 897, 913 (1984). In deciding whether the good faith exception applies, this Court must consider "whether a reasonably well trained officer would have known that the search was illegal despite the magistrate's authorization." Id. at 922 n.23. This inquiry is objective in nature, depending upon the understanding of a reasonable officer in light of the totality of the circumstances. See *Hyppolite,* 65 F.3d at 1156.

In light of the totality of the circumstances, we conclude that the warrant in this case was not so facially deficient as to preclude reasonable reliance upon it. First, the warrant specified that the items to be seized consisted of evidence associated with bank robbery. Thus, it did not fail to provide the searching officers any guidance whatsoever as to the subject of the search.

Second, this Court considers the knowledge of the searching officers in assessing the objective reasonableness of reliance upon a warrant. See *United States* v. *Curry,* 911 F.2d 72, 78 (8th Cir. 1990) (noting that "in assessing whether reliance on a search warrant was objectively reasonable under the totality of the circumstances, it is appropriate to take into account the knowledge that an officer in the searching officer's position would have possessed"). Agent Wenko, who was the lead agent during the search of Dickerson's apartment, was familiar not only with the specifics of the bank robbery in question, but, perhaps as important, had been investigating bank robberies for seven years and thus was very familiar with the type of evidence to look for (e.g., guns, money, bait bills, dye-stained money and clothes, disguises, carrying bags, and gloves).

---

[23] The agents also found a small quantity of drugs in plain view.

For the foregoing reasons, we conclude that the district court erred in finding that the agents could not have acted in good-faith reliance on the warrant.

V.

In Conclusion, we find that the admissibility of confessions in federal court is governed by 18 U.S.C.A. § 3501 (West 1985), rather than *Miranda,* that the warrant was sufficiently particular in describing the items to be seized, and that the officers executing the warrant acted in good faith. Accordingly, the district court's order suppressing the statements Dickerson made at the FBI Field Office and the physical evidence obtained during the search of his apartment is reversed, and the case is remanded for further proceedings.

REVERSED AND REMANDED

MICHAEL, Circuit Judge, Dissenting in part and Concurring in part:

Thirty years have passed since Congress enacted 18 U.S.C. § 3501 in reaction to *Miranda.* We are nearing the end of the seventh consecutive Administration that has made the judgment not to use § 3501 in the prosecution of criminal cases. Now, after all this time, the majority supplants the Department of Justice's judgment with its own and says that § 3501 must be invoked. After making that judgment call, the majority holds that the section is constitutional, without the benefit of any briefing in opposition. In pressing § 3501 into the prosecution of a case against the express wishes of the Department of Justice, the majority takes on more than any court should. I therefore respectfully Dissent from the parts of the majority opinion that deal with § 3501. As for the search warrant, I would uphold it under *Leon's* good faith exception, but I Dissent from the holding that the warrant is sufficiently specific.

I.

The majority begins its reach to inject § 3501 into this case with an overstatement. It says that the § 3501 issue is "squarely presented." Ante at 2; see also ante at 4 ("the question of whether § 3501 governs the admissibility of confessions in federal court is squarely before us today"). In its brief to us the government has said plainly, "we are not making an argument based on § 3501 in this appeal." Appellant's Opening Br. at 34. The defendant, of course, does not mention § 3501. Thus, we are not being urged to inject § 3501 into this case by anyone except the amici, the Washington Legal Foundation and the Safe Streets Coalition. That is not enough to put the issue of § 3501's constitutionality and application squarely before us. Perhaps the majority recognizes as much, for it quickly moves to an argument about why the court itself should force § 3501 into this case.

The majority's argument for taking up § 3501 is as follows. First, the Department of Justice will not defend the constitutionality of § 3501, so the question whether the statute or Miranda governs the admission of federal confessions will not be decided unless we act on our own. Second, Dickerson's confession in this case is admissible under § 3501 but not under Miranda. "As a result," the majority concludes, "we are required to consider the issue now." Ante at 26 (emphasis added). One thing I am sure of is that we are not required to consider a § 3501 issue when it is raised only in an amicus brief. See *Davis* v. *United States,* 512 U.S. 452, 457 n.* (1994) ("declin[ing] the invitation of some amici to consider" § 3501). Indeed, the only issues not raised by the parties that we are required to consider are those of subject matter jurisdiction and justiciability. See e.g., *Mt. Healthy City School District Board of Education* v. *Doyle,* 429 U.S. 274, 278 (1977) ("we are obliged to inquire sua sponte whenever a doubt arises as to the existence of federal jurisdiction"); *Juidice* v. *Vail,* 430 U.S. 327,

331 (1977) ("Although raised by neither of the parties, we are first obliged to examine the standing of appellees, as a matter of the case-or-controversy requirement associated with Art. III"); *LaFaut* v. *Smith,* 834 F.2d 389, 394-95 n.9 (4th Cir. 1987) (concluding that whether a claim is moot "is a jurisdictional question that the court is obliged to consider sua sponte whenever it arises") (citations omitted). We have jurisdiction in this case, and it is fit for adjudication. The real question, therefore, is whether we should exercise our discretion and consider § 3501, when no party has invoked the statute. I believe that the situation calls for the exercise of judicial restraint; we should stay away from the § 3501 issue.

To start with, I cannot agree with the majority's accusation that the Department of Justice "elevat[ed] politics over law" when it prevented the United States Attorney from invoking § 3501 in an effort to save Dickerson's confession. See ante at 4. A move to admit more confessions could be touted as aggressive prosecution, so I would think it might be better politics to invoke § 3501. In any event, I see no evidence that the Department of Justice is putting politics over law when it comes to § 3501. The Department's view—that § 3501 cannot be used to admit confessions that Miranda would exclude—is a view that I accept as genuine.

I believe that *Davis* v. *United States,* 512 U.S. 452 (1994), remains sound authority for us to decline consideration of § 3501 on the invitation of an amicus. In *Davis* the Court did not take up § 3501 because "the issue is one of first impression involving the interpretation of a federal statute on which the Department of Justice expressly declines to take a position." Id. at 457 n.*. Our panel majority says that everything has changed since Davis because the Attorney General has now written Congress, saying that the Department of Justice will not defend the constitutionality of § 3501. See ante at 3-4, 25. I do not think the Attorney General's letter changes anything. It simply confirms what the Supreme Court already knew in *Davis,* that is, that the Department of Justice was not going to invoke the statute to try to salvage confessions. See *Davis,* 512 U.S. at 463 (Scalia, J., Concurring) ("This is not the first case in which the United States has declined to invoke § 3501 before us—nor even the first case in which that failure has been called to its attention."). The majority also contends that *Davis* is distinguishable because the Supreme Court saved that confession on another ground, making consideration of § 3501 unnecessary. That is not why the Court declined to consider § 3501. The Court said specifically "that the Government has not sought to rely in this case on 18 U.S.C. § 3501, . . . and we therefore decline the invitation of some amici to consider it." Davis, 512 U.S. at 457 n.*. See also id. at 462 n.* ("the Court today bases its refusal to consider § 3501 not upon the fact that the provision is inapplicable, but upon the fact that the Government failed to argue it") (Scalia, J., Concurring). Thus, we are faced with essentially the same situation that the Supreme Court confronted in *Davis* when it refused to take up § 3501: the government has expressly declined to "mak[e] an argument based on § 3501 in this appeal," Appellant's Opening Br. at 34, and we are free to reject amici's call for its consideration.

It is a mistake for our court to push § 3501 into this case for several reasons. First, courts as a general rule do not interfere with the executive's broad discretion in the initiation and conduct of criminal prosecutions. See generally *United States* v. *Armstrong,* 116 S. Ct. 1480, 1486 (1996); *United States* v. *Juvenile Male J.A.J.,* 134 F.3d 905, 907 (8th Cir. 1998). Forcing the use of § 3501 upon a United States Attorney gets uncomfortably close to encroaching upon the prosecutor's routine discretion. I recognize, of course, that courts have a large measure of control over the course of a case once it is filed. But a decision not to invoke § 3501 in response to a motion to suppress a confession is a matter of prosecutorial strategy. We should leave that to the executive. There is also a related point. In invoking § 3501, the majority overrides 30 years of Department of Justice prosecutorial policy. Any change in this policy should come from Justice.

Second, it is "a sound prudential practice" for us to avoid issues not raised by the parties. See *Davis,* 512 U.S. at 464 (Scalia, J., Concurring). This is because "[t]he premise of our adversarial system is that appellate courts do not sit as self-directed boards of legal inquiry and research, but essentially as arbiters of legal questions presented and argued by the parties before them." *Carducci* v. *Regan,* 714 F.2d 171, 177 (D.C. Cir. 1983) (Scalia, J.). We perform our role as neutral arbiter best when we let the parties raise the issues, and both sides brief and argue them fully. That did not happen here. By invoking § 3501, the majority injects into this case the overriding constitutional question of whether § 3501 can supersede *Miranda.* It then decides the question against the defendant, when the only briefing we have on the issue is about two pages from amici that the majority agrees with. The majority holds that § 3501 governs the admissibility of confessions in federal court because *Miranda* is not a constitutional rule. I don't know whether it is or not, but before I had to decide, I would want thoughtful lawyers on both sides to answer one question for me. If *Miranda* is not a constitutional rule, why does the Supreme Court continue to apply it in prosecutions arising in state courts? See, e.g., *Stansberry* v. *California,* 511 U.S. 318 (1994) (per curiam); see also *Mu'Min* v. *Virginia,* 500 U.S. 415, 422 (1996) (noting that with respect to cases tried in state court, the Supreme Court's "authority is limited to enforcing the commands of the United States Constitution"). This question illustrates that the § 3501 issue is so sweeping that we should not be delving into it on our own. In this case, we should follow our usual practice of deciding only the issues raised by the parties.[footnote 24] The majority's fallback position is that if we do not press the use of § 3501, no one else will. See ante at 26. This overlooks Congress. If another branch is to question and investigate the executive's 30 year policy of not using § 3501, it should be Congress. After all, Congress—consistent with separation of powers principles—uses the public hearings process to examine the policies and conduct of the executive. That process has been used on occasion to question the executive's exercise of prosecutorial discretion and the formulation of litigation strategy. See *Ameron, Inc.* v. *United States Army Corps of Engineers,* 809 F.2d 979, 991 n.8 (3d Cir. 1986). Congress therefore may legitimately investigate why the executive has ignored § 3501 and what the consequences are. The legislative branch is better equipped than we are to investigate, for example, the question raised by Justice Scalia in his Concurring opinion in Davis: whether the government's failure to invoke § 3501 "may have produced . . . the acquittal and the non-prosecution of many dangerous felons." Davis, 512 U.S. at 465 (emphasis added). Whether the answer to that question or other considerations should be used to prod the executive into changing its policy with respect to § 3501 is a matter that I would leave to Congress.

Because I would not invoke § 3501, I would affirm the district court's order denying the government's motion to reconsider the admissibility of Dickerson's confession for the reasons stated in part II.A. of the majority opinion.

II.

As for the physical evidence seized from Dickerson's apartment, I agree with the majority's Conclusion that it should have been admitted under the good faith exception. I respectfully disagree, however, with the majority's Conclusion that a warrant

---

[24]The majority misses my point when it erroneously suggests that I have examined all of the relevant authority and cannot conclude that *Miranda* renders § 3501 unconstitutional. See ante at n.21, 42. My point is that we should not be examining the question at all, much less deciding it. For the record, however, not everyone agrees with the majority. See Charles Alan Wright, Federal Practice and Procedure § 76 (2d ed. 1982) ("Unless the [Supreme] Court overrules Miranda, or holds that the 1968 statute [§ 3501] has successfully accomplished this, lower courts must follow the decision rather than the statute."); 1 Wayne R. LaFave & Jerold H. Israel, Criminal Procedure § 6.5(e) (1984) (§ 3501 "is unconstitutional to the extent that it purports to repeal *Miranda.*").

permitting a search for "evidence of the crime of bank robbery" is sufficiently particular under the Fourth Amendment.

A warrant must guide the executing officer with a particular description of the items to be seized. See *United States* v. *Wolfenbarger,* 696 F.2d 750, 752 (10th Cir. 1982) ("A description is sufficiently particular when it enables the searcher to reasonably ascertain and identify the things authorized to be seized.") (citation omitted). Thus, a warrant authorizing seizure of "address books, diaries, business records, documents, receipts, warranty books, guns, stereo equipment, [and] color television which are evidence of violation of Georgia State Statute 16-8-2 Theft by Taking" is sufficiently particular because it identifies the universe of items to be seized. See *United States* v. *Fawole,* 785 F.2d 1141, 1144 (4th Cir. 1986). On the other hand, a warrant for seizure of "'any other evidence relating to the commission of a crime' plainly is not sufficiently particular with respect to the things to be seized." *United States* v. *George,* 975 F.2d 72, 75 (2d Cir. 1992).

I recognize that courts on occasion have upheld warrants authorizing the seizure of the "instrumentalities" of certain distinctive crimes. Nevertheless, I believe "evidence of the crime of bank robbery" is far too general. That description does nothing to confine the discretion of an executing officer, especially if the warrant is relayed for execution by an officer who has never served on a bank robbery squad. A search for evidence of bank robbery would surely include a search for guns, masks, and cash. But what else? It might be construed to allow a search through all financial records, as well as a search for any items purchased. Under this interpretation, virtually no piece of paper or property would be beyond the bounds of a search. The description in the warrant here was simply too general to satisfy Fourth Amendment standards.

SECTION VI

Dickerson Brief

Nos. 99-5525

In The Supreme Court of the United States

CHARLES THOMAS DICKERSON,

Petitioner,

V.

UNITED STATES OF AMERICA

Respondent.

On Writ of Certiorari to the
United States Court of Appeals
for the Fourth Circuit

BRIEF OF PETITIONER

Carter G. Phillips James W. Hundley*
Jeffrey T. Green Briglia & Hundley, P.C.
Kurt H. Jacobs The Mosby Professional Building
Sidley & Austin 10560 Main Street, Suite 314
1722 Eye Street, N.W. Fairfax, Virginia 22030 Washington, D.C. 20006 (703) 385-8005
(202) 736-8000
Paul F. Washington
75 Rockefeller Plaza
New York, New York 10019

Counsel for Petitioner
January 28, 2000 *Counsel of Record

QUESTION PRESENTED

Whether Congress' enactment of 18 U.S.C. § 3501 constitutes an unconstitutional attempt legislatively to narrow the protections in the Self-Incrimination Clause of the Fifth Amendment embodied in this Court's opinion in *Miranda* v. *Arizona*, 384 U.S. 436 (1966)?

TABLE OF AUTHORITIES

CASES

Brown v. *Board of Educ.*, 347 U.S. 483 (1954)
Bruton v. *United States*, 391 U.S. 123 (1968)
Butler v. *McKellar*, 494 U.S. 407 (1990)
Carter v. *Kentucky*, 450 U.S. 288 (1981)
Colorado v. *Connelly*, 479 U.S. 157 (1986)
Colten v. *Kentucky*, 407 U.S. 104 (1972)
Connecticut v. *Barrett*, 479 U.S. 523 (1987)
Culombe v. *Connecticut*, 367 U.S. 568 (1961)
Davis v. *United States*, 512 U.S. 452 (1994)
Doe v. *United States*, 487 U.S. 201 (1988)
Edwards v. *Arizona*, 451 U.S. 477 (1981)
Escobedo v. *Illinois*, 378 U.S. 478 (1964)
Fare v. *Michael C.*, 442 U.S. 707 (1979)
Faretta v. *California*, 422 U.S. 806 (1975)
Freedman v. *Maryland*, 380 U.S. 51 (1965)
Garcia v. *San Antonio Metro. Transit Auth.*, 469 U.S. 528 (1985)
Gertz v. *Robert Welch, Inc.*, 418 U.S. 323 (1974)
Gideon v. *Wainwright*, 372 U.S. 335 (1963)
Gray v. *Maryland*, 523 U.S. 185 (1998)
Greenwald v. *Wisconsin*, 390 U.S. 519 (1968)
Griffin v. *California*, 380 U.S. 609 (1965)
Harris v. *Rivera*, 454 U.S. 339 (1981)
Illinois v. *Perkins*, 496 U.S. 292 (1990)
Jackson v. *Denno*, 378 U.S. 368 (1964)
Johnson v. *Zerbst*, 304 U.S. 458 (1938)
Lisenba v. *California*, 314 U.S. 219 (1941)
Maine v. *Moulton*, 474 U.S. 159 (1985)
Malloy v. *Hogan*, 378 U.S. 1 (1964)
Marbury v. *Madison*, 5 U.S. (1 Cranch) 137 (1803)
Massiah v. *United States*, 377 U.S. 201 (1964)
Mathis v. *United*, 391 U.S. 1 (1968)
McNabb v. *United States*, 318 U.S. 332 (1943)
Michigan v. *Harvey*, 494 U.S. 344 (1990)
Michigan v. *Jackson*, 475 U.S. 625 (1986)
Michigan v. *Payne*, 412 U.S. 47 (1973)
Michigan v. *Tucker*, 417 U.S. 433 (1974)
Mincey v. *Arizona*, 437 U.S. 385 (1978)
Minnick v. *Mississippi*, 498 U.S. 146 (1990)
Miranda v. *Arizona*, 384 U.S. 436 (1966)
Mitchell v. *United States*, 119 S. Ct. 1307 (1999)
Moran v. *Burbine*, 475 U.S. 412 (1986)
Mu'Min v. *Virginia*, 500 U.S. 415 (1991)
New York v. *Quarles*, 467 U.S. 649 (1984)
North Carolina v. *Pearce*, 395 U.S. 711 (1969)
Oregon v. *Elstad*, 470 U.S. 298 (1985)
Orozoco v. *Texas*, 394 U.S. 324 (1969)
Patterson v. *McLean Credit Union*, 491 U.S. 164 (1989)
Payne v. *Arkansas*, 356 U.S. 560 (1958)
Payne v. *Tennessee*, 501 U.S. 808 (1991)
Pennsylvania v. *Muniz*, 496 U.S. 582 (1990)
Planned Parenthood v. *Casey*, 505 U.S. 833 (1992)
Rhode Island v. *Innis*, 446 U.S. 291 (1980)
Rock v. *Arkansas*, 483 U.S. 44 (1987)
Tennessee v. *Street*, 471 U.S. 409 (1985)

United States v. *Balsys,* 118 S. Ct. 2218 (1998)
United States v. *Goodwin,* 457 U.S. 368 (1982)
United States v. *Title Ins. & Trust Co.,* 265 U.S. 472 (1924)
Vasquez v. *Hillary,* 474 U.S. 254 (1986)
Wasman v. *United States,* 468 U.S. 559 (1984)
Withrow v. *Williams,* 507 U.S. 680 (1993)
Wong Sun v. *United States,* 371 U.S. 471 (1963)

CONSTITUTION

U.S. Const. amend. V

FEDERAL STATUTES

2 U.S.C. § 288k(b)
18 U.S.C. § 3501
28 U.S.C. § 2254(a)

CONGRESSIONAL HISTORY

114 Cong. Rec. 16,074 (1968)
16,295 (1968)
S. Rep. No. 90-1097 (1968), *reprinted in* 1968 U.S.C.C.A.N. 2112

SCHOLARLY AUTHORITIES

Stephen I. Schulhofer, *Reconsidering Miranda,* 54 U. Chi. L. Rev. 435 (1987)
Yale Kamisar, *Can (Did) Congress "Overrule" Miranda?,* 85 Cornell L. Rev. (2000) (forthcoming)

OTHER AUTHORITY

Albert W. Alschuler, *A Peculiar Privilege in Historical Perspective, in The Privilege Against Self-Incrimination* 181 (R.H. Helmholz et al. eds., 1997)
Charles M. Gray, *Self-Incrimination in Interjurisdictional Law: The Sixteenth and Seventeenth Centuries, in The Privilege Against Self-Incrimination* 47 (R.H. Helmholz et al. eds., 1997)
R.H. Helmholz, *Introduction, in The Privilege Against Self-Incrimination* 1 (R.H. Helmholz et al. eds., 1997)
R.H. Helmholz, *The Privilege and the Jus Commune: The Middle Ages to the Seventeenth Century, in The Privilege Against Self-Incrimination* 17 (R.H. Helmholz et al. eds., 1997)
John H. Langbein, *The Privilege and Common Law Criminal Procedure: The Sixteenth to the Eighteenth Centuries, in The Privilege Against Self-Incrimination* 82 (R.H. Helmholz et al. eds., 1997)
Eben Moglen, *The Privilege in British North America: The Colonial Period to the Fifth Amendment, in The Privilege Against Self-Incrimination* 109 (R.H. Helmholz et al. eds., 1997)

Henry E. Smith, *The Modern Privilege: Its Nineteenth-Century Origins, in The Privilege Against Self-Incrimination* 145 (R.H. Helmholz et al. eds., 1997)

BRIEF OF PETITIONER
OPINIONS BELOW

The opinion of the court of appeals is reported at 166 F.3d 667 (4th Cir. 1999), and is reproduced in the Joint Appendix (J.A.) at ___. That opinion reversed an unpublished opinion and order of the district court, reproduced in the J.A. at ___. Following the district court's ruling, both the government and petitioner filed motions requesting that the district court reconsider aspects of its initial ruling. J.A. 75, 86. The district court's opinion denying both motions is reported at 971 F. Supp. 1023 (E.D. Va. 1997) and is reproduced in the J.A. at ___.

STATEMENT OF JURISDICTION

The United States Court of Appeals for the Fourth Circuit issued its opinion on February 8, 1999. The petitioner filed a Petition for Rehearing and Petition for Rehearing En Banc which the Fourth Circuit denied on April 1, 1999. The Court extended the time for filing the Petition for Certiorari until July 30, 1999. The Petition for Certiorari was filed on July 30, 1999, and the Court granted the Petition for Certiorari on December 6, 1999. This Court has jurisdiction under 28 U.S.C. § 1254.

CONSTITUTIONAL AND STATUTORY
PROVISIONS INVOLVED

U.S. Const. amend. V; 18 U.S.C. § 3501. [footnote 1]

STATEMENT OF THE CASE

The issue in this case is whether this Court's landmark holding in *Miranda* v. *Arizona*, 384 U.S. 436 (1966), which precludes admitting into evidence unwarned statements made by an individual during a custodial interrogation, is based on the Fifth Amendment and therefore beyond the power of Congress to overrule statutorily. The district court found that certain statements of petitioner, Charles Thomas Dickerson, were unwarned and therefore inadmissible under *Miranda*. The Fourth Circuit, *sua sponte*, held that Congress, in enacting § 3501, superseded *Miranda's* warning requirements. Accordingly, the Fourth Circuit applied § 3501's "totality of the circumstances" test to determine the admissibility of petitioner's statements.

The Fourth Circuit erred. Pursuant to *Miranda* and its progeny the Fifth Amendment's privilege against self-incrimination is not solely a privilege to be free from abuse at the station house. It is also a privilege not to become an unwitting or unwilling witness against oneself while being subjected to the pressures inherent in private custodial interrogation. Accordingly, *Miranda's* minimum constitutional threshold requires that an individual be apprised of his rights, that officials respect

---

[1]The text of the pertinent constitutional and statutory provisions are reproduced in the Appendix ("App.") to this brief.

the exercise of those rights and that any waiver be knowingly, intelligently and voluntarily made before a statement made to law enforcement officials during custodial interrogation may be admitted in the prosecution's case-in-chief.

Incriminating statements therefore are admissible only if they are made in the absence of overt coercion and after warnings or other procedures fully effective in apprising persons of their rights. Without knowledge on the part of the individual being questioned as to what choices are available to him, statements cannot be deemed truly voluntary. If the government is allowed to keep its suspect in a state of ignorance, the Fifth Amendment protections are reduced to a mere "'form of words.'" *Miranda*, 384 U.S. at 444 (quoting *Silverthorne Lumber Co.* v. *United States,* 251 U.S. 385, 392 (1920)). Section 3501, which makes apprising an individual of his rights merely optional, directly contradicts *Miranda*'s minimum threshold requirement that an individual be apprised of his rights and that the exercise of those rights be respected. Because *Miranda*'s minimum threshold is a matter of constitutional law, and because *stare decisis* requires continued adherence to *Miranda*'s threshold requirements, § 3501 is invalid.

Given the notoriety of this matter, it should be noted at the outset that petitioner has not (and never before has been) convicted of bank robbery in this or any other case. This matter is before the Court on a successful suppression motion and no trial has been held. Petitioner therefore is entitled to the full protections of the presumption that he is innocent. Moreover, contrary to numerous and nationwide media reports [footnote 2], petitioner did not confess to any bank robbery, much less "multiple" bank robberies. His "statements" concerned only his whereabout and activities. Nor has petitioner been "let off on a technicality." Petitioner remains under indictment. At this point only the statements petitioner made in custody remain suppressed.

A. Factual Background.

The facts material to consideration of the question presented are as follows: On January 24, 1997, a Nations Bank in Alexandria, Virginia was robbed. Witnesses saw the robber, later identified as James Rochester, leave the bank and enter an Oldsmobile Cierra. Using the description of the getaway car, including its license plate number, the FBI determined that petitioner was the car's owner.

At approximately 5:30 p.m. on the evening of January 27, 1997, law enforcement officers went to petitioner's home in Takoma Park, Maryland. An Oldsmobile Cierra registered to petitioner was parked in the vicinity. The officers set-up surveillance. After waiting for more than a hour, they knocked on petitioner's door. Approximately ten FBI agents and local police officers arrived at the door of petitioner's apartment with their guns drawn as he opened the door. Three or four, including Special FBI Agent Lawlor, entered petitioner's apartment without a warrant and without his consent. The officers asked him to accompany them to the FBI field office in Washington, D.C. Only when leaving did the officers ask petitioner whether he would consent to a search of the residence. He refused and was driven by the officers to the FBI field office.

Once at the Field Office, Agent Lawlor and another FBI agent interviewed petitioner. He was not advised of his *Miranda* rights prior to this interrogation. Petitioner denied any knowledge of incidents that might relate to the robbery. He admitted only that he had been in the vicinity of the bank at the time it was robbed. After obtaining this statement, Agent Lawlor left the interrogation room and telephoned a United

---

[2] *See* Michael Dorman, *Imagine You're Arrested. First, They Read Your Rights. (Right?),* Newsday, October 14, 1999, at A25; Stephen Seplow, *Miranda Rights Case Revisited,* Dayton Daily News, November 25, 1999, at 2A; Tony Mauro, *Supreme Court Agrees to Revisit Miranda Warning,* USA Today, December 7, 1999, at 4A; Joan Biskupic, *High Court to Reconsider Miranda Ruling,* Washington Post, December 7, 1999, at A1; Orrin G. Hatch, *Miranda Warnings and Voluntary Confessions Can Co-Exist,* Wall Street Journal, at A35.

States Magistrate Judge for the District of Maryland, to obtain a search warrant for petitioner's home. The warrant issued at 8:50 p.m.

After obtaining the warrant, Agent Lawlor returned to the interrogation room and told petitioner that his home was going to be searched. Petitioner then made another statement, still denying his involvement, but providing information about James ("Jimmy") Rochester, the man who had committed the robberies. [footnote 3] It was only after giving this statement that petitioner was, for the first time, advised of his rights as mandated by *Miranda* v. *Arizona*, 384 U.S. 436 (1966). This was done using a rights waiver form which petitioner signed. After completing this form, petitioner was formally placed under arrest. He then left the field office with the agents and showed them Rochester's apartment in Oxon Hill, Maryland. Based on this information, the FBI arrested James Rochester, who was a suspect in connection with a number of bank robberies in various states on the east coast. Following his arrest, James Rochester admitted that he had robbed several banks, including the Nations Bank in Alexandria on January 24, 1997. Petitioner, however, was charged with one count of conspiracy to commit bank robbery in violation of 18 U.S.C. § 2113(a) and (d), and three counts of using a firearm during a bank robbery in violation of 18 U.S.C. § 924(c). [footnote 4]

B. Procedural Background.

Petitioner filed a motion to suppress the statements given at the FBI field office. After careful examination of the facts as presented by both petitioner and the prosecution, the district court granted the motion. Regarding the statements, the district court observed that Agent Lawlor had obtained a search warrant for petitioner's residence at 8:50 pm. At the suppression hearing, Agent Lawlor testified that when he informed petitioner about the warrant, petitioner reacted by saying he wanted to make a further statement. It was at this point, Agent Lawlor said he "Mirandized" petitioner and obtained a signed waiver form. Although at most only a few minutes had passed since the warrant was issued, the time written on petitioner's waiver form was 9:41 p.m. The District Court found that "Agent Lawlor's testimony is in direct conflict with the documentary evidence, which shows that the warrant issued at 8:50 p.m., and petitioner's testimony that he was Mirandized at the end of 'a half hour' long interview." J.A. ___. The court suppressed petitioner's statements, finding that "Dickerson was not advised of his *Miranda* rights until after he had completed his statement." *Id.* at ___. [footnote 5]

---

[3]Petitioner's statement to the agent was as follows: Petitioner had gone to Alexandria on January 24, 1997, with a man named Jimmy. Petitioner knew Jimmy because Jimmy was married to petitioner's cousin. Petitioner further stated that, while in Alexandria, he parked his car and went into a bagel shop. Initially, Jimmy waited in the car, but as petitioner walked away, he saw Jimmy get out of the car. When petitioner returned to his car, Jimmy was already back in it. When petitioner began to drive away, Jimmy told him to pull over. He complied, thinking Jimmy had to use the bathroom. Jimmy got out and returned after a few minutes. When petitioner stopped at a stop sign, Jimmy got out of the car and put something in the trunk. When petitioner again stopped at a red light a short distance down the street, Jimmy told him to run it. It was at this point that petitioner began to suspect that Jimmy may have committed a robbery. Petitioner knew that Jimmy had come to the Washington, D.C. area after committing a number of robberies in Georgia.

[4]A superseding indictment was issued on June 24, 1997. It charged the same offenses except it alleged that petitioner acted as an aider and abettor to the bank robberies and firearm offenses in violation of 18 U.S.C. § 2.

[5]Central to the district court's ruling was its finding that "the content of Agent Lawlor's testimony, which was impeached by the government's own exhibits, and his demeanor lacked credibility." J.A. at ___. As an example, the court observed that Agent Lawlor "dodged questions" about whether officers entered petitioner's home with their guns drawn, even after the officers had taken a hour to plan their entry and after petitioner had initially stalled when the officers first knocked and announced themselves. *Id.* Agent Lawlor also testified that petitioner was not under arrest when this group of officers took him from Maryland to the FBI Field Office in Southwestern D.C. and therefore *Miranda* warnings were unnecessary. The District Court specifically noted that it made a "first hand assessment of witness credibility, based on demeanor, voice inflection and a totality of other factors not well reflected by an inanimate record, for which the district court is uniquely suited." *Id.* at ___ (citing cases).

The parties filed cross-motions for reconsideration, which the district court denied. [footnote 6] The District Court did not address § 3501 in either of its orders, nor did it make any specific finding as to whether petitioner's statements were voluntary.

A divided panel of the Fourth Circuit Court of Appeals reversed the district court. The Fourth Circuit held that it had discretion to consider § 3501's applicability, despite the fact that no party had raised the issue. In explaining this unusual exercise of discretion, the court of appeals observed that in recent years "career prosecutors" (but not the Department of Justice), political groups and politicians had repeatedly urged the court of appeals to address § 3501. J.A. ___ ("the Washington Legal Foundation and the Safe Streets Coalition . . . took the government to task . . . . As a result, we ordered the Department of Justice to address the effect of § 3501") (citing *United States* v. *Leong,* 116 F.3d 1474 (4th Cir. 1997) (table)). In the instant case, because the DOJ had expressed its view that § 3501 was unconstitutional, and in order to ensure "the proper administration of the criminal law," J.A. ___, the Fourth Circuit determined that it would accede to the urgings of amici.

In examining *Miranda,* the Fourth Circuit was surprised that "the sixty-page opinion does not specifically state the basis for its holding." J.A. ___. The Court, however, found that

the opinion "strongly suggested . . . that the basis for the rule was identical to that set forth in *McNabb* and *Malloy, i.e.,* an exercise of the Court's power to prescribe nonconstitutional 'rules of procedure and evidence.' " *Id.* at ___ (quoting *Palermo* v. *United States,* 360 U.S. 343, 353 n.11 (1959)).

The Fourth Circuit conceded that Congress, in enacting § 3501 had the "express purpose of returning to the pre-*Miranda* case-by-case determination of whether a confession was voluntary." J.A. ___. Nonetheless, the court of appeals concluded that Congress had the authority to do so. In addition to the court of appeal's conclusion that *Miranda*'s holding was an exercise of only supervisory powers, the Fourth Circuit also cited subsequent cases from the Court describing *Miranda*'s rules as "prophylactic." *Id.* at ___. However, the Fourth Circuit cited only its own opinion in declaring that "it is certainly 'well established that the failure to deliver *Miranda* warnings is not itself a constitutional violation'." *Id.* at ___ (quoting *United States* v. *Elie,* 111 F.3d 1135, 1142 (4th Cir. 1997)). In response to the dissent's objection that *Miranda*'s application in state cases proves its constitutional force, the Fourth Circuit merely said "the dissent raises an interesting academic question." *Id.* at ___.

C. Statutory Background.

Congress enacted 18 U.S.C. § 3501 on June 19, 1968, just two years after the Court issued *Miranda.* Under § 3501, whether a confession is "voluntarily given" and therefore admissible is to be determined by the trial judge, "tak[ing] into consideration all the circumstances surrounding the giving of the confession." *Id.* § 3501(b). On its face, the statute directly conflicts with *Miranda*'s holding that a statement made in custodial interrogation is inadmissible unless "the accused [is] adequately and effectively apprised of his rights and the exercise of those rights [is] fully honored." 384 U.S. at 467. This conflict was intentional. Congress enacted § 3501 to re-

---

[6]In their cross-motion, prosecutors attached an affidavit from Agent Durkin that contradicted Agent Lawlor's testimony. The affidavit stated that petitioner had initially refused to give a statement after Agent Lawlor told him about the warrant, and that petitioner did not make a statement until after the search was concluded. Prosecutors also attached a hand-written statement from petitioner (separate from the "9:41 pm" waiver form) in which petitioner wrote that he had been read his rights at 7:30 pm and denied involvement. This statement, however, is plainly incorrect as to time in that petitioner also states he was brought to the FBI field house at 5:30 pm. Officers had only first arrived at petitioner's apartment at 5:30 pm and did not knock and enter until "over an hour" later. Though the times given in the statement are demonstrably inaccurate, the statement is consistent with petitioner's testimony that there was a two-hour gap between petitioner's arrival at the Field Office and his being apprised of his rights. In denying the cross-motion, the District Court ruled that the government had not proffered any "new and heretofore unavailable evidence supporting reversal of this Court's July 1, 1997 Order." J.A. ___.

place *Miranda*'s standard for determining whether a statement is admissible under the Fifth Amendment with a broader totality of the circumstances test. See S. Rep. No. 90-1097 (1968), *reprinted in* 1968 U.S.C.C.A.N. 2112, 2141; see *id.* at 2210-11.

Congress also left no doubt that *Miranda*'s holding that the accused be apprised of his rights was a matter of constitutional interpretation. The Senate Judiciary Committee expressed its view that *Miranda*'s "majority opinion . . . misconstrues the Constitution." S. Rep. 90-1097 (1968), *reprinted in* 1968 U.S.C.C.A.N. 2112, 2136. Section 3501 further reflected the mistaken view that Congress could override the Court on such constitutional rulings: "I say that we would be derelict in our duty if we as Representatives of the people did not declare once and for all time the equality of this Congress of the United States with the Supreme Court of the United States and put the Court in its place." 114 Cong. Rec. 16,074 (1968) (statement of Rep. Whitten); see *id.* at 16,295 (statement of Rep. Reid) ("In my judgment, this title constitutes an emotional backlash at the Supreme Court").

Precisely because of § 3501's unconstitutionality, the Executive Branch has largely refused to enforce it since it was enacted over thirty years ago. See *Davis* v. *United States,* 512 U.S. 452, 463-64 (1994) (Scalia, J. concurring) (noting that "[i]n fact, with limited exceptions the provision has been studiously avoided by every Administration, not only in this Court but in the lower courts, since its enactment 25 years ago"). Pursuant to 2 U.S.C. § 288k(b) (requiring the Department of Justice to notify Congress whenever it will not defend the constitutionality of a federal statute), Attorney General Janet Reno has notified Congress that the Department will not defend the constitutionality of § 3501. See J.A.___. For the past 33 years, therefore, *Miranda*, not § 3501, has governed the admissibility at trial of statements procured during custodial interrogation.

SUMMARY OF ARGUMENT

In *Miranda* v. *Arizona,* 384 U.S. 436 (1966), the Court engaged in a conventional exercise of constitutional interpretation. The Court held that the Fifth Amendment privilege against self-incrimination is fully applicable to custodial interrogation. After reviewing the scope of the privilege, the Court concluded that it secures for individuals the right to make a free, "intelligent" choice regarding whether to talk, or not talk, to law enforcement officers during interrogations. Therefore, to permit a full opportunity to exercise the privilege and to overcome pressures inherent in the custodial interrogation process, the privilege requires that there be procedures fully effective in apprising persons *prior to* interrogation of their right to remain silent and ensuring that attempts to exercise the privilege *during* interrogation are fully honored. To provide "constitutional guidelines," the Court set forth specific warnings that must be given *prior to* interrogation and procedures followed *during* interrogation as a constitutional minimum. The Court held that these measures, or other procedures at least as effective in apprising persons of their right to remain silent and assuring that exercise of such rights would be honored, must be provided to give effect to the privilege.

In subsequent years, the Court has continued to refer to *Miranda*'s specific requirements as constitutionally based. The Court has also applied *Miranda*'s holding to a myriad of cases arising in State courts, and on habeas review. While the Court has sometimes referred to these requirements as "prophylactic rules," it cannot be that they are not required by the Constitution. "Prophylactic" is not a synonym for "non-constitutional." If it were, then for 33 years the Court has violated federalism and acted utterly lawlessly in requiring States to comply with *Miranda*'s rules and numerous other prophylactic rules that are not required by the Constitution. Because *Miranda*'s rules have been applied against the States and are constitutionally required, neither Congress nor the

States may ignore them. Section 3501 utterly fails to comply with *Miranda*'s constitutional rules. It fails to provide the warnings and additional procedures specified in *Miranda*, and makes no provision whatsoever for procedures at least as effective in apprising individuals of their right to remain silent and assuring that exercise of the right will be honored. Section 3501 is therefore unconstitutional.

Only the Supreme Court may alter *Miranda*'s requirements and 33 years after *Miranda* was decided, principles of *stare decisis* counsel against doing so. *Miranda* has proved to be workable, is a ruling on which there has been considerable reliance and has not been overtaken by doctrinal developments or changes in its factual underpinnings. *Miranda* is a well-reasoned, principled decision. Moreover, it is one of the Court's most famous opinions of the twentieth century. *Miranda*'s specific holdings have been widely popularized through the media and accepted in the legal culture. Departing from them would erode public confidence in the legitimacy of the criminal justice system and the legitimacy of the Court's exercise of its authority.

ARGUMENT

I. *MIRANDA* ENUNCIATED A CONSTITUTIONAL RULE THAT CANNOT BE REVERSED BY CONGRESS.

A. Miranda's Core Constitutional Holdings.

This Court's decision in *Miranda* was, first and foremost, a construction and analysis of what the Fifth Amendment requires in the context of custodial interrogations. In deciding *Miranda*, the Court was doing more than "judicially creat[ing] rules of evidence and procedure that are not required by the Constitution." J.A. ___. Rather, it announced three core constitutional holdings. *First,* the Court held that the Fifth Amendment "privilege [against self-incrimination] is fully applicable during a period of custodial interrogation." *Miranda* v. *Arizona,* 384 U.S. 436, 460 (1966).

Second, the Fifth Amendment prohibition against compelled self-incrimination requires that the decision whether to speak to officers while in custody must be proven to be both intelligently made and entirely voluntary. Accordingly, interrogating officials must inform the individual of his rights and provide assurances that the individual's decision will be honored.

Third, the *Miranda* Court elaborated on the nature and content of the "concrete constitutional guidelines for law enforcement agencies and courts to follow," 384 U.S. at 442, specifying the information that must be provided as a minimum constitutional threshold. Specifically, the Court held: *prior to any questioning,* the person must be warned that he has a right to remain silent, that any statement he does make may be used as evidence against him, and that the has a right to the presence of an attorney, either retained or appointed. The defendant may waive effectuation of these rights, *provided the waiver is made voluntarily, knowingly and intelligently.* If, however, he indicates in any manner and at any stage of the process that he wishes to consult with an attorney before speaking *there can be no questioning.* Likewise, if the individual is alone and indicates in any manner that he does not wish to be interrogated, *the police may not question him. Miranda* v. *Arizona,* 384 U.S. 436, 444-45 (1966). While the Court did not insist that its own wording of the warnings must be followed, it expressly held that alternative procedures must be "at least as effective in apprising accused persons of their right of silence and in assuring a continuous opportunity to exercise it." *Id.* at 467; see also *id.* at 444 (specifying either the Court's "procedural safeguards" or "other fully effective means . . . to inform accused persons of their right of silence and to assure a continuous opportunity to exercise it"); *id.* at 476 (specifying the Court's warnings or "a fully effective equivalent" to warn accused of rights and protect exercise thereof); *id.* at 478-79 (same); *id.* at 490-91 (same). Thus, these protections are part of our irreducable minimum protection embraced by the privilege against self-incrimination in the Fifth Amendment.

Too often, analyses of the *Miranda* decision focuses on the precise formulation of the now famous warnings and fail to address the carefully crafted constitutional analysis which led to the rule. [footnote 7] While the Court invited alternative procedures, it did not invite procedures that dispensed with apprising persons in custody at the outset of their rights and assuring that their exercise of those rights would be honored. Moreover, the Court expressly rejected an after the fact "totality of the circumstances" test. Such procedures (including what Congress ultimately passed in § 3501) are constitutionally infirm because, even where an individual may be otherwise aware of his rights, warnings are nonetheless required and the individual must still be assured by his interrogators that they will respect his exercise of his rights.

1. The Court's first core constitutional holding was to confirm that "there can be no doubt that the Fifth Amendment privilege is available outside of criminal court proceedings and serves to protect persons in all settings in which their freedom of action is curtailed in any significant way from being compelled to incriminate themselves." *Id.* at 467. In reaching this conclusion, the Court clarified issues raised in its prior holdings in *Malloy* v. *Hogan,* 378 U.S. 1 (1964), and *Escobedo* v. *Illinois,* 378 U.S. 478 (1964). See *Miranda,* 384 U.S. at 440, 463-66. [footnote 8] The Court held that "all the principles embodied in the privilege apply to informal compulsion exerted by law-enforcement officers during in-custody questioning," finding that the "question, in fact, could have been taken as settled in federal courts almost 70 years ago, when, in *Bram* v. *United States,* 168 U.S. 532, 542 . . . (1897), this Court held: ". . . wherever a question arises whether a confession is incompetent because not voluntary, the issue is controlled by that portion of the fifth amendment . . . commanding that no person 'shall be compelled in any criminal case to be a witness against himself.' " *Id.* at 461 (second omission in original). The Court, however, granted certiorari in *Miranda* to address "problems" exposed in "debate" engendered by *Escobedo,* regarding "applying the privilege against self-incrimination to in-custody interrogation, and to give concrete constitutional guidelines" regarding such application. *Id.* at 440-41.

2. The Court's second core holding was that the Fifth Amendment requires that statements made during custodial interrogation are inadmissible at trial in the prosecution's case-in-chief unless, before making those statements, "the accused [is] adequately and effectively apprised of his rights and the exercise of those rights [is] fully honored." *Miranda,* 384 U.S. at 467. This second holding emerged from the Court's lengthy review of the history of the privilege, see *id.* at 458-66. The Court emphasized that a decision to make a statement in any situation in which an individual has become a

---

[7] *See generally* Stephen I. Schulhofer, *Reconsidering Miranda,* 54 U. Chi. L. Rev. 435 (1987).

[8] In *Malloy* v. *Hogan,* the Court squarely held that "the Fifth Amendment's exception from compulsory self-incrimination is also protected by the Fourteenth Amendment against abridgement by the States," 378 U.S. 1, 6 (1964), and therefore applied to an "interrogation" of the petitioner conducted as part of a state "inquiry" into alleged criminal activities. *Id.* at 12-14. One week later, in *Escobedo* v. *Illinois,* the Court held inadmissible all statements extracted during an interrogation where the accused had requested and been refused an opportunity to consult with counsel and had not been warned of his constitutional right to remain silent, finding that the accused had been denied the assistance of counsel in violation of the Sixth and Fourteenth Amendments. 378 U.S. 478, 490-91 (1964). Among the prior opinions relied on in reaching this conclusion were the Court's holding in *Gideon* v. *Wainwright,* 372 U.S. 335, 342 (1963), that the Sixth Amendment applied to the states, and its holding in *Massiah* v. *United States,* 377 U.S. 201, 204 (1964), that the Sixth Amendment right to the aid of counsel surely applied "to an indicted defendant under interrogation by police in a completely extrajudicial proceeding."

"suspect" or "the accused" must both be intelligently made and unfettered. See *id.* at 460 ("the privilege is fulfilled only when the person is guaranteed the right 'to remain silent unless he chooses to speak in the unfettered exercise of his own free will' " (quoting *Malloy* v. *Hogan,* 378 U.S. 1, 8 (1964))); see also *id.* at 468 (the decision must be "intelligent"). Simply put, no decision is intelligently made where the decider is ignorant of the available options, and no choice is voluntary where an inquisitor withholds critical information about the choice.

The *Miranda* Court further recognized the simple reality that compulsion may come in many forms, not only those traditionally associated with plainly unconstitutional "third degree" tactics. Instead, the risk of compulsion is inherent in any proceeding where an accused has been deprived of his freedom, taken to a strange place and subjected to questioning by those trained to elicit answers. When the subject of such a proceeding makes a decision to speak, the voluntariness—and reliability—of such a decision is suspect unless it can be shown that the subject had been made aware that he was free to do otherwise. This is true "whatever the background of the person interrogated," for even one who is aware of his rights needs reassurance that "he is free to exercise this privilege at that point in time." *Miranda*, 384 U.S. at 469.

Accordingly, the constitutional command that an individual be free from compelled self-incrimination and that any waiver of such right be voluntary necessitates, at a minimum, that the individual be warned at the outset of interrogation of his rights and that the individual be told that his decision to invoke those rights will be honored. See *id.* at 444 (there must be "fully effective means . . . devised to inform accused persons of their right of silence and to assure a continuous opportunity to exercise it"); *id.* at 478-79 ("[p]rocedural safeguards must be employed to protect the privilege [that are] fully effective means . . . to notify the person of his right of silence and to assure that the exercise of the right will be scrupulously honored"); *id.* at 490 (requiring "safeguards for the privilege . . . as effective as those described above in informing accused persons of their right of silence and in affording a continuous opportunity to exercise it").

This minimum threshold requirement supplanted the "totality of the circumstances" analysis that the Court had used under the Fourteenth Amendment to determine whether the statements made during custodial interrogation were voluntary. See, *e.g., Michigan* v. *Tucker,* 417 U.S. 433, 441 (1974) ("[b]efore *Miranda* the principal issue in these cases was not whether a defendant had waived his privilege against compulsory self-incrimination but simply whether his statement was 'voluntary.' In state cases the Court applied the Due Process Clause of the Fourteenth Amendment"); *id.* at 442 ("it was not until this Court's decision in *Miranda* that the privilege against compulsory self-incrimination *was seen as the principal protection for a person facing police interrogation*") (emphasis added).

3. The "concrete constitutional guidelines" which the Court delineated encompass the third core constitutional holding in *Miranda.* The Court justified each of the warnings required in *Miranda* as "absolute prerequisite[s]," 384 U.S. at 468, to interrogation on the constitutional grounds that they were necessary and sufficient conditions to the intelligent exercise of the privilege in a custodial context. *First,* the Court held that a warning that the accused has the right to remain silent is indispensable "for an intelligent decision as to its exercise" as well as "an absolute prerequisite in overcoming the inherent pressures of the interrogation atmosphere." *Id. Second,* the Court held that "[t]he warning of the right to remain silent *must* be accom-

panied by the explanation that anything said can and will be used against the individual in court." *Id.* at 469 (emphasis added). The Court explained "This warning may serve to make the individual more acutely aware that *he is faced with a phase of the adversary system—that he is not in the presence of persons acting solely in his interest.*" *Id.* at 469 (emphasis added).

Third, the Court recognized that the "circumstances surrounding in-custody interrogation can operate very quickly to overbear the will of one merely made aware of his privilege by his interrogators," *id.,* and that "[e]ven preliminary advice given to the accused by his own attorney can be swiftly overcome by the secret interrogation process." *Id.* at 470. To remedy this, the Court held that "an individual held for interrogation *must* be clearly informed that he has the right to consult with a lawyer and to have the lawyer with him during interrogation," *id.* at 471 (emphasis added), and noted that "the right to be furnished counsel does not depend on a request." See *id.* at 471 (quoting *Carnley* v. *Cochran,* 369 U.S. 506, 513 (1962)). The Court held that "[a]n individual need not make a pre-interrogation request for a lawyer" for the right to counsel to attach to custodial interrogation. *Id.* at 470. "The accused who does not know his rights and therefore does not make a request may be the person who most needs counsel." *Id.* at 470-71.

Fourth, the Court required that a person interrogated be informed that "if he is indigent a lawyer will be appointed to represent him." *Id.* at 473. This step was held to be necessary to assure that the accused was in a position to knowingly exercise or waive this right: "As with the warnings of the *right* to remain silent and of the *general right* to counsel, only by effective and express explanation to the indigent of *this right* can there be assurance *that he was truly in a position to exercise it.*" *Id.* at 473 (emphasis added).

Although *Miranda* invited Congress and the states to develop other "fully . . . effective" procedures to "safeguard[] . . . the privilege," *id.* at 490, it emphasized that "unless we are shown other procedures which are *at least as effective in apprising accused persons of their right of silence* and in as-suring a continuous opportunity to exercise it," *id.* at 467 (emphasis added), the alternative procedures would fall short of the Fifth Amendment's re-quirements. *Miranda* did *not* leave Congress free to supplant the requisite warnings with procedures that altogether fail to "appris[e] accused persons" at the outset of interrogation of their right to remain silent, their right to counsel, and assurance that exercise of these rights would be honored.

B. The Court's Subsequent Application Of Miranda To The States And On Habeas.

The Supreme Court's jurisprudence following *Miranda* further demonstrates that this Court in *Miranda* established constitutional, not merely supervisory, rules. In numerous subsequent opinions, the Court has referred to *Miranda*'s rules as con-stitutional requirements and extensions of its holding as constitutionally based. See *Edwards* v. *Arizona,* 451 U.S. 477, 481-82 (1981) (explaining that "[i]n *Miranda* v. *Arizona,* the Court determined that the Fifth and Fourteenth Amendments' prohibi-tion against compelled self-incrimination *required* that custodial interrogation be preceded by advice to the putative defendant that he has the right to remain silent and also the right to the presence of an attorney") (emphasis added). [footnote 9]

---

[9] *See, e.g., Illinois* v. *Perkins,* 496 U.S. 292, 296 (1990) (*Miranda* rules rest on "the Fifth Amendment privilege against self-incrimination"); *Butler* v. *McKellar,* 494 U.S. 407, 411 (1990) (noting holding of *Arizona* v. *Roberson* "that the Fifth Amendment bars police-initiated interrogations following a suspect's request for counsel in the context of a separate investigation"); *Michigan* v. *Jackson,* 475 U.S. 625, 629 (1986) ("[t]he Fifth Amendment protection against compelled self-incrimination provides the right to counsel at custodial interrogations"); *Moran* v. *Burbine,* 475 U.S. 412, 427 (1986) (*Miranda* is "our interpretation of the Federal Constitution").

Perhaps the clearest indication that the Court has never regarded *Miranda* as resting simply on its supervisory powers is the fact that the Court consistently has applied the *Miranda* rules to cases arising in state courts. See, *e.g., Stansbury* v. *California,* 511 U.S. 318, 322-27 (1994); *Minnick* v. *Mississippi,* 498 U.S. 146 (1990); *Arizona* v. *Roberson,* 486 U.S. 675 (1988). (Indeed, three of the four consolidated cases which comprise *Miranda* arose in state courts.) Although the Court has the authority to announce rules of procedure and evidence binding on federal courts, fundamental principles of federalism preclude the exercise of any such supervisory authority over the state courts. With respect to cases tried before state tribunals, the Court's "authority is limited to enforcing the commands of the United States Constitution." *Mu'Min* v. *Virginia,* 500 U.S. 415, 422 (1991). The federal judiciary "may not require the observance of any special procedures" in state courts "except when necessary to assure compliance with the dictates of the Federal Constitution." *Harris* v. *Rivera,* 454 U.S. 339, 344-45 (1981); see *McNabb* v. *United States,* 318 U.S. 332, 340 (1943) ("the power of this Court to undo convictions in state courts is limited to enforcement of those 'fundamental principles of liberty and justice' which are secured by the Fourteenth Amendment") (citation omitted) (quoting *Hebert* v. *Louisiana,* 272 U.S. 312, 316 (1926)). Therefore, the Court's continued application of *Miranda*'s exclusionary rule in state cases is conclusive proof that *Miranda* rests on constitutional underpinnings. The Fourth Circuit's effort cavalierly to dismiss this fact as "an interesting academic question . . . [that] has no bearing on our conclusion that *Miranda*'s conclusive presumption is not required by the Constitution," J.A. ___ n.21, simply disregards the profound importance of this limit on the Court's authority. In effect, the Court of Appeals is suggesting that this Court has exceeded its authority in scores of cases over the past 30 years. This is no matter of mere academic musings. [footnote 10]

Finally, the Supreme Court has held that claims that a conviction rests on statements obtained in violation of *Miranda* are cognizable on federal habeas review. *Withrow,* 507 U.S. at 690-95. Habeas review is only available for claims that a person "is in custody in violation of the Constitution or the laws or treaties of the United States." 28 U.S.C. § 2254(a). *Miranda* certainly does not involve laws or treaties. Thus, the Court's holding in *Withrow* depends on the conclusion that the requirements of *Miranda* arise from and protect constitutional rights. In reaching its conclusion, the Court rejected the government's argument that since the *Miranda* rules "are not constitutional in character, but merely 'prophylactic,' " federal habeas review should not extend to claims based on violations of these rules. *Withrow,* 507 U.S. at 690. The Court declined to reach this conclusion and observed that *Miranda* safeguards a "fundamental trial right." *Id.* at 691.

C. Miranda's "Prophylactic" Rules Have Constitutional Weight.

The Fourth Circuit, citing no support, relies on the theory that "prophylactic" rules created by the Court to protect rights enumerated in the Constitution are subject to reversal by Congress and the states. See J.A. ___. First, the Fourth Circuit's theory is clearly at odds with *Miranda*'s express holding that Congress and the States could not override its requirements. See, e.g., *Miranda,* 384 U.S. at 490 (Congress and the States must adopt "safeguards for the privilege" that are "fully effective . . . in informing accused persons of their right of silence and in affording a continuous opportunity to exercise it"). While the Court in subsequent opinions has referred to *Miranda*'s specific warnings as "prophylactic" rules that safeguard constitutional rights, that does not mean that *Miranda*'s holdings lack constitutional force and may

---

[10]Indeed, *Michigan* v. *Tucker,* 417 U.S. 433 (1974), and *Oregon* v. *Elstad,* 470 U.S. 298 (1985), cases relied upon by the panel to support its conclusion that *Miranda* is not a constitutionally based decision, arose in state courts. In both decisions, the Supreme Court reaffirmed *Miranda*'s basic conclusion that unwarned statements must be excluded from the government's case-in-chief. *Tucker,* 417 U.S. at 445; *Elstad,* 470 U.S. at 307.

be overridden by Congress. Those same opinions recognize their constitutional underpinnings of the rules and do not hold, or even suggest, that Congress and the States are free to reverse them. Moreover, the Court's many other opinions involving "prophylactic" rules that guard fundamental constitutional rights do not suggest that Congress and the States are free to override such rules.

Miranda's four warnings are flexible only in the sense that that they may be replaced by procedures "at least as effective in apprising accused persons of their right of silence and in assuring a continuous opportunity to exercise it." *Miranda*, 384 U.S. at 467. They create a safe harbor when followed. But that does not mean the legislative branches are precluded from devising equally effective methods of presenting the privilege against self-incrimination. *Miranda* itself noted that one alternative procedure that would meet this requirement would be to require "[t]he presence of counsel" during interrogation. *Id.* at 466. Nonetheless, *Miranda* established constitutional minimum protection to protect the right to silence and to counsel during custodial interrogation—*i.e.*, *Miranda*'s procedures or "other fully effective means . . . to inform accused persons of their right of silence and to assure a continuous opportunity to exercise it." *Id.* at 444; see *id.* at 467, 476, 478-79.

Indeed, the specific opinions the Fourth Circuit relied upon referring to the *Miranda* rules as "prophylactic" recognized the constitutional underpinnings of *Miranda*'s rules. In *Tucker,* 417 U.S. at 444, the Court held that the specific *Miranda* warnings were "not themselves *rights* protected by the Constitution but were instead measures to *insure* that the right against compulsory self-incrimination was protected," and referred to *Miranda*'s own explanation that its prescribed warnings were not a "'constitutional straightjacket.'" *Id.* (quoting *Miranda*, 384 U.S. at 467). Thus, *Tucker* is entirely consistent with *Miranda*'s understanding that the specific safeguards it prescribed were not required by the Constitution in the sense that other "procedures" or "solution[s]" could replace them so long as they were "at least as effective in apprising accused persons of their right of silence and in assuring a continuous opportunity to exercise it." *Miranda*, 384 U.S. at 467.

In *New York* v. *Quarles,* 467 U.S. 649, 654 (1983), the Court simply reiterated *Tucker*'s observation that the "*Miranda* warnings . . . are 'not themselves rights protected by the Constitution but [are] instead measures to insure that the right against compulsory self-incrimination [is] protected.'" *Id.* at 654 (alteration in original) (quoting *Michigan* v. Tucker, 417 U.S. 413, 444 (1974)). In *Elstad,* 470 U.S. at 318, the Court held that "a suspect who has once responded to unwarned yet uncoercive questioning is not thereby disabled from waiving his rights and confessing after he has been given the requisite *Miranda* warnings." In reaching this conclusion, the Court observed that the *Miranda*'s exclusionary rule is prophylactic in that it "*serves the Fifth Amendment and sweeps more broadly than the Fifth Amendment itself.*" *Id.* at 306 (emphasis added). [footnote 11] The Court nonetheless reaffirmed that a *Miranda* violation "affords a bright-line, legal presumption of coercion, requiring suppression of all unwarned statements." *Id.* at 306 n.1.

Each of these cases does no more than adjust the contours of the prophylaxis. When, for example, public safety or good faith on the part of officials warrant limitations on the scope of the underlying constitutional provision, this Court (and not

---

[11]The Court has also adopted constitutional prophylactic rules that predictably overprotect constitutional rights in a variety of other settings. *See, e.g., Gertz* v. *Robert Welsh, Inc.,* 418 U.S. 323, 340, 342 (1974) (explaining that, even though "there is no constitutional value in false statements of fact," the Court in *New York Times Co.* v. *Sullivan,* 376 U.S. 254 (1964), and its progeny nevertheless "extended a measure of strategic protection to defamatory falsehood" in cases involving public officials and public figures); *Freedman* v. *Maryland,* 380 U.S. 51, 58 (1965) (setting forth "procedural safeguards designed to obviate the dangers of a censorship system" with respect to motion picture obscenity).

Congress or state legislatures) has carefully crafted adjustments. [footnote 12] The existence of such cases does not strip *Miranda*'s requirements of constitutional dimension. If it did, and if *Miranda*'s minimum threshold requirements represented nothing more than an exercise of the Court's supervisory powers, then there is no reason why such requirements should have been applicable to the States. It is fallacious to reason as the Fourth Circuit has that because this Court has made such adjustments to the prophylactic reach of *Miranda*, it was merely exercising a supervisory power rather than applying a constitutional requirement to a new type of circumstance.

Moreover, *Miranda* is just one of many instances in which the Court has announced prophylatic rules to protect underlying constitutional rights. For example, to "avoid[] otherwise difficult line-drawing problems" and adopt a test with "relatively few problems with proof," the Court has established a prophylatic rule that a permanent physical occupation is per se a taking. *Loretto* v. *Teleprompter Manhattan CATV Corp.*, 458 U.S. 419, 436-37 (1982). The Court has created numerous "prophylatic constitutional rules," *Michigan* v. *Payne*, 412 U.S. 47, 53, regarding criminal procedure. See North *Carolina* v. *Pearce*, 395 U.S. 711, 726 (1969) (to protect Due Process Clause right to appeal, "whenever a judge imposes a more severe sentence upon a defendant after a new trial, the reasons for his doing so must affirmatively appear," or vindictiveness will be presumed); *Michigan* v. *Payne*, 412 U.S. 47, 53 (1973) explaining that "[i]t is an inherent attribute of prophylactic constitutional rules, such as those established in *Miranda* and *Pearce*, that their [. . .] application will occasion windfall benefits for some defendants who have suffered no constitutional deprivation"); *Blackledge* v. *Perry*, 417 U.S. 21, 28-29 (1974) (although there was "no evidence that the prosecutor in this case acted in bad faith," it was not constitutionally permissible for the State to respond to Perry's invocation of his statutory right of appeal by bringing a more serious charge against him prior to the trial *de novo*); *Maine* v. *Moulton*, 474 U.S. 159, 168 (1985) (requiring suppression of accused's statements relating to pending charges at trial on the charges when obtained by law enforcement officials conducting surveillance of accused relating to new or additional crimes, despite assertions of the legitimate reasons for the surveillance, to protect the accused Sixth Amendment right to communicate only through counsel with police regarding the pending charges); *Michigan* v. *Jackson*, 475 U.S. 625, 636 (1986) (holding that where "police initiate an interrogation after the defendant's assertion, at an arraignment or similar proceeding, of his right to counsel, any waiver of the defendant's [Sixth Amendment] right to counsel for that police-initiated interrogation is invalid" and resulting confessions inadmissible); *Michigan* v. *Harvey*, 494 U.S. 344, 345-46 (1990) (holding that statement inadmissible in prosecution's case in chief order *Michigan* v. *Jackson's* "prophylactic rule" may nonetheless be used "to impeach a defendant's false or inconsistent testimony"). Nothing in the language of those decisions suggests that their prophylactic character makes these rules not constitutionally required. Indeed, the fact that rule is strongly prophylactic often reflects the importance of the underlying constitutional right and preventing less than fully intelligent waiver of such right. As the Court has explained, "we should 'indulge every reasonable presumption against waiver of fundamental constitutional rights.'" *Jackson*, 475 U.S. at 633 (quoting *Johnson* v. *Zerbst*, 304 U.S. 458, 464 (1938)).

In sum, it cannot be that prophylatic rules designed to protect constitutional rights and applied against the States are not constitutionally required. "Prophylatic" is not a synonym for "non-constitutional." If it was, and Congress could alter *Miranda*'s rules, then for 33 years the Court has engaged in the rankest violation of federal-state

---

[12]*See, e.g., Tennessee* v. *Street*, 471 U.S. 409, 417 (1985) (confession that is inadmissible under *Bruton* rule is admissible for impeachment); *United States* v. *Leon*, 468 U.S. 897, 913 (1984) (officer's reasonable reliance on search warrant ultimately held invalid does not bar admission of evidence obtained in prosecution's case-in-chief); *Oregon* v. *Haas*, 420 U.S. 714, ___ (1975) (evidence obtained in violation of Fourth Amendment admissible for impeachment purposes).

relations and utterly lawless by requiring States to comply with *Miranda* rules that are not constitutionally required and requiring compliance with a host of other prophylatic rules not required by the Constitution.

D. Section 3501 Is Constitutionally Infirm.

In enacting 18 U.S.C. § 3501, Congress attempted to secure the admissibility in federal courts of statements that would otherwise be suppressed under this Court's decision in *Miranda*. [footnote 13] By its terms, § 3501 makes "whether or not [a] defendant was advised or knew that he was not required to make any statement and that any such statement could be used against him" simply one of many factors a trial judge may consider in determining whether a statement is "voluntary" and hence admissible. 18 U.S.C. § 3501(b)(3). Similarly, whether a defendant was advised of his right to counsel is but another factor to be considered. *Id.* § 3501(b)(4). The purpose and effect of § 3501 would be to establish the totality of the circumstances test for determining the admissibility of custodial statements, despite *Miranda's* rejection of that test. Section 3501 therefore squarely conflicts with *Miranda's* core holding that "the accused must be . . . apprised of his rights and the exercise of those rights must be fully honored." 384 U.S. at 467.

In addition, because § 3501 does not require the four specific warnings and additional procedures outlined in *Miranda*, nor does it provide procedures "at least as effective in apprising accused persons of their right of silence and in assuring continuing opportunity to exercise it," *id.* at 468, it fails to meet the minimum protections *Miranda* determined the Constitution required. Section 3501's procedures are not "as effective" as those specified in *Miranda*. Section 3501 does not require "appropriate safeguards *at the outset* of the interrogation," *id.* at 457 (emphasis added), nor does it impose *any* affirmative obligation upon the part of officials to ensure that any statements are "truly the product of free choice." *Id.* at 457.

Similarly, § 3501's procedures, by failing to require that accused persons be informed of their right to silence and right to counsel, fail to require the knowing and intelligent waiver of these constitutional rights. *Miranda* specifically held that the "high standards of proof for the waiver of constitutional rights . . . applied to in-custody interrogation." *Id.* at 475 (citation omitted). The Court "ha[s] adhered to the principle that nothing less than the *Zerbst* standard for the waiver of constitutional rights applies to the waiver of *Miranda* rights." *Minnick,* 498 U.S. at 160 (Scalia, J., dissenting). Section 3501 conflicts with *Miranda's* requirement that the government demonstrate knowing and intelligent waiver of the right to remain silent and to have assistance of counsel during custodial interrogation.

Congress has no power to overrule the Court's interpretations of the Constitution. City of *Boerne* v. *Flores,* 521 U.S. 507, 517-21 (1997). If that is the end, the proper course is to pursue the consitutional amendment process. Because § 3501 clearly conflicts with *Miranda*, and *Miranda* represents the Court's interpretation of the Constitution, § 3501 is invalid. If Congress could overturn any Supreme Court interpretation of the Constitution it disliked simply be enacting contrary legislation, then the Constitution would no longer be "superior, paramount law" but "on a level with or-

---

[13] *See* S. Rep. No. 90-1097 (1968), *reprinted in* 1968 U.S.C.C.A.N. 2112. Congress also explicitly sought to overrule the now displaced holding of *Escobedo* v. *Illinois,* 378 U.S. 478, 490-91 (1964) which applied the Sixth Amendment right to counsel to interrogations conducted as part of a police investigation that had "focus[ed]" on a particular suspect in police custody. Although not raised in the Congressional debate (nor addressed in the Fourth Circuit's opinion below), § 501 would also appear to render admissible statements obtained in violation of the holdings in *Massiah,* 377 U.S. at 206 (suppressing under the Sixth Amendment's right to counsel statements obtained through government efforts to "deliberately elicit[]" incriminating statements after adversarial proceedings have commenced) and *Wong Sun* v. *United States,* 371 U.S. 471, 484-87 (1963) (holding that even voluntary statements may be inadmissible if derived from an illegal arrest or search or otherwise the "fruit" of a Fourth Amendment violation). *See* Yale Kamisar, *Can (Did) Congress "Overrule" Miranda?* 85 Cornell L. Rev n. 5 (2000) (forthcoming).

dinary legislative acts, and like other acts . . . alterable when the legislature shall please to alter it." *Marbury* v. *Madison,* 5 U.S. (1 Cranch) 137, 177 (1803).

II. THERE IS NO REASON TO DISLODGE *MIRANDA'S* CONSTITUTIONAL RULING.

Principles of *stare decisis* dictate that *Miranda* not be overruled, now, 33 years after the decision. *Miranda* constituted a fully warranted exercise of the Court's power to interpret the Constitution, which should not be disturbed. *Miranda* involved elucidation of a fundamental right that has become deeply ingrained in the Court's own subsequent opinions, in law enforcement practices, and in the public's understanding of the Constitution in a criminal justice setting.

The doctrine of stare decisis "permits society to presume that bedrock principles are founded in the law rather than in the proclivities of individuals, and thereby contributes to the integrity of our constitutional system of government, both in appearance and in fact." *Vasquez* v. *Hillary,* 474 U.S. 254, 265-66 (1986). Adhering to precedent "'is usually the wise policy, because in most matters it is more important that the applicable rule of law be settled than that it be settled right.'" *Payne* v. *Tennessee,* 501 U.S. 808, 827 (1991) (quoting *Burnet* v. *Coronado Oil & Gas Co.,* 285 U.S. 393, 406 (1932) (Brandeis, J., dissenting)). "Indeed, the very concept of the rule of law underlying our own Constitution requires such continuity over time that a respect for precedent is, by definition, indispensable." *Planned Parenthood* v. *Casey,* 505 U.S. 833, 854 (1992). Although "the rule of *stare decisis* is not an 'inexorable command,'" *id.,* "[e]ven in constitutional cases, the doctrine carries such persuasive force that [the Court] ha[s] always required a departure from precedent to be supported by some 'special justification.'" *United States* v. *International Bus. Mach. Corp.,* 514 U.S. 843, 856 (1996) (quoting *Payne* v. *Tennessee,* 501 U.S. 808, 842 (1991) (Souter, J., concurring)).

Traditional considerations in stare decisis analysis are whether the "governing decisions are unworkable," *Payne* v. *Tennessee,* 501 U.S. at 827; whether the governing decisions are subject to a kind of reliance that would lead to special hardship were those decisions abandoned, see *id.* at 827-28; *United States* v. *Title Ins. & Trust Co.,* 265 U.S. 472, 486 (1924); *Casey,* 505 U.S. at 854-56; whether the law's development in intervening years has rendered the prior holding a "remnant of abandoned doctrine," *id.* at 855; see *Patterson* v. *McLean Credit Union,* 491 U.S. 164, 173-74 (1989); whether any factual premises underlying the prior holding have so changed as to render the holding irrelevant or unjustifiable, see *Casey,* 505 U.S. at 855; *Vasquez,* 474 U.S. at 266; and whether the governing decision was "unsound in principle." *Garcia* v. *San Antonio Metro. Transit Auth.,* 469 U.S. 528, 546-47 (1985). Each of these considerations is addressed below. Each demonstrates that *Miranda* should be reaffirmed.

A. Workability.

Miranda's holdings have in no sense proven "unworkable" in practice. [footnote 14] To the contrary, *Miranda*'s core holding that there must be procedures to apprise an individual in custody of his rights and its specific rules have proven easy to administer by law enforcement officers and the courts. The United States has represented that "Federal agents do not find it difficult, in general, to read a suspect his rights and determine whether the suspect wishes to answer questions." Gov't Br. 21. This Court has repeatedly held that a virtue of *Miranda* is the ease and clarity of its application by police and courts. See *Moran* v. *Burbine,* 475 U.S. 412, 425 (1986)

---

[14]*Cf. Garcia* v. *San Antonio Metro. Transit Auth.,* 469 U.S. 528, 546-47 (1985) (finding approval of whether particular governmental function is "'integral'" or "'traditional'" to be "unsound in principle and unworkable in practice").

("[a]s we have stressed on numerous occasions, '[o]ne of the principal advantages' of *Miranda* is the ease and clarity of its application") (second alteration in original); *Berkemer* v. *McCarty,* 468 U.S. 420, 432 (1984) (noting "the simplicity and clarity" of *Miranda*); see also *New York* v. *Quarles,* 467 U.S. 649, 664 (1984) (O'Connor, J., concurring in and dissenting in part) (*Miranda* rules have "'afforded police and courts clear guidance on the manner in which to conduct a custodial investigation.'"). Even 19 years ago, Chief Justice Burger declared: "[t]he meaning of *Miranda* has become reasonably clear and law enforcement practices have adjusted to its strictures; I would neither overrule *Miranda,* [nor] disparage it . . . at this late date." *Rhode Island* v. *Innis,* 446 U.S. 291, 304 (1980) (Burger, C.J., concurring).

Although the Court has noted that *Miranda*'s requirements may have led in some instances to the exclusion of statements that were not the product of physical or psychological coercion, [footnote 15] application of *Miranda* has not been shown to undermine law enforcement. Indeed, it is just as likely that the simplicity and lack of ambiguity in a *Miranda* waiver form have resulted in the admission of statements that might otherwise have been found to be compelled. At bottom, the "judgment and experience of federal law enforcement agencies is that *Miranda* is workable in practice and serves several significant law enforcement objectives." Gov't Br. 20. The minimum burdens *Miranda* imposes are in fact likely outweighed by the decision's benefits. See *Fare* v. *Michael C.,* 442 U.S. 707, 718 (1979) (noting that the "gain in specificity, which benefits the accused and the State alike, has been thought to outweigh the burdens that the decision in *Miranda* imposes on law enforcement agencies and the courts"). The benefit to the administration of justice is reflected in the fact that some federal agencies have expanded use of *Miranda* warnings to non-custodial settings. See Gov't Br. 21-22.

The ease with which *Miranda* is applied by courts, contrasts markedly with the difficulties that courts experienced attempting to apply the former Due Process Clause totality of the circumstances test for voluntariness, as even the dissent in *Miranda* reveals. See *Miranda,* 384 U.S. at 507 (Harlan, J., dissenting) (describing that in "more than 30 full opinions" "the voluntariness rubric was . . . never pinned down to a single meaning but on the contrary [the Court] infused it with a number of different values . . . . The outcome was a continuing re-evaluation on the facts of each case of *how much* pressure on the subject was permissible") (citation omitted).

B. Reliance.

While the Court has held that the "classic case for weighing reliance heavily in favor of following [an] earlier rule occurs in the commercial context," *Casey,* 505 U.S. at 855-56 (citing *Payne* v. *Tennessee,* 501 U.S. 808, 828 (1991), the Court has also considered whether reversal of a precedent would result in "significant damage to the stability of the society governed by it." *Id.,* at 855. For nearly thirty-five years, *Miranda*'s requirements have shaped law enforcement training, police conduct, the provision of counsel to those subjected to custodial interrogation and public expectations with respect to custodial interrogation. The *Miranda* warnings themselves have been widely popularized, and for good reason; they promote a perception of fairness, integrity and respect for the Constitution and criminal justice system. See Gov't Br. 36.

C. Subsequent Doctrinal Developments.

It cannot be said that "intervening development of the law, through . . . the growth of judicial doctrine," has removed *Miranda*'s doctrinal underpinnings. *Patterson,* 491 U.S. at 173 (year?). Just the opposite is true. The Court has consistently premised subsequent decisions on the continuing validity of *Miranda*'s core holding requiring the

---

[15] *See, e.g., Michigan* v. *Harvey,* 494 U.S. 344, 350 (1990) (*Miranda*'s exclusionary rule "result[s] in the exclusion of some voluntary and reliable statements").

suppression of unwarned statements in the prosecution's case-in-chief. See, *e.g., Minnick* v. *Mississippi,* 498 U.S. 146, 156 (1990) (suppressing statement given after defendant had requested and consulted with counsel, but while counsel was not present); *Pennsylvania* v. *Muniz,* 496 U.S. 582, 599 (1990) (suppressing unwarned response to question asked during station house sobriety test); *Berkemer,* 468 U.S. at 434 (holding unanimously that *Miranda* applies to questioning on misdemeanor charges).

In fact, the Court has expanded and clarified *Miranda*'s requirements with respect to the exclusion of unwarned statements in the prosecution's case in chief. For example, *Miranda* held that the police must terminate interrogation of an accused in custody if the accused requests assistance of counsel. 384 U.S. at 474. The Court reinforced the protections of *Miranda* in *Edwards* v. *Arizona,* 451 U.S. 477 (1981), which held that once the accused requests counsel, officials may not reinitiate questioning "until counsel has been made available to him, unless the accused himself initiates further communication, exchanges, or conversations with police." *Id.* at 484-85. *Edwards* is "designed to prevent police from badgering a defendant into waiving his previously asserted *Miranda* rights." *Michigan* v. *Harvey,* 494 U.S. 344, 350 (1990). In *Minnick,* the Court reinforced *Edwards,* holding that "when counsel is requested, interrogation must cease, and officials may not reinitiate interrogation *without counsel present, whether or not the accused has consulted with his attorney."* 498 U.S. at 153 (emphasis added). The Court stated that its holding in *Minnick* was consistent with *Miranda*'s observation that "'the need for counsel to protect the Fifth Amendment privilege comprehends not merely a right to consult with counsel prior to questioning, but also to have counsel present during any questioning if the defendant so desires.'" *Id.* at 154 (quoting *Miranda,* 384 U.S. at 470).

The Court's subsequent opinions have never suggested that Congress or the States could ignore *Miranda*'s core holdings and adopt procedures, such as those embodied in § 3501, that fail to require apprising accused persons of their Fifth Amendment rights. To the contrary, the Court has repeatedly imposed a heightened standard for waiver during custodial interrogation of the right to remain silent and the right to counsel. "The right to counsel recognized in *Miranda* is sufficiently important to suspects in criminal investigations, [the Court] ha[s] held, that it 'requir[es] the special protection of the knowing and intelligent waiver standard.'" *Davis* v. *United States,* 512 U.S. 452, 458 (1994) (third alteration in original) (quoting *Edwards* v. *Arizona,* 451 U.S. 477, 483 (1981)).

The Court has, under certain circumstances, continued to examine the application of *Miranda*'s exclusionary requirements to situations not considered in *Miranda.* The Court has also declined to extend *Miranda*'s exclusionary requirements to situations or types of evidence not considered in *Miranda.* See, *e.g., Michigan* v. *Tucker,* 417 U.S. 433, 449 (1974) (declining to extend exclusionary rule to testimony of witness discovered as a result of accused's statements); *Oregon* v. *Elstad,* 470 U.S. 298, 314-17 (1985) (declining to suppress statement made after warnings and valid waiver of rights where police had obtained earlier voluntary but unwarned statement); *Quarles,* 467 U.S. at 659-60 (refusing to suppress weapon found as a result of unwarned statements based on public safety exception to *Miranda*). The Court's carefully justified decisions not to extend *Miranda* in certain contexts in no way suggest that *Miranda*'s holdings are a "doctrinal anachronism." *Casey,* 505 U.S. at 855.

D. Unchanged Factual Premises.

In the intervening years since *Miranda,* the characteristics and circumstances of police interrogations have not changed in a manner that robs *Miranda*'s rule "of significant application or justification." *Casey,* 505 U.S. at 855. A cursory review of reported decisions demonstrates the point. See, *e.g., Cooper* v. *Dupnik,* 963 F.2d 1220, 1224 (9th Cir. 1992) (en banc) (according to pre-arranged plan, officers ignored subject's requests for counsel and interrogated him for four hours in hopes of obtaining a confession which they knew would be inadmissible, but could be used for impeachment); *Weaver v. Brenner*, 40 F.3d 527, 537 (2d Cir. 1994) (officers who had probably cause for arrest nonetheless conducted allegedly coercive interrogation in order to obtain confession). Even if, overall, the instances of "brutality" and physical coercion may have declined since 1966, any such decline is likely the result of adoption of *Miranda*'s rule requiring "procedures . . . effective in apprising accused persons of their right of silence and in assuring a continuous opportunity to exercise it," 384 U.S. at 467, thus fulfilling the Court's hope, if not prophecy, that the "proper limitation upon custodial interrogation" set forth in *Miranda* would "eradicate[]" physical coercion "in the foreseeable future." *Id.* at 447.

Moreover, it cannot be said that the psychological coercion that *Miranda* found inherent in private interrogations of citizens no longer exists. Custodial interrogations are still largely conducted in private, with accused citizens cut off from relatives, friends and attorneys. Individuals are still "thrust into an unfamiliar atmosphere and run through menacing police interrogation procedures." *Id.* at 457. This Court's own cases reflect this fact. See, *e.g., Minnick*, 498 U.S. at 153-54 ("The case before us well illustrates the pressures, and abuses, that may be concomitants of custody. . . . [T]hough [petitioner] resisted, he was required to submit to both the FBI and the [Sheriff] Denham interviews."). Put simply, the nature of the interrogation process has not changed so markedly since issuance of *Miranda* as to rob the Court's decision of significant application and justification.

Even were it found that *Miranda* has been so successful that most persons subjected to interrogation are aware of their right to remain silent, the *Miranda* warnings retain their importance. The warnings "show the individual that his interrogators are prepared to recognize his privilege should he choose to exercise it." *Id.* at 468. Further, *Miranda*'s procedures are necessary to ensure that an accused's attempt to exercise his rights is "fully honored." *Id.* at 467.

E. Miranda Is Not "Unsound In Principle."

Miranda's holdings are certainly neither unreasoned nor "unsound in principle." *Garcia*, 469 U.S. at 546-47. To the contrary, the decision was a proper act of constitutional interpretation. [footnote 16] First, *Miranda*'s minimum threshold requirements are consistent with the text and history of the Fifth Amendment. Second, it flows logically from, and closely matches, the scope of the underlying Fifth Amendment right. Third, these requirements were a natural outgrowth of judicial precedent and law enforcement experience. And fourth, having proven to be far easier to administer in courts, and by law enforcement, *Miranda*'s minimum requirements more effectively serve the purposes of the Fifth Amendment than the totality-of-the-circumstances test.

First, Miranda's minimum threshold requirements are consistent with the text of the Fifth Amendment, which states that "[n]o person . . . shall be compelled in any criminal case to be a witness against himself." U.S. Const. amend. V. (App. 1a). While expressed as a limitation on government power, the Fifth Amendment's prohibition against government efforts to coerce an individual to make incriminating statements necessarily means that the individual has an affirmative right to remain silent, and must be knowing, intelligent, and voluntary. See *Miranda*, 384 U.S. at 465. *Miranda*'s requirements simply assure that individuals can freely choose to exercise the right to remain silent.

The history of the Fifth Amendment also supports *Miranda*'s minimum threshold requirements. As the Court has noted, the Framers likely understood the Fifth

---

[16]While the method and result of the constitutional analysis were routine, *Miranda was* remarkable in that Court interpreted a "fundamental" right at the core of our democratic system.

Amendment to reflect common law rights, see *United States* v. *Balbys,* 118 S. Ct. 2218, 2232 & nn.13,14 (1998). The Framers certainly understood that the common-law and Constitutional rights against self-incrimination not only were part of a complex of other trial rights, but also were *evolving* rights that changed as criminal procedures developed. [footnote 17] The *Miranda* Court's crafting of the minimum threshold requirements in light of contemporary practices in the criminal justice system is fully consistent with this tradition. In addition, the core aspects of *Miranda*'s requirements echo views at the time of the framing. For example, it was understood that the privilege against self-incrimination, among other things, entitled a defendant to remain silent, rather than answer questions under oath posed by a government interrogator before trial. [footnote 18] And by the mid-nineteenth century, interrogators in both America and England advised defendants of their right to remain silent. [footnote 19] In that manner, too, *Miranda*'s requirements are consistent with the historical understanding of the right. [footnote 20] And more fundamentally, throughout its history, the principle against self-incrimination has stood as an expanding bulwark to protect the private interests enunciated by *Miranda,* including guarding individual conscience against government intrusion. [footnote 21]

Second, Miranda's minimum threshold requirements closely adhere to the scope of the underlying Fifth Amendment right. While phrasing the principle in somewhat different ways, the Court has repeatedly held for over a century, both before and after *Miranda,* that the "Fifth Amendment guarantees . . . the right of a person to remain silent unless he chooses to speak in the unfettered exercise of his own will, and to suffer no penalty . . . for such silence." *Malloy,* 378 U.S. at 7-8. Thus, the prohibition against "compelled" statements means that the statement must be "truly

---

[17]*See* Eben Moglen, *The Privilege in British North America: The Colonial Period to the Fifth Amendment, in The Privilege Against Self-Incrimination* 109, 136-41 (R.H. Helmholz et al. eds., 1997) ("*The Privilege*"); Henry E. Smith, *The Modern Privilege: Its Nineteenth-Century Origins, in The Privilege* 145, 148-59; *United States* v. *Balsys,* 118 S. Ct. 2218, 2223 (1998); *cf. Miranda,* 384 U.S. at 460; *id.* at 507-08 (Harlan, J., dissenting).

[18]*See* Albert W. Alschuler, *A Peculiar Privilege in Historical Perspective, in The Privilege* 181, 192.

[19]See *id.* at 198.

[20]The historical record is admittedly less clear as to the extent to which, at the time of the framing, interrogators could require defendants to make *unsworn* pretrial statements. Although the Marian committal statute of 1555 directed magistrates to interrogate suspects, and this practice was carried over into the manuals distributed to justices of the peace in Colonial America. John H. Langbein, *The Privilege and Common Law Criminal Procedure: The Sixteenth to the Eighteenth Centuries, in The Privilege* 82, 91-94; Moglen, *supra* at 116-17, there is evidence that commentators and a number of practitioners concluded that the right to remain silent applied to unsworn pre-trial statements as well. Moglen, *supra* at 141-43; Langbein, *supra* at 97. Moreover, it would be inappropriate to read the Fifth Amendment right as merely prohibiting the specific practices that were prohibited by statute or the common-law at the time of its adoption. First, such a venture is risky, because the historical record is spare and the Framers' understanding of the precise scope of the right is unclear. R.H. Helmholz, *Introduction, in The Privilege* 1, 11; Moglen, *supra* at 136-38. Second, as noted in the text, the right against self-incrimination was part of a cluster of other trial rights and was itself an evolving right that changed as criminal procedures changed. Third, to return to the practices at the time just before the Framing would be to revert to a world in which defendants were prohibited from testifying under oath on their own behalf, Langbein, *supra* at 88; Alschuler, *supra* at 198, which would require overruling *Rock* v. *Arkansas,* 483 U.S. 44 (1987); where, because counsel was generally unavailable as a matter of right or practice, defendants were effectively *required* to speak as unsworn advocates on their own behalf (which of course rendered any right against self-incrimination largely meaningless), Langbein, *supra* at 82-88; Alschuler, *supra* at 194-95, which would require overruling not only countless Fifth Amendment cases, but also *Gideon* v. *Wainwright,* 372 U.S. 335 (1963); and where the trier of fact could make unfavorable inferences from the defendants' failure to speak, Langbein, *supra* at 92, which would require overruling *Griffin* v. *California,* 380 U.S. 609 (1965).

[21]*See, e.g.,* R.H. Helmholz, *The Privilege and the Jus Commune: The Middle Ages to the Seventeenth Century, in The Privilege* 17, 21-29, 44; Charles M. Gray, *Self-Incrimination in Interjurisdictional Law: The Sixteenth and Seventeenth Centuries, in The Privilege* 47, 61-63; Langbein, *supra* at 103, 108.

the product of free choice." *Miranda*, 384 U.S. at 457, 458. [footnote 22] That is, the individual must make a knowing, intelligent, and voluntary choice not to remain silent. See, *e.g., id.* at 465. Given this scope of the underlying right, as well as the nature of custodial interrogation, it only makes sense that the individual be reminded of his right to remain silent and that other safeguards be put in place to assure that the individual's right is observed. See *id.* at 469-75.

Third, Miranda's holding was the natural outgrowth of more than 30 years of judicial experience with the totality-of-the-circumstances test. On the one hand, it *continued* the natural advancement in the Court's understanding of the nature of compulsion, which, as the principal dissent in *Miranda* noted, had evolved to require "close attention to the individual's state of mind and capacity for effective choice." *Id.* at 507 (Harlan, J., dissenting); see also, *e.g., Colorado v. Connelly*, 479 U.S. 157, 164 (1986) (Rehnquist, C.J.); *Blackburn v. Alabama*, 361 U.S. 199, 206 (1960). It also was faithful to the Court's longstanding admonition that the Fifth Amendment right be generously interpreted. See *Miranda*, 384 U.S. at 461 (citing cases); *id.* at 508 (Harlan, J., dissenting) (noting that the trend in the Court's decisions was "usually in the direction of restricting admissibility").

On the other hand, based up on 30 years of judicial experience, the *Miranda* Court *rejected* the totality of the circumstances test for measuring compulsion under the Fifth Amendment. In over 30 cases in as many years, the Court's analysis constantly changed, see *id.* at 507-08 (Harlan, J., dissenting), and the Court recognized that, given the proper focus on the mental state and capacity of the accused, continuing to engage in a totality-of-the circumstances analysis would involve pure "speculation." *Id.* at 468-69. Yet, this was not all. Even if the speculative exercise could be undertaken, *Miranda* also held that it was necessary for officials to inform even a suspect aware of his rights that his interrogators—these particular interrogators—themselves understood and would respect his rights. *Id.* This further requirement also flows from the need to ensure an unfettered choice. At bottom, then the inquiry necessary under a "totality of the circumstances" test, in order to ensure a knowing and voluntary waiver, would look no further than the "ascertainable fact" of whether the accused had been apprised of his rights. Thus, the Court quite properly recognized that *Miranda*'s minimum requirements were the only appropriate response.

Similarly, *Miranda*'s minimum threshold requirements were based on Court's understanding of the extensive practical experience of law enforcement. On the one hand, the core requirement of apprising the accused of his rights, safeguarding exercise of those rights, as well as the specific warnings, were based on similar rules in place for federal enforcement personnel. See *Miranda, id.* at 481-86. On the other hand, the imposition of the requirements as a matter of constitutional law reflected the Court's own institutional experience in analyzing the nature of police interrogations, *id.* at 448, 456, as well as its understanding of the difficulty of reconstructing what actually occurs during interrogations, see *id.* at 448. Moreover, the *Miranda* Court was mindful to minimize the burden imposed on law enforcement all it

---

[22]*See Withrow*, 507 U.S. at 689; *Doe v. United States*, 487 U.S. 201, 214 n.12 (1988); *Carter v. Kentucky*, 450 U.S. 288, 304 (1981); *Mincey v. Arizona*, 437 U.S. 385, 398 (1978) ("It is hard to imagine a situation less conducive to the exercise of 'a rational intellect and a free will' than Mincey's"); *Greenwald v. Wisconsin*, 390 U.S. 519, 521 (1968) ("Considering the totality of these circumstances, we do not think it credible that petitioner's statements were the product of his free and rational choice."); *Culombe v. Connecticut*, 367 U.S. 568, 583 (1961) ("[A]n extra-judicial confession, if it was to be offered in evidence against a man, must be the product of his own free choice."); *Payne v. Arkansas*, 356 U.S. 560, 567 (1958) ("It seems obvious from the *totality* of this course of conduct, and particularly the culminating threat of mob violence, that the confession was coerced and did not constitute an 'expression of free choice.'") (footnotes omitted); *Lisenba v. California*, 314 U.S. 219, 241 (1941) (no evidence that statements "were the result of the deprivation of his free choice to admit, to deny, or to refuse to answer"); *Bram v. United States*, 168 U.S. 532, 549 (1897) ("accused must be free of hope or fear in respect to the crime charged").

required were warnings and attendant procedural safeguards, with which law enforcement could easily comply. And it provided the political branches of both the States and federal government with flexibility to adopt alternative procedures, as long as they complied with the constitutional requirements that the accused be informed of his or her rights through the used of procedures as fully as effective as those announced by the Court.

Finally, over 30 years of additional experience since *Miranda* have proven that *Miranda*'s minimum requirements better serve the policies underlying the Fifth Amendment. While the Fifth Amendment serves a number of purposes, at bottom, it serves to protect "the dignity and integrity of its citizens," by striking a "'fair state-individual balance.'" *Id.* at 460 (quoting 8 Wigmore, *Evidence* 317 (McNaughton rev. 1961); see *Balsys*, 118 S. Ct. at 2232 (balancing private and governmental interests in determining the scope of the Fifth Amendment right). *Miranda*'s requirements strike a "fair[er]" balance than the totality-of-the-circumstances test. These minimum requirements better serve law enforcement, by providing a clear-cut rule for interrogating witnesses, rather than subjecting police to second guessing based on a more amorphous totality-of-the-circumstances test. They better serve the judiciary, by providing a test that is more easily and consistently administered, rather than reconstructing all of the circumstances of an interrogation and attempting to divine the defendant's state of mind. They better serve the individual, by helping to assure that the individual is aware of his rights and that those rights are respected. And adherence comes at little cost—it only requires that the warnings be administered, something that is an extraordinarily simple act.

F. Considerations That Transcend Traditional Factors.

Miranda has become one of the Court's most famous opinions of the twentieth century. Where the rules of cases have found "'"wide acceptance in the legal culture,'"" this "is adequate reason not to overrule these cases." *Mitchell* v. *United States,* 119 S. Ct. 1307, 1316 (1999), (Scalia, J. , dissenting). *Miranda*'s widespread acceptance extends beyond the legal culture. *Miranda*'s specific holding has become widely popularized through television and film and hence is emblazoned on the public's consciousness. Whatever concerns arose immediately in the aftermath of *Miranda* as to guilty defendants being released on a technicality has been replaced by an abiding respect for *Miranda* rights. The public correctly understands that the Court held in *Miranda* that to protect an individual's constitutional right to remain silent, law enforcement officers must inform suspects subjected to interrogation of their right to remain silent, that what they say can and will be used against them, that they have a right to an attorney, and if they cannot afford one, an attorney will be appointed for them, and that law enforcement officers must honor a suspect's request to remain silent or to have counsel.

Adherence to *Miranda*'s requirements has promoted public confidence that law enforcement officers and the courts are treating individuals subjected to custodial interrogation in a similar, fair and lawful manner that respects their constitutional right to remain silent. Overruling *Miranda* would thus erode public confidence that police and the courts are treating persons subjected to police custodial interrogation in a manner that appropriately and fairly respects their constitutional rights. As the United States notes, law enforcement depends on citizen cooperation and support, and a step such as overruling *Miranda*, which could undermine that support, should not be taken lightly. See Gov't Br. at 36.

Moreover, departing from *Miranda* would erode public confidence in the legitimacy of the Court's elucidation of constitutional principles. "The Court's power lies . . . in its legitimacy, a product of substance and perception that shows itself in the people's acceptance of the Judiciary as fit to determine what the Nation's law means and to declare what it demands." *Casey,* 505 U.S. at 865. Because neither the factual underpinnings of *Miranda*'s central holding nor subsequent evolution in the Court's jurisprudence justify abandoning *Miranda*, "the Court could not pretend to be reexamining [*Miranda*] with any justification beyond a present doctrinal disposition to come out differently." *Id.* at 864. A substantial reduction in the protections afforded by *Miranda* would, under these circumstances, needlessly upset "a carefully crafted balance designed to fully protect both the defendant's and society's interests." *Moran* v. *Burbine,* 475 U.S. 412, 433 n.4 (1986).

CONCLUSION

For the reasons stated above, the judgment of the court of appeals should be reversed. Respectfully submitted.

Carter G. Phillips James W. Hundley*

Jeffrey T. Green Briglia & Hundley, P.C.

Kurt H. Jacobs The Mosby Professional Building

Sidley & Austin 10560 Main Street, Suite 314

1722 Eye Street, N.W. Fairfax, Virginia 22030 Washington, D.C. 20006 (703) 385-8005 (202) 736-8000

Paul F. Washington

75 Rockefeller Plaza

New York, NY 10019

Counsel for Petitioner

January 28, 2000 * Counsel of Record

APPENDIX
RELEVANT CONSTITUTIONAL AND STATUTORY PROVISIONS

U.S. Const. amend. V.

No person shall be held to answer for a capital, or otherwise infamous crime, unless on a presentment or indictment of a grand jury, except in cases arising in the land or naval forces, or in the militia, when in actual service in time of war or public danger; nor shall any person be subject for the same offense to be twice put in jeopardy of life or limb, nor shall be compelled in any criminal case to be a witness against himself, nor be deprived of life, liberty, or property, without due process of law; nor shall private property be taken for public use, without just compensation.

18 U.S.C. § 3501 Admissibility of Confessions

(a) In any criminal prosecution brought by the United States or by the District of Columbia, a confession, as defined in subsection (e) hereof, shall be admissible in evidence if it is voluntarily given. Before such confession is received in evidence, the trial judge shall, out of the presence of the jury, determine any issue as to voluntariness. If the trial judge determines that the confession was voluntarily made it shall be admitted in evidence and the trial judge shall permit the jury to hear relevant evidence on the issue of voluntariness and shall instruct the jury to give weight to the confession as the jury feels it deserves under all the circumstances.

(b) The trial judge in determining the issue of voluntariness shall take into consideration all the circumstances surrounding the giving of the confession, including (1) the time elapsing between arrest and arraignment of the defendant making the confession, if it was made after arrest and before arraignment, (2) whether such defendant knew the nature of the offense with which he was charged or of which he was suspected at the time of making the confession, (3) whether or not such defendant was advised or knew that he was not required to make any statement and that any such statement could be used against him, (4) whether or not such defendant had been advised prior to questioning of his right to the assistance of counsel; and (5) whether or not such defendant was without the assistance of counsel when questioned and when giving such confession.

The presence of absence of any of the above-mentioned factors to be taken into consideration by the judge need not be conclusive on the issue of voluntariness of the confession.

(c) In any criminal prosecution by the United States or by the District of Columbia, a confession made or given by a person who is a defendant therein, while such person was under arrest or other detention in the custody of any law-enforcement officer or law-enforcement agency, shall not be inadmissible solely because of delay in bringing such person before a magistrate or other officer empowered to commit persons charged with offenses against the laws of the United States or of District of Columbia if such confession is found by the trial judge to have been made voluntarily and if the weight to be given the confession is left to the jury and if such confession was made or given by such person within six hours immediately following his arrest or other detention. *Provided,* That the time limitation contained in this subsection shall not apply in any case in which the delay in bringing such person before such magistrate or other officer beyond such six-hour period is found by the trial judge to be reasonable considering the means of transportation and the distance to be traveled to the nearest available such magistrate or other officer.

(d) Nothing contained in this section shall bar the admission in evidence of any confession made or given voluntarily by any person to any other person without interrogation by anyone, or at any time at which the person who made or gave such confession was not under arrest or other detention.

(e) As used in this section, the term "confession" means any confession of guilt of any criminal offense or any self-incriminating statement made or given orally or in writing.

SECTION
VII

Government Brief

NO. 99-5525

In the Supreme Court of the United States

CHARLES THOMAS DICKERSON, PETITIONER
V.
UNITED STATES OF AMERICA

ON WRIT OF CERTIORARI
TO THE UNITED STATES COURT OF APPEALS
FOR THE FOURTH CIRCUIT

BRIEF FOR THE UNITED STATES

JANET RENO
Attorney General

SETH P. WAXMAN
Solicitor General
Counsel of Record

JAMES K. ROBINSON
Assistant Attorney General

MICHAEL R. DREEBEN
Deputy Solicitor General

JAMES A. FELDMAN
LISA S. BLATT
Assistants to the Solicitor General

Department of Justice
Washington, D.C. 20530-0001
(202) 514-2217

QUESTION PRESENTED

Whether a voluntary confession may be admitted into evidence in the government's case-in-chief under 18 U.S.C. 3501, notwithstanding that the confession was taken in violation of the requirements of *Miranda* v. *Arizona,* 384 U.S. 436 (1966).

STATEMENT

1. On January 24, 1997, the First Virginia Bank in Alexandria, Virginia, was robbed of approximately $876. The robber carried a silver semi-automatic handgun and a black leather bag. Immediately after the robbery, a witness saw the robber place something into the trunk of a white Oldsmobile Ciera, get into the passenger side of the car, and ride away. The witness observed the getaway car's license plate number, and law enforcement agents determined that the car was registered to petitioner. J.A. 36-37, 140-141, 167.

On January 27, 1997, at around 5:30 p.m., a team including agents of the Federal Bureau of Investigation (FBI) and an Alexandria police detective went to petitioner's apartment in Takoma Park, Maryland. Several agents entered the apartment. [footnote 1] While the agents were there, FBI Special Agent Lawlor saw a large amount of cash (later determined to be $552) on petitioner's bed. Petitioner refused to allow the agents to search his apartment. Petitioner then accompanied the agents to the FBI field office in Washington, D.C. J.A. 37, 141-142, 167-168.

Agent Lawlor and Alexandria Detective Durkin interviewed petitioner at the FBI field office. Agent Lawlor testified that petitioner initially stated only that he had driven his white Oldsmobile Ciera to the Old Town area of Alexandria at about 10 a.m. to look at a restaurant. Petitioner also said that he parked his car and went to get a bagel. Agent Lawlor testified that the area in which petitioner was parked was near the scene of the bank robbery. J.A. 43, 168. Agent Lawlor testified that he then left the room and obtained by telephone a warrant to search petitioner's apartment. Id. at 43, 168-169. Lawlor testified that he returned to the interview room and told petitioner that other agents were about to search his apartment. Lawlor further testified that petitioner was then advised of his rights under *Miranda* v. *Arizona,* 384 U.S. 436 (1966), and waived those rights in writing. J.A. 44-46, 170.

According to Lawlor, after the waiver, petitioner admitted that he had been with Jimmy Rochester on the morning of the robbery, and that Rochester had previously committed numerous robberies and might have robbed the First Virginia Bank. Petitioner stated that both he and Rochester left petitioner's car to go separate places, and that when he returned, Rochester was already in the car and the two drove away. He also stated that he stopped the car at Rochester's request, and Rochester put something in the trunk. Later, Rochester told him to run a red light, and petitioner began to surmise that Rochester might have robbed a bank. Petitioner also said that later that day Rochester gave him a silver .45-caliber pistol, and that the agents might find the gun and dye-stained money in petitioner's apartment. J.A. 46-47, 170. Officers subsequently searched petitioner's apartment and found a .45-caliber handgun, dye-stained money and a bait bill from another robbery or robberies, ammunition, and masks. Id. at 56, 170.

---

[1] At the suppression hearing, the testimony of Special Agent Christopher Lawlor and that of petitioner diverged on several issues. See J.A. 141. For example, Agent Lawlor testified that the entry was by consent after he knocked on the door, ibid., while petitioner testified that the agents entered without being invited in, id. at 142.

2. A grand jury sitting in the Eastern District of Virginia indicted petitioner on one count of conspiracy to commit bank robbery, in violation of 18 U.S.C. 371, three counts of bank robbery, in violation of 18 U.S.C. 2113(a) and (d), and three counts of using a firearm during and in relation to a crime of violence, in violation of 18 U.S.C. 924(c). Petitioner moved to suppress his statements and the evidence seized from his apartment. The district court held a hearing at which Agent Lawlor and petitioner both testified. Petitioner testified that, contrary to Agent Lawlor's testimony, he had not been advised of his *Miranda* rights until after he had made all of the statements at issue.

Following the hearing, the district court granted petitioner's suppression motions. J.A. 140-155. With respect to the statements, the district court found that petitioner had been in custody during the questioning, and the court credited petitioner's testimony that he had not been read his *Miranda* rights and had not executed a waiver until after he had made all of the statements at issue. Id. at 151-155. The court also suppressed the evidence seized from petitioner's apartment pursuant to a search warrant. [footnote 2]

3. The government filed a motion for reconsideration. In support of its motion, the government submitted the affidavit of Detective Durkin, who was present throughout petitioner's interview. In his affidavit, Detective Durkin stated that petitioner had been read *Miranda* warnings and executed the written waiver before petitioner gave his more elaborate statement acknowledging his activities with Rochester on the day of the robbery. J.A. 102-103. The government further submitted petitioner's own handwritten statement acknowledging that he had been advised of his rights. Id. at 105. The government also argued (id. at 87) that even if petitioner's statements had been elicited in violation of *Miranda,* they were voluntary and therefore admissible under 18 U.S.C. 3501, which provides in relevant part that "[i]n any criminal prosecution brought by the United States or by the District of Columbia, a confession * * * shall be admissible in evidence if it is voluntarily given," 18 U.S.C. 3501(a), that "[t]he trial judge in determining the issue of voluntariness shall take into consideration all the circumstances surrounding the giving of the confession," and that the "presence or absence" of any particular factors "need not be conclusive on the issue of voluntariness of the confession," 18 U.S.C. 3501(b).

The district court denied the motion for reconsideration on the ground that the government had failed to establish that the additional evidence it proffered had been unavailable at the time of the suppression hearing. J.A. 159. The district court did not address Section 3501. See id. at 157-161.

4. The government appealed, and a divided panel of the court of appeals reversed. J.A. 162-225.

a. With respect to petitioner's statements, the court first held that the district court did not abuse its discretion in denying the government's motion for reconsideration, because the government had not availed itself of earlier opportunities to offer the additional evidence that petitioner had received *Miranda* warnings. J.A. 177-184. The court then turned to Section 3501. Although the majority noted that the government explicitly declined to make any argument based on 18 U.S.C. 3501 on appeal, Gov't C.A. Br. 34 n.19, the majority found that it was required to consider whether petitioner's statements were admissible under Section 3501 notwithstanding the absence of prior *Miranda* warnings. J.A. 184-191.

---

[2] Petitioner also moved to suppress a leather backpack and solvent used to clean dye-stained money, which were recovered from a search of the getaway car. The district court denied that motion. J.A. 144-145 & n.2.

The majority held that "[Section] 3501, rather than the judicially created rule of *Miranda*," governs the admissibility of confessions in federal court. J.A. 211. The majority noted that Congress had enacted Section 3501 "with the express purpose of legislatively overruling *Miranda*," id. at 197, and that Congress had the authority to do so only if the rules set forth in *Miranda* were not required by the Constitution, id. at 201. Relying on cases decided after *Miranda* in which this Court "referred to the warnings as 'prophylactic,' and 'not themselves rights protected by the Constitution,' " id. at 203-207 (citations omitted), the court of appeals held that "Congress necessarily possesses the legislative authority to supersede the conclusive presumption created by *Miranda* pursuant to its authority to prescribe the rules of procedure and evidence in the federal courts," id. at 207-208. The majority noted the dissent's contention that, under the majority's theory, it remained unexplained how this Court could continue to apply *Miranda* to state prosecutions if *Miranda* is not a constitutional rule. But the majority found that to be an "interesting academic question" that "has no bearing on our conclusion that *Miranda's* conclusive presumption is not required by the Constitution." Id. at 208 n.21.

The court of appeals therefore reversed the district court's order suppressing petitioner's statements. J.A. 211-212. Because the district court had refused to suppress the fruits of petitioner's statements, the court of appeals also concluded that the district court had "necessarily found that [petitioner's] statements were voluntary under the Fifth Amendment" and thus admissible under Section 3501. Ibid. [footnote 3]

b. Judge Michael dissented in part. He would not have addressed the applicability of Section 3501, because the government had not invoked the statute and the court of appeals did not have the benefit of full briefing and argument on the issue. J.A. 218-223. In his view, it was "a mistake for our court to push 3501 into this case." Id. at 221.

5. Petitioner sought rehearing en banc. The government filed a brief in support of partial rehearing en banc. In that brief (at 12), the government argued that the *Miranda* jurisprudence has a constitutional basis, and, accordingly, the lower federal courts are bound by *Miranda* unless and until the Supreme Court itself overrules it. Id. at 6 (citing *Agostini* v. *Felton,* 521 U.S. 203, 237 (1997)). The government thus concluded that the lower federal courts "may not apply Section 3501 to admit confessions that *Miranda* would exclude." Id. at 12.

The court of appeals denied rehearing en banc by an 8-5 vote. J.A. 226. This Court granted certiorari, limited to the first question presented by the petition, i.e., whether Section 3501 "was an unconstitutional attempt by Congress to legislatively overrule the Supreme Court's decision in *Miranda*." Pet. i; 120 S. Ct. 578 (1999). [footnote 4]

---

[3]The court of appeals also reversed the district court's order suppressing the physical evidence seized from petitioner's apartment. J.A. 212-217. Judge Michael disagreed with the majority's conclusion that the search warrant was sufficiently particular, but agreed that the evidence seized was nonetheless admissible pursuant to the good-faith exception. Id. at 224-225. This Court did not grant certiorari on this issue.

[4]We continue to believe that the court of appeals erred in concluding that it was free to depart from this Court's decision in *Miranda* based on a perception that that case was undermined by other precedents, and we also note (as we did in our brief in support of partial rehearing en banc at 13 n.5 and in our brief at the petition stage at 37-38 n.24) that, if the court of appeals had ordered the district court to consider the evidence presented by the government on motion for reconsideration, it might have avoided an unnecessary decision of a constitutional question, see *Ashwander* v. *TVA,* 297 U.S. 288, 347 (1936) (Brandeis, J., concurring). The Fourth Circuit nevertheless reached the validity of Section 3501. If this Court reverses the Fourth Circuit on that issue, and if the Fourth Circuit determines not to revisit its affirmance of the district court's refusal to hear the government's supplemental evidence on motion for reconsideration, the case will return to the district court for trial of petitioner based on the physical and testimonial evidence that shows petitioner's complicity in the charged bank-robbery and firearms offenses.

INTRODUCTION AND SUMMARY OF ARGUMENT

Section 3501 cannot constitutionally authorize the admission of a confession that would be excluded from evidence under this Court's *Miranda* cases. *Miranda* and its progeny represent an exercise of this Court's authority to implement and effectuate constitutional rights, and, accordingly, those decisions are binding on Congress. See *City of Boerne* v. *Flores,* 521 U.S. 507, 516-529 (1997); *Marbury* v. *Madison,* 5 U.S. (1 Cranch) 137 (1803). The voluntariness test in Section 3501 cannot supersede *Miranda* on the theory that *Miranda* represents only supervisory "rules of procedure and evidence," J.A. 208, because this Court's consistent application of *Miranda* to the States demonstrates that *Miranda* is a constitutionally based ruling. Section 3501 could be validly applied to require the admission in evidence of confessions that would be inadmissible under *Miranda* and its progeny only if this Court overrules its decisions in *Miranda* and the cases that have followed it. Taking into account principles of stare decisis and the role *Miranda* has come to play in the criminal justice system, we do not believe that *Miranda* should be overruled. Rather, we believe, as this Court concluded more than a decade ago, that *Miranda* "strikes the proper balance between society's legitimate law enforcement interests and the protection of the defendant's Fifth Amendment rights." *Moran* v. *Burbine,* 475 U.S. 412, 424 (1986).

I. Before this Court's decision in *Miranda* in 1966, the admissibility of a confession was judged under a voluntariness test, developed under the Due Process Clause, that took into account the totality of the circumstances. *Miranda* prescribed an additional inquiry based on the Fifth Amendment's Self-Incrimination Clause, which had been made applicable to the States in 1964. Two years after the decision in *Miranda,* Congress enacted Section 3501 to overrule *Miranda* in federal prosecutions and to return the law to the due process test that this Court had found inadequate in *Miranda.* Section 3501(a) accordingly provides that "a confession * * * shall be admissible in evidence if it is voluntarily given." Section 3501(b) specifies a list of non-exclusive factors that a judge "shall take into consideration" in making the voluntariness determination, but it provides that "[t]he presence or absence of any of [those factors] need not be conclusive." Because the factors listed in Section 3501(b) are non-exclusive, the weight to be given them is not specified, and their presence or absence is not determinative, Section 3501 would, if valid, return the law applied in federal prosecutions to its pre-*Miranda* state.

Returning the law to its pre-*Miranda* state is beyond Congress's power, because this Court's decision in *Miranda* was a constitutional decision and Congress may not overrule constitutional decisions of this Court. It is true that this Court has referred to the rule of *Miranda* as a "prophylactic rule" that sweeps more broadly than does the Fifth Amendment itself and that requires the suppression of some confessions that would be deemed voluntary under the due process totality-of-the-circumstances test. Nonetheless, this Court has also frequently stated that *Miranda's* requirements are based on its power to interpret and apply the Constitution. In addition, this Court has consistently applied *Miranda* to the States, including in three of the four consolidated cases that were resolved in the *Miranda* decision itself. Although the court of appeals believed that the application of *Miranda* to the States presented only an "interesting academic question," such application would not be permissible under the "supervisory" authority of this Court. The application of *Miranda* to the States therefore establishes that *Miranda's* requirements are constitutional in nature. This Court has also held that the *Miranda* rules are applicable on federal habeas review of state convictions-a holding that can be explained only on the premise that *Miranda* states a rule of constitutional law.

The court of appeals relied in part on this Court's statements in *Miranda* itself that it did not intend to create a "constitutional straitjacket" that would preclude any legislative action in this area, 384 U.S. at 467, and that "the Constitution does not require any specific code of procedures for protecting the privilege against self-incrimination during custodial interrogation," id. at 490. But the Court added several times in its opinion that any such legislative solution must be "fully as effective as [the *Miranda* rules themselves] in informing accused persons of their right of silence and in affording a continuous opportunity to exercise it." Ibid. The Court thus made clear that while the Constitution does not itself require that any particular measures be taken, nonetheless some measures must be taken that will be adequate for the purpose at hand-here, the protection of the Fifth Amendment privilege. Congress may not simply overrule *Miranda* and enact legislation like Section 3501 that provides no more protection to the Fifth Amendment privilege than did pre-*Miranda* law. The recognition in *Miranda* that Congress may choose to play a role in this area provides no support for the proposition that Congress may override a determination by this Court regarding what is necessary to provide adequate protection to constitutional rights.

II. Because the *Miranda* decision is of constitutional dimension, Congress may not legislate a contrary rule unless this Court were to overrule *Miranda*. We submit that principles of stare decisis do not favor the overruling of *Miranda*, and we do not request the Court to take that step. In the thirty-four years since that decision was handed down, it has become embedded in the law and defined through the decisions of this Court. If *Miranda* were to be overruled, this Court would have to disavow a long line of its cases that have interpreted *Miranda*, and it would have to overrule directly at least eleven cases that have reaffirmed that a confession obtained in violation of *Miranda* must be suppressed in the government's case-in-chief. At this date, there is no sufficient justification to overrule the balance struck in *Miranda* between the need for police questioning and the privilege against compelled self-incrimination, and there are substantial benefits to retaining that balance.

We acknowledge that there is a profound cost to the truthfinding function of a criminal trial when probative evidence is suppressed. That value necessarily must weigh heavily in this Court's appraisal of the continued validity of *Miranda*. In many respects, however, *Miranda* is beneficial to law enforcement. Its core procedures provide clear guidance to law enforcement officers, and thus are not difficult to administer. If those procedures are followed, a defendant will frequently forgo any challenge to the voluntariness of an ensuing confession, because the fact that a defendant chooses to speak after receiving *Miranda* warnings is highly probative that his confession was voluntary. By contrast, the totality-of-the-circumstances test that was the sole measure of a confession's admissibility before *Miranda*, and that would govern in its absence, would be much more difficult for the police and the courts to apply and much more uncertain in application.

There is no sufficient change in the factual premises on which this Court based its decision in *Miranda* that would justify revisiting its holding. Although technological changes-such as the availability of videotaping-might be of relevance as a part of a package of safeguards intended to provide alternative protection for the Fifth Amendment privilege, Section 3501 does not adopt those safeguards or any others to ensure that a suspect is aware of his rights and has an opportunity to exercise them.

Finally, both the confidence of the public in the fairness of the criminal justice system and the stability of this Court's constitutional jurisprudence are of surpassing importance to the system of justice, and each may be expected to suffer if *Miranda* were overruled. Those values weigh heavily against discarding the essence of the balance that the Court struck in *Miranda*. Accordingly, *Miranda* should not be overruled, and Section 3501 cannot constitutionally authorize the admission of a statement that would be excluded under this Court's *Miranda* cases.

ARGUMENT

I. SECTION 3501 COULD BE VALIDLY APPLIED TO REQUIRE THE ADMISSION IN EVIDENCE OF CONFESSIONS THAT WOULD BE INADMISSIBLE UNDER *MIRANDA* AND ITS PROGENY ONLY IF THIS COURT WERE TO OVERRULE ITS DECISIONS IN *MIRANDA* AND THE CASES THAT HAVE FOLLOWED IT

The text and legislative history of Section 3501 demonstrate that it was intended to restore the pre-*Miranda* totality-of-the-circumstances voluntariness test as the sole test for admitting confessions in federal court. [footnote 5] An examination of this Court's cases, however, reveals that this Court decided *Miranda*, and has continued to apply it in numerous subsequent cases, in the exercise of its power to interpret and apply the Constitution. Accordingly, unless this Court overrules its decision in *Miranda*, Congress does not have the authority to return the law to its pre-*Miranda* state. *City of Boerne* v. *Flores*, 521 U.S. 507, 516-529 (1997). Section 3501 therefore may not validly be applied to permit the admission of a confession that would be inadmissible under *Miranda* and its progeny.

A. Section 3501 Was Intended To And Does Return To The Pre-*Miranda* Voluntariness Test

1. In *Brown* v. *Mississippi,* 297 U.S. 278 (1936), this Court first reversed a criminal conviction on the ground that it was based on a confession that was obtained by physical force in violation of the Due Process Clause. As the Court explained in *Schneckloth* v. *Bustamonte,* 412 U.S. 218, 223 (1973), "[i]n some 30 different cases decided during the era that intervened between *Brown and Escobedo* v. *Illinois,* 378 U.S. 478 [(1964)], the Court was faced with the necessity of determining whether in fact the confessions in issue had been 'voluntarily' given." The due process "voluntariness" test that emerged from those cases demands an inquiry into "whether a defendant's will was overborne," id. at 226, and it requires a reviewing court to "assess[] the totality of all the surrounding circumstances-both the characteristics of the accused and the details of the interrogation," ibid. The Court emphasized in *Schneckloth* that "none of [the confession cases] turned on the presence or absence of a single controlling criterion; each reflected a careful scrutiny of all the surrounding circumstances." Ibid.

2. In 1964, the Supreme Court decided *Malloy* v. *Hogan,* 378 U.S. 1 (1964), which held that the Fifth Amendment's Self-Incrimination Clause is applicable to the States because it is incorporated in the Fourteenth Amendment's Due Process Clause. [footnote 6] Two years later in *Miranda,* the Court thus addressed afresh the issue of the admissibility of confessions in state courts, operating for the first time under the Self-Incrimination Clause, rather than the Fourteenth Amendment's Due Process Clause. The Court reached the now-familiar conclusion that statements stemming from custodial interrogation of a suspect are inadmissible at trial unless the police first provide the suspect with a set of four specific warnings. [footnote 7] 384 U.S. at 444. The Court noted that, while it might not find statements taken without the warnings "to have been involuntary in traditional terms," id. at 457, procedural safeguards were necessary because custodial interrogation is inherently coercive. The Court thus reasoned that, "[u]nless adequate protective devices are employed to dispel the compulsion inherent in custodial surroundings, no statement obtained from the defendant can truly be the product of his free choice." Id. at 458; see id. at 467.

---

[5]Except where otherwise indicated, our references to Section 3501 refer only to Section 3501(a) and (b). The balance of Section 3501 addresses other issues not pertinent here. See note 14, infra.

[6]*See Michigan* v. *Tucker,* 417 U.S. 433, 442-443 (1974) ("Th[e] privilege had been made applicable to the States in *Malloy* v. *Hogan* * * * and was thought to offer a more comprehensive and less subjective protection than the doctrine of previous cases.").

[7]Those warnings are that (1) the defendant has the right to remain silent; (2) any statement he makes may be used as evidence against him; (3) he has the right to the presence of an attorney; and (4) if he cannot afford an attorney, one will be appointed for him. 384 U.S. at 479. The Court made clear that, in specifying warnings-and-waiver procedures, it did not preclude Congress and the States from "develop[ing] their own safeguards for the privilege, so long as they are fully as effective as those described above in informing accused persons of their right of silence and in affording a continuous opportunity to exercise it." Id. at 490. See pp. 26-29, infra.

3. In 1968, Congress enacted Section 3501. As the court of appeals noted, "[b]ased on the statutory language alone, it is clear that Congress enacted 3501 with the express purpose of returning to the pre-*Miranda* case-by-case determination of whether a confession was voluntary." J.A. 199. [footnote 8] Section §3501(a) provides in pertinent part that "[i]n any criminal prosecution brought by the United States or by the District of Columbia, a confession * * * shall be admissible in evidence if it is voluntarily given." Section 3501(b) provides that a trial judge "determining the issue of voluntariness shall take into consideration all the circumstances surrounding the giving of the confession, including" five factors. Those factors are

(1) the time elapsing between arrest and arraignment of the defendant making the confession, * * * (2) whether such defendant knew the nature of the offense with which he was charged or of which he was suspected at the time of making the confession, (3) whether or not such defendant was advised or knew that he was not required to make any statement and that any such statement could be used against him, (4) whether or not such defendant had been advised prior to questioning of his right to the assistance of counsel; and (5) whether or not such defendant was without the assistance of counsel when questioned and when giving such confession.

18 U.S.C. 3501(b). Section 3501(b) goes on to specify, however, that "[t]he presence or absence of any of the above-mentioned factors to be taken into consideration by the judge need not be conclusive on the issue of voluntariness of the confession."

In setting forth the basic rule that a confession "shall be admissible in evidence if it is voluntarily given," Section 3501(a) restates the due process "voluntariness" test that governed the admissibility of confessions before this Court decided *Miranda.* Section 3501(b) confirms that the statute's "voluntariness" test is identical to that applied under pre-*Miranda* law by providing that "the issue of voluntariness shall take into consideration all the circumstances surrounding the giving of the confession." Compare *Schneckloth,* 412 U.S. at 226 (before *Miranda,* admissibility of confession was based on "totality of all the surrounding circumstances"); *Haynes* v. *Washington,* 373 U.S. 503, 513 (1963) ("an examination of all of the attendant circumstances"); *Gallegos* v. *Colorado,* 370 U.S. 49, 55 (1962) ("There is no guide to the decision of cases such as this, except the totality of circumstances."); *Reck* v. *Pate,* 367 U.S. 433, 440 (1961) ("all the circumstances attendant upon the confession must be taken into account"); *Malinski* v. *New York,* 324 U.S. 401, 404 (1945) ("If all the attendant circumstances indicate that the confession was coerced or compelled, it may not be used to convict a defendant.").

The listing of five specific factors in Section 3501(b) that a court "shall take into consideration" does not alter the conclusion that Section 3501 purports to reinstate the pre-*Miranda* voluntariness test. It is difficult to see how the enumeration of any number of non-exclusive factors would differ from the pre-existing analysis, which required consideration of all factors that might bear on voluntariness. In this respect, it is significant that the five factors are neither exclusive nor determinative-as Section 3501(b) states, their "presence or absence * * * need not be conclusive on the issue of voluntariness." Nor are they necessarily the most

---

[8]The language of Section 3501 requires the admission of all voluntary confessions. Accordingly, it would logically extend to post-arraignment confessions that are taken in violation of the Sixth Amendment and would be inadmissible under *Massiah* v. *United States,* 377 U.S. 201 (1964), and to confessions that were the fruits of a Fourth Amendment violation and hence inadmissible under *Wong Sun* v. *United States,* 371 U.S. 471 (1963). Applying Section 3501 according to its terms would therefore apparently require that two additional lines of cases be overruled. Neither, however, is at issue in this case.

significant factors; the use or threat of violence or other similar treatment by an interrogator, for example, could easily dictate the conclusion that a confession is involuntary without regard to any other factors. [footnote 9]

Furthermore, the five factors had specifically been recognized by this Court as significant under the pre-*Miranda* voluntariness test, so that their listing in Section 3501(b) marked no change from pre-*Miranda* law. For example, the presence of counsel during interrogation had always been an important factor in establishing voluntariness. [footnote 10] Two other factors-the defendant's knowledge of his right to remain silent and of his right to the assistance of counsel-had also been a regular part of the analysis. [footnote 11] Since its decision in *Brown,* the Court had frequently adverted to the length of time the defendant had been held in custody as an important factor in determining voluntariness, and that factor had apparently been dispositive in some cases. [footnote 12]

---

[9] *See, e.g., Stein* v. *New York,* 346 U.S. 156, 182 (1953) ("Physical violence or threat of it * * * serves no lawful purpose, invalidates confessions that otherwise would be convincing, and is universally condemned by the law. When present, there is no need to weigh or measure its effects on the will of the individual victim."); *Brown* v. *Mississippi,* 297 U.S. 278, 285-286 (1936) ("The rack and torture chamber may not be substituted for the witness stand."); *cf. Ashcraft* v. *Tennessee,* 322 U.S. 143, 151 (1944) (defendant questioned by relays of interrogators for 36 hours without sleep).

[10] *See, e.g., Haynes* v. *Washington,* 373 U.S. 503, 507 (1963) (holding confession involuntary where police refused defendant's requests to call attorney); *Gallegos* v. *Colorado,* 370 U.S. 49, 55 (1962) (holding confession involuntary where there was a "failure to see to it that [the defendant] had the advice of a lawyer or a friend"); *Spano* v. *New York,* 360 U.S. 315, 323 (1959) (holding confession involuntary where police "ignored [the defendant's] reasonable requests to contact the local attorney whom he had already retained"); *Cicenia* v. *Lagay,* 357 U.S. 504, 509 (1958) (holding confession voluntary, but noting that "defendant's lack of counsel [is] one pertinent element"); *Leyra* v. *Denno,* 347 U.S. 556, 561 (1954) (holding confession involuntary where defendant was "unprotected by counsel" at time of confession); *Haley* v. *Ohio,* 332 U.S. 596, 600 (1948) (plurality opinion) (holding confession involuntary where "[n]o lawyer stood guard * * * to see to it that [the police] stopped short of the point where [the defendant] became the victim of coercion"); *Malinski* v. *New York,* 324 U.S. 401, 405 (1945) (holding confession involuntary where among the "circumstances [that] stand out" are that defendant "was not allowed to see a lawyer, though he asked for one"); *Lisenba* v. *California,* 314 U.S. 219, 240 (1941) (holding confession voluntary where "[c]ounsel had been afforded full opportunity to see [defendant] and had advised him," but noting that special scrutiny is required where defendant "is subjected to questioning by officers for long periods, and deprived of the advice of counsel").

[11] *See, e.g., Haynes,* 373 U.S. at 510-511 (holding confession involuntary where defendant not "advised by authorities of his right to remain silent, warned that his answers might be used against him, or told of his rights respecting consultation with an attorney"); *Culombe* v. *Connecticut,* 367 U.S. 568, 609-610 (1961) (opinion of Frankfurter, J.) (holding confession involuntary where "[t]here is no indication that at any time [the defendant] was warned of his right to keep silent."); *Crooker* v. *California,* 357 U.S. 433, 438 (1958) (holding confession voluntary where there was "police statement to [the defendant] that he did not have to answer questions"); *Ashdown* v. *Utah,* 357 U.S. 426, 428 (1958) (holding confession voluntary where, inter alia, interrogator "advised [the defendant] that she did not have to answer any questions and that she was entitled to consult with an attorney"); *Payne* v. *Arkansas,* 356 U.S. 560, 567 (1958) (holding confession involuntary where defendant "was not advised of his right to remain silent or of his right to counsel"); *Brown* v. *Allen,* 344 U.S. 443, 476 (1953) (holding confession voluntary where "[t]here is evidence that petitioner was told he could remain silent and that any statement he might make could be used against him"); *Harris* v. *South Carolina,* 338 U.S. 68, 70 (1949) (opinion of Frankfurter, J.) (holding confession involuntary where there was "failure to advise the petitioner of his rights"); *Turner* v. *Pennsylvania,* 338 U.S. 62, 64 (1949) (opinion of Frankfurter, J.) (holding confession involuntary where defendant was "not informed of his right to remain silent until after he had been under the pressure of a long process of interrogation and had actually yielded to it"); *Haley,* 332 U.S. at 598 (plurality opinion) (holding confession involuntary where "[a]t no time was [the defendant] advised of his right to counsel.").

[12] *See Stein* v. *New York,* 346 U.S. at 187 (Because "[t]o delay arraignment, meanwhile holding the suspect incommunicado, facilitates and usually accompanies use of 'third-degree' methods, * * * we regard such occurrences as relevant circumstantial evidence in the inquiry as to physical or psychological coercion."); see also *Reck* v. *Pate,* 367 U.S. 433, 440 (1961) (holding confession involuntary where defendant held four days before first confession and an additional four days before arraignment); *Thomas* v. *Arizona,* 356 U.S. 390, 401 n.8 (1958) (holding confession voluntary where, "[u]nlike many cases where this Court has found coercion, there apparently was no failure here to comply with the state statute requiring that a prisoner be taken before a magistrate without unnecessary delay after arrest"); *Fikes* v. *Alabama,* 352 U.S. 191, 194-197 (1957) (holding confession involuntary where defendant held without arraignment five days before first confession and an additional five days before second confession); *Watts* v. *Indiana,* 338 U.S. 49, 52-53 (1949) (opinion of Frankfurter, J.) (holding confession involuntary where defendant held five days without arraignment before confessing); *Turner,* 338 U.S. at 64 (opinion of Frankfurter, J.) (holding confession involuntary where defendant held five days without arraignment before confessing); *Chambers* v. *Florida,* 309 U.S. 227, 239 (1940) (holding confession involuntary where defendants held without arraignment incommunicado five days).

One Section 3501(b) factor that had received less attention in this Court's pre-*Miranda* confession cases was whether the "defendant knew the nature of the offense with which he was charged or of which he was suspected." 18 U.S.C. 3501(b). In at least one case, however, in determining the voluntariness of a confession, the Court had referred to the fact that "[n]o warrant was read to [the defendant] and he was not informed of the charge against him." *Harris* v. *South Carolina,* 338 U.S. 68, 69 (1949); see also id. at 72 (Douglas, J., concurring) (mentioning same factor). In any event, Section 3501 does not dictate the weight to be given this factor in the analysis of whether a confession is voluntary. In *Colorado* v. *Spring,* 479 U.S. 564, 577 (1987), the Court "h[e]ld that a suspect's awareness of all the possible subjects of questioning in advance of interrogation is not relevant to determining whether the suspect voluntarily, knowingly, and intelligently waived his Fifth Amendment privilege." Accordingly, the defendant's knowledge of the crimes of which he is suspected is an insignificant factor in the voluntariness inquiry. [footnote 13]

4. The history of Section 3501 confirms that Congress intended Section 3501 to overrule this Court's decision in *Miranda* and restore the totality-of-the-circumstances test of voluntariness in federal prosecutions. Senator McClellan introduced the original bill, S. 674, to "rectify" what he perceived as "the mockery of justice" reflected in the "5-to-4" *Miranda* decision and to restore "voluntariness [as] the only test" for determining the admissibility of a confession. 113 Cong. Rec. 1583, 1584 (1967). [footnote 14] Senator McClellan expressed similar views during the Senate hearings on the bill in the Spring and Summer of 1967. Controlling Crime Through More Effective Law Enforcement: Hearings Before the Subcomm. on Crim. Laws and Procedures of the Senate Comm. on the Judiciary, 90th Cong., 1st Sess. 1174 (1967) (Hearings) ("In view of the *Miranda* decision, we have the bill that I introduced which would restore what had been a traditional procedure heretofore."). And Attorney General Ramsey Clark advised the Senate that S. 674 was unconstitutional to the extent it "intended to dispense with the requirement that [*Miranda*] warnings be given and to substitute a flexible standard that the presence or absence of such warnings need only be considered on the issue of voluntariness." Id. at 82. [footnote 15]

---

[13]Indeed, because a defendant's knowledge of the crimes of which he is suspected is "not relevant" to the validity of a defendant's waiver of his rights under *Spring,* even if Section 3501 expressly gave that factor great weight in determining whether a confession was admissible, it would not accomplish any purpose in protecting the defendant's Fifth Amendment rights. It would therefore not respond to any concern underlying this Court's determination in *Miranda* that exclusive reliance on the pre-*Miranda* "voluntariness" test was inadequate.

[14]The bill was part of Title II of the Omnibus Crime Control and Safe Streets Act of 1967. Title II also contained provisions designed to overturn this Court's decisions in *McNabb* v. *United States,* 318 U.S. 332 (1943), and *Mallory* v. *United States,* 354 U.S. 449 (1957), which held that delay before bringing an accused before a magistrate bars the admission of the accused's pre-arraignment confession, and *United States* v. *Wade,* 388 U.S. 218 (1967), which established the right of an accused to have counsel at police line-ups. Those provisions ultimately were enacted as 18 U.S.C. 3501(c) and 3502, which are not at issue in this case. Title II also contained provisions that the Senate failed to pass which would have stripped the Supreme Court and federal courts of jurisdiction to review state-court decisions admitting confessions and would have abolished federal habeas corpus review of state-court judgments. See S. Rep. No. 1097, 90th Cong., 2d Sess. 10 (1968); 114 Cong. Rec. 11,189 (1968).

[15]In its original form, S. 674 provided in subsection (b) that a court "shall take into consideration all the circumstances surrounding the giving of the confession," but nothing in the bill expressly stated that a court could find a confession voluntary in the absence of the warnings set forth in *Miranda.* Hearings 74. The Attorney General of California therefore testified that the Senate should close that "possible loophole" by amending S. 674 "to provide that the presence or absence of any of the factors listed in subsection (b) shall not be conclusive on the issue of voluntariness." Hearings 926 (statement of Thomas C. Lynch). The bill was subsequently amended to provide, as it presently does, that "[t]he presence or absence of any of the above-mentioned factors to be taken into consideration by the judge need not be conclusive of the issue of voluntariness," thereby removing any doubt that Congress intended to dispense with the requirements laid down in *Miranda.*

The Senate Committee Report accompanying Section 3501 stated that the Committee was convinced by the evidence presented during the Senate hearings "that the rigid and inflexible requirements of the majority opinion in the *Miranda* case are unreasonable, unrealistic, and extremely harmful to law enforcement" and that the proper test for admissibility should be the traditional "totality of circumstances" test of voluntariness that was endorsed by the dissenting Justices in *Miranda*. S. Rep. No. 1097, 90th Cong., 2d Sess. 46, 49-51 (1968).[16] During the weeks of debate concerning Section 3501, members of both the House and Senate similarly expressed their understanding that the statute was designed to restore the law on the admissibility of confessions as it existed before *Miranda*. [footnote 17]

B. This Court's Decisions In *Miranda* And The Cases That Have Followed It Reveal That The *Miranda* Rule Is Based On This Court's Authority To Interpret And Apply The Constitution

1. In *Miranda* itself, the Court left no doubt that it was basing its decision on the Court's authority to interpret and apply the Constitution. The Court began its opinion by noting that it had granted certiorari "to explore some facets of the problems * * * of applying the privilege against self-incrimination to incustody interrogation, and to give concrete constitutional guidelines for law enforcement agencies and courts to follow." 384 U.S. at 441-442. The balance of the opinion is replete with references to the constitutional basis for the decision-"rights grounded in a specific requirement of the Fifth Amendment of the Constitution." Id. at 489. As the Court held, the unwarned confessions in the four cases before the Court in *Miranda* "were obtained from the defendant under circumstances that did not meet constitutional standards for protection of the privilege." Id. at 491. [footnote 18]

---

[16]The committee members in the minority agreed that Section 3501 "repeal[ed]" *Miranda* by making "voluntariness the sole criterion of the admissibility of a confession in a Federal court." S. Rep. No. 1097, supra, at 148.

[17]See, e.g., 114 Cong. Rec. 11,206 (1968) (Sen. McClellan) (statute would "restore" voluntariness test as "the only test * * * in determining admissibility"); id. at 11,594 (Sen. Morse) (Section 3501 "would overrule" *Miranda*); id. at 11,612 (Sen. Thurmond) (statute "would restore the test for admissibility of confessions in criminal cases to that time-tested and well-founded standard of voluntariness"); id. at 13,202 (Sen. Scott) (statute "would restore the test which had been in use and considered constitutional until recent Supreme Court decisions, most notably *Miranda* v. *Arizona*"); id. at 14,136 (Sen. Fong) ("Sections 3501(a) and (b) * * * would overrule all of the *Miranda* standards and render them merely as guidelines to determine the admissibility and the weight to be given a confession."); id. at 14,158 (Sen. Hart) (statute "would repeal" *Miranda*); id. at 14,167 (Sen. McIntyre) (statute "would overrule [*Miranda*], whereby the Court established a constitutional requirement * * * above and beyond the traditional test of voluntariness"); id. at 14,176 (Sen. Erin) ("John Marshall said that voluntary confessions are admissible. And this is what the Constitution meant until the 13th day of June, 1966, when an attempt was made by five Judges to change the Constitution over the opposition of the other four Judges."); id. at 16,066 (Rep. Cellar) ("the main purpose * * * is to overrule [*Miranda*]"); id. at 16,075 (Rep. Rogers) (statute "is the first step to reverse the actions of the Supreme Court of the United States in favoring the criminals"); id. at 16,296 (Rep. Randall) (statute "simply provides that confessions may be voluntarily given, notwithstanding the line of decisions announced by the U.S. Supreme Court").

[18]See also 384 U.S. at 445 ("The constitutional issue we decide in each of these cases is the admissibility of statements obtained from a defendant questioned while in custody.") (emphasis added), 457 (referring to the Court's "concern for adequate safeguards to protect precious Fifth Amendment rights") (emphasis added), 458 (examining "history and precedent underlying the Self-Incrimination Clause to determine its applicability in this situation") (emphasis added), 476 ("The requirement of warnings and waiver of rights is a fundamental with respect to the Fifth Amendment privilege and not simply a preliminary ritual to existing methods of interrogation.") (emphasis added), 478 ("The fundamental import of the privilege while an individual is in custody is not whether he is allowed to talk to the police without the benefit of warnings and counsel, but whether he can be interrogated.") (emphasis added), 479 ("The whole thrust of our foregoing discussion demonstrates that the Constitution has prescribed the rights of the individual when confronted with the power of government when it provided in the Fifth Amendment that an individual cannot be compelled to be a witness against himself.") (emphasis added), 481 n.52 ("[d]ealing as we do here with constitutional standards in relation to statements made") (emphasis added), 490 ("the issues presented are of constitutional dimensions and must be determined by the courts") (emphasis added).

2. In a line of cases beginning with *Michigan* v. *Tucker,* 417 U.S. 433 (1974), the Court has held that a failure to apply *Miranda's* interrogation safeguards is not per se a constitutional violation and that a statement will not invariably be deemed "compelled" in violation of the Fifth Amendment simply because it was unwarned. In *Tucker,* the Court declined to suppress the testimony of a witness whose identity was learned from a statement taken from the defendant in violation of *Miranda,* because the Court found that the police conduct at issue did not "breach the right against compulsory self-incrimination[,] * * * but departed only from the prophylactic standards later laid down by this Court in *Miranda* to safeguard that privilege," 417 U.S. at 445-446, and because "[t]he deterrent purpose of the exclusionary rule" would not have been served in that case, id. at 447.

   Since *Tucker,* this Court has frequently observed that the *Miranda* rules are "prophylactic" in character and that an unwarned statement is not necessarily "compelled" in violation of the Fifth Amendment. See, e.g., *Davis* v. *United States,* 512 U.S. 452, 457 (1994); *Duckworth* v. *Eagan,* 492 U.S. 195, 203 (1989); *Connecticut* v. *Barrett,* 479 U.S. 523, 528 (1987). Consistent with the description of *Miranda's* procedures as prophylactic, the Court has weighed the advantages and disadvantages of *Miranda* in defining its application. In *Oregon* v. *Elstad,* 470 U.S. 298 (1985), the Court declined to suppress the fruits of an unwarned statement, emphasizing that the "fruit of the poisonous tree" doctrine "assumes the existence of a constitutional violation" (id. at 305), but that "[t]he *Miranda* exclusionary rule * * * may be triggered even in the absence of a Fifth Amendment violation." Id. at 306. The Court has also recognized a "public safety" exception to *Miranda's* "prophylactic rule," stating that a violation of the procedural safeguards of *Miranda* is not itself a violation of the Fifth Amendment. *New York* v. *Quarles,* 467 U.S. 649, 657 (1984). And the Court has concluded that unwarned statements may be used to impeach a testifying defendant at trial, notwithstanding the violation of *Miranda,* if the traditional test for "voluntariness" is satisfied. See *Oregon* v. *Hass,* 420 U.S. 714, 722-723 (1975); *Harris* v. *New York,* 401 U.S. 222, 224 (1971).

   Considered in isolation, the language used in *Tucker* and its progeny that a violation of *Miranda* is not itself a violation of the Constitution could be read to support an inference that *Miranda* is not a constitutional rule. Indeed, the Fourth Circuit read those statements to mean that *Miranda* is simply a "judicially created rule" that may be supplanted by legislation. J.A. 211. A well-established line of this Court's cases, however, requires the conclusion that *Miranda,* as applied by this Court, does indeed rest on a constitutional basis.

3. Beginning with *Miranda* itself, this Court has repeatedly applied the warnings requirement, and its associated suppression remedy, to cases arising in state courts. [footnote 19] See, e.g., *Stansbury* v. *California,* 511 U.S. 318 (1994) (per curiam); *Minnick* v. *Mississippi,* 498 U.S. 146 (1990); *Arizona* v. *Roberson,* 486 U.S. 675 (1988); *Edwards* v. *Arizona,* 451 U.S. 477, 481-482 (1981). Although this Court has the power to announce rules of procedure and evidence binding on federal courts, it has consistently disclaimed-both before and after *Miranda*-any such supervisory authority over state courts. The Court's authority in state cases "is limited to enforcing the commands of the United States Constitution." *Mu'Min* v. *Virginia,* 500 U.S. 415, 422

---

[19]Three of the four consolidated cases in *Miranda* itself arose in state courts, as did *Tucker, Elstad, Quarles,* and other cases on which the court of appeals relied in concluding that *Miranda* lacks a constitutional basis. The fourth of the consolidated cases in *Miranda* involved a federal conviction (*Westover* v. *United States,* No. 761).

(1991). See *Smith* v. *Phillips,* 455 U.S. 209, 221 (1982) ("Federal courts hold no supervisory authority over state judicial proceedings and may intervene only to correct wrongs of constitutional dimension."); *Cicenia* v. *Lagay,* 357 U.S. 504, 508-509 (1958) ("Were this a federal prosecution we would have little difficulty in dealing with [the admissibility of the confession] under our general supervisory power over the administration of justice in the federal courts. But to hold that what happened here violated the Constitution of the United States is another matter.") (citation omitted). Because federal judges "may not require the observance of any special procedures" in state courts "except when necessary to assure compliance with the dictates of the Federal Constitution," *Harris* v. *Rivera,* 454 U.S. 339, 344-345 (1981) (per curiam), the Court's continued application of *Miranda's* exclusionary rule in state cases necessarily means that *Miranda* rests on the Court's authority to apply the Constitution.

The same point is manifest in this Court's holding that claims of *Miranda* violations are cognizable on federal habeas review. See *Withrow* v. *Williams,* 507 U.S. 680, 690-695 (1993); see also *Thompson* v. *Keohane,* 516 U.S. 99 (1995). Habeas corpus is available only for claims that a person "is in custody in violation of the Constitution or laws or treaties of the United States." 28 U.S.C. 2254(a). Because *Miranda* is not a "law" or a "treaty," the Court's holding in *Withrow* necessarily depends on the premise that the requirements of *Miranda* implement and protect constitutional rights.

Significantly, this Court has regularly described the *Miranda* holding, and subsequent extensions of that holding, as resting on constitutional grounds. See, e.g., *Illinois* v. *Perkins,* 496 U.S. 292, 296 (1990) (describing *Miranda* rules as resting on "the Fifth Amendment privilege against self-incrimination"); *Butler* v. *McKellar,* 494 U.S. 407, 411 (1990) (noting holding of *Arizona* v. *Roberson* "that the Fifth Amendment bars police-initiated interrogation following a suspect's request for counsel in the context of a separate investigation"); *Michigan* v. *Jackson,* 475 U.S. 625, 629 (1986) ("The Fifth Amendment protection against compelled self-incrimination provides the right to counsel at custodial interrogations."); *Moran* v. *Burbine,* 475 U.S. 412, 427 (1986) (describing *Miranda* as "our interpretation of the Federal Constitution"); *Edwards* v. *Arizona,* 451 U.S. 477, 481-482 (1981) (describing *Miranda* as having "determined that the Fifth and Fourteenth Amendments[]" required custodial interrogation to be preceded by advice concerning the suspect's rights). As those cases highlight, the Court's description of the *Miranda* rules as "prophylactic" does not mean that the rules are therefore extra-constitutional. As the Court stated in Withrow: " '[p]rophylactic' though it may be, in protecting a defendant's Fifth Amendment privilege against self-incrimination, *Miranda* safeguards 'a fundamental trial right.' " 507 U.S. at 691 (emphasis omitted).

The court of appeals in this case did not confront the import of this Court's application of *Miranda* to the States and on habeas review, nor did the court of appeals address the Court's own description of its *Miranda*-based holdings as constitutional in nature. Rather, the court stated that, although it "raises an interesting academic question," this Court's application of *Miranda* in state prosecutions "has no bearing on our conclusion that *Miranda's* conclusive presumption is not required by the Constitution." J.A. 208 n.21. Any conclusion about the legal source of *Miranda,* however, must take into account the fact that the Court has applied that case to the States and on habeas review, since this Court could not do so if *Miranda* were a non-constitutional decision.

C. Congress May Not Overrule This Court's Decision In *Miranda,* Because That Decision Is Based On The Constitution And Congress May Not Overrule Constitutional Decisions Of This Court

When this Court decides a case on a statutory or supervisory basis, Congress has general authority to alter the law and undo the decision, within otherwise applicable constitutional limits. *Miranda,* however, was not a statutory or supervisory power case, but instead rests on constitutional grounds. Accordingly, unless this Court overrules *Miranda,* Section 3501 may not constitutionally be applied to permit admission of a confession that would be inadmissible under *Miranda.*

1. The court of appeals in this case suggested that Section 3501 is valid because "the Court [in *Miranda*] acknowledged that the Constitution did not require the warnings, disclaimed any intent to create a 'constitutional straitjacket,' repeatedly referred to the warnings as 'procedural safeguards,' and invited Congress and the States 'to develop their own safeguards for [protecting] the privilege.'" J.A. 203 (citations omitted; quoting *Miranda,* 384 U.S. at 467, 444, 490). That represents, however, a fundamental misunderstanding of this Court's decision in *Miranda,* based on truncated quotations from the Court's opinion and an untenable theory of this Court's authority to impose rules on the States.

2. The court of appeals' quotation of the *Miranda* opinion omits the crucial portion of the sentence that follows the portion quoted by the court. The full sentence in this Court's opinion in *Miranda* states that "Congress and the States are free to develop their own safeguards for the privilege, so long as they are fully as effective as those described above in informing accused persons of their right of silence and in affording a continuous opportunity to exercise it." 384 U.S. at 490 (emphasis added). The Court therefore clearly did not merely invite Congress and the States to develop "their own safeguards," regardless of their efficacy or adequacy, to replace the Court's *Miranda* holding. Instead, the Court invited Congress and the States to develop "their own safeguards" only if they were "fully as effective" as the *Miranda* rules to "inform[] accused persons of their right of silence and * * * afford[] a continuous opportunity to exercise it."

Indeed, the Court consistently emphasized in *Miranda* that legislation providing alternative safeguards had to satisfy the test of constitutional adequacy that the Court set forth in *Miranda.* For example, earlier in its opinion, the Court set forth the standard with even greater precision:

It is impossible for us to foresee the potential alternatives for protecting the privilege which might be devised by Congress or the States in the exercise of their creative rule-making capacities. Therefore we cannot say that the Constitution necessarily requires adherence to any particular solution for the inherent compulsions of the interrogation process as it is presently conducted. Our decision in no way creates a constitutional straitjacket which will handicap sound efforts at reform, nor is it intended to have this effect. We encourage Congress and the States to continue their laudable search for increasingly effective ways of protecting the rights of the individual while promoting efficient enforcement of our criminal laws. However, unless we are shown other procedures which are at least as effective in apprising accused persons of their right of silence and in assuring a continuous opportunity to exercise it, the following safeguards must be observed.

384 U.S. at 467 (emphasis added). In at least two other places in its opinion, the Court similarly emphasized that any legislative alternative must meet this standard of adequacy. See id. at 476 ("The warnings required * * * in accordance with our opinion today are, in the absence of a fully effective equivalent, prerequisites to the admissibility of any statement made by a defendant.") (emphasis added), 478-479 ("Procedural safeguards must

be employed to protect the privilege, and unless other fully effective means are adopted to notify the person of his right of silence and to assure that the exercise of the right will be scrupulously honored, the following measures are required.") (emphasis added). [footnote 20]

This could not be clearer. Although Congress and the States could surely seek to provide alternative safeguards for the Fifth Amendment privilege, such legislation would be valid only if the safeguards satisfied the constitutional standard of adequacy stated in *Miranda*. [footnote 21] Section 3501 does not satisfy that standard. Indeed, it does not attempt to do so. As Professor Wright has noted, "It is one thing to devise alternative safeguards and quite another to provide, as the 1968 legislation does, that no safeguards are needed." 1 Charles Alan Wright, Federal Practice and Procedure: Criminal 76, at 185 (3d ed. 1999).

3. In sum, the Court in *Miranda* expressly rested its decision on constitutional grounds, and the Court's continued application of *Miranda's* requirements to the States and on habeas review cannot be explained on any ground other than that the Court regards those requirements as implementing and effectuating constitutional rights. The specific warnings articulated in *Miranda* are not required by the Fifth Amendment. But *Miranda* is of constitutional dimension and cannot be superseded by legislation that would return the law to its pre-*Miranda* state, as does Section 3501. "Where rights secured by the Constitution are involved, there can be no rule making or legislation which would abrogate them." *Miranda,* 384 U.S. at 491. Accord City of *Boerne* v. *Flores,* 521 U.S. at 516-529. That principle has long been a fundamental feature of our constitutional structure of government. See *Marbury* v. *Madison,* 5 U.S. (1 Cranch) 137 (1803). Accordingly, before Section 3501 could be applied in a manner that is inconsistent with this Court's *Miranda* jurisprudence, the Court would have to reconsider and overrule *Miranda.*

II. *MIRANDA* SHOULD NOT BE OVERRULED

The resolution of whether *Miranda* should be overruled or reaffirmed raises fundamental questions and implicates competing interests of the highest order. Weighing those interests is not an easy task. But in our view, sound application of principles of stare decisis dictates that at this point in time, thirty-four years after *Miranda* was decided and many years after it has been absorbed into police practices, judicial procedures, and the public understanding, the *Miranda* decision should not be overruled. As Chief Justice Burger stated twenty years ago: "The meaning of *Miranda* has become reasonably clear and law enforcement practices have adjusted to its strictures; I would neither overrule *Miranda,* disparage it, nor extend it at this late date." *Rhode Island* v. *Innis,* 446 U.S. 291, 304 (1980) (Burger, C.J., concurring).

---

[20]Amicus Washington Legal Foundation argues that various post-violation remedies, such as criminal actions under 18 U.S.C. 241 and 242, civil actions under *Bivens* v. *Six Unknown Named Agents,* 403 U.S. 388 (1971), and administrative actions under the Federal Tort Claims Act, are available to ensure that officers comply with the Fifth Amendment. Amicus Br. 14 (filed Nov. 1, 1999). None of those remedies-even if they are as readily available as amicus contends-purports to satisfy *Miranda's* holding that alternatives must "notify the person of his right of silence and * * * assure that the exercise of the right will be scrupulously honored." 384 U.S. at 479.

[21]This circumstance-in which there is a goal that must be reached, but a variety of different means by which a legislature may reach that goal -is not unfamiliar in constitutional law. In its procedural due process cases, for example, this Court has made clear that the Constitution sets various minimum standards that must be satisfied, but that the legislature may select between a variety of possible procedures that would satisfy those standards. See, e.g., *Bell* v. *Burson,* 402 U.S. 535, 542 (1971) (stating that "[w]e deem it inappropriate in this case to do more than lay down this requirement" and noting that "[t]he alternative methods of compliance are several"). See also Henry J. Friendly, Some Kind of Hearing, 123 U. Pa. L. Rev. 1267, 1279 (1975) ("[T]he elements of a fair hearing should not be considered separately; if an agency chooses to go further than is constitutionally demanded with respect to one item, this may afford good reason for diminishing or even eliminating another.").

Stare decisis "permits society to presume that bedrock principles are founded in the law rather than in the proclivities of individuals, and thereby contributes to the integrity of our constitutional system of government, both in appearance and in fact." *Vasquez* v. *Hillary,* 474 U.S. 254, 265-266 (1986). While "stare decisis is not an 'inexorable command,' " especially in a constitutional case, *Planned Parenthood of Southeastern Pennsylvania* v. *Casey,* 505 U.S. 833, 854 (1992), "[e]ven in constitutional cases, the doctrine carries such persuasive force that [the Court] ha[s] always required a departure from precedent to be supported by some 'special justification.' " *United States* v. *International Business Machines Corp.,* 517 U.S. 843, 856 (1996).

The Court's judgment regarding whether to overrule prior cases "is customarily informed by a series of prudential and pragmatic considerations designed to test the consistency of overruling a prior decision with the ideal of the rule of law, and to gauge the respective costs of reaffirming and overruling a prior case." *Casey,* 505 U.S. at 854. Among the considerations that govern are

whether the rule has proven to be intolerable simply in defying practical workability, whether the rule is subject to a kind of reliance that would lend a special hardship to the consequences of overruling and add inequity to the cost of repudiation, whether related principles of law have so far developed as to have left the old rule no more than a remnant of abandoned doctrine, or whether facts have so changed, or come to be seen so differently, as to have robbed the old rule of significant application or justification.

Id. at 854-855 (citations omitted). The Court has regularly sought guidance by applying these factors-costs and workability, reliance, developments in the law that have affected the validity of the past precedent, and a change or perceived change in factual premises-to determine whether prior precedents should be reconsidered or overruled. See, e.g., *Payne* v. *Tennessee,* 501 U.S. 808, 827-830 (1991); *Vasquez,* 474 U.S. at 265-266. In addition, in a case involving a precedent of the significance of *Miranda,* larger considerations enter into the calculus as well. Cf. *Casey,* 505 U.S. at 861.

A. Costs And Workability

The core holding of *Miranda* is that, absent a "fully effective equivalent," 384 U.S. at 476, see pp. 26-28, supra, statements that are obtained in custodial interrogation are inadmissible in the prosecution's case-in-chief unless the suspect, before speaking, was given the prescribed warnings and waived his rights to remain silent and to consult counsel. Any consideration of whether that holding should be overruled must begin with an assessment of *Miranda's* costs and benefits, and whether *Miranda* has proven workable in practice.

1. There are undeniably instances in which the exclusionary rule of *Miranda* imposes costs on the truth-seeking function of a trial, by depriving the trier of fact of "what concededly is relevant evidence." *Colorado* v. *Connelly,* 479 U.S. 157, 166 (1986); see also, e.g., *McNeil* v. *Wisconsin,* 501 U.S. 171, 181 (1991) (the "ready ability to obtain uncoerced confessions is not an evil but an unmitigated good"); *Michigan* v. *Harvey,* 494 U.S. 344, 350 (1990) (Miranda's exclusionary rule "result[s] in the exclusion of some voluntary and reliable statements"); *Oregon* v. *Elstad,* 470 U.S. 298, 312 (1985) (loss of "highly probative evidence of a voluntary confession" is a "high cost to legitimate law enforcement"). [footnote 22] In our view, however, the cost

---

[22]The Court has made the same point in discussing the Fourth Amendment exclusionary rule. See, e.g., *Pennsylvania Bd. of Probation & Parole* v. *Scott,* 524 U.S. 357, 364 (1998) ("Because the exclusionary rule precludes consideration of reliable, probative evidence, it imposes significant costs: It undeniably detracts from the truthfinding process and allows many who would otherwise be incarcerated to escape the consequences of their actions."); *United States* v. *Leon,* 468 U.S. 897, 907 & n.6 (1984) ("The substantial social costs exacted by the exclusionary rule * * * have long been a source of concern. * * * 'Any rule of evidence that denies the jury access to clearly probative and reliable evidence must bear a heavy burden of justification, and must be carefully limited to the circumstances in which it will pay its way by deterring official lawlessness.' ") (quoting *Illinois* v. *Gates,* 462 U.S. 213, 257-258 (1983) (White, J., concurring)).

of *Miranda's* exclusionary rule does not so impede or undermine law enforcement that the overruling of *Miranda* is warranted. Rather, the judgment and experience of federal law enforcement agencies is that *Miranda* is workable in practice and serves several significant law enforcement objectives. [footnote 23] Indeed, in the thirty-two years since the enactment of Section 3501, the United States has never asked this Court to reconsider its decision in *Miranda.*

2. *Miranda's* core procedures are not difficult to administer. Federal agents do not find it difficult, in general, to read a suspect his rights and determine whether the suspect wishes to answer questions. And the administration of *Miranda* warnings is useful, for a defendant who waives his rights will often forgo any challenge to the admissibility of an ensuing confession. In those instances in which such challenges nonetheless are made, compliance with *Miranda* helps ensure that statements will be found admissible because they were voluntary. Indeed, long before *Miranda* was decided, the Federal Bureau of Investigation had adopted a practice of administering warnings similar to those required by *Miranda* to all suspects before questioning them. See 384 U.S. at 483-488 & n.54. That practice was instituted to ensure that agents treat suspects fairly while simultaneously obtaining important investigative information and reliable statements that are admissible in court. See id. at 483 n.54 (noting statement of J. Edgar Hoover, then-Director of the FBI, explaining that the FBI's policy of giving warnings was based on the principle that "[l]aw enforcement, * * * in defeating the criminal, must maintain inviolate the historic liberties of the individual."). The FBI's policy was workable before *Miranda,* and the FBI has had very little difficulty complying with the bright-line core mandates of the *Miranda* decision since 1966.

   The experience of other federal law enforcement agencies since *Miranda* has also confirmed that *Miranda* has proved workable in practice and is in many respects beneficial to law enforcement. It is the policy of some agencies, such as the Internal Revenue Service and the Bureau of Alcohol, Tobacco, and Firearms, to provide *Miranda* warnings not only before engaging in custodial interrogation, but also in some non-custodial settings. The experience of those agencies is that the core *Miranda* warnings and waiver framework is administrable and does not impede law enforcement. In short, federal law enforcement agencies have concluded that the *Miranda* decision itself generally does not hinder their investigations and the issuance of *Miranda* warnings at the outset of a custodial interrogation is in the best interests of law enforcement as well as the suspect.

3. This Court has frequently noted that it is a virtue of *Miranda* that it provides bright-line rules that can be readily applied by the police and the courts to a

---

[23] A lively debate in the law reviews has considered whether the social scientific evidence demonstrates that *Miranda* has had any effect on the rates at which criminals are prosecuted and convicted. In our view, the social scientific evidence is at best inconclusive and certainly insufficient on which to base a decision to overrule an important constitutional precedent. Compare Paul G. Cassel & Richard Fowles, Handcuffing the Cops? A Thirty-Year Perspective on *Miranda's* Harmful Effects on Law Enforcement, 50 Stan. L. Rev. 1055 (1998), with Stephen J. Schulhofer, *Miranda's* Practical Effect: Substantial Benefits and Vanishingly Small Social Costs, 90 Nw. U.L. Rev. 500 (1996), and John J. Donahue III, Did *Miranda* Diminish Police Effectiveness?, 50 Stan. L. Rev. 1147 (1998). See also Richard A. Leo & Welsh S. White, Adapting to *Miranda:* Modern Interrogators' Strategies for Dealing with the Obstacles Posed by *Miranda,* 84 Minn. L. Rev. 397 (1999). The argument that *Miranda* should be superseded by Section 3501 to increase the number of confessions is also hopelessly at odds with the argument of amicus that Section 3501 continues to give law enforcement agents sufficient incentives to give *Miranda* warnings. See Br. Amicus Curiae of Washington Legal Found. 13 (filed Nov. 1, 1999). If amicus's appraisal of the incentives provided by Section 3501 to give warnings is correct, replacing *Miranda* with Section 3501 would have little or no benefit in increasing the rate at which offenders confess.

large variety of factual circumstances. [footnote 24] Indeed, even when, as in *New York* v. *Quarles,* 467 U.S. 649 (1984), the Court recognized an exception to the *Miranda* rules for public safety, the Court explained that "the exception will not be difficult for police officers to apply," 467 U.S. at 658, and that "police officers can and will distinguish almost instinctively" between questions permitted and prohibited under the exception, id. at 658-659.

While *Miranda* itself is generally workable, federal law enforcement agencies have encountered difficulties with some of the extensions of *Miranda in Edwards* v. *Arizona,* 451 U.S. 477, 480 (1981), and later cases. Those cases require that, once a suspect invokes his right to counsel during custodial interrogation, law enforcement agents may not later reinitiate questioning without counsel present, even on matters unrelated to the crime for which the suspect was being held and questioned. See *Arizona* v. *Roberson,* 486 U.S. 675 (1988); *Minnick* v. *Mississippi,* 498 U.S. 146 (1990). Whatever difficulty is caused by those decisions, however, is more properly charged to the account of *Edwards* and *Roberson* than to *Miranda,* and any such difficulty would properly be far more relevant should the Court be faced with reconsideration of those decisions rather than *Miranda* itself. The *Miranda* doctrine has undergone a continuous course of development in this Court since 1966. [footnote 25] Insofar as it is shown that some applications of *Miranda* create inequity or are otherwise unworkable, there is no reason to believe that the doctrine will not continue to develop in future years as appropriate. [footnote 26]

4. Finally, a return to a totality-of-the-circumstances test in all settings is unlikely to be more workable in practice than is the *Miranda* rule itself. Rather, it is likely to be more difficult to apply both for agents and courts. The underlying due process rule that confessions are inadmissible unless

---

[24] *See Arizona* v. *Roberson,* 486 U.S. 675, 681 (1988) ("We have repeatedly emphasized the virtues of a bright-line rule in cases following *Edwards* as well as *Miranda.*"); *Colorado* v. *Spring,* 479 U.S. 564, 577 n.9 (1987) (*Miranda* has the "important virtue of informing police and prosecutors with specificity as to how a pretrial questioning of a suspect must be conducted.") (internal quotation marks omitted); *Moran* v. *Burbine,* 475 U.S. 412, 425 (1986) ("As we have stressed on numerous occasions, '[o]ne of the principal advantages' of *Miranda* is the ease and clarity of its application."); *Berkemer* v. *McCarty,* 468 U.S. 420, 432 (1984) (noting "the simplicity and clarity" of *Miranda*); *Fare* v. *Michael C.,* 442 U.S. 707, 718 (1979) (*Miranda's* "gain in specificity, which benefits the accused and the State alike, has been thought to outweigh the burdens that the decision in *Miranda* imposes on law enforcement agencies and the courts."); see also *New York* v. *Quarles,* 467 U.S. 649, 664 (1984) (O'Connor, J., concurring in the judgment and dissenting in part) (*Miranda* rules have "afforded police and courts clear guidance on the manner in which to conduct a custodial investigation."). The Court has thus noted that "there is little reason to believe that the police today are unable, or even generally unwilling, to satisfy *Miranda's* requirements." *Withrow* v. *Williams,* 507 U.S. 680, 695 (1993).

[25] In many respects, the Court has tailored the *Miranda* doctrine as necessary to make it more workable. See, e.g., *Davis* v. *United States,* 512 U.S. 452 (1994) (ambiguous invocation of right to counsel does not require cessation of all questioning); *Berkemer* v. *McCarty,* 468 U.S. 420 (1984) (*Miranda* warnings not required in a routine traffic stop); *Quarles,* 467 U.S. at 657 (public safety exception). The Court has not recently decided an *Edwards* issue, but in *United States* v. *Green,* 504 U.S. 908 (1992) (No. 91-5121), the Court granted certiorari to review "[w]hether *Edwards* * * * requires the suppression of a voluntary confession because law enforcement officers initiated interrogation of the suspect five months after he invoked his right to counsel in connection with an unrelated offense, where the suspect consulted with counsel and pleaded guilty to the unrelated offense prior to the interrogation." The case became moot after oral argument when the respondent died. See 507 U.S. 545 (1993). Had the case not become moot, the Court would have decided whether a further refinement to the *Edwards-Roberson* rules was appropriate.

[26] Another problem that can occur in applying *Miranda* is that officers who have detained or are questioning a suspect without arresting him may be found by a court to have applied a "restraint on freedom of movement of the degree associated with a formal arrest." *Thompson* v. *Keohane,* 516 U.S. 99, 112 (1995) (internal quotation marks omitted). In that situation, an officer may inadvertently fail to issue *Miranda* warnings. As this Court has noted, "the task of defining 'custody' is a slippery one, and 'policemen investigating serious crimes [cannot realistically be expected to] make no errors whatsoever.' " *Oregon* v. *Elstad,* 470 U.S. at 309. It therefore stands to reason that in some close cases, the officers will make a mistake, but it will be a "reasonable" one under all the circumstances. While the Court has not considered whether to recognize an exception to *Miranda's* suppression rule in such a case, it has adopted a rule in the Fourth Amendment exclusionary rule context for cases in which police acted in good-faith reliance on a warrant or authorization by another governmental actor. See *United States* v. *Leon,* 468 U.S. at 906-913; *Arizona* v. *Evans,* 514 U.S. 1, 15 (1995).

they are found voluntary under the traditional totality-of-the-circumstances test remains applicable, even if the *Miranda* warnings have been administered. See, e.g., *Miller* v. *Fenton,* 474 U.S. 104 (1985). As a general matter, however, "cases in which a defendant can make a colorable argument that a self-incriminating statement was 'compelled' despite the fact that the law enforcement authorities adhered to the dictates of *Miranda* are rare." *Berkemer* v. *McCarty,* 468 U.S. at 433 n.20. See also *Oregon* v. *Elstad,* 470 U.S. at 318 ("The fact that a suspect chooses to speak after being informed of his rights is, of course, highly probative [on the voluntariness of his statements]."); *Colorado* v. *Spring,* 479 U.S. at 576 ("Indeed, it seems self-evident that one who is told he is free to refuse to answer questions is in a curious posture to later complain that his answers were compelled."). In the absence of *Miranda,* additional pressure would be placed on the voluntariness doctrine to determine the result in close and difficult cases. Although many law enforcement agencies would continue to observe the *Miranda* procedures to help ensure the admissibility of confessions they obtain, it is likely that some police departments would become less rigorous in requiring warnings, others might significantly modify them, and some police officers would, in the "often competitive enterprise of ferreting out crime," *Johnson* v. *United States,* 333 U.S. 10, 14 (1948), fail to issue warnings at all before conducting custodial interrogation.

If *Miranda* warnings are not required, the result will be uncertainty for the police and an additional volume of litigation focusing on the totality-of-the-circumstances voluntariness standard. That approach takes into account not only what the agents say and do, see, e.g., *Miller,* 474 U.S. at 116, but also facts about the particular suspect (such as his maturity, education, physical condition, mental health, and knowledge of constitutional rights, see *Withrow,* 507 U.S. at 693 (citing cases)), about the circumstances of the questioning (the length of the detention, the length and nature of the interrogation, the physical constraints or deprivations imposed, the suspect's access to friends and relatives, see id. at 693-694; *Schneckloth* v. *Bustamonte,* 412 U.S. 218, 226 (1973); *Miranda,* 384 U.S. at 445-446), and other factors. [footnote27] As demonstrated by the thirty pre-*Miranda* confession cases decided by this Court under the due process test, see pp. 14-18, supra (discussing cases), the totality-of-the-circumstances voluntariness test is more difficult and uncertain in application than *Miranda*. Cf. *Minnick* v. *Mississippi,* 498 U.S. at 151 ("*Edwards* conserves judicial resources which would otherwise be expended in making difficult determinations of voluntariness"). Its many variables would complicate the task of law enforcement in assessing what procedures would reliably secure admissible confessions.

B. Reliance Interests

Reliance interests are also an important factor, and rules of criminal procedure do not in general give rise to substantial reliance interests. See *Payne* v. *Tennessee,* 501 U.S. at 828. [footnote 28] As we note below, see pp. 49-50, infra, it is of significance,

---

[27] See also *Culombe* v. *Connecticut,* 367 U.S. at 601-602 (opinion of Frankfurter, J.) (relevant factors include "extensive cross-questioning," "undue delay in arraignment," "failure to caution a prisoner," "refusal to permit communication with friends and legal counsel," "the duration and conditions of detention," "the manifest attitude of the police toward [the suspect], his physical and mental state, the diverse pressures which sap or sustain his powers of resistance and self-control").

[28] Criminal defendants are unlikely to have given unwarned confessions in reliance on the belief that they would not be used in the prosecution's case-in-chief. Insofar as the government has taken action to foster such a belief in a given case, cf. *California Attorneys for Criminal Justice* v. *Butts,* 195 F.3d 1039, 1042-1043 (9th Cir. 1999), the defendant might advance a claim that the government had failed to fulfill a promise it made; such a claim would be analyzed under due process cases such as *Doyle* v. *Ohio,* 426 U.S. 610 (1976), as well as under the voluntariness test.

however, that the requirements of *Miranda* have shaped years of police conduct and governed decades of criminal prosecutions. Moreover, upsetting settled public expectations by overruling a constitutional precedent as well-known and widely applied as *Miranda* would tend to have a destabilizing effect on public confidence in the fairness of the criminal justice system and public trust in this Court's legitimacy.

C. Developments In The Law That Have Affected The Validity Of The Past Precedent

1. Perhaps the feature of *Miranda* that has raised the greatest doctrinal doubt about that decision's validity is the tension that has emerged in this Court's cases that followed the *Miranda* decision itself. The Court has consistently premised those decisions on the proposition that *Miranda's* holding requires the suppression of unwarned statements in the government's case-in-chief in state and federal cases. The one exception is the Court's holding in *New York* v. *Quarles,* 467 U.S. 649 (1984), recognizing a "public safety" exception to *Miranda.* But that case did not question the general rule against the use of unwarned statements in the government's case-in-chief, which the Court restated the following year in *Oregon* v. *Elstad,* 470 U.S. at 306-307. [footnote 29] The Court has never suggested that the core holding of *Miranda* should be overruled. Indeed, if this Court were to overrule *Miranda,* it would not only have to disavow the line of its cases that have addressed the Miranda rule, but would also have to overrule directly at least eleven cases that have reaffirmed that a confession obtained in violation of *Miranda* must be suppressed in the government's case-in-chief. [footnote 30]

   The Court's decision in *Quarles* and its holdings limiting the application of *Miranda's* suppression rule outside the government's case-in-chief, however, have led some observers to conclude that *Miranda* has lost its character as a rule that protects constitutional rights. The Court's decisions in *Tucker* and later cases rest on the conclusion that the procedural safeguards articulated in *Miranda* are not themselves required by the Constitution and that a violation of *Miranda's* prophylactic rules does not necessarily produce statements that are themselves "compelled." That reasoning is the foundation of the public-safety exception and of this Court's holdings that unwarned, but voluntary, statements may be used for impeachment and for the acquisition of derivative evidence that may be admitted at trial. [footnote 31] Since the Court has said that a *Miranda* violation does not necessarily involve a violation of the Constitution, the question arises whether this Court has properly determined to apply a suppression remedy in the government's case-in-chief in all prosecutions, federal and state, for the violation of judicially imposed prophylactic rules.

2. In our judgment, the Court's statements that *Miranda's* "prophylactic" requirements sweep more broadly than does the Self-Incrimination Clause itself do not invalidate *Miranda's* status as a Fifth Amendment decision. It is worth recalling that this Court adopted the procedural safeguards of *Mi-*

---

[29]Elstad made this crystal clear: "When police ask questions of a suspect in custody without administering the required warnings, *Miranda* dictates that the answers received be presumed compelled and that they be excluded from evidence at trial in the State's case in chief. * * * The Court today in no way retreats from the bright-line rule of *Miranda.*" 470 U.S. at 317.

[30]*Thompson* v. *Keohane,* 516 U.S. 99 (1995); *Withrow* v. *Williams,* 507 U.S. 680 (1993); *Minnick* v. *Mississippi,* 498 U.S. 146 (1990); *Pennsylvania* v. *Muniz,* 496 U.S. 582 (1990); *Arizona* v. *Roberson,* 486 U.S. 675 (1988); *Berkemer* v. *McCarty,* 468 U.S. 420 (1984); *Smith* v. *Illinois,* 469 U.S. 91 (1984) (per curiam); *Edwards* v. *Arizona,* 451 U.S. 477 (1981); *Estelle* v. *Smith,* 451 U.S. 454 (1981); *Orozco* v. *Texas,* 394 U.S. 324 (1969); *Mathis* v. *United States,* 391 U.S. 1 (1968).

[31]In contrast, statements "compelled" under a grant of immunity may generally not be used, consistent with the Fifth Amendment, either for impeachment, see *New Jersey* v. *Portash,* 440 U.S. 450, 458-459 (1979), or for the acquisition of derivative evidence that may be introduced against the defendant, see *Kastigar* v. *United States,* 406 U.S. 441 (1972).

randa only after more than thirty years of applying a case-by-case voluntariness test. That judicial experience led the Court to conclude that Fifth Amendment rights in the setting of custodial interrogation could not adequately be protected through case-specific adjudication of claims of police coercion, and that procedural safeguards were required. See, e.g., *Haynes* v. *Washington,* 373 U.S. at 515 ("The line between proper and permissible police conduct and techniques and methods offensive to due process is, at best, a difficult one to draw, particularly in cases such as this where it is necessary to make fine judgments as to the effect of psychologically coercive pressures and inducements on the mind and will of an accused."). [footnote 32] The objective of the *Miranda* safeguards "is not to mold police conduct for its own sake. Nothing in the Constitution vests in us the authority to mandate a code of behavior for state officials wholly unconnected to any federal right or privilege. The purpose of the *Miranda* warnings instead is to dissipate the compulsion inherent in custodial interrogation and, in so doing, guard against abridgement of the suspect's Fifth Amendment rights." *Moran* v. *Burbine,* 475 U.S. at 425.

The Court has explained the balance struck in *Miranda* as follows:

Custodial interrogations implicate two competing concerns. On the one hand, the need for police questioning as a tool for effective enforcement of criminal laws cannot be doubted. Admissions of guilt are more than merely desirable; they are essential to society's compelling interest in finding, convicting, and punishing those who violate the law. On the other hand, the Court has recognized that the interrogation process is inherently coercive and that, as a consequence, there exists a substantial risk that the police will inadvertently traverse the fine line between legitimate efforts to elicit admissions and constitutionally impermissible compulsion. *Miranda* attempted to reconcile these opposing concerns by giving the defendant the power to exert some control over the course of the interrogation. Declining to adopt the more extreme position that the actual presence of a lawyer was necessary to dispel the coercion inherent in custodial interrogation, the Court found that the suspect's Fifth Amendment rights could be adequately protected by less intrusive means. Police questioning, often an essential part of the investigatory process, could continue in its traditional form, the Court held, but only if the suspect clearly understood that, at any time, he could bring the proceeding to a halt or, short of that, call in an attorney to give advice and monitor the conduct of his interrogators.

Moran, 475 U.S. at 426-427 (citations and internal quotation marks omitted). *Miranda* thereby serves individual and systemic interests in safeguarding Fifth Amendment rights. Although "[b]oth waiver of rights and admission of guilt are consistent with the affirmation of individual responsibility that is a principle of the criminal justice system, * * * neither admissions nor waivers are effective unless there are both particular and systemic assurances that the coercive pressures of custody were not the inducing cause." *Minnick* v. *Mississippi,* 498 U.S. at 155.

---

[32]*Blackburn* v. *Alabama,* 361 U.S. 199, 207 (1960) ("[A] complex of values underlies the stricture against use by the state of confessions which, by way of convenient shorthand, this Court terms involuntary, and the role played by each in any situation varies according to the particular circumstances of the case."); *Spano* v. *New York,* 360 U.S. 315, 321 (1959) ("[A]s law enforcement officers become more responsible, and the methods used to extract confessions more sophisticated, our duty to enforce federal constitutional protections does not cease. It only becomes more difficult because of the more delicate judgments to be made."); *Haley* v. *Ohio,* 332 U.S. 596, 605 (1948) (Frankfurter, J., concurring in the judgment) ("Because of their inherent vagueness the tests by which we are to be guided are most unsatisfactory, but such as they are we must apply them."); id. at 606 ("Unhappily we have neither physical nor intellectual weights and measures by which judicial judgment can determine when pressures in securing a confession reach the coercive intensity that calls for the exclusion of a statement so secured.").

3. The Court has explained not only the need for safeguards in custodial interrogation, but also how *Miranda's* status as a prophylactic rule is linked to the constitutional provision on which it is based. In *Oregon v. Elstad,* the Court explained that the "[f]ailure to administer *Miranda* warnings creates a presumption of compulsion [that is] * * * irrebuttable for purposes of the prosecution's case in chief." 470 U.S. at 307. Because a confession obtained in violation of *Miranda* is subject to an "irrebuttable presumption of compulsion" in the prosecution's case-in-chief, the suppression of confessions in that context is consistent with the Self-Incrimination Clause's requirement that a person not be "compelled" to be a witness against himself. The conclusive presumption is a rule of law that the Court applies to serve systemic goals in protecting Fifth Amendment rights. See Elstad, 470 U.S. at 307 n.1 ("A *Miranda* violation does not constitute coercion but rather affords a bright-line, legal presumption of coercion, requiring suppression of all unwarned statements [in the government's case-in-chief].") (emphasis in original).

  The Court in *Elstad* also explained that, outside the government's case-in-chief, a confession obtained in violation of *Miranda* is subject only to a rebuttable presumption of compulsion. Accordingly, it may be permissible to use an unwarned confession for impeachment or to obtain evidence. 470 U.S. at 307 ("But the *Miranda* presumption, though irrebuttable for purposes of the prosecution's case in chief, does not require that the statements and their fruits be discarded as inherently tainted."). The rule in those settings thus permits use of the unwarned confession so long as the presumption of compulsion is overcome by a showing under the totality of the circumstances that the statement was made voluntarily. Ibid.; see *Lego* v. *Twomey,* 404 U.S. 477, 489 (1972).

4. There are other contexts in which this Court similarly has recognized prophylactic rules that are designed to safeguard constitutional rights, even when those rules may in particular cases sweep more broadly than the constitutional right upon which they are based. For example, in *Douglas* v. *California,* 372 U.S. 353 (1963), this Court held that States must provide appointed counsel to indigent criminal defendants on appeal. Subsequently, in *Anders* v. *California,* 386 U.S. 738 (1967), the Court set forth a procedure to be used by appellate counsel representing an indigent defendant when counsel concludes that there is no non-frivolous ground for appeal and he wishes to withdraw from representation. The *Anders* procedure, however, "is not 'an independent constitutional command,' " but " 'a prophylactic framework' * * * established to vindicate the constitutional right to appellate counsel." *Smith* v. *Robbins,* No. 98-1037 (Jan. 19, 2000), slip op. at 10 (quoting *Pennsylvania* v. *Finley,* 481 U.S. 551, 555 (1987)). The Court has recently reaffirmed that some such prophylactic procedure is necessary. In *Smith,* the Court explained that "the States are free to adopt different procedures [from those outlined in *Anders*], so long as those procedures adequately safeguard a defendant's right to appellate counsel." Slip op. 2; see also id. at 15 ("In determining whether a particular state procedure satisfies this standard, it is important to focus on the underlying goals that the procedure should serve-to ensure that those indigents whose appeals are not frivolous receive the counsel and merits brief required by *Douglas,* and also to enable the State to protect itself so that frivolous appeals are not subsidized and public moneys not needlessly spent.") (internal quotation marks omitted).

  Similarly, in *Michigan* v. *Jackson,* 475 U.S. 625, 636 (1986), the Court held that, once a defendant has invoked his Sixth Amendment right to counsel at an arraignment or similar proceeding, "any waiver of the defendant's right to counsel for * * * police-initiated interrogation is invalid." In

Michigan v. *Harvey,* 494 U.S. 344 (1990), however, the Court held that such invalidity requires suppression of a confession obtained in violation of *Jackson* only in the prosecution's case-in-chief, but not when it is offered for impeachment. The Court explained that distinction on the ground that *Jackson* is "not compelled directly by the Constitution," 494 U.S. at 351-352, but sets forth a "prophylactic rule," id. at 345, 346, 349, 351, 353, "designed to ensure voluntary, knowing, and intelligent waivers of the Sixth Amendment right to counsel," id. at 351. The Court acknowledged in *Harvey* that the rationale of this line of Sixth Amendment decisions is based on the rationale underlying *Miranda.* See 494 U.S. at 349-352. [footnote 33]

In *North Carolina* v. *Pearce,* 395 U.S. 711 (1969), the Court held that an increased sentence imposed on a defendant after a successful appeal and reconviction is presumed to be the product of vindictiveness and therefore unconstitutional unless non-vindictive reasons for the increased sentence appear on the record. The Court has explained that *Pearce* is a "prophylactic rule" and has noted the similarities between the "prophylactic rules" in *Pearce* and *Miranda. Michigan* v. *Payne,* 412 U.S. 47, 53-54 (1973); see also *Wasman* v. *United States,* 468 U.S. 559, 562-563 (1984); *United States* v. *Goodwin,* 457 U.S. 368, 372-377 (1982); *Colten* v. *Kentucky,* 407 U.S. 104, 116 (1972). The Court reached a similar conclusion in *Blackledge* v. *Perry,* 417 U.S. 21 (1974), holding that a State may not respond to a defendant's attempt to seek a trial de novo in a higher tier of a two-tier court system by charging the defendant with a more serious offense. The Court has recognized that the rules announced in *Pearce* and *Blackledge,* like the rules in *Miranda* and *Jackson,* require a decision in favor of the defendant in some cases even though the underlying constitutional right being protected may not have been shown to have been violated in a particular case. [footnote 34] But the Court determined that such rules were necessary to provide full effectuation of constitutional rights. [footnote 35]

Our point is not that such rules are always correct, or that prophylactic rules that lead to the suppression of evidence in a criminal case are often justified. In most criminal settings, the heavy costs of such rules would not outweigh the potential marginal protection they offer for the underlying constitutional right. Ordinarily, therefore, this Court requires proof of an individualized constitutional harm before framing a remedy. See, e.g., *United States* v. *Morrison,* 449 U.S. 361, 364 (1981). That does not, however, deprive the *Miranda* rules, or other constitutional prophylactic rules, of their constitutional status. Prophylactic rules are now and have been for many years a feature of this Court's constitutional adjudication. *Miranda* is distinctive in the detail with which the Court specified particular procedural safeguards.

---

[33] Another example of a prophylactic rule is the Confrontation Clause doctrine of *Bruton* v. *United States,* 391 U.S. 123 (1968), which forbids the admission of a nontestifying co-defendant's confession in a joint trial, even with a limiting instruction. The purpose of the *Bruton* rule is to avoid the risk that the jury will disregard its instructions. See *Gray* v. *Maryland,* 523 U.S. 185, 189, 192, 197 (1998) (referring to "protective rule" of *Bruton*). Although some juries might be able to follow a limiting instruction, the Court concluded that the risk that many could not do so warranted a conclusion that the Confrontation Clause itself protects the defendant against the latter possibility. But in a situation in which competing values outweigh that risk, the co-defendant's confession may be used. See *Tennessee* v. *Street,* 471 U.S. 409 (1985) (confession that is inadmissible under Bruton rule is admissible for impeachment).

[34] See *Blackledge,* 417 U.S. at 28 (applying the rule notwithstanding that there was "no evidence that the prosecutor in this case acted in bad faith or maliciously"); *Payne,* 412 U.S. at 54 (noting that *Pearce* adopted presumption of vindictiveness notwithstanding that "nothing in *Pearce* intimates that the Court regarded [judicial vindictiveness] as anything more than an infrequently appearing blemish on the sentencing process").

[35] The Court has also adopted constitutional prophylactic rules to safeguard constitutional rights in a variety of other settings. See, e.g., *Gertz* v. *Robert Welch, Inc.,* 418 U.S. 323, 340, 342 (1974) (explaining that, even though "there is no constitutional value in false statements of fact," the Court in *New York Times Co.* v. *Sullivan,* 376 U.S. 254 (1964), and its progeny nevertheless "extended a measure of strategic protection to defamatory falsehood" in cases involving public officials and public figures); *Freedman* v. *Maryland,* 380 U.S. 51, 58 (1965) (setting forth "procedural safeguards designed to obviate the dangers of a censorship system" with respect to motion picture obscenity).

But *Miranda's* adoption of a prophylactic rule- which has since been applied where necessary but not, as *Tucker, Quarles,* and *Elstad* show, in categories of cases where its adverse effects would outweigh any benefits- does not uniquely depart from the Court's constitutional jurisprudence.

D. Change In Factual Premises

There appear to be at least two key factual assumptions underlying *Miranda.* First, "the process of in-custody interrogation of persons suspected or accused of crime contains inherently compelling pressures." 384 U.S. at 467. Second, "without proper safeguards"-provided by the administration of the *Miranda* warnings or a fully effective equivalent -there is a great risk that those pressures may "undermine the individual's will to resist and to compel him to speak where he would not otherwise do so freely." Ibid. Debate concerning each of those premises is possible, as it was at the time *Miranda* was decided. The inquiry for purposes of stare decisis, however, focuses on changes in circumstance, because the rule of stare decisis would provide little stability if the factual premises of previous decisions were constantly subject to reconsideration, even when the evidence showed no change of circumstance. We cannot conclude that the passage of time or other developments in our society have substantially altered the validity of either of the key factual premises on which *Miranda* was based. [footnote 36]

The Court's perception of custodial interrogation as inherently coercive was based on the Court's prior "voluntariness" cases and its review of police interrogation manuals. See *Miranda,* 384 U.S. at 445-456. The Court's conclusion was not driven solely by cases of physical abuse; to the contrary, the Court "stress[ed] that the modern practice of in-custody interrogation is psychologically rather than physically oriented." Id. at 448. Custodial interrogation is an important and necessary procedure of law enforcement, and law enforcement agents today are generally better trained than they were in 1966. It cannot be said, however, that the interrogation process is so uniformly different now than at the time of *Miranda* that changes have undercut the validity of that decision.

Likewise, the Court's view that warnings (or other safeguards) would be an effective antidote to the coercive pressures of custodial interrogation has not been undercut by changed circumstances. Some modern technologies-videotaping, for example-could offer promise in documenting that a particular confession was not produced by any coercion inherent in the custodial setting. But no assurance currently exists that such technological substitutes could provide a suitable replacement for the by-now well-understood *Miranda* warnings on a large-scale basis, and in any event the statute at issue in this case does not present the question whether such a technological fix could form part of an adequate substitute for the *Miranda* warnings. See pp. 13-20, supra. Nor does the widespread public familiarity with the *Miranda* warnings suggest that they are no longer necessary. Not all members of our society are conversant with their rights. And, if *Miranda* were overruled, it is difficult to predict how long even general public familiarity would persist. [footnote 37] Finally, even if a suspect held in custody already knows of his rights, the Court in *Miranda* concluded that the provision of warnings in each case "show[s] the individual that

---

[36]In a companion federal case decided with *Miranda,* the United States argued that, in deciding whether a suspect's statements during in-custody questioning were the product of compulsion, the Court should require consideration of the totality of the circumstances, rather than adopting a constitutional rule turning on the presence or absence of warnings. Brief for the United States at 28-38, *Westover* v. *United States,* 383 U.S. 903 (1966) (No. 761). The calculus of whether to retain *Miranda's* rule with respect to unwarned statements, thirty-four years after the Court announced it, presents very different considerations.

[37]Federal law enforcement agencies would, as a matter of policy, continue to comply with the warnings requirements of *Miranda.* We are unable to predict whether state and local law enforcement would do so. More to the point here, there would be no basis for the Court to draw a firm conclusion about what practices would ensue were it to overrule *Miranda.*

his interrogators are prepared to recognize his privilege should he choose to exercise it." 384 U.S. at 468. Once again, there is no basis for a conclusion that changed circumstances or a changed perception of the facts warrants reassessment of that view.

* * * * *

In considering whether the Court should revisit *Miranda,* it is appropriate to make an observation that transcends the usual factors considered under the rubric of stare decisis. In our view, *Miranda* has come to play a unique and important role in the nation's conception of our criminal justice system: it promotes public confidence that the criminal justice system is fair. Overruling *Miranda*-at this juncture, more than three decades after it was announced and after law enforcement has accommodated to its basic requirements- would thus tend to undermine public confidence in the fairness of that system. The law enforcement system depends on citizen cooperation and support in myriad ways. Steps that may damage that confidence should not be taken lightly.

There is no doubt that the public pays a heavy price if technical violations of *Miranda* result in suppression of otherwise probative evidence, and non-prosecution or acquittal of felons ensues. But there are concrete benefits of *Miranda* as well: it establishes clear guidelines of conduct for agents; it facilitates the admission in evidence of confessions that follow administration of the warnings; it bolsters the credibility of such confessions in the eyes of jurors; and it generally contributes to the perceived fairness of the criminal justice system. The stability of this Court's constitutional jurisprudence is also of surpassing importance to the system of justice. Especially in light of those factors, we do not urge the Court that *Miranda* be overruled.

CONCLUSION

The decision of the court of appeals should be reversed.
Respectfully submitted.

JANET RENO
Attorney General

SETH P. WAXMAN
Solicitor General

JAMES K. ROBINSON
Assistant Attorney General

MICHAEL R. DREEBEN
Deputy Solicitor General

JAMES A. FELDMAN
LISA S. BLATT
Assistants to the Solicitor General

JANUARY 2000

APPENDIX

1. The Fifth Amendment of the United States Constitution provides in relevant part that "[n]o person shall * * * be compelled in any criminal case to be a witness against himself."

2. Section 3501 of Title 18 provides as follows:

   (a) In any criminal prosecution brought by the United States or by the District of Columbia, a confession, as defined in subsection (e) hereof, shall be admissible in evidence if it is voluntarily given. Before such confession is received in evidence, the trial judge shall, out of the presence of the jury, determine any issue as to voluntariness. If the trial judge determines that the confession was voluntarily made it shall be admitted in evidence and the trial judge shall permit the jury to hear relevant evidence on the issue of voluntariness and shall instruct the jury to give such weight to the confession as the jury feels it deserves under all the circumstances.

   (b) The trial judge in determining the issue of voluntariness shall take into consideration all the circumstances surrounding the giving of the confession, including (1) the time elapsing between arrest and arraignment of the defendant making the confession, if it was made after arrest and before arraignment, (2) whether such defendant knew the nature of the offense with which he was charged or of which he was suspected at the time of making the confession, (3) whether or not such defendant was advised or knew that he was not required to make any statement and that any such statement could be used against him, (4) whether or not such defendant had been advised prior to questioning of his right to the assistance of counsel; and (5) whether or not such defendant was without the assistance of counsel when questioned and when giving such confession.

      The presence or absence of any of the abovementioned factors to be taken into consideration by the judge need not be conclusive on the issue of voluntariness of the confession.

   (c) In any criminal prosecution by the United States or by the District of Columbia, a confession made or given by a person who is a defendant therein, while such person was under arrest or other detention in the custody of any law-enforcement officer or law-enforcement agency, shall not be inadmissible solely because of delay in bringing such person before a magistrate or other official empowered to commit persons charged with offenses against the laws of the United States or of the District of Columbia if such confession is found by the trial judge to have been made voluntarily and if the weight to be given the confession is left to the jury and if such confession was made or given by such person within six hours immediately following his arrest or other detention: Provided, That the time limitation contained in this subsection shall not apply in any case in which the delay in bringing such person before such magistrate or other official beyond such six-hour period is found by the trial judge to be reasonable considering the means of transportation and the distance to be traveled to the nearest available such magistrate or other officer.

   (d) Nothing contained in this section shall bar the admission in evidence of any confession made or given voluntarily by any person to any other person without interrogation by anyone, or at any time at which the person who made or gave such confession was not under arrest or other detention.

   (e) As used in this section, the term "confession" means any confession of guilt of any criminal offense or any self-incriminating statement made or given orally or in writing.

SECTION VIII

𝕮𝖆𝖘𝖘𝖊𝖑𝖑 𝕭𝖗𝖎𝖊𝖋

STATEMENT

The facts of this case and proceedings below have been adequately summarized by the parties. We emphasize only that this case is before this Court with a district court finding that petitioner Dickerson's incriminating statements were voluntary. J.A. 155, 158, 212. [footnote 1]

INTRODUCTION AND SUMMARY OF ARGUMENT

The ultimate question in this case is whether the federal criminal justice system must exclude from evidence a criminal suspect's voluntary statement, despite an Act of Congress to the contrary. *Miranda* v. *Arizona,* 384 U.S. 436 (1966), automatically excludes such a statement if it was given in response to custodial questioning without the required warnings. It enforces that exclusion on the basis of an irrebuttable presumption that such questioning by police must in every case have coerced the confession. This presumption controls regardless of how frequently it is false; regardless of how much it costs the integrity and truthfulness of the trial, if a trial is still possible; and regardless of how abundant the evidence may be in a particular case that the suspect understood his situation and made his own decision to speak. Nothing in the Constitution requires this uncompromising rule or strips the elected branches of their authority to modify it.

Congress' decision to enact Section 3501 was consistent with the Constitution. *Miranda* did not, and of course could not, simply redraft the Fifth Amendment to include a new constitutional right (or, as the *Miranda* Court put it, create a "constitutional straitjacket," 384 U.S. at 467) prohibiting the use of unwarned, though voluntary, statements. Later pronouncements by the Court have confirmed that *Miranda's* exclusionary rule was instead a preventive measure—part of a "series of recommended procedural safeguards," *Davis* v. *United States,* 512 U.S. 452, 457-458 (1994), that "sweep[] more broadly than the Fifth Amendment itself," *Oregon* v. *Elstad,* 470 U.S. 298, 306 (1985). Because *Miranda's* exclusionary rule was in this sense judicially improvised, rather than constitutionally required, *Miranda* necessarily

---

[1]The case at this stage presents no challenge to the way in which 18 U.S.C. 3501 was raised below. In the district court, career prosecutors argued that Section 3501 required reconsideration of the court's decision suppressing Dickerson's confession. J.A. 94-6. On appeal to the Fourth Circuit, the prosecutors' superiors in the Department of Justice did not permit them to continue pressing that position. This led the Washington Legal Foundation to seek and obtain leave of the court to brief and argue as amicus curiae in defense of the statute, a defense which was successful. J.A. 184-85. Dickerson's petition for certiorari also sought review of the question whether Section 3501 was "properly raised" below, but the Court declined to consider the issue.

accommodates legislative modification. Accordingly, there is neither need nor reason to overrule *Miranda* in order to uphold Section 3501.

The benefits of *Miranda* are preserved virtually intact by Section 3501. There is ample reason to conclude that *Miranda* warnings will remain a standard law enforcement practice, because the statute, as well as numerous other legal rules, makes it very much in every officer's interest to continue to give them. What Section 3501 changes is not so much the officer's incentive to give warnings, but rather *Miranda's* draconian remedy for any defect in giving them (or, as here, just in proving they were given). As Congress understood, the *automatic* character of *Miranda's* exclusionary rule is excessive because, heedless of the costs, it excludes confessions that manifestly were not produced by the police coercion that was *Miranda's* principal target.

So long as *in*voluntary confessions remain banned, as they are under Section 3501, and so long as trial courts are empowered without limitation to examine and thwart any police behavior that produces involuntary confessions—again as they are under the statute—*Miranda's* automatic exclusionary rule is unnecessary to preserve the full breadth of a suspect's Fifth Amendment right not to be compelled to be a witness against himself. Because *Miranda's* automatic rule excluding *unwarned* statements extends beyond the Fifth Amendment's bar on *actually compelled* statements, Congress was free to balance for itself the costs and benefits of that automatic rule, and to supersede it with a rule more in keeping with the facts of each case and more faithful to the text of the Fifth Amendment.

In Section I below, we show that Congress had the authority to modify *Miranda's* exclusionary rule as it did in Section 3501. The rule was an exercise by the Court of its power to devise, in the absence of legislation, prophylactic measures that may extend beyond constitutional requirements in order to protect the underlying constitutional right. In cases such as *New York* v. *Quarles,* 467 U.S. 649 (1984), *Harris v. New York,* 401 U.S. 222, 224 (1971), and *Oregon* v. *Hass,* 420 U.S. 714, 722 (1975), the Court has made clear that there is "no constitutional imperative," 467 U.S. at 658 n.7, requiring the exclusion of an unwarned yet voluntary statement. Section 3501 is built on this understanding, while fully honoring the requirements of the Fifth Amendment by continuing a blanket ban on involuntary confessions. Nothing in the Constitution provides grounds for the Court to invalidate the decision of Congress to modify the overprotective and extraconstitutional features of the court-devised rule.

In Section II, we show that even if the judicial branch properly may require some measure of prophylaxis beyond what the Constitution requires, Section 3501, taken together with the considerable development over the last 34 years of other statutes, rules and remedies regulating police behavior, amply provides the needed measure of protection. By listing the rendition of warnings as a factor a court *must* consider in making voluntariness determinations, Section 3501 itself provides strong incentives for federal officers to continue delivering warnings. Moreover, Section 3501 should not be examined in a vacuum. Congress has bolstered the protections the statute provides with other rules such as a 1974 provision allowing suits against federal agencies that produce coerced confessions. These measures, along with post-Miranda judicial doctrines like *Bivens* v. *Six Unknown Named Agents,* 403 U.S. 388 (1971), and improved training of federal law enforcement officers, adequately protect Fifth Amendment values.

In Section III, we show that, whether or not Section 3501 supersedes *Miranda* of its own force, the Court itself should modify *Miranda's* irrebuttable, but certainly factually incorrect, presumption that every unwarned confession is *ipso facto* involuntary and hence must be excluded. In *City of Boerne* v. *Flores,* 521 U.S. 507 (1997), the Court held that when Congress legislates to protect constitutional rights, its remedy should be both congruent and proportional to the evil it aims to address. Applying the proportionality standard to the Court's prophylactic rules, it follows that the now-automatic exclusionary rule of *Miranda* should be changed to allow the government to prove, if it can, that in a given case an unwarned or imperfectly warned statement was nonetheless a product of free will.

ARGUMENT

I. SECTION 3501 IS A PERMISSIBLE RESTRUCTURING BY CONGRESS OF A PROPHYLACTIC RULE THAT SWEEPS MORE BROADLY THAN THE CONSTITUTION.

The question whether *Miranda's* automatic exclusionary rule or Section 3501 governs the admissibility of confessions turns on whether *Miranda's* rule is constitutionally required. If it is, then plainly Congress could not change it. *See City of Boerne* v. *Flores,* 521 U.S. 507 (1997). If otherwise—if instead it is, as the Court often has stated, a judicially-devised remedy that "serves" the Fifth Amendment but "sweeps more broadly than the Fifth Amendment itself," *Oregon* v. *Elstad,* 470 U.S. 298, 306 (1985)—then it is equally plain that Congress does have the power to modify it. *See Smith* v. *Robbins,* 120 S.Ct. 746 (2000); *Palermo* v. *United States,* 360 U.S. 343 (1959). Congress may substitute a different remedial regime so long as that regime honors what the Constitution requires.

The court below determined that *Miranda's* exclusionary rule is not constitutionally required, and that Section 3501 is a permissible modification.[footnote 2] Both conclusions are correct.

A. Miranda Did Not Create a New Constitutional Right Empowering the Defendant to Exclude at Trial His Unwarned, But Voluntarily Given, Statement

The *Miranda* rule "is not itself required by the Fifth Amendment's prohibition on coerced confessions. . . ." *Davis* v. *United States,* 512 U.S. at 458. This conclusion is supported by the text and history of the Fifth Amendment, the structure of the *Miranda* decision, and numerous subsequent holdings from the Court interpreting *Miranda.*

1. Miranda Created Non-Constitutional, Prophylactic Rules

Until 1966, no special rule governed the admissibility in federal court of incriminating statements made by a suspect in police custody. Instead, as the court below explained, the approach regarding such statements "remained the same for nearly 180 years: confessions were admissible at trial if made voluntarily." J.A. 194. *See generally* Joseph D. Grano, Confessions, Truth and the Law 87-144 (1993); *Dept. of Justice Office of Legal Policy, Report to the Attorney General on the Law of Pretrial Interrogation, reprinted in* 22 U. Mich. J.L. Ref. 437, 453-91 (1989) ("*DOJ Report*"). In 1966, however, the Court considered whether there should be additional protection for a suspect during custodial police questioning. In *Miranda* v. *Arizona,* 384 U.S. 436 (1966), the Court concluded that in such circumstances, the voluntariness rule should be supplemented with the now well-known warnings and waiver procedure.

The parties view these supplements as virtual—although they concede, not actual—requirements of the Fifth Amendment's prohibition against any person being "compelled in any criminal case to be a witness against himself." U.S. Const. amend. V. They are then left to wonder about the conceded "tension" their view creates with numerous later cases repeatedly emphasizing that those safeguards are "not themselves rights protected by the Constitution," *e.g., New York* v. *Quarles,* 467 U.S. 649, 654 (1984) (internal quotation omitted). Govt. Br. at 39. The parties make no effort to sketch a consistent theory that would reconcile the holdings of these later cases, *see*

---

[2]The other courts that have squarely decided the issue have reached the same conclusion as the court below. *See United States* v. *Crocker,* 510 F.2d 1129, 1136-38 (10th Cir. 1975) (alternative holding); *United States* v. *Rivas-Lopez,* 988 F. Supp. 1424, 1430-36 (D. Utah 1997); *United States* v. *Tapia-Mendoza,* 41 F.Supp.2d 1250, 1256 (D. Utah 1999); *but cf. United States* v. *Cheely,* 21 F.3d 914, 923 (9th Cir. 1994) (two-sentence conclusion that Section 3501 does not "trump" *Edwards* v. *Arizona*).

infra, at p.16, n.10, with the features of those cases (*Miranda's* application to the states and the like) that the parties favor. The failure to advance a reconciling theory, or any theory specifically explaining *Miranda's* constitutional basis, is the conceptual black hole in the parties' case. Their failure to resolve this central analytical issue impeaches the fundamentals of their claim that *Miranda* is immune from legislative change. [footnote 3]

There is certainly language in *Miranda* that can be read as imposing constitutional requirements. *See* Pet. Br. at 18-20. But even without reference to later opinions that remove any doubt, *Miranda* is better read as creating safeguards rather than establishing previously unseen requirements of the Fifth Amendment itself.

The *Miranda* Court stated that it had no intention of "creat[ing] a constitutional straitjacket." *Miranda,* 384 U.S. at 467. This disclaimer is difficult to explain if the Court believed the specific rules it announced were ordained by the Constitution. The opinion characteristically speaks of the "potentiality" of compulsion and the need for "appropriate safeguards" designed "to insure" that statements are the product of free choice, as well as the possibility of Fifth Amendment rights being "jeopardized" by custodial interrogation. 384 U.S. at 457, 479. But potential compulsion is different from actual compulsion; jeopardizing Fifth Amendment rights is different from violating them; and assuring that Fifth Amendment rights are protected is different from concluding that they are always infringed without those protections. *Miranda's* rationale is, therefore, prophylactic in precisely the sense the Court's later cases have used that term.

2. The Court's More Recent Decisions Leave No Doubt that Compliance with Miranda's Rules is not a Constitutional Prerequisite for Admitting Confessions.
More than a quarter century of this Court's jurisprudence, starting with *Michigan* v. *Tucker,* 417 U.S. 433, 443-444 (1974), establishes beyond argument that the Constitution does not require *Miranda* warnings. Still less does it require the rule that a demonstrably voluntary confession must be excluded simply because the warnings were absent, defective as to some particular, or (as here) inadequately proved because of a later prosecutorial misstep unrelated to the suspect's questioning. Rather, *Miranda's* rules were, as the Court often has said, put forth as "a series of recommended procedural safeguards," *Davis* v. *United States,* 512 U.S. at 457-458, that are "not themselves rights protected by the Constitution" and are "not constitutional in character," *Withrow* v. *Williams,* 507 U.S. 689, 690-691 (1993); *see Oregon* v. *Elstad,* 470 U.S. at 306-07. The *Miranda* rules "are preventative and do not . . . stem from violations of a constitutional right." *Arizona* v. *Roberson,* 486 U.S. 675, 691 (1988) (Kennedy, J., dissenting).

This view of *Miranda's* rules as judicially crafted safeguards rather than constitutional rights is no mere loose shorthand. The holdings of three of the Court's most important *Miranda*-related cases rest directly on *Miranda's* non-constitutional status. In each of those cases, the Court allowed the admission into evidence of un-Mirandized but voluntary confessions. In *New York* v. *Quarles,* 467 U.S. 649, 654 (1984), the Court held that an incriminating statement obtained by police questioning of a rape suspect they had just captured was admissible despite the failure to give *Miranda* warnings. Similarly, in *Harris* v. *New York,* 401 U.S. 222, 224 (1971), and *Oregon* v. *Hass,* 420 U.S. 714, 722 (1975), the Court held that statements obtained in violation of *Miranda* could be used to impeach the testimony of a defendant who took the stand. The Court reasoned that the central truth-seeking purpose of the trial would be too far undermined if the defendant were permitted to keep from the jury his previous voluntary, though un-Mirandized, account.

---

[3]Dickerson does at times appear to offer a theory of *Miranda,* albeit one that cannot and does not seriously purport to survive *Quarles* and similar cases. Pet. Br. at 22-27. The Department offers no theory.

The basis for these rulings was that *Miranda's* exclusionary rule is not constitutionally required. Other considerations—including, significantly for purposes of this case, a reluctance to put the public safety at risk or to allow distortion of the truth—could take precedence over that rule, which rested on a *policy* decision by the *Miranda* majority to bolster the Fifth Amendment with an additional layer of protection. *See Quarles*, 467 U.S. at 658 n.7; *Hass*, 420 U.S. at 721-24; *Harris*, 401 U.S. at 224-26.

The competing theory of *Miranda's* exclusionary rule is that un-Mirandized statements are excluded because the failure to give the suspect warnings means his statements are *necessarily* "compelled" as that term is used in the Fifth Amendment. *See* Pet. Br. at 19. This theory cannot be squared with these decisions. Under that reading, *any* use of an un-Mirandized statement at trial, including the ones allowed in *Quarles, Harris,* and *Hass* would also have to be barred, since those uses too would amount to "compelled" self-incriminating testimony. *See Mincey* v. *Arizona,* 437 U.S. 385, 397-98 (1978); *New Jersey* v. *Portash,* 440 U.S. 450, 458-59 (1979). [footnote 4] Accordingly, the Court's admission of un-Mirandized statements in *Quarles, Harris,* and *Hass* proves that Miranda's rule excluding unwarned but voluntary statements is not required by the Constitution.[footnote 5] That is the starting point from which to analyze Congress's authority to adopt Section 3501.

B. The Miranda Rules are Best Viewed as an Exercise of the Court's Power to Craft Safeguards for Constitutional Rights in the Absence of Legislative Action.

The parties argue that the statute cannot stand because it adopts an approach different from what is said to be *Miranda's* constitutionally "based" regime. Conspicuously absent from this analysis is any specific explanation of what *Miranda's* constitutional "basis" is. Instead, the parties employ gossamer phrases to the effect that, for example, Miranda has "constitutional dimension," Pet. Br. at 25, or that *Miranda* represented "an exercise of this Court's authority to implement and effectuate constitutional rights . . . ." Govt. Br at 6. A more determined effort to understand *Miranda's* actual status demonstrates, however, that Section 3501 is compatible with Miranda's legal foundations. Accordingly, there is no need to overrule *Miranda* in order to uphold the statute.

Miranda's exclusionary rule is best understood as an exercise of the Court's authority to improvise measures to assist in the protection of constitutional rights where neither the Constitution nor the legislature has specified a particular mechanism for protecting those rights. *See, e.g.,* Bivens v. *Six Unknown Agents,* 403 U. S. 388 (1971); *Mapp v. Ohio,* 367 U.S. 643 (1961).[footnote 6] The judicially devised regime may and sometimes does sweep more broadly than is strictly necessary to vindicate the right involved, *Bivens,* 403 U.S. at 397; *see also id.* at 406-08 (Harlan, J.,

---

[4]While emphasizing at length the importance of stare decisis (*see* Pet. Br. at 30-45; Govt. Br. at 29-49), the parties fail to explain how, without overruling *Quarles, Harris* and *Hass,* the Court could conclude that the Constitution requires the suppression of an unwarned but voluntary statement. To pass off *Quarles* as the "public safety exception" to *Miranda* of course explains nothing. The question is not whether *Quarles* is such an "exception," but under what principle of law that or any exception is possible. *Miranda's* exclusionary rule is no more and no less "constitutionally based" when public safety is at stake than at any other time. And certainly neither public safety nor anything else could authorize the prosecution to use as evidence a statement obtained by what the Fifth Amendment actually forbids, namely compulsion. *See Mincey,* 437 U.S. at 398 ("*any* use criminal trial use against a defendant of his *involuntary* statement is a denial of due process of law) (emphases in original).

[5]These three cases are by no means the only ones reaching such a conclusion. For example, another well-developed line of cases allows evidence derived from statements obtained in violation of *Miranda* to be used because *Miranda's* "procedural safeguards were not themselves rights protected by the Constitution," *Michigan* v. *Tucker,* 417 U.S. 433, 444 (1974), and "may be triggered even in the absence of a Fifth Amendment violation," *Oregon* v. *Elstad,* 470 U.S. 298, 306 (1985).

[6]The search and seizure exclusionary rule is different from *Miranda's* because it is a remedy for *actual violations* of the Fourth Amendment. Adopting an analogous approach in the Fifth Amendment context would mean suppressing evidence only in cases in which a defendant's constitutional right against compelled self-incrimination has actually been violated. This is precisely the approach of Section 3501.

concurring). [footnote 7] Because the Court has crafted such measures to protect constitutional rights against infringement by the states as well as the federal government, *see, e.g., Mapp; Bush* v. *Lucas,* 462 U.S. 367, 374-75 (1983), this understanding of *Miranda's* exclusionary rule is consistent with its application to the states.

Since *Miranda's* exclusionary rule is not a requirement of the Fifth Amendment, but is instead, in the mold of *Bivens,* an exercise of the Court's power to improvise a more sweeping, albeit prophylactic, measure designed to assist in protecting Fifth Amendment rights, it follows that Congress had the authority to modify it. The existence of such authority is presumed throughout *Bivens* itself, for example, and lies at the heart of the Court's later holding in *Bush* v. *Lucas,* 462 U.S. 367 (1983). In that case, the Court refused to allow a *Bivens* remedy for money damages in an action by a federal employee for the government's breach of his First Amendment rights. The Court concluded the *Bivens* remedy was precluded because Congress had provided for a different remedy—not including money damages—through various federal personnel statutes. In *Bush,* the Court reached this conclusion while assuming that civil service remedies were *not* as fully effective as a *Bivens* remedy would be either in compensating the plaintiff or in deterring the unconstitutional exercise of authority by supervisors. 462 U.S. at 372-73, 377. According to the Court, the touchstone for assessing the constitutionality of the remedial regime Congress chose was not the judicially-devised regime for which it substituted. Rather, the touchstone was whether the congressional regime provided "meaningful" relief for the constitutional violation at issue. *Id.* at 368, 386. If it did, then how it compared to the judicially-devised scheme was irrelevant. *Id.* at 368, 386-90; *see also Schweiker* v. *Chilicky,* 487 U.S. 412, 425 (1988) (remedial regime replacing judicially-devised one upheld because it contained "meaningful safeguards" for the constitutional rights at issue even though it failed to provide as "complete relief" as a *Bivens* remedy).

Analogously, in *Smith* v. *Robbins,* 120 S.Ct. 746 (2000), the Court upheld as constitutional a state scheme concerning withdrawal by appointed appellate counsel when faced with a frivolous appeal. The issue, the Court declared, was "what is constitutionally compelled," *id.* at 763, not how closely the state's procedure—indeed the only procedure—resembled the procedure the Court suggested in *Anders* v. *California,* 386 U.S. 738 (1967). The *Robbins* Court warned that "any view . . . that converted [the *Anders* procedure] from a suggestion into a straitjacket would contravene [our] established practice of allowing the States wide discretion, subject to the minimum requirements of the [Constitution], to experiment with solutions to difficult policy problems." *Id.* at 11.

Like the regimes at issue in *Bush, Chilicky,* and *Robbins,* the modification to *Miranda's* automatic exclusionary rule that Congress adopted in Section 3501 is proper because it too fully protects the underlying constitutional right: the citizen's right not to be compelled to be a witness against himself. Indeed, it protects the underlying right more fully than the regime at issue in *Bush,* since in that case the Court assumed that the legislative remedy for the constitutional violation at issue was "less than complete." 462 U.S. at 373. That cannot be said of Section 3501: Under the statute, statements found for any reason to have been involuntary *are always* inadmissible, thereby preventing the defendant from incurring *any* constitutional harm under the Self-Incrimination Clause. [footnote 8]

---

[7] The crafting of interim remedies not themselves required by the Constitution, but designed in the absence of legislation to assist in protecting constitutional rights, has become known as the exercise by the Court of the power to create "constitutional common law." *See* Henry P. Monaghan, *Foreword: Constitutional Common Law,* 89 Harv. L. Rev. 1, 42 (1975).

[8] *See United States* v. *Balsys,* 118 S.Ct. 2218, 2232 n.12 (1999) ("Although conduct by law enforcement officials prior to trial may ultimately impair [the Self-Incrimination] right, a constitutional violation occurs only at trial") (internal citation omitted).

Congress of course has no authority to modify the content of constitutional rights whether directly or under the guise of its remedial powers. *See City of Boerne v. Flores,* 521 U.S. 507 (1997). By the same token, we assume it could not abrogate a judicially devised protective measure essential to the survival of a constitutional right. But that is very different from saying that Congress likewise has no authority to modify a ruling that "overprotects" a constitutional right, as is clearly the case with *Miranda's* automatic rule excluding all unwarned statements. *See, e.g., Oregon v. Elstad,* 470 U.S. at 306 (*Miranda* "sweeps more broadly than the Fifth Amendment itself"); *Duckworth v. Eagan,* 492 U.S. 195, 209 (1989) (O'Connor, J., concurring) ("the *Miranda* rule 'overprotects' the value at stake"). Overprotection *means* protection beyond what the Constitution requires. It is in precisely that area that Congress must be free to fashion or modify rules as it thinks wisest. *See Smith v. Robbins,* 120 S.Ct. at 763 ("We address not what is prudent or appropriate, but only what is constitutionally compelled") (internal quotation omitted); *cf. Palermo v. United States,* 360 U.S. 343, 353 n.11 (1959).

Indeed, if Congress had no role in making independent judgments about what the law should be once constitutional requirements are satisfied, it is difficult to see that it would have any role at all. Rules required by the Constitution and rules beyond those required by the Constitution together exhaust the universe of rules. If the judicial branch is empowered to establish for all time the latter as well as the former, then there is nothing left for Congress to do. *Cf. Boerne,* 521 U.S. at 535-36 ("Our national experience teaches that the Constitution is preserved best when each part of the Government respects both the Constitution and the proper actions and determinations of the other branches.").

In considering the legislation that became Section 3501, Congress balanced the costs and benefits of a rule excluding all unwarned confessions against the costs and benefits of allowing the trial court to decide on the facts of each case whether the suspect spoke voluntarily. It knew what is obvious, namely, that a court is distinctly less likely to find an unwarned statement to have been voluntary, but that sometimes the court would decide that other circumstances proved the statement's voluntary character. It also knew that there would be some cases where allowing the jury to hear that statement would be the difference between successful and unsuccessful prosecution of a dangerous criminal. Finally, it understood the damage to public confidence in the criminal justice system, not to mention the risk to public safety, that results when the jury reaches the wrong result because it is not allowed to hear highly probative evidence.

Weighing all these considerations, Congress concluded that the cost of slightly less police deterrence—that is, marginally diminished deterrence resulting from the significant risk (as opposed to the certainty) of excluding an unwarned confession—was outweighed by the benefits of admitting such a confession, so long as it is voluntary. Because Congress' modification of *Miranda's* extraconstitutional and overprotective exclusionary rule continues to forbid in all instances the government's use of involuntary statements, it fully affords defendants their rights under the Fifth Amendment, and thus is constitutionally sound.

The parties' answer to this argument depends on clouding the distinction between constitutional requirements and nonconstitutional protective measures. The strategy of this response is carried off with a virtual army of seemingly refined phrases—"constitutionally rooted," "of constitutional dimension" and the like—used to characterize *Miranda's* status.[footnote 9] But these characterizations turn

---

[9]The list is not unimpressive. We are, for example, told that the *Miranda* rules have "constitutional weight," "constitutional force," "constitutional underpinnings," "constitutional dimension," and "constitutional footings"; that they are "constitutionally based"; that they rest on "a constitutional basis," "a constitutional foundation," and "constitutional grounds"; and finally that they "implement and protect constitutional rights." Pet. Br. at 22, 23 25; Govt. Br. at 23, 25, Govt. Cert. Br. at 7-9, 16-17.

out to be not so much refinement as equivocation impersonating refinement. They do nothing to resolve, and in fact seem designed to obscure, the fundamental incoherence of the parties' position: admitting that confessions obtained in violation of *Miranda* do not always amount to compelled self-incrimination, but maintaining nonetheless that it is unconstitutional for Congress to permit the admission of such statements even if they have been shown to be voluntary.

The parties' position rests on the implicit assumption that courts, in order to provide an additional shield for the exercise of a constitutional right, have the authority to invalidate an Act of Congress even if it is fully adequate to protect against the actual violation of that right. That, however, is precisely the authority the Court refused to exercise in *Bush* and *Chilicky.* In those cases, the Court found that Congress was in a better position than the courts to evaluate the costs and benefits of differing approaches, *Bush,* 462 U.S. at 387-90, and that the Court had "no legal basis that would allow [it] to revise [Congress's] decisions." *Chilicky,* 487 U.S. at 429.

The same is true here. It is not possible through any feasible set of rules to assure that custodial questioning never becomes coercive. The only way to foreclose that possibility completely would be to prohibit custodial questioning altogether, just as the only way to provide complete assurance against violations of defendants' rights at trial would be to prohibit all prosecutions. The *Miranda* Court declined to impose either prohibition, and with good reason.

Because perfection is not possible, the effectiveness of laws intended to decrease the number of constitutional violations, the estimation of how many there are to be decreased, and the assessment of the cost to other values that one preventive rule or another is likely to impose, are necessarily matters of judgment and degree. "Congressional competence at 'balancing governmental efficiency and the rights of [individuals],' . . . is no more questionable" in the context of custodial interrogations than in other settings. *See Chilicky,* 487 U.S. at 425, *quoting Bush,* 462 U.S. at 389 (internal citation omitted); *see also Palermo,* 360 U.S. at 343 n.11 (discovery rules for criminal defendants). Accordingly, there is no more basis for disturbing Congress's judgment as to what measures are best designed to effectuate that balance fairly in this instance than there was in *Bush* or *Chilicky.*

C. The Application of Miranda's Rules in State Cases Does Not Demonstrate that the Rules are Constitutional Requirements.

The parties acknowledge the Court's repeated statements that *Miranda's* rules are not themselves required by the Constitution and are not constitutional in character. Pet. Br. at 22-24; Govt. Br. at 21-26. They nonetheless contend that *Miranda's* application to the States by implication must mean that the rules *are* constitutional in character.

The parties' contention on this point requires disregarding much of what the Court has said in numerous state cases concerning *Miranda's* non-constitutional status in favor of an implication concerning an issue that the parties in those cases did not even raise. The implication seems dubious for that reason alone. It would be unusual for the Court to have considered that issue *sua sponte* in reviewing the state cases, given its normal disinclination to go beyond the issues that the parties have presented. *See, e.g., Michigan* v. *Mosley,* 423 U.S. 96, 100 (1975) ("Neither party in the present case challenges the continued validity of the *Miranda* decision. . . ."); *Minnick* v. *Mississippi,* 498 U.S. 146, 161 (1990) (Scalia, J., dissenting) ("we have not been called upon to reconsider *Edwards.* . . .").

In any event, the implication about *Miranda's* status that the parties seek to draw cannot be reconciled with the holdings of many of the very state cases they cite. As explained, *supra,* at pp. 8-9, the Court's decision to admit un-Mirandized but voluntary statements in *Quarles, Harris,* and *Hass,* all three of which were state cases, *turned* on the non-constitutional status of *Miranda's* exclusionary rule. Similarly, the decision in *Oregon* v. *Elstad,* to admit a confession that was the fruit of an un-Mirandized earlier statement rests squarely on the ground that "a simple failure to administer *Miranda* warnings is not in itself a violation of the Fifth Amendment." 470 U.S. at 306 n.1. [footnote 10]

If the holdings in these cases are still good law, the most that could follow from the state review cases is that, in the absence of legislation taking a different approach, the Court has some authority to impose on the states nonconstitutional measures designed to protect constitutional rights. Of course we have not disputed that this is so. To the contrary, that theory lies at the heart of our explanation of the legal basis of *Miranda* as a form of constitutional common law—an explanation to which the parties fail to provide a coherent alternative.

To be sure, *Miranda's* application to the States despite the fact that its rules are not constitutionally required implies that the Court has some authority to impose on the States measures that are not strictly constitutionally necessary, but are designed to assist in enforcing constitutional rights. This, of course, is hardly the revolutionary proposition the parties suggest. It is consistent with what the *Miranda* Court itself said on the subject, since for whatever else is in dispute about the decision, it is at a minimum clear that the Court believed that its specific rules were not constitutionally mandated and could be legislatively superseded by others. Thus, the recognition that the Court could impose nonconstitutional rules in the review of state cases provides no basis for the further step of inferring that Congress has no authority to modify those rules in federal jurisdiction.

Miranda is not the only instance in which the Court has found that it has this power. In addition to the cases discussed, *supra,* at pp. 10-12, the Court has engaged in a similar task in several other areas. One illustration is the Act of State doctrine, which bars federal and state courts from inquiring into the validity of the public acts of foreign governments. As explained in *Banco Nacional de Cuba* v. *Sabbatino,* 376 U.S. 398 (1964):

The text of the Constitution does not require the act of state doctrine * * * * The act of state doctrine does, however, have "constitutional" underpinnings. It arises out of the basic relationships between branches of government in a system of separation of powers * * * * [T]here are enclaves of federal judge-made law which bind the States * * * * [T]he act of state doctrine is a principle of decision binding on federal and state courts alike but compelled by neither international law nor the Constitution * * * *

376 U.S. at 423-24, 426-27. Like the *Miranda* rules, the Act of State doctrine is also subject to revision and restriction by Congress as a judicially developed, nonconstitutional rule, even while the Court's authority to craft it in the first instance is not seriously in doubt. *See Banco Nacional de Cuba* v. *Farr,* 383 F.2d 166, 180-81 (2d Cir. 1967), *cert. denied,* 390 U.S. 956 (1968). [footnote 11]

---

[10]The parties collect general language in several cases referring to the *Miranda* rules in constitutional terms. *See, e.g.,* Pet. Br. at 20 & n.9; Govt. Br. at 24-25. Such language is invariably dicta, however, set out in contexts in which the constitutional or nonconstitutional character of the rules was not an issue and no greater precision in expression was called for. None of the dicta purports to supersede more detailed statements about *Miranda's* non-constitutional status in, for example, *Quarles* and *Elstad,* which is clearly part of the logic and holding of these decisions. Numerous other statements are to similar effect *See, e.g., Davis* v. *United States,* 512 U.S. 452, 457 (1994) (*Miranda* rights are "not themselves rights protected by the Constitution") (internal citation omitted); *Michigan* v. *Harvey,* 494 U.S. 344, 350 (1990) (*Miranda* rules are "not themselves rights protected in the Constitution") (internal citation omitted); *Connecticut* v. *Barrett,* 479 U.S. 523, 528 (1987) ("the *Miranda* Court adopted prophylactic rules designed to insulate the exercise of Fifth Amendment rights from government compulsion"); *Moran* v. *Burbine,* 475 U.S. 412, 424 (1986) ("As is now well established, the *Miranda* warnings are not themselves rights protected by the Constitution") (internal quotation omitted).

[11]Another illustration is the dormant commerce clause doctrine. This doctrine furthers the constitutional "right to engage in interstate trade," Dennis v. *Higgins,* 498 U.S. 439, 448 (1991) (internal quotations omitted), by invalidating state laws that unduly burden or interfere with such commerce. The Court's decisions in this area are certainly "constitutionally based" on the Commerce Clause. Nonetheless, Congress is free to validate state actions that would otherwise be prohibited under the Court's decisions. *See, e.g., Northeast Bancorp* v. *Board of Governors,* 472 U.S. 159, 174-75 (1985); *Pennsylvania* v. *Wheeling & Belmont Bridge Co.,* 59 U.S. 421, 436 (1856).

This in turn means that language in some cases outside the *Miranda* context that seems to suggest that the Court uniformly lacks the authority to impose nonconstitutional measures on the States has been overly broad. [footnote 12] Such language perhaps should be read to be limited to circumstances where the measures being advocated are not sufficiently connected to the enforcement of a constitutional provision. That was the distinction the Court suggested in *Moran* v. *Burbine,* 475 U.S. 412 (1986). There the Court drew a line between *Miranda's* prophylactic measures, which in its view could permissibly be imposed on the States—not because they were constitutionally required but because they were sufficiently closely connected to the protection of Fifth Amendment rights—and the rule the defendant was urging. See *id.* at 424-25. That rule would have excluded statements on account of police deception of an attorney seeking to represent a suspect who had agreed to talk voluntarily. The Court held that it could not impose that rule, because its lack of connection to the Fifth Amendment meant that its imposition would cross the line between a permissible prophylactic measure and an impermissible supervisory power exercise. [footnote 13]

D. The Application of Miranda's Rules in Habeas Proceedings Does Not Demonstrate that The Rules Are Constitutional Requirements
The parties also claim that the application of the *Miranda* rules in habeas proceedings, see *Withrow* v. *Williams,* 507 U.S. 689 (1993), demonstrates that the rules are constitutional requirements. In *Withrow,* Dickerson asserts, the Court "rejected the government's argument that since the *Miranda* rules are not constitutional in character, but merely 'prophylactic,' federal habeas review should not extend to claims based on violations of these rules. *Withrow,* 507 U.S. at 690." Pet. Br. at 22 (internal quotation omitted).

This is true as far as it goes. What Dickerson neglects to mention, however, is that the Court made clear it was rejecting *not* the government's *premise* about the non-constitutional status of the *Miranda* rules, but rather the *consequence* the government argued flowed from that premise. The full paragraph reads as follows:

Petitioner, supported by the United States as *amicus curiae,* argues that *Miranda's* safeguards are not constitutional in character, but merely "prophylactic," and that in consequence habeas review should not extend to a claim that a state conviction rests on statements obtained in the absence of these safeguards. *We accept petitioner's premise for purposes of this case, but not her conclusion.* 507 U.S. at 691

---

[12]Many of these statements are also susceptible to more than one reading. For example, *Mu'Min* v. *Virginia,* 500 U.S. 415, 422 (1991), indicates that the Court's power over the states "is limited to *enforcing* the commands of the United States Constitution" (emphasis added). Of course, if the Court can "enforce" constitutional commands with non-constitutional prophylactic rules, as the *Miranda* doctrine indicates, then this statement provides no basis for concluding that the *Miranda* rules are somehow constitutionally required.

[13]As a final argument supporting the constitutional character of the *Miranda* regime, the parties claim that it is analogous to various other rules promulgated by the Court that are said to "sweep more broadly than the constitutional right upon which they are based." Govt. Br. at 44; *see* Pet. Br. at 25-27. With one irrelevant exception, these analogies prove nothing of the sort. Instead, the cited rules, while prophylactic in the sense that they instrumentally guard against various evils, are constitutional *requirements* of the Due Process Clause or other constitutional provisions. *See generally* Joseph D. Grano, *Miranda's Constitutional Difficulties: A Reply to Professor Schulhofer,* 55 U. Chi. L. Rev. 174, 188-89 (1988). For instance, it may be true that the evil guarded against by *North Carolina* v. *Pearce,* 395 U.S. 711 (1969)—vindictive increases in sentences and defendants' inhibitions from the fear of such increases—would not invariably occur otherwise. Nonetheless, the Court has held that, where the risk of the threatened evil is sufficiently grave, measures to prevent them must be observed as a matter of constitutional due process. *See, e.g., Blackledge* v. *Perry,* 417 U.S. 21, 28 (1974) (holding that *Pearce* applies in two-tiered system because "[d]ue process of law *requires* that such a potential for vindictiveness must not enter into" the system) (emphasis added). In contrast, the *Miranda* rules cannot be understood as a due process requirement on a par with *Pearce,* because the Constitution does not bar the admission of un-Mirandized but voluntary statements.

The irrelevant example provided by the parties is *Michigan* v. *Jackson,* 475 U.S. 625 (1986). But that case "simply superimpos[es] the Fifth Amendment analysis of *Edwards* [and related *Miranda* doctrine] onto the Sixth Amendment." *Michigan* v. *Harvey,* 494 U.S. 344, 350 (1990). Because the *Jackson* rules are merely an offshoot of *Miranda,* they provide no independent guidance on interpreting the *Miranda* rules.

(emphasis added). Moreover, also contrary to what Dickerson's brief suggests, the Court did not reject that conclusion for purposes of determining whether Miranda violations provided a sufficient *jurisdictional* basis for a habeas claim, a point petitioner declined to press at argument. [footnote 14] Rather, the question the Court decided was on what basis habeas review of such claims should proceed: under ordinary habeas standards, or the judicially-created rule of *Stone* v. *Powell,* 428 U.S. 465 (1976), imposing special extra-statutory limitations on review of Fourth Amendment habeas challenges.

This leaves the parties to argue that, despite its statement to the contrary, the *Withrow* Court must nevertheless have implicitly decided that the Miranda rules were constitutional; otherwise, instead of reaching the merits, the Court should have reversed the district court on jurisdictional grounds. This must be so, according to the parties, because federal habeas review of state court decisions is available only for claims that a person "is in custody in violation of the Constitution or the laws or treaties of the United States." 28 U.S.C. 2254(a). In their view, a *Miranda* violation "certainly does not involve laws or treaties," Pet. Br. at 22; *see* Govt. Br. at 24. Therefore, the only theory on which *Miranda* claims could be cognizable on habeas is if a *Miranda* violation were a violation of the Constitution.

As with their argument about *Miranda's* application to the States, this means that once again the parties are arguing that the true holding of *Withrow* is the opposite of what the Court said was the premise of that holding. And as with that argument as well, the parties ignore an easy reconciling solution.

Contrary to the parties' hasty dismissal of the possibility, it seems far more likely that the Court's implicit finding of jurisdiction in *Withrow* rests on the proposition that *Miranda,* while not part of the Constitution, is part of the "laws of the United States," which for purposes of Section 2254(a), includes not only federal statutes but also decisional law designed to help effectuate the federal Constitution or statutes. *See generally* Larry W. Yackle, Post Conviction Remedies § 97, at 371 (1981 & 1996 Supp.) (concluding *Miranda* rules can be viewed as "federal 'law' which, under the [habeas] statute, may form the basis for habeas relief"). That view was the one taken on the question at the time by the Department of Justice; [footnote 15] it accords with the interpretation the Court has given of the same phrase used in a similar context in the federal question jurisdictional statute, 28 U.S.C. 1331, *see National Farmers Union Ins. Companies* v. *Crow Tribe of Indians,* 471 U.S. 845, 850-51 (1985) (federal common law as articulated in rules that are fashioned by court decisions constitutes "laws" as that term is used in Section 1331); and it parallels the construction the Court gave to the words "laws of the several States" to include state decisional law in *Erie Railroad Co.* v. *Tompkins,* 304 U.S. 64 (1938). Thus, the cognizability of *Miranda* violations on habeas provides no basis for concluding that *Miranda's* exclusionary rule is constitutionally required or immune from legislative modification.

E. Considerations of Stare Decisis Support Upholding Section 3501

Since, as the Court has held repeatedly, the *Miranda* rules are nonconstitutional, there is no need to overrule *Miranda* to uphold Section 3501. Rather, if the Court affirms the judgment below, it will ratify a statute that supersedes nonconstitutional case law rules while continuing to preserve both the constitutional right itself and the courts' ability to enforce that right. There is no affront to stare decisis in doing so,

---

[14] *See Withrow* v. *Williams,* No. 91-1030, tr. of oral argument at 12.

[15] When *Withrow* was argued, the Deputy Solicitor General told the Court directly that *Miranda* could indeed be viewed as a "law" of the United States under the habeas statute. *See Withrow* v. *Williams,* No. 91-1030, tr. of oral argument at 15-16.

only a recognition that Congress has the final say on matters that the Constitution does not resolve.

On the other hand, holding Section 3501 unconstitutional could not avoid creating serious stare decisis difficulties. It would require overruling *Quarles, Harris, Hass,* and *Elstad* for starters, and indeed every one of the Court's cases whose judgment has depended on the long-held view that *Miranda* provides only "a series of recommended procedural safeguards." *Tucker,* 417 U.S. at 444. It would also require the Court to retract statements in two recent cases that Section 3501 is "the statute governing the admissibility of confessions in federal prosecutions." *Davis* v. *United States,* 512 U.S. 452, 457 n.* (1994); *United States* v. *Alvarez-Sanchez,* 511 U.S. 350, 351 (1994) (upholding Section 3501(c)). [footnote 16]

The most one could say for the parties' argument is that the *Miranda* decision in some places apparently indicated that actual compulsion in violation of the Fifth Amendment necessarily occurs unless the *Miranda* procedures or other equally restrictive procedures are observed in custodial questioning. *See* 384 U.S. at 457-58, 467-74. As we have shown, however, this view was abandoned years ago. Hence, any "overruling" of the aspect of *Miranda* which might have implied immunity from legislative modification has already happened. As the government has conceded, "The Court has retreated from [the inherent compulsion] aspect of its reasoning in *Miranda.*" Govt. Cert. Br. at 13-14; *see also Planned Parenthood* v. *Casey,* 505 U.S. 833, 855 (1992) (it weighs against following a precedent if "related principles of law have so far developed as to have left the old rule no more than a remnant of abandoned doctrine"). [footnote 17]

F. Policy Considerations Support Upholding Section 3501

Since stare decisis does not support the parties' attack on Section 3501, their accompanying analysis of policy considerations that allegedly support the *Miranda* rules is just that and nothing more: arguments of an essentially legislative nature as to why the *Miranda* rules are beneficial. In our constitutional system, arguments of this type are properly addressed to the legislature and afford no basis for invalidating a statute which is consistent with the Constitution.

Moreover, even considered on their own terms, the parties' arguments are unpersuasive. Even if it were true that *Miranda's* procedures are on the whole beneficial to law enforcement, a question we address momentarily, it would not advance the parties' cause. First, for obvious reasons the parties do not even purport to say that *Miranda's* automatic exclusionary rule, the only aspect of *Miranda* directly before the Court, has such beneficial effects. Second, nothing in 18 U.S.C. 3501 prevents or discourages law enforcement agencies from continuing to give *Miranda* warnings. As to the government's suggestion that *Miranda* is not a problem for federal law enforcement agencies, the overwhelming support for the court of appeals' decision by prosecutors and law enforcement organizations who have filed amicus briefs in this case including representatives of federal law enforcement agents suggests otherwise.

Indeed, contrary to the impression conveyed in the government's brief, the actual views of federal law enforcement agencies that have been lodged with the Court reveal serious difficulties with *Miranda's* automatic exclusionary rule. While the brief reports that "federal law enforcement agencies have concluded that the

---

[16]The statement in *Alvarez-Sanchez* came at the urging of the government. *See* Br. for the U.S. at 32, *United States* v. *Alvarez-Sanchez,* 511 U.S. 350 (1994) (No. 92-1812) (urging the admission of a confession under Section 3501(c) and explaining that Section 3501(a) "requires the admission" of voluntary statements). In its earlier submission to the Court, the government did not address any of the complex severability issues that arise under its current position that the major provision of the statute is actually unconstitutional.

[17]It is also interesting that government asserts in its brief that for many years the *Miranda* rules have been stable, clear, and helpful to law enforcement, *see* Govt. Br. at 35, while in a footnote it reports that "[i]n many respects, the Court has tailored the *Miranda* doctrine as necessary to make it more workable." *Id.* at 35, n.25. A rule that has been changed in "many respects" is not the strongest candidate for rigorous application of stare decisis, and the frequent changes themselves attest to the problems *Miranda* creates.

Miranda decision itself generally does not hinder their investigations," Govt. Br. at 34, that conclusion appears to rest on the position of such agencies as the Internal Revenue Service and the Customs Service, which typically conduct non-custodial interviews, to which *Miranda* is inapplicable. *See, e.g., Beckwith* v. *United States,* 425 U.S. 341 (1976); *United States* v. *Leasure,* 122 F.3d 837, 840 (9th Cir. 1997), *cert. denied,* 522 U.S. 1065 (1998). On the other hand, the Drug Enforcement Administration, which perhaps conducts a higher percentage of custodial interrogations than any other federal agency, concluded that the "methods used by DEA to investigate drug organizations highlight the need to reform the formal, prophylactic requirements of *Miranda.*" Letter from Richard A. Fiano, DEA's Chief of Operations, to Frank A.S. Campbell (Oct. 13, 1999). [footnote 18] Similarly, the FBI reports that offshoots of the *Miranda* requirements, such as the rule of *Edwards* v. *Arizona,* 451 U.S. 477 (1981), have had "an impact on numerous FBI investigations." Letter from Larry R. Parkinson to Eleanor D. Acheson (Oct. 19, 1999). Moreover, while the government cannot conceal the fact that it opposed the *Miranda* rules at their inception, *see* Govt. Br. at 48 n.36, it neglects to mention that the Department has for many years supported the constitutionality of Section 3501. *See DOJ Report, supra,* 22 U. Mich. J.L. Ref. at 520-21; Paul G. Cassell, *The Statute that Time Forgot: 18 U.S.C. § 3501 and the Overhauling of* Miranda, 85 Iowa L. Rev. 175, 197-203 (1999); *see also United States* v. *Crocker,* 510 F.2d 1129, 1136-38 (10th Cir. 1975) (upholding statute at government request).

Even apart from this information, the government's own brief admits that the *Miranda* system has harmed federal law enforcement, but claims those harms, which it avoids detailing, can be dealt with by other means. Stripped of euphemism, the government's position appears to be essentially as follows: (1) The Court should hold Section 3501 unconstitutional, thereby perpetuating *Miranda* in all respects; (2) The Court should thereafter ameliorate the harm resulting from its refusal to uphold the statute by overruling or modifying such decisions as *Edwards* v. *Arizona,* 451 U.S. 477 (1981). Govt. Br. at 35 (discussing considerations that would apply "should the Court be faced with reconsideration" of *Edwards* other cases); and (3) The Court should perhaps, in the future, further ameliorate the harm resulting from its refusal to uphold the statute by adopting a "good faith" exception to *Miranda.* Govt. Br. at 36 n.26.

Obviously, upholding Section 3501 would resolve the problems identified by the government. In contrast, the government's approach would require a repudiation of the current precedents in order to invalidate Section 3501, and would then require an overruling of additional precedents to deal with the resulting harm to law enforcement. As an approach supposedly dictated by respect for stare decisis, the course urged by the government is, to say the least, peculiar.

A final point about the Department's claim that *Miranda* has not harmed law enforcement is that Congress—the branch empowered to make such factual determinations—disagrees. After extensive hearings on *Miranda's* real world effects, the Senate Judiciary Committee recommended adoption of Section 3501 because "the rigid and inflexible requirements of the majority opinion in the *Miranda* case are . . . extremely harmful to law enforcement." S. Rep. 90-1097, 90th Cong., 2d Sess. at 46, *reprinted in* 1968 U.S.C.C.A.N. at 2132. This finding on an "essentially

---

[18]The Solicitor General lodged this correspondence with the Court on February 24, 2000. Curiously, one of the lodged documents is a letter from the DEA General Counsel's Office written just two days before the lodging. While supporting Section 3501, that letter conflicts in important respects with the views quoted above by DEA's Chief of Operations, Richard A. Fiano, which were written well before the filing of the government's brief. It should be noted that the DEA General Counsel's letter was written only *after* two United States Senators had attempted to obtain from the Justice Department the earlier written views of the DEA supporting Section 3501. *See* 146 Cong. Rec. S760-02 (Feb. 24, 2000) (statement of Sen. Thurmond) (raising questions about why DEA's previous written position was not referenced in the Department's brief to the Court). Undersigned counsel also wrote the Department, seeking information about the views of the United States Attorneys in addition to the other law enforcement components whose opinions the Department has selected for disclosure. The Department, however, has declined to provide those views. So that the record may be complete on these issues, we will lodge this correspondence with the Court.

factual issue" is "of course entitled to a great deal of deference, inasmuch as Congress is an institution better equipped to amass and evaluate the vast amounts of data bearing on such an issue." *Walters* v. *Nat'l Ass'n of Radiation Survivors,* 473 U.S. 305, 331 n.12 (1985).

If Congress's factual finding is correct, as the Court must assume, *see Turner Broadcasting System, Inc.* v. *FCC,* 512 U.S. 622, 666 (1994) (plurality opinion), [footnote 19] many dangerous criminals are escaping justice in the teeth of a federal statute that would permit their successful prosecution. And this stands to reason. Over time, a rule that automatically excludes voluntary confessions whenever there is a deviation from the *Miranda* regime is going to exact a significant toll on the system. The Court has recognized, for example, that "the task of defining 'custody' [under *Miranda*] is a slippery one, and policemen investigating serious crimes cannot realistically be expected to make no errors whatsoever." *Oregon* v. *Elstad,* 470 U.S. 298, 309 (1985). [footnote 20] One of the most worthwhile aspects of the statute is that it does not punish society when the officer fails to adhere to every aspect of *Miranda's* requirements but nonetheless treats the suspect in a way that assures courts—as both courts below felt assured—that the suspect's statement was voluntary. Thus, to the extent public policy considerations are relevant to the Court's conclusion, they support upholding Section 3501.

II. EVEN IF THE COURT IS EMPOWERED TO DEMAND SOME LEVEL OF PROHPYLAXIS BEYOND CONSTITUTIONAL REQUIREMENTS, SECTION 3501, TAKEN TOGETHER WITH OTHER PROVISIONS OF LAW, PROVIDES ADEQUATE PROTECTION

We have argued up to now that Section 3501 is a valid exercise of Congress' authority to modify *Miranda's* extraconstitutional exclusionary rule. The parties disagree, effectively maintaining that Section 3501 is invalid because it violates a rule that in some sense is constitutional, and that even if Congress has a proper role, this particular statute fails to satisfy some additional requirement of prophylactic adequacy. Pet. Br. at 28-29; Govt. Br. at 27-29.

In this section, we demonstrate that the statute, taken together with the legal landscape that surrounds it, provides more than adequate protection to safeguard suspects from police compulsion. A word is useful at the outset, however, to address the premise of the parties' claim.

That premise is that the Constitution requires more than the Constitution requires. In particular, what the parties seek by insisting on *some* protection beyond

---

[19]Recent empirical scholarship also supports the congressional conclusion. *See* Paul G. Cassell & Richard Fowles, *Handcuffing the Cops? A Thirty-Year Perspective on* Miranda's *Harmful Effects on Law Enforcement,* 50 Stan. L. Rev. 1055 (1998) (precipitous drop in FBI crime clearance rates after Miranda, as shown in Appendix A to this brief); Paul G. Cassell, Miranda's *Social Costs: An Empirical Reassessment,* 90 Nw. U.L. Rev. 387 (1996) (before-and-after *Miranda* studies show drop in confession rates); *see also* Paul G. Cassell & Bret S. Hayman, *Police Interrogation in the 1990s: An Empirical Study of the Effects of* Miranda, 43 UCLA L. Rev. 839, 871-76 (1994) (similar findings).

[20]The difficulties in defining "custody" should be enough to demonstrate that *Miranda's* "bright line" rules are blurry and that, if anything, the *Miranda* rules actually increase litigation. Under *Miranda,* a federal court must determine (if requested by the defendant) both (1) *Miranda* compliance (including a determination that the suspect "voluntarily" waived his *Miranda* rights, *see North Carolina* v. *Butler,* 441 U.S. 369, 373 (1979)) *and* (2) the ultimate voluntariness of the statement. Even if the officer complied with Miranda, the Court must still consider a defendant's voluntariness arguments. *See Withrow* v. *Williams,* 507 U.S. 680, 693 (1993) (concluding "virtually all *Miranda* claims" can "simply be recast" as voluntariness arguments). On the other hand, if the officer violated *Miranda,* the court must typically still determine the voluntariness of the statement, since this governs its use for impeachment and derivative evidence purposes. Thus, the *Miranda* rules do not reduce the burden on the courts. *See DOJ Report,* supra, 22 U. Mich. J.L. Ref. at 547-48 ("[There] is no reason to believe that [*Miranda*] has had any effect of reducing the volume of litigation relating to the admission of pretrial statements by defendants").

the Constitution's text is for the Court to rewrite the Fifth Amendment to require the police *affirmatively to assist* the suspect in making what they view as a more enlightened, or at least a shrewder, decision about whether to talk. Imposing such an obligation on the police arguably would be a good idea; it would appeal to some as improving the fairness of the process, although it would disturb others as going too far in handicapping unobjectionable police work. In other words, it is precisely the sort of reasonably debatable policy choice that, because of its extraconstitutional character, is properly committed to popular, rather than judicial, judgment.

And that, we believe, is the crucial point for purposes of this case. For whatever else may be said of it, any obligation *affirmatively to assist* a suspect is not even arguably required by the Fifth Amendment as the Framers wrote it. [footnote 21] The Fifth Amendment simply forbids the police from *compelling* the suspect to talk. In other words, it prevents the police from in any way forcing, but not from causing, a confession. Causation can, certainly, escalate to the point of compulsion, but the parties have produced no evidence that this happens typically or even particularly frequently. When it does, Section 3501 provides the courts with the means to ferret it out and, by suppressing a statement that is *for any reason* found to be involuntary, deny the police any advantage they might have hoped to achieve by such behavior.

Society might conclude that, notwithstanding the absence of a Fifth Amendment violation, a suspect's unwarned confession *should* be suppressed. Some states might decide—indeed several have already decided—that a failure to give warnings *does* warrant automatic suppression. [footnote 22] Others might adopt the middle course Congress chose in Section 3501, in which warnings are pointedly encouraged, but a failure to give them does not automatically require suppression. Ariz. Rev. Stat. Ann. § 13-3988. Still other states might opt, for example, to require video or audio recording; *see Stephan* v. *State,* 711 P.2d 1156, 1158 (Alaska 1985); *State* v. *Scales,* 518 N.W.2d 587, 591-93 (Minn. 1994), or to insure that any questioning be undertaken only in the presence of magistrate, *see* Akhil Reed Amar, The Constitution and Criminal Procedure: First Principles 77 (1997). But we believe it beyond the proper reach of judicial authority and judicial competence, *see Walters* v. *Nat'l Ass'n of Radiation Survivors,* 473 U.S. 305, 331 n.12 (1985), to ossify as a constitutional mandate any of these extraconstitutional policy choices.

In any event, Section 3501—read in combination with other bodies of law providing criminal, civil, and administrative sanctions for coercion during interrogation, along with the Fifth Amendment's own exclusionary rule banning use of compelled statements—leaves in place a significant degree of protection for the exercise of a suspect's rights.

A. Section 3501 Contains Protective Measures Against Compelled Confessions.
Section 3501 preserves much of the prophylactic value of *Miranda's* exclusionary rule, albeit through a different and more refined mechanism. The statute requires that in making the voluntariness determination, the court "shall take into consideration all the circumstances surrounding the giving of the confession." 18 U.S.C. 3501(b). The statute also, however, specifically enumerates five factors that courts *must* consider. Among the most prominent of these is whether the suspect received *Miranda* warnings.

---

[21]The same is true of the Fourth Amendment's ban on unreasonable searches. For example, the police need not inform a suspect of his right to refuse consent to a search, notwithstanding that the results of a search may be as thoroughly incriminating as a confession. Although where the suspect is in custody, his unwarned consent to the search should receive heightened scrutiny, it can nonetheless be valid so long as it is voluntary under all the circumstances. *See Schneckloth* v. *Bustamonte,* 412 U.S. 218, 227-47 (1973). Section 3501 virtually replicates this standard in the Fifth Amendment context.

[22]*See, e.g.,* La. Const. Art. I, § 13. *See generally* Barry Latzer, State Constitutional Criminal Law 1995 & 1999 Supp.) §§ 4.1 - 4.18 (describing independent state approaches to aspects of *Miranda* doctrine).

Specifically, Section 3501 directs the courts to consider the following when making voluntariness determinations:

(1) the time elapsing between arrest and arraignment of the defendant making the confession, if it was made after arrest and before arraignment, (2) whether such defendant knew the nature of the offense with which he was charged or of which he was suspected at the time of making the confession, *(3) whether or not such defendant was advised or knew that he was not required to make any statement and that any such statement could be used against him, (4) whether or not such defendant had been advised prior to questioning of his right to the assistance of counsel;* and (5) whether or not such defendant was without the assistance of counsel when questioned and when giving such confession. 18 U.S.C. 3501(b) (emphasis added).

The prominence that *Miranda* warnings enjoy in Section 3501 means that, if the Court upholds the statute, federal law enforcement officers will almost certainly continue to give them. They will do so for much the same reason as they do so now: self interest. Taking this precautionary measure will assist in obtaining a favorable ruling on the admissibility of the statement at trial, whereas failing to do so will make such a decision much less likely. *See Berkemer* v. *McCarty,* 468 U.S. 420, 433 n.20 (1984) (Mirandized statements rarely found to be involuntary). Therefore, it is not surprising that in a footnote at the very end of its brief, the Department of Justice states categorically that whether *Miranda* or Section 3501 is the law, "Federal law enforcement agencies would, as a matter of policy, continue to comply with the warnings requirements of *Miranda.*" *See* Govt. Br. at 49 n.37. [footnote 23] This assurance provides real-world confirmation for the view of the court below that "nothing [in the statutory standard] provides those in law enforcement with an incentive to stop giving the now familiar *Miranda* warnings." J.A. 210. What is most likely to happen is that rather than reading warnings from *Miranda* cards, officers will read them from Section 3501 cards.

The parties nevertheless suggest that Section 3501 adds nothing to pre-*Miranda* law on the warnings question, citing various pre-*Miranda* cases in which courts also considered the presence or absence of warnings as a factor in voluntariness determinations. *See* Govt. Br. at 16 n.11. But at most all those cases show is that before *Miranda,* whether warnings were given was relevant evidence of voluntariness if the parties sought to have the court consider it. There is a significant difference between the prophylactic value of that occasionally vigilant system, and the rule of Section 3501, under which the judge *must consider in every case* whether the warnings were given. The incentives to warn that Section 3501 provides are much stronger than those in pre-*Miranda* law, since under the statute officers know that in every federal criminal prosecution the giving of the warnings will be an issue.

Section 3501 provides greater protection to suspects than pre-*Miranda* law in other ways as well. *See* Fred Graham, The Self-Inflicted Wound 324 (1970) ("parts of [Section 3501] would have been a progressive expansion of suspect's rights if Congress had passed it prior to *Miranda*"). Indeed, in at least one respect, Section 3501 extends protection beyond *Miranda* and current voluntariness caselaw standards. The statute directs the district court to consider whether the "defendant knew the nature of the offense with which he was charged or of which he was suspected at the time of the confession." 18 U.S.C. 3501(b)(2). Under current law, no such inquiry is relevant in order to assess the voluntariness of a suspect's confession. *See Colorado*

---

[23]This point alone creates considerable doubt about the parties' appeal to "transcend[ent]" factors as weighing against Section 3501, namely the "unique and important role" *Miranda* is said to have come to play in the nation's criminal justice system. Govt. Br. at 49; *see* Pet. Br. at 44. The subtext of this argument is that Section 3501 will be the death knell for *Miranda* warnings. Yet any federal officer who fails to give warnings will be taking a remarkably foolish risk, endangering the usefulness of the whole enterprise of questioning the suspect. Moreover, although state cases are not at issue here, the nation's leading law enforcement groups have filed *amicus* briefs indicating that they would continue to give *Miranda* warnings should the Section 3501 standards become applicable to their state officers.

v. *Spring,* 479 U.S. 564, 577 (1987) (suspect's awareness of all the crimes about which he may be questioned is not relevant to determining the validity of his decision to waive the Fifth Amendment privilege). [footnote 24]

Contrary to the parties' claims, then, Section 3501 does not simply return the law of custodial interrogation to its pre-*Miranda* status. Rather, through the incentives it creates, it preserves the best prophylactic features of *Miranda* while eliminating its worst and most socially damaging rigidities. It thus produces "win-win" regime, under which federal law enforcement officers will continue to deliver *Miranda* warnings to suspects, while in cases with technical disputes over *Miranda* compliance (this case being a prime example, *see* J.A. 180-84), the suspect's statement will be admitted if, but only if, it is voluntary.

B. Other Protective Measures Against Compelled Confessions Have Expanded Considerably Since 1966.

The interrogation practices of federal law enforcement officers are addressed not only in Section 3501, but also by other federal statutes and related bodies of law holding out the possibility of civil, criminal, and administrative penalties against officers who coerce suspects. Almost all this law was created or significantly expanded after *Miranda*. Thus, the legal incentives for non-coercive police questioning today are almost unrecognizably greater than when *Miranda* was decided.

Since 1966, civil penalties against federal officers who violate constitutional rights have become available. When *Miranda* was written, it was quite difficult as a practical matter to obtain damages in federal court from federal law enforcement officers who violated Fifth Amendment rights. *See Bell* v. *Hood,* 327 U.S. 678 (1946). That changed in 1971, with *Bivens* v. *Six Unknown Named Agents,* 403 U.S. 388 (1971), in which the Court held that a complaint alleging that the Fourth Amendment had been violated by federal agents acting under color of their authority gives rise to a federal cause of action. Since then, courts have held that *Bivens* actions apply to abusive police interrogations. *See, e.g., Wilkins* v. *May,* 872 F.2d 190, 194 (7th Cir. 1989) (allowing a *Bivens* claim under the Due Process Clause for police misconduct during custodial interrogation).

Likewise, when *Miranda* was decided, the federal government was effectively exempt from civil suits arising out of Fifth Amendment violations. At the time, sovereign immunity barred recovery for many intentional torts which might normally form the basis for such suits. *See* S. Rep. No. 93-588, *reprinted in* 1974 U.S.C.C.A.N. 2789, 2791. After *Miranda*, Congress acted to provide that the federal government is civilly liable for damages for conduct that could implicate Fifth Amendment concerns. In 1974, Congress amended the Federal Tort Claims Act to make it applicable "to acts or omissions of investigative or law enforcement officers of the United States Government" on any subsequent claim arising "out of assault, battery, false imprisonment, false arrest, abuse of process, or malicious prosecution." 28 U.S.C. 2680(h).

Supplementing these expansions of civil liability for coerced confessions is the enforcement of criminal law in the area. Thus, 18 U.S.C. 241 and 242 prohibit the deprivation of constitutional rights under color of law. While Congress adopted these

---

[24]The government concedes that a suspect's awareness of charges "received less attention in this Court's pre-*Miranda* confession cases," Govt. Br. at 17, but claims that this factor was "referred to" in one case. *Id.* (citing *Harris* v. *South Carolina,* 338 U.S. 68, 69 (1949)). The government's brief inaccurately cites this reference as coming from a decision of the Court, rather than a mere *plurality* opinion. *See* 338 U.S. at 69 (Frankfurter, J. writing for three members of the Court); *id.* at 72 (Douglas, J., concurring). Thus, the government is unable to find even a single decision of this Court substantively discussing this factor as part of the pre- (or post-) *Miranda* voluntariness decisions. Clearly, then, some suspects will receive more protection under Section 3501 than under *Miranda*— *e.g.,* the respondent in *Colorado* v. *Spring; see also State* v. *Randolph,* 370 S.W.2d 741 (W. Va. 1988) (rejecting *Spring* under state law and suppressing confession because suspect not aware of suspected charges). Moreover, it is plausible that law enforcement agencies would respond to a favorable decision on Section 3501 by adding an additional warning to their "*Miranda*" cards addressing this point.

statutes during the Reconstruction Era, post-*Miranda* cases now make clear these statutes apply to federal law enforcement officers, *United States* v. *Otherson,* 637 F.2d 1276, 1278-79 (9th Cir. 1980), who obtain coerced confessions, *see United States* v. *Lanier,* 520 U.S. 259, 271 (1997) (noting that "beating to obtain a confession plainly violates § 242") (internal citation omitted). Also, the Justice Department's Civil Rights Division and the FBI now more effectively support enforcement of these statutes against federal officials. *See generally* 28 C.F.R. § 0.50 (establishing Justice Department's Civil Rights Division).

Also, just last year, Congress adopted legislation requiring federal prosecutors (and, by extension, agents acting as their proxies) to comply with the state rules of ethics in the jurisdictions in which they practice. 28 U.S.C. 530B. A number of state ethics rules forbid contact with suspects who are represented by counsel, even during preliminary stages of an investigation. *See* Model Rules of Professional Conduct Rule 4.2. The effect of Congress' action is to create a hybrid federal-state prophylactic rule restricting the opportunities for federal investigators to question suspects in ways that can extend well beyond *Miranda*'s requirements. *Cf. Moran* v. *Burbine,* 475 U.S. 412 (1986).[25]

The government also admits that the risk of Fifth Amendment violations is now less than at the time of the *Miranda* decision, acknowledging that "law enforcement agents today are generally better trained than they were in 1966." U.S. Br. at 48. This is, of course, only a part of the picture. As the Department of Justice has more fully explained in connection with the Fourth Amendment exclusionary rule, devices for preventing constitutional violations include not only better training but also specific rules and regulations governing the conduct of employees, and the use of investigative techniques such as searches and seizures; . . . institutional arrangements for conducting internal investigations of alleged violations of the rules and regulations; and . . . disciplinary measures that may be imposed for unlawful or improper conduct.

Dept. of Justice Office of Legal Policy, Report to the Attorney General on the Search and Seizure Exclusionary Rule, reprinted in 22 U. Mich. J.L. Ref. 573, 622 (1989).

Finally, it is important to remember that the Fifth Amendment itself provides its own exclusionary remedy. Actual violations of the Fifth Amendment, as opposed to "technical *Miranda* violation[s]," *Quarles,* 467 U.S. at 668, will always lead to the exclusion of evidence. [footnote 26]

C. Section 3501, Combined with Civil Rights Actions and Other Remedies, Creates a Constitutionally Adequate Alternative to the Miranda Rules.

Taken together, the combination of Section 3501 and the changes outlined above to prevent coerced confessions—along with the Fifth Amendment's exclusion of involuntary statements—renders *Miranda*'s automatic exclusionary rule unnecessary. Unlike the *Miranda* rule, which "sweeps more broadly than the Fifth Amendment itself" and "may be triggered even in the absence of a Fifth Amendment violation," *Oregon* v. *Elstad,* 470 U.S. 298, 306-10 (1985), the civil and criminal sanctions

---

[25]The provisions are highly controversial. *See, e.g., Ethical Standards for Federal Prosecutors Act of 1996: Hearing Before the Subcomm. on Courts of the House Judiciary Comm.,* 104th Cong., 2d Sess. 49 (1996) (statement of then-Associate Deputy Attorney Gen. Seth P. Waxman) (restrictions have "the potential to wreak havoc on federal law enforcement efforts"). Efforts are underway in Congress to amend or even repeal them. The provisions are significant, however, because they demonstrate Congress fully considers the need to protect criminal suspects in crafting legislation.

[26]While Section 3501 does not directly affect state cases, similar points can be made in relation to the adequacy of remedies and deterrents there. Available remedies and sanctions for actual Fifth Amendment violations by state officers include the constitutional exclusionary sanction, suits under 42 U.S.C. 1983 (which has been expansively interpreted since 1966), state tort suits, and criminal prosecution under 18 U.S.C. §§ 241, 242. In addition, if there is reasonable cause to believe that a pattern or practice of Fifth Amendment violations exists in a state or local law enforcement agency, the Attorney General has the authority to seek systemic injunctive and declaratory relief under 42 U.S.C. 14141 (adopted in 1994). Moreover, the federal judiciary, through direct appeals and habeas proceedings, can review all state court voluntariness determinations. *See Miller* v. *Fenton,* 474 U.S. 104 (1985).

adopted by Congress focus more directly on conduct that squarely implicates the Fifth Amendment proscription against compelled self-incrimination. At the same time, they provide stronger remedies against federal agents who coerce confessions than does the *Miranda* exclusionary rule. The exclusion of evidence of course "does not apply any direct sanction to the individual official whose illegal conduct" is at issue. *Bivens* v. *Six Unknown Named Agents,* 403 U.S. 388, 416 (1971) (Burger, C.J., dissenting). In contrast, civil remedies directly affect the offending officer. Similarly, civil actions against the United States provide a tangible financial incentive to insure that federal practices comport with constitutional requirements. Training and internal disciplinary actions against federal agents must also be considered an important part of the calculus. Thus, "[b]y all appearances," Congress, the Executive (and the Court in *Bivens*) have "already taken sensible and reasonable steps to deter [Fifth] Amendment violations by" police officers, and "his makes the likely additional deterrent value of the [*Miranda*] exclusionary rule small." *INS* v. *Lopez-Mendoza,* 468 U.S. 1032, 1049 (1984).

The parties do not challenge our contention that the combination of Section 3501 and the other measures we have identified provides as much prophylactic protection as the *Miranda* rules against actual Fifth Amendment violations. Their only response is contained in a footnote in the government's brief. Govt. Br. at 28 n. 20. The government maintains that, even assuming this combination is *more* effective than *Miranda* in preventing such violations, it still cannot be preferred. Relying on language from *Miranda*, the government contends that alternatives must be shown to be "at least as effective [as *Miranda*] in apprising the accused persons of their rights of silence and in assuring a continuous opportunity to exercise it." Govt. Br. at 27 (*quoting Miranda*, 384 U.S. at 467).

This language obviously was not necessary to the decision in *Miranda*. Compare Harris, 401 U.S. at 224 ("Some comments in the *Miranda* opinion can indeed be read as indicating a bar to use of an uncounseled statement for any purpose, but discussion of that issue was not at all necessary to the Court's holding and cannot be regarded as controlling.") Moreover, these statements cannot be reconciled with the present understanding of *Miranda*.

Miranda's various statements about the need for equally effective alternatives cited by the parties all occur in those parts of the opinion where the Court seems to be saying that any statement obtained without a prior explanation to the defendant of his rights is necessarily compelled. But as we explain *supra* at pp. 8-9, *Quarles, Harris,* and *Hass* make it clear that those portions of *Miranda* are not good law, since in each case, suspects' statements were found voluntary and admissible despite having been obtained without either compliance with *Miranda* or any "equally effective" alternative to make sure the suspects were aware of their rights.

Once those portions of *Miranda* fall, the force of the "equally effective" langauge falls with it. The Court would only have the authority to insist on warnings or their equivalents if the admission of a statement obtained without these measures would violate the Constitution. Under the only interpretation of *Miranda* that can be squared with *Quarles, Harris,* and *Hass,* that is not the case. The surviving justification for a "warnings or equivalent" requirement, and thus the one informing how that "requirement" should be interpreted today, is instead to help prevent future Fifth Amendment violations. In that case, however, other prophylactic measures that provide equivalent protection against the use of actually compelled statements are constitutionally sufficient even if they do not provide equivalent assurance that the suspect was informed of his rights. *Cf. Smith* v. *Robbins,* 120 S.Ct. at 759 (upholding against constitutional challenge an alternative to *Anders* procedure that provided protection for constitutional right at issue at least as good as contained in *Anders.*) In other words, the *Miranda* Court's authority to order Congress to enact (if it was to enact anything) a regime mostly identical in terms of warnings to the one the Court devised has been undermined by the Court's own understanding, evident in its more recent cases, that the regime itself was never constitutionally mandated. [footnote 27]

A final reason for upholding the statute is the Court's traditional reluctance "to avoid imposing a single solution on [the Congress and] the States from the top down." *Smith* v. *Robbins,* 120 S.Ct. at 750. So far as custodial police questioning is concerned, the law has remained immobilized in *Miranda*'s 1960's gaze, as foreseen by *Miranda's* dissenters. *See* 384 U.S. at 524 (Harlan, J., dissenting) ("[d]espite the Court's disclaimer, the practical effect of the decision made today must inevitably be to handicap serious efforts at reform."). Today police do not generally use such potentially desirable reforms such as videotaping. No doubt such alternatives could be made more appealing to legislators and administrators if some trade-off were allowed in relaxing features of the *Miranda* system not required by the Constitution and detrimental to law enforcement. More than three decades of experience, however, shows that it is impossible as a practical matter to explore such alternatives under the *Miranda* regime. As the Court has warned in other contexts, " '[J]udicial imposition of a categorical remedy . . . [has] pretermit[ted] other responsible solutions being considered in Congress and state legislatures.' " *Smith* v. *Robbins,* 120 S.Ct. at 758 (*quoting Murray* v. *Giarratano,* 492 U.S. 1, 13 (1989) (Kennedy, J., concurring in the judgment)).

III. IF CONGRESS CANNOT ALTER *MIRANDA'S* IRREBUTTABLE PRESUMPTION, THIS COURT SHOULD.

If, contrary to our submission, the Court concludes that congressional modification of *Miranda* was impermissible, the Court should nevertheless affirm the Fourth Circuit's judgment by making its own modification to *Miranda.* Specifically, it should abandon the irrebuttable presumption that confessions obtained without compliance with the *Miranda* procedures are always involuntary, and instead make clear that that presumption may be rebutted. Such a modification would then permit the Court to uphold the constitutionality of Section 3501.

Modification of *Miranda* in this fashion would bring that case into harmony with the principles of the Court's landmark decision in *City of Boerne* v. *Flores,* 521 U.S. 507 (1997). There, the Court distinguished between permissible prophylactic measures adopted to remedy or prevent unconstitutional actions, and impermissible attempts to rewrite constitutional protections disguised as prophylactic or remedial measures. For a prophylactic measure to be upheld as truly remedial or preventive, there must be "congruence and proportionality between the injury to be prevented or remedied and the means adopted to that end." *Id.* at 508; *see Kimel* v. *Florida Board of Regents,* 120 S.Ct. 631 (2000). In its current form, *Miranda*'s prophylactic regime does not satisfy these requirements. If, however, the Court modifies that regime to allow rebuttal of the currently irrebuttable presumption of involuntariness covering all non-complying custodial confessions, the modified regime would be consonant with *Boerne.*

---

[27]Finally, we would note that even if *Miranda* could somehow insist that any substitute for its regime be "at least as effective" in assuring that suspects are advised of their rights, we believe Section 3501 would actually satisfy that standard, or at least that there is sufficient reason to believe that it would, that this Court should defer to Congress's judgment on that point. *Cf. Bush; Chilicky.* Since the judgment of the court of appeals over a year ago upholding Section 3501 in the Fourth Circuit, it does appear that in practice, Section 3501 has indeed been at least as effective as the *Miranda* regime.

*A. Miranda's Irrebuttable Presumption Is Not Congruent and Proportional
to the Problem of Involuntary Confessions.*

In *Boerne,* the Court held that there are significant limits even on Congress' power to devise remedial measures. [footnote 28] Otherwise, the power to enforce the right at issue would be transformed into the power to make "a substantive change in constitutional protections." *Id.* at 532. To insure against rewriting the Constitution in the guise of remediation, the Court has considered whether a response is "out of proportion to its supposed remedial . . . objectives." *Kimel,* 120 S.Ct. at 644.

Miranda's rules are out of proportion because they "prohibit[] substantially more" police practices than would "likely be held unconstitutional under the applicable" Fifth Amendment standard. *Id.* at 647. To be sure, confessions obtained without complying with *Miranda's* procedures may sometimes be involuntary. But there is little reason to believe that this will be true all the time or even most of the time:

In case after case, the courts are asked . . . to decide purely technical *Miranda* questions that contain not even a hint of police overreaching. And in case after case, no voluntariness issue is raised, primarily because none exists. Whether the suspect was in "custody," whether or not there was "interrogation," whether warnings were given or were adequate, whether the defendant's equivocal statement constituted an invocation of rights, whether waiver was knowing and intelligent—this is the stuff that *Miranda* claims are made of. While these questions create litigable issues under *Miranda,* they generally do not indicate the existence of coercion . . . sufficient to establish involuntariness. *Withrow* v. *Williams,* 507 U.S. at 709-10 (O'Connor, J., dissenting) (collecting numerous illustrations). In this very case, for example, the district court found Dickerson's unwarned statements voluntary under the Fifth Amendment. J.A. 158 n.1. [footnote 29]

Miranda's lack of proportionality is shown not only by its overbroad reach in particular cases, but also by its unlimited application. *Miranda's* automatic exclusionary rule applies to every episode of custodial questioning conducted by every level of government, federal, state, and local, numbering in the hundreds of thousands each year. It is not limited to a particular period of time or to jurisdictions with a particular history of abuse. It contains no mechanism for a jurisdiction to extricate itself by showing that it has had a long history of compliance with the Self-Incrimination Clause. *Cf. Boerne,* 521 U.S. at 533 (commenting favorably on the presence of such devices as a means of assuring proportionality). The "indiscriminate scope" of the rules is itself strong evidence that they are disproportionate. *Kimel,* 120 S.Ct. at 650.

Finally, *Miranda's* irrebuttable presumption is disproportionate in another sense as well: it rigidly excludes confessions obtained without compliance with *Miranda* regardless of any other circumstances. This can lead to "disparity in particular cases between the error committed by the police officer and the windfall afforded a guilty defendant by application of the rule [that] is contrary to the idea of proportionality that is essential to the concept of justice." *Stone* v. *Powell,* 428 U.S. at 491.

---

[28]Because Congress has Section 5 "enforcement" power under the Fourteenth Amendment, as well as the power to craft "necessary and proper" legislation under U.S. Const., art. I, § 8, its authority to craft prophylactic measures is presumably broader than the Court's. *Compare Katzenbach* v. *Morgan,* 384 U.S. 641, 649-50 (1966) (upholding congressional ban on literacy tests) with *Lassiter* v. *Northampton Bd. of Elections,* 360 U.S. 45, 51-54 (1959) (Court refuses to strike down literacy tests under its own authority to enforce the Equal Protection Clause). Because, as we show in this section, even Congress could not apply *Miranda*-style prophylactic legislation to the States under *Boerne,* this case does not present the important question of how much narrower the Court's power to craft prophylactic rules may be.

[29]The voluntariness of the statements in this case is typical of *Miranda* violations that have reached this Court over the years. *See, e.g., United States* v. *Green,* 504 U.S. 908 (1992) (No. 91-1521) (statement specifically found to be voluntary below, *see* 592 A.2d 985, 986 n.2 (D.C. 1991)), *cert. dismissed,* 507 U.S. 545 (1993); *Oregon* v. *Elstad,* 470 U.S. 298, 315 (1985) ("It is beyond dispute that respondent's earlier [un-Mirandized] remark was voluntary"); *Oregon* v. *Hass,* 420 U.S. 714, 722 (1975) ("There is no evidence or suggestion that Hass' statements to [police]. . . were involuntary or coerced."); *Michigan* v. *Tucker,* 417 U.S. 433, 444 (1974) ("the interrogation in this case involved no compulsion sufficient to breach the right against compulsory self-incrimination").

The Court has also looked to the scope of the problem Congress is addressing when considering the breadth of prophylactic rules. The scope of the problem to which *Miranda* was responding remains unclear, but the evidence of epidemic police abuse was, and is, quite limited. *Miranda* did refer to "anecdotal evidence" concerning abusive police interrogation, *id.* at 645, [footnote 30] which no doubt was a problem in exceptional cases before *Miranda*—just as it remains a problem in some exceptional cases today. But the bulk of the justification in the opinion came from an examination of "police manuals and texts" on techniques for questioning suspects. *Miranda,* 384 U.S. at 448. The difficulties with this material as evidence of pervasive coercion in custodial interrogations, however, are legion. *See generally id.* at 532-33 (White, J., dissenting). In fact, the *Miranda* majority acknowledged that it had little idea about typical practices. *Id.* at 448. Moreover, while the police manuals were offered as evidence of compulsion, the *Miranda* court in fact concluded only that they created the "potentiality for compulsion." *Id.* at 457. Thus the opinion in effect admitted its failure to demonstrate that the techniques and circumstances it characterized as giving rise to potential compulsion pervasively resulted in *actual* compulsion. [footnote 31] Nor is that particularly surprising, for it is clear that the *Miranda* Court's true concern was with the potentially coercive circumstances themselves, not with actual compulsion—just as it is clear that "[the 103d] Congress' concern was with the incidental burdens imposed" on religion by neutral laws, not with "deliberate persecution." *Boerne,* 521 U.S. at 531-32.

B. Changing Miranda's Irrebuttable Presumption to a Rebuttable One Would Create a Remedial Measure Congruent and Proportionate to the Problem of Coercive Police Conduct.

The lack of congruence and proportionality between *Miranda's* rules and Fifth Amendment violations can be cured by changing *Miranda's* irrebuttable presumption to a rebuttable one. Today, the "[f]ailure to administer *Miranda* warnings creates a presumption of compulsion" which is "irrebuttable for purposes of the prosecution's case in chief." *Oregon* v. *Elstad,* 470 U.S. at 307. In other contexts, such rigid presumptions are typically justified on the ground that they "avoid the costs of excessive inquiry where a *per se* rule will achieve the correct result in almost all cases." *Coleman* v. *Thompson,* 501 U.S. 722, 737 (1991).[32] Here, however, the presumption operates to achieve incorrect results in many cases.

"Per se rules should not be applied . . . in situations where the generalization is incorrect as an empirical matter; the justification for a conclusive presumption disappears when application of the presumption will not reach the correct result most

---

[30]Interestingly, *Miranda* did not cite any contemporary cases in which the police had extracted a confession through threatened force. For this point, it relied on such dated information as the Wickersham Report in 1931 and a few Supreme Court cases in the 1940s and early 1950s. 384 U.S. at 445-46. *Miranda* went on to conclude that police coercion "is not, unfortunately, relegated to the past or to any part of the country," *id.* at 446, resting this assertion on a few additional isolated and dated reports. *Id.* The Court conceded, however, that "the examples given above are undoubtedly the exception now." *Id.* at 447.

[31]It is also noteworthy that both the executive and legislative branches reached their own conclusions, contemporaneously with *Miranda,* that coercion as traditionally understood was not pervasive in custodial interrogations. *See* President's Comm'n on Law Enforcement and Admin. of Justice, The Challenge of Crime in a Free Society 93 (1967) (stating, based on pre-*Miranda* data, that "today the third degree is almost nonexistent"); S. Rep. 90-1097, *reprinted in 1968* U.S.C.C.A.N. 2112, 2134 (1968) (reviewing congressional testimony from expert witnesses on lack of coercive techniques and concluding *Miranda's* contrary findings were based on an "overreact[ion] to defense claims that police brutality is widespread"); *see generally* Cassell, *Miranda's Social Costs,* supra, 90 Nw. U.L. Rev at 473-78 (collecting evidence on limited number of involuntary confessions in 1966).

[32]Per se rules are also sometimes justified on the grounds that exceptions are not sufficiently "important to justify the time and expense necessary to identify them." *Coleman,* 501 U.S. at 737 (internal quotation omitted). This rationale has no application here. Congress has determined to the contrary that the judiciary should devote such additional energy as may be needed (if any) to making accurate (rather than presumptive) voluntariness determinations in federal criminal cases. Moreover, because confessions are "essential to society's compelling interest in finding, convicting, and punishing those who violate the law," *Moran* v. *Burbine,* 475 U.S. 412, 426 (1986), individualized voluntariness determinations will be time well spent.

of the time." *Id.* Under *Kimel* and *Boerne,* the present irrebuttable presumption creates a jarring lack of "congruence and proportionality." Indeed, to apply an irrebuttable presumption is effectively to change the Fifth Amendment's compulsion standard to a new, warnings-and-waiver standard, thus "alter[ing] the meaning" of the Fifth Amendment, *Boerne,* 521 U.S. at 519, and "substantively redefin[ing] the State's legal obligations" during custodial interrogation, *Kimel,* 120 S.Ct. at 648. *See generally* J. Grano, *supra,* at 198 (*Miranda* "substituted for the constitutional rule a new substantive rule of its own making").

These problems would be substantially resolved if this Court modifies *Miranda* so that it operates as a rebuttable presumption—that is, confessions taken without following the *Miranda* procedures would be presumed involuntary unless the state can prove otherwise. Justice Clark suggested this approach in his dissent in *Miranda* as an intermediate position between the majority and the other dissenters. He proposed that "[i]n the absence of warnings, the burden would be on the State to prove . . . that in the totality of the circumstances, including the failure to give the necessary warnings, the confession was clearly voluntary." 384 U.S. at 503 (Clark, J., dissenting).

This allocation of burdens, superimposed on Section 3501 (which can easily be read in this fashion [footnote 33]), brings Section 3501's prophylactic effect even closer to that of *Miranda's* exclusionary rule by explicitly conferring a preferred status to confessions obtained in compliance with *Miranda.* At the same time, it eliminates the single feature of *Miranda's* irrebuttable presumption most objectionable under *Boerne:* the imposition of a standard for the admissibility of custodial confessions more stringent than the constitutional voluntariness standard, and the attendant automatic exclusion of many statements that in fact comply with the constitutional standard. In contrast, a rebuttable presumption would be a proportionate response to the various risks identified by the *Miranda* Court. It would also preserve the assistance to the courts that the *Miranda* factors have provided in structuring to the voluntariness inquiry, while bringing to an end the irrationally mechanical application of those factors to exclude unwarned confessions, no matter what the circumstances, even when the confession is unquestionably voluntary.

In *Illinois* v. *Gates,* 462 U.S. 213 (1983), the Court performed a similar modification to a test it had previously suggested but came to regard as overly rigid. In *Gates,* the Court rejected the two-pronged "*Spinelli-Aguilar*" test for determining probable cause in favor of a totality-of-the-circumstances approach. Raising a concern that applies equally to the *Miranda* doctrine, the Court explained that "the 'two-pronged test' has encouraged an excessively technical dissection of informants' tips, with undue attention being focused on isolated issues that cannot sensibly be divorced from the other facts. . . ." *Id.* at 234-35. Yet, in restoring the totality-of-the-circumstances approach, the Court emphasized that the *Spinelli-Aguilar* factors remained "highly relevant" in determining probable cause, *id.* at 230, and later cases have examined them, *see Alabama* v. *White,* 496 U.S. 325, 328 (1990). Thus, just as the *Spinelli-Aguilar* factors now serve "not as inflexible, independent requirements applicable in every case," but rather as "guides to a magistrate's determination of probable case," *Gates,* 462 U.S. at 230, so too the *Miranda* factors would guide determination of voluntariness issues.

Changing the *Miranda* presumption to a rebuttable one would not merely return the law to its pre-*Miranda* state. When *Miranda* was decided, the constitutional assignment of the burden for establishing voluntariness was unclear. *See Developments in the Law—Confessions,* 79 Harv. L. Rev. 938, 1069-70 (1966) (noting majority rule that state proves voluntariness and minority rule that defendant proves

---

[33]Section 3501(a) provides that a confession "shall be admissible in evidence *if* it is voluntarily given" (emphasis added), implying that the presumption is against admissibility unless and until voluntariness is established.

involuntariness). [footnote 34] A rebuttable *Miranda* presumption could be crafted that would place the burden on the government to establish voluntariness while making delivery of *Miranda* warnings an important part of the calculus.

The parties spend little time justifying the inflexibility of the *Miranda* rules, relying instead almost exclusively on a general argument against overruling *Miranda*. But the irrebuttable presumption that underlies the automatic exclusionary rule has been effectively repudiated by cases such as *Quarles* and numerous others we have discussed. Even without that doctrinal development, however, there would be ample grounds for changing the inflexible presumption. "*Stare decisis* is not an inexorable command" and "[t]his is particularly true in a constitutional case." *Payne* v. *Tennessee,* 501 U.S. 808, 828 (1991). "The justifications for the case system and stare decisis must rest upon the Court's capacity, and responsibility, to acknowledge its missteps." *Nixon* v. *Shrink Missouri Government PAC,* 120 S.Ct. 897, 914 (2000) (Kennedy, J., dissenting). Most importantly, "when governing decisions are . . . badly reasoned, this Court has never felt constrained to follow precedent." *Payne,* 501 U.S. at 827 (internal quotation omitted).

This criticism applies with special force to the *Miranda* decision. That 5-to-4 decision was flatly in conflict with 180 years of common law and constitutional history, and with substantially all prior judicial precedent, which required the suppression of pretrial statements only in cases involving actual compulsion by the government, and explicitly rejected the complex of procedural rules that *Miranda* imposed. *See DOJ Report,* supra, 22 U. Mich. J. L. Ref. at 453-84, 491-506. Against that backdrop, stare decisis provides no basis for preserving the anachronistic, yet sweeping and irrebuttable, presumption that anchors Mi*randa*'s exclusionary rule.

* * * * *

The parties close their briefs with an appeal to "transcend[ent]" factors allegedly arguing against Section 3501, namely what is said to be the "important role" *Miranda* has come to play in maintaining confidence in the nation's criminal justice system. Govt. Br. at 49; *see* Pet. Br. at 44. We agree that important factors are at stake here, but they argue for upholding the statute.

Foremost among these factors is the importance of the search for truth. "The central purpose of a criminal trial is to decide the factual question of the defendant's guilt or innocence." *Colorado* v. *Connelly,* 479 U.S. 157, 166 (1986) (internal quotation omitted). Public confidence in the criminal justice system cannot possibly be enhanced by a rule that conceals from the jury truthful and voluntarily given confessions. Public confidence cannot be enhanced by the result of that concealment, namely, a significantly increased risk that an admitted criminal will go free. Public confidence cannot be enhanced by a rule that turns its back on discovering the facts in favor of an irrebuttable presumption that is always slanted and often wrong. And lastly, with all due respect to *Miranda*, public confidence cannot be enhanced by a ruling of this Court bottomed on the 1960's view that law enforcement officers are so much to be distrusted that the law of confessions will start by presuming their penchant for lawless, strong-arm tactics.

Public confidence is, instead, best served by permitting citizens to give voice to their views through their elected representatives. By substantial bi-partisan majorities, those representatives adopted Section 3501 precisely for the purpose of changing *Miranda's* automatic exclusionary rule while preserving a strong incentive to

---

[34]The issue has been clarified, but not been definitively resolved, after *Miranda. Lego* v. *Twomey,* 404 U.S. 477, 489 (1972), definitely suggests that the prosecution must prove voluntariness. *See generally* 3 Wayne R. LaFave et al., Criminal Procedure § 10.3(c) at 429 (2d ed. 1999) (noting *Lego* "raises serious doubts" about placing burden on defendant to prove involuntariness). But some states continue to place the burden on the defendant to show involuntariness. *See, e.g., Chambers* v. *States,* 742 So.2d 466, 476 (Fla. Dist. Ct. App. 1999).

continue advising suspects of their rights. This judgment was in our view balanced and wise, but for however that may be, it fully honored the requirements of the Fifth Amendment and thus merits this Court's approval.

CONCLUSION

For the foregoing reasons, the judgment of the court of appeals should be affirmed. Respectfully submitted.

Paul G. Cassell
(*Court Appointed Amicus*)
University of Utah
College of Law
332 S. 1440 E. Front
Salt Lake City, UT 84112
(801) 585-5202

Daniel J. Popeo
Paul D. Kamenar
Washington Legal Foundation
2009 Massachusetts Ave., N.W.
Washington, D.C. 20036
(202) 588-0302
Date: March 9, 2000

APPENDIX A

[Figure 1—Violent Crime Clearance Rates from 1950 to 1995, reprinted from Paul G. Cassell & Richard Fowles, *Handcuffing the Cops? A Thirty-Year Perspective on Miranda's Harmful Effects on Law Enforcement*, 50 Stan. L. Rev. 1055, 1069 (1998).]

APPENDIX B

1. The Fifth Amendment of the United States Constitution provides in relevant part that "[n]o person shall . . . be compelled in any criminal case to be a witness against himself."

2. Section 3501 of Title 18 provides as follows:

   (a) In any criminal prosecution brought by the United States or by the District of Columbia, a confession, as defined in subsection (e) hereof, shall be admissible in evidence if it is voluntarily given. Before such confession is received in evidence, the trial judge shall, out of the presence of the jury, determine any issue as to voluntariness. If the trial judge determines that the confession was voluntarily made it shall be admitted in evidence and the trial judge shall permit the jury to hear relevant evidence on the issue of voluntariness and shall instruct the jury to give such weight to the confession as the jury feels it deserves under all the circumstances.

   (b) The trial judge in determining the issue of voluntariness shall take into consideration all the circumstances surrounding the giving of the confession, including (1) the time elapsing between arrest and arraignment of the defendant making the confession, if it was made after arrest and before arraignment, (2) whether such defendant knew the nature of the offense with which he was charged or of which he was suspected at the time of making the confession, (3) whether or not such defendant was advised or knew that he was not required to make any statement and that any such statement could be used against him, (4) whether or not such defendant had been advised prior to questioning of his right to the assistance of counsel; and (5) whether or not such defendant was without the assistance of counsel when questioned and when giving such confession.

The presence or absence of any of the abovementioned factors to be taken into consideration by the judge need not be conclusive on the issue of voluntariness of the confession.

(c) In any criminal prosecution by the United States or by the District of Columbia, a confession made or given by a person who is a defendant therein, while such person was under arrest or other detention in the custody of any law-enforcement officer or law-enforcement agency, shall not be inadmissible solely because of delay in bringing such person before a magistrate or other official empowered to commit persons charged with offenses against the laws of the United States or of the District of Columbia if such confession is found by the trial judge to have been made voluntarily and if the weight to be given the confession is left to the jury and if such confession was made or given by such person within six hours immediately following his arrest or other detention:

Provided, That the time limitation contained in this subsection shall not apply in any case in which the delay in bringing such person before such magistrate or other official beyond such six-hour period is found by the trial judge to be reasonable considering the means of transportation and the distance to be traveled to the nearest available such magistrate or other officer.

(d) Nothing contained in this section shall bar the admission in evidence of any confession made or given voluntarily by any person to any other person without interrogation by anyone, or at any time at which the person who made or gave such confession was not under arrest or other detention.

(e) As used in this section, the term "confession" means any confession of guilt of any criminal offense or any self-incriminating statement made or given orally or in writing.

SECTION
IX

Cite as: 530 U.S. ____ (2000)

Opinion of the Court

Supreme Court of the United States

NO. 99—5525

CHARLES THOMAS DICKERSON, PETITIONER *V.* UNITED STATES

ON WRIT OF CERTIORARI TO THE UNITED STATES COURT OF APPEALS FOR THE FOURTH CIRCUIT
[June 26, 2000]

CHIEF JUSTICE REHNQUIST delivered the opinion of the Court.

In *Miranda* v. *Arizona,* 384 U.S. 436 (1966), we held that certain warnings must be given before a suspect's statement made during custodial interrogation could be admitted in evidence. In the wake of that decision, Congress enacted 18 U.S.C. §3501 which in essence laid down a rule that the admissibility of such statements should turn only on whether or not they were voluntarily made. We hold that *Miranda,* being a constitutional decision of this Court, may not be in effect overruled by an Act of Congress, and we decline to overrule *Miranda* ourselves. We therefore hold that *Miranda* and its progeny in this Court govern the admissibility of statements made during custodial interrogation in both state and federal courts.

Petitioner Dickerson was indicted for bank robbery, conspiracy to commit bank robbery, and using a firearm in the course of committing a crime of violence, all in violation of the applicable provisions of Title 18 of the United States Code. Before trial, Dickerson moved to suppress a statement he had made at a Federal Bureau of Investigation field office, on the grounds that he had not received "*Miranda* warnings" before being interrogated. The District Court granted his motion to suppress, and the Government took an interlocutory appeal to the United States Court of Appeals for the Fourth Circuit. That court, by a divided vote, reversed the District Court's suppression order. It agreed with the District Court's conclusion that petitioner had not received *Miranda* warnings before making his statement. But it went on to hold that §3501, which in effect makes the admissibility of statements such as Dickerson's turn solely on whether they were made voluntarily, was satisfied in this case. It then concluded that our decision in *Miranda* was not a constitutional hold-ing, and that therefore Congress could by statute have the final say on the question of admissibility. 166 F.3d 667 (1999).

Because of the importance of the questions raised by the Court of Appeals' de-cision, we granted certiorari, 528 U.S. 1045 (1999), and now reverse.

We begin with a brief historical account of the law governing the admission of confessions. Prior to *Miranda,* we evaluated the admissibility of a suspect's confes-sion under a voluntariness test. The roots of this test developed in the common law, as the courts of England and then the United States recognized that coerced confes-sions are inherently untrustworthy. See, *e.g., King* v. *Rudd,* 1 Leach 115, 117–118, 122–123, 168 Eng. Rep. 160, 161, 164 (K. B. 1783) (Lord Mansfield, C. J.) (stating that the English courts excluded confessions obtained by threats and promises); *King* v. *Warickshall,* 1 Leach 262, 263–264, 168 Eng. Rep. 234, 235 (K. B. 1783) ("A free and voluntary confession is deserving of the highest credit, because it is presumed to flow from the strongest sense of guilt . . . but a confession forced from the mind by the flat-tery of hope, or by the torture of fear, comes in so questionable a shape . . . that no credit ought to be given to it; and therefore it is rejected"); *King* v. *Parratt,* 4 Car. & P. 570, 172 Eng. Rep. 829 (N. P. 1831); *Queen* v. *Garner,* 1 Den. 329, 169 Eng. Rep. 267 (Ct. Crim. App. 1848); *Queen* v. *Baldry,* 2 Den. 430, 169 Eng. Rep. 568 (Ct. Crim. App. 1852); *Hopt* v. *Territory of Utah,* 110 U.S. 574 (1884); *Pierce* v. *United States,* 160 U.S. 355, 357 (1896). Over time, our cases recognized two constitutional bases for the re-quirement that a confession be voluntary to be admitted into evidence: the Fifth Amendment right against self-incrimination and the Due Process Clause of the Four-teenth Amendment. See, *e.g., Bram* v. *United States,* 168 U.S. 532, 542 (1897) (stat-ing that the voluntariness test "is controlled by that portion of the Fifth Amendment . . . commanding that no person 'shall be compelled in any criminal case to be a wit-ness against himself' "); *Brown* v. *Mississippi,* 297 U.S. 278 (1936) (reversing a crim-inal conviction under the Due Process Clause because it was based on a confession obtained by physical coercion).

While *Bram* was decided before *Brown* and its progeny, for the middle third of the 20th century our cases based the rule against admitting coerced confessions pri-marily, if not exclusively, on notions of due process. We applied the due process vol-untariness test in "some 30 different cases decided during the era that intervened be-tween *Brown* and *Escobedo* v. *Illinois,* 378 U.S. 478 [(1964)]." *Schneckcloth* v. *Bustamonte,* 412 U.S. 218, 223 (1973). See, *e.g., Haynes* v. *Washington,* 373 U.S. 503 (1963); *Ashcraft* v. *Tennessee,* 322 U.S. 143 (1944); *Chambers* v. *Florida,* 309 U.S. 227 (1940). Those cases refined the test into an inquiry that examines "whether a defen-dant's will was overborne" by the circumstances surrounding the giving of a confes-sion. *Schneckcloth,* 412 U.S., at 226. The due process test takes into consideration "the totality of all the surrounding circumstances—both the characteristics of the ac-cused and the details of the interrogation." *Ibid.* See also, *Haynes, supra,* at 513; *Gal-legos* v. *Colorado,* 370 U.S. 49, 55 (1962); *Reck* v. *Pate,* 367 U.S. 433, 440 (1961) ("[A]ll the circumstances attendant upon the confession must be taken into account"); *Ma-linski* v. *New York,* 324 U.S. 401, 404 (1945) ("If all the attendant circumstances in-dicate that the confession was coerced or compelled, it may not be used to convict a defendant"). The determination "depend[s] upon a weighing of the circumstances of pressure against the power of resistance of the person confessing." *Stein* v. *New York,* 346 U.S. 156, 185 (1953).

We have never abandoned this due process jurisprudence, and thus continue to exclude confessions that were obtained involuntarily. But our decisions in *Malloy* v. *Hogan,* 378 U.S. 1 (1964), and *Miranda* changed the focus of much of the inquiry in determining the admissibility of suspects' incriminating statements. In *Malloy,* we held that the Fifth Amendment's Self-Incrimination Clause is incorporated in the Due Process Clause of the Fourteenth Amendment and thus applies to the States. *Id.,* at 6–11. We decided *Miranda* on the heels of *Malloy.*

In *Miranda,* we noted that the advent of modern custodial police interrogation brought with it an increased concern about confessions obtained by coercion.[footnote 1] 384 U.S., at 445–458. Because custodial police interrogation, by its very nature, isolates and pressures the individual, we stated that "[e]ven without employing brutality, the 'third degree' or [other] specific stratagems, . . . custodial interrogation exacts a heavy toll on individual liberty and trades on the weakness of individuals." *Id.,* at 455. We concluded that the coercion inherent in custodial interrogation blurs the line between voluntary and involuntary statements, and thus heightens the risk that an individual will not be "accorded his privilege under the Fifth Amendment . . . not to be compelled to incriminate himself." *Id.,* at 439. Accordingly, we laid down "concrete constitutional guidelines for law enforcement agencies and courts to follow." *Id.,* at 442. Those guidelines established that the admissibility in evidence of any statement given during custodial interrogation of a suspect would depend on whether the police provided the suspect with four warnings. These warnings (which have come to be known colloquially as "*Miranda* rights") are: a suspect "has the right to remain silent, that anything he says can be used against him in a court of law, that he has the right to the presence of an attorney, and that if he cannot afford an attorney one will be appointed for him prior to any questioning if he so desires." *Id.,* at 479.

Two years after *Miranda* was decided, Congress enacted §3501. That section provides, in relevant part:

"(a) In any criminal prosecution brought by the United States or by the District of Columbia, a confession . . . shall be admissible in evidence if it is voluntarily given. Before such confession is received in evidence, the trial judge shall, out of the presence of the jury, determine any issue as to voluntariness. If the trial judge determines that the confession was voluntarily made it shall be admitted in evidence and the trial judge shall permit the jury to hear relevant evidence on the issue of voluntariness and shall instruct the jury to give such weight to the confession as the jury feels it deserves under all the circumstances.

"(b) The trial judge in determining the issue of voluntariness shall take into consideration all the circumstances surrounding the giving of the confession, including (1) the time elapsing between arrest and arraignment of the defendant making the confession, if it was made after arrest and before arraignment, (2) whether such defendant knew the nature of the offense with which he was charged or of which he was suspected at the time of making the confession, (3) whether or not such defendant was advised or knew that he was not required to make any statement and that any such statement could be used against him, (4) whether or not such defendant had been advised prior to questioning of his right to the assistance of counsel; and (5) whether or not such defendant was without the assistance of counsel when questioned and when giving such confession.

"The presence or absence of any of the above mentioned factors to be taken into consideration by the judge need not be conclusive on the issue of voluntariness of the confession."

Given §3501's express designation of voluntariness as the touchstone of admissibility, its omission of any warning requirement, and the instruction for trial courts to consider a nonexclusive list of factors relevant to the circumstances of a confession, we agree with the Court of Appeals that Congress intended by its enactment to overrule *Miranda.* See also *Davis* v. *United States,* 512 U.S. 452, 464 (1994) (SCALIA, J., concurring) (stating that, prior to *Miranda,* "voluntariness *vel non* was the touchstone of admissibility of confessions"). Because of the obvious conflict between our decision in *Miranda* and §3501, we must address whether Congress has constitutional authority to thus supersede *Miranda.* If Congress has such authority, §3501's

---

[1]While our cases have long interpreted the Due Process and Self-Incrimination Clauses to require that a suspect be accorded a fair trial free from coerced testimony, our application of those Clauses to the context of custodial police interrogation is relatively recent because the routine practice of such interrogation is itself a relatively new development. See, *e.g., Miranda,* 384 U.S., at 445–458.

totality-of-the-circumstances approach must prevail over *Miranda*'s requirement of warnings; if not, that section must yield to *Miranda*'s more specific requirements.

The law in this area is clear. This Court has supervisory authority over the federal courts, and we may use that authority to prescribe rules of evidence and procedure that are binding in those tribunals. *Carlisle* v. *United States,* 517 U.S. 416, 426 (1996). However, the power to judicially create and enforce nonconstitutional "rules of procedure and evidence for the federal courts exists only in the absence of a relevant Act of Congress." *Palermo* v. *United States,* 360 U.S. 343, 353, n. 11 (1959) (citing *Funk* v. *United States,* 290 U.S. 371, 382 (1933), and *Gordon* v. *United States,* 344 U.S. 414, 418 (1953)). Congress retains the ultimate authority to modify or set aside any judicially created rules of evidence and procedure that are not required by the Constitution. *Palermo, supra,* at 345–348; *Carlisle, supra,* at 426; *Vance* v. *Terrazas,* 444 U.S. 252, 265 (1980).

But Congress may not legislatively supersede our decisions interpreting and applying the Constitution. See, *e.g., City of Boerne* v. *Flores,* 521 U.S. 507, 517–521 (1997). This case therefore turns on whether the *Miranda* Court announced a constitutional rule or merely exercised its supervisory authority to regulate evidence in the absence of congressional direction. Recognizing this point, the Court of Appeals surveyed *Miranda* and its progeny to determine the constitutional status of the *Miranda* decision. 166 F.3d, at 687–692. Relying on the fact that we have created several exceptions to *Miranda*'s warnings requirement and that we have repeatedly referred to the *Miranda* warnings as "prophylactic," *New York* v. *Quarles,* 467 U.S. 649, 653 (1984), and "not themselves rights protected by the Constitution," *Michigan* v. *Tucker,* 417 U.S. 433, 444 (1974), [footnote 2] the Court of Appeals concluded that the protections announced in *Miranda* are not constitutionally required. 166 F.3d, at 687–690.

We disagree with the Court of Appeals' conclusion, although we concede that there is language in some of our opinions that supports the view taken by that court. But first and foremost of the factors on the other side—that *Miranda* is a constitutional decision—is that both *Miranda* and two of its companion cases applied the rule to proceedings in state courts—to wit, Arizona, California, and New York. See 384 U.S., at 491–494, 497–499. Since that time, we have consistently applied *Miranda*'s rule to prosecutions arising in state courts. See, *e.g., Stansbury* v. *California,* 511 U.S. 318 (1994) (*per curiam*); *Minnick* v. *Mississippi,* 498 U.S. 146 (1990); *Arizona* v. *Roberson,* 486 U.S. 675 (1988); *Edwards* v. *Arizona,* 451 U.S. 477, 481–482 (1981). It is beyond dispute that we do not hold a supervisory power over the courts of the several States. *Smith* v. *Phillips,* 455 U.S. 209, 221 (1982) ("Federal courts hold no supervisory authority over state judicial proceedings and may intervene only to correct wrongs of constitutional dimension"); *Cicenia* v. *Lagay,* 357 U. S 504, 508–509 (1958). With respect to proceedings in state courts, our "authority is limited to enforcing the commands of the United States Constitution." *Mu'Min* v. *Virginia,* 500 U.S. 415, 422 (1991). See also *Harris* v. *Rivera,* 454 U.S. 339, 344–345 (1981) (*per curiam*) (stating that "[f]ederal judges may not require the observance of any special procedures" in state courts "except when necessary to assure compliance with the dictates of the Federal Constitution"). [footnote 3]

---

[2] *See also Davis* v. *United States,* 512 U. S 452, 457–458 (1994); *Withrow* v. *Williams,* 507 U.S. 680, 690–691 (1993) ("*Miranda*'s safeguards are not constitutional in character"); *Duckworth* v. *Eagan,* 492 U.S. 195, 203 (1989); *Connecticut* v. *Barrett,* 479 U.S. 523, 528 (1987) ("[T]he *Miranda* Court adopted prophylactic rules designed to insulate the exercise of Fifth Amendment rights"); *Oregon* v. *Elstad,* 470 U.S. 298, 306 (1985); *Edwards* v. *Arizona,* 451 U.S. 477, 492 (1981) (Powell, J., concurring in result).

[3] Our conclusion regarding *Miranda*'s constitutional basis is further buttressed by the fact that we have allowed prisoners to bring alleged *Miranda* violations before the federal courts in habeas corpus proceedings. See *Thompson* v. *Keohane,* 516 U.S. 99 (1995); *Withrow, supra,* at 690–695. Habeas corpus proceedings are available only for claims that a person "is in custody in violation of the Constitution or laws or treaties of the United States." 28 U.S.C. § 2254(a). Since the *Miranda* rule is clearly not based on federal laws or treaties, our decision allowing habeas review for *Miranda* claims obviously assumes that *Miranda* is of constitutional origin.

The *Miranda* opinion itself begins by stating that the Court granted certiorari "to explore some facets of the problems . . . of applying the privilege against self-incrimination to in-custody interrogation, *and to give concrete constitutional guidelines for law enforcement agencies and courts to follow.*" 384 U.S., at 441–442 (emphasis added). In fact, the majority opinion is replete with statements indicating that the majority thought it was announcing a constitutional rule. [footnote 4] Indeed, the Court's ultimate conclusion was that the unwarned confessions obtained in the four cases before the Court in *Miranda* "were obtained from the defendant under circumstances that did not meet constitutional standards for protection of the privilege." [footnote 5] *Id.,* at 491.

Additional support for our conclusion that *Miranda* is constitutionally based is found in the *Miranda* Court's invitation for legislative action to protect the constitutional right against coerced self-incrimination. After discussing the "compelling pressures" inherent in custodial police interrogation, the *Miranda* Court concluded that, "[i]n order to combat these pressures and to permit a full opportunity to exercise the privilege against self-incrimination, the accused must be adequately and effectively appraised of his rights and the exercise of those rights must be fully honored." *Id.,* at 467. However, the Court emphasized that it could not foresee "the potential alternatives for protecting the privilege which might be devised by Congress or the States," and it accordingly opined that the Constitution would not preclude legislative solutions that differed from the prescribed *Miranda* warnings but which were "at least as effective in apprising accused persons of their right of silence and in assuring a continuous opportunity to exercise it." [footnote 6] *Ibid.*

The Court of Appeals also relied on the fact that we have, after our *Miranda* decision, made exceptions from its rule in cases such as *New York* v. *Quarles,* 467 U.S. 649 (1984), and *Harris* v. *New York,* 401 U.S. 222 (1971). See 166 F.3d, at 672, 689–691. But we have also broadened the application of the *Miranda* doctrine in cases such as *Doyle* v. *Ohio,* 426 U.S. 610 (1976), and *Arizona* v. *Roberson,* 486 U.S. 675 (1988). These decisions illustrate the principle–not that *Miranda* is not a constitutional rule—but that no constitutional rule is immutable. No court laying down a general rule can possibly foresee the various circumstances in which counsel will seek to apply it, and the sort of modifications represented by these cases are as much a normal part of constitutional law as the original decision.

---

[4] See 384 U.S., at 445 ("The constitutional issue we decide in each of these cases is the admissibility of statements obtained from a defendant questioned while in custody"), 457 (stating that the *Miranda* Court was concerned with "adequate safeguards to protect precious Fifth Amendment rights"), 458 (examining the "history and precedent underlying the Self-Incrimination Clause to determine its applicability in this situation"), 476 ("The requirement of warnings and waiver of rights is . . . fundamental with respect to the Fifth Amendment privilege and not simply a preliminary ritual to existing methods of interrogation"), 479 ("The whole thrust of our foregoing discussion demonstrates that the Constitution has prescribed the rights of the individual when confronted with the power of government when it provided in the Fifth Amendment that an individual cannot be compelled to be a witness against himself"), 481, n. 52 (stating that the Court dealt with "constitutional standards in relation to statements made"), 490 ("[T]he issues presented are of constitutional dimensions and must be determined by the courts"), 489 (stating that the *Miranda* Court was dealing "with rights grounded in a specific requirement of the Fifth Amendment of the Constitution").

[5] Many of our subsequent cases have also referred to *Miranda*'s constitutional underpinnings. See, *e.g., Withrow,* 507 U.S., at 691 (" 'Prophylactic' though it may be, in protecting a defendant's Fifth Amendment privilege against self-incrimination, *Miranda* safeguards a 'fundamental trial right' "); *Illinois* v. *Perkins,* 496 U.S. 292, 296 (1990) (describing *Miranda*'s warning requirement as resting on "the Fifth Amendment privilege against self-incrimination"); *Butler* v. *McKellar,* 494 U.S. 407, 411 (1990) ("[T]he Fifth Amendment bars police-initiated interrogation following a suspect's request for counsel in the context of a separate investigation"); *Michigan* v. *Jackson,* 475 U.S. 625, 629 (1986) ("The Fifth Amendment protection against compelled self-incrimination provides the right to counsel at custodial interrogations"); *Moran* v. *Burbine,* 475 U.S. 412, 427 (1986) (referring to *Miranda* as "our interpretation of the Federal Constitution"); *Edwards,* 451 U.S., at 481–482.

[6] The Court of Appeals relied in part on our statement that the *Miranda* decision in no way "creates a 'constitutional straightjacket.' " See 166 F.3d, at 672 (quoting *Miranda,* 384 U.S., at 467). However, a review of our opinion in *Miranda* clarifies that this disclaimer was intended to indicate that the Constitution does not require police to administer the particular *Miranda* warnings, not that the Constitution does not require a procedure that is effective in securing Fifth Amendment rights.

The Court of Appeals also noted that in *Oregon* v. *Elstad,* 470 U.S. 298 (1985), we stated that " '[t]he *Miranda* exclusionary rule . . . serves the Fifth Amendment and sweeps more broadly than the Fifth Amendment itself.' " 166 F.3d, at 690 (quoting *Elstad, supra,* at 306). Our decision in that case—refusing to apply the traditional "fruits" doctrine developed in Fourth Amendment cases—does not prove that *Miranda* is a nonconstitutional decision, but simply recognizes the fact that unreasonable searches under the Fourth Amendment are different from unwarned interrogation under the Fifth Amendment.

As an alternative argument for sustaining the Court of Appeals' decision, the court-invited *amicus curiae* [footnote 7] contends that the section complies with the requirement that a legislative alternative to *Miranda* be equally as effective in preventing coerced confessions. See Brief for Paul G. Cassell as *Amicus Curiae* 28–39. We agree with the *amicus'* contention that there are more remedies available for abusive police conduct than there were at the time *Miranda* was decided, see, *e.g., Wilkins* v. *May,* 872 F.2d 190, 194 (CA7 1989) (applying *Bivens* v. *Six Unknown Fed. Narcotics Agents,* 403 U.S. 388 (1971), to hold that a suspect may bring a federal cause of action under the Due Process Clause for police misconduct during custodial interrogation). But we do not agree that these additional measures supplement §3501's protections sufficiently to meet the constitutional minimum. *Miranda* requires procedures that will warn a suspect in custody of his right to remain silent and which will assure the suspect that the exercise of that right will be honored. See, *e.g.,* 384 U.S., at 467. As discussed above, §3501 explicitly eschews a requirement of preinterrogation warnings in favor of an approach that looks to the administration of such warnings as only one factor in determining the voluntariness of a suspect's confession. The additional remedies cited by *amicus* do not, in our view, render them, together with §3501 an adequate substitute for the warnings required by *Miranda.*

The dissent argues that it is judicial overreaching for this Court to hold §3501 unconstitutional unless we hold that the *Miranda* warnings are required by the Constitution, in the sense that nothing else will suffice to satisfy constitutional requirements. *Post,* at 10–11, 22–23. But we need not go farther than *Miranda* to decide this case. In *Miranda,* the Court noted that reliance on the traditional totality-of-the-circumstances test raised a risk of overlooking an involuntary custodial confession, 384 U. S, at 457, a risk that the Court found unacceptably great when the confession is offered in the case in chief to prove guilt. The Court therefore concluded that something more than the totality test was necessary. See *ibid.;* see also *id.,* at 467, 490–491. As discussed above, §3501 reinstates the totality test as sufficient. Section 3501 therefore cannot be sustained if *Miranda* is to remain the law.

Whether or not we would agree with *Miranda*'s reasoning and its resulting rule, were we addressing the issue in the first instance, the principles of *stare decisis* weigh heavily against overruling it now. See, *e.g., Rhode Island* v. *Innis,* 446 U.S. 291, 304 (1980) (Burger, C. J., concurring in judgment) ("The meaning of *Miranda* has become reasonably clear and law enforcement practices have adjusted to its strictures; I would neither overrule *Miranda,* disparage it, nor extend it at this late date"). While " '*stare decisis* is not an inexorable command,' " *State Oil Co.* v. *Khan,* 522 U.S. 3, 20 (1997) (quoting *Payne* v. *Tennessee,* 501 U.S. 808, 828 (1991)), particularly when we are interpreting the Constitution, *Agostini* v. *Felton,* 521 U.S. 203, 235 (1997), "even in constitutional cases, the doctrine carries such persuasive force that we have always required a departure from precedent to be supported by some 'special justification.' " *United States* v. *International Business Machines Corp.,* 517 U.S. 843, 856 (1996) (quoting *Payne, supra,* at 842 (SOUTER, J., concurring) (in turn quoting *Arizona* v. *Rumsey,* 467 U.S. 203, 212 (1984))).

---

[7]Because no party to the underlying litigation argued in favor of §3501's constitutionality in this Court, we invited Professor Paul Cassell to assist our deliberations by arguing in support of the judgment below.

We do not think there is such justification for overruling *Miranda. Miranda* has become embedded in routine police practice to the point where the warnings have become part of our national culture. See *Mitchell* v. *United States,* 526 U.S. 314, 331–332 (1999) (SCALIA, J., dissenting) (stating that the fact that a rule has found " 'wide acceptance in the legal culture' " is "adequate reason not to overrule" it). While we have overruled our precedents when subsequent cases have undermined their doctrinal underpinnings, see, *e.g., Patterson* v. *McLean Credit Union,* 491 U.S. 164, 173 (1989), we do not believe that this has happened to the *Miranda* decision. If anything, our subsequent cases have reduced the impact of the *Miranda* rule on legitimate law enforcement while reaffirming the decision's core ruling that unwarned statements may not be used as evidence in the prosecution's case in chief.

The disadvantage of the *Miranda* rule is that statements which may be by no means involuntary, made by a defendant who is aware of his "rights," may nonetheless be excluded and a guilty defendant go free as a result. But experience suggests that the totality-of-the-circumstances test which §3501 seeks to revive is more difficult than *Miranda* for law enforcement officers to conform to, and for courts to apply in a consistent manner. See, *e.g., Haynes* v. *Washington,* 373 U.S., at 515 ("The line between proper and permissible police conduct and techniques and methods offensive to due process is, at best, a difficult one to draw"). The requirement that *Miranda* warnings be given does not, of course, dispense with the voluntariness inquiry. But as we said in *Berkemer* v. *McCarty,* 468 U.S. 420 (1984), "[c]ases in which a defendant can make a colorable argument that a self-incriminating statement was 'compelled' despite the fact that the law enforcement authorities adhered to the dictates of *Miranda* are rare." *Id.,* at 433, n. 20.

In sum, we conclude that *Miranda* announced a constitutional rule that Congress may not supersede legislatively. Following the rule of *stare decisis,* we decline to overrule *Miranda* ourselves. [footnote 8] The judgment of the Court of Appeals is therefore

Reversed.

---

[8]Various other contentions and suggestions have been pressed by the numerous *amici,* but because of the procedural posture of this case we do not think it appropriate to consider them. See *United Parcel Service, Inc.* v. *Mitchell,* 451 U.S. 56, 60, n. 2 (1981); *Bell* v. *Wolfish,* 441 U.S. 520, 531–532, n. 13 (1979); *Knetsch* v. *United States,* 364 U.S. 361, 370 (1960).

Supreme Court of the United States

NO. 99—5525

CHARLES THOMAS DICKERSON, PETITIONER *V.* UNITED STATES

ON WRIT OF CERTIORARI TO THE UNITED STATES COURT OF APPEALS FOR THE FOURTH CIRCUIT
[June 26, 2000]

Justice Scalia, with whom Justice Thomas joins, dissenting.

Those to whom judicial decisions are an unconnected series of judgments that produce either favored or disfavored results will doubtless greet today's decision as a paragon of moderation, since it declines to overrule *Miranda* v. *Arizona,* 384 U.S. 436 (1966). Those who understand the judicial process will appreciate that today's decision is not a reaffirmation of *Miranda,* but a radical revision of the most significant element of *Miranda* (as of all cases): the rationale that gives it a permanent place in our jurisprudence.

Marbury v. *Madison,* 1 Cranch 137 (1803), held that an Act of Congress will not be enforced by the courts if what it prescribes violates the Constitution of the United States. That was the basis on which *Miranda* was decided. One will search today's opinion in vain, however, for a statement (surely simple enough to make) that what 18 U.S.C. § 3501 prescribes–the use at trial of a voluntary confession, even when a *Miranda* warning or its equivalent has failed to be given—violates the Constitution. The reason the statement does not appear is not only (and perhaps not so much) that it would be absurd, inasmuch as §3501 excludes from trial precisely what the Constitution excludes from trial, viz., compelled confessions; but also that Justices whose votes are needed to compose today's majority are on record as believing that a violation of *Miranda* is *not* a violation of the Constitution. See *Davis* v. *United States,* 512 U.S. 452, 457–458 (1994) (opinion of the Court, in which Kennedy, J., joined); *Duckworth* v. *Eagan,* 492 U.S. 195, 203 (1989) (opinion of the Court, in which Kennedy, J., joined); *Oregon* v. *Elstad,* 470 U.S. 298 (1985) (opinion of the Court by O'Connor, J.); *New York* v. *Quarles,* 467 U.S. 649 (1984) (opinion of the Court by Rehnquist, J.). And so, to justify today's agreed-upon result, the Court must adopt a significant *new,* if not entirely comprehensible, principle of constitutional law. As the Court chooses to describe that principle, statutes of Congress can be disregarded, not only when what they prescribe violates the Constitution, but when what they prescribe contradicts a decision of this Court that "announced a constitutional rule," *ante,* at 7. As I shall discuss in some detail, the only thing that can possibly mean in the context of this case is that this Court has the power, not merely to apply the Constitution but to expand it, imposing what it regards as useful "prophylactic" restrictions upon Congress and the States. That is an immense and frightening antidemocratic power, and it does not exist.

170

It takes only a small step to bring today's opinion out of the realm of power-judging and into the mainstream of legal reasoning: The Court need only go beyond its carefully couched iterations that "*Miranda* is a constitutional decision," *ante,* at 8, that "*Miranda* is constitutionally based," *ante,* at 10, that *Miranda* has "constitutional underpinnings," *ante,* at 10, n. 5, and come out and say quite clearly: "We reaffirm today that custodial interrogation that is not preceded by *Miranda* warnings or their equivalent violates the Constitution of the United States." It cannot say that, because a majority of the Court does not believe it. The Court therefore acts in plain violation of the Constitution when it denies effect to this Act of Congress.

I.

Early in this Nation's history, this Court established the sound proposition that constitutional government in a system of separated powers requires judges to regard as inoperative any legislative act, even of Congress itself, that is "repugnant to the Constitution."

> "So if a law be in opposition to the constitution; if both the law and the constitution apply to a particular case, so that the court must either decide that case conformably to the law, disregarding the constitution; or conformably to the constitution, disregarding the law; the court must determine which of these conflicting rules governs the case." *Marbury, supra,* at 178.

The power we recognized in *Marbury* will thus permit us, indeed require us, to "disregar[d]" §3501, a duly enacted statute governing the admissibility of evidence in the federal courts, only if it "be in opposition to the constitution"—here, assertedly, the dictates of the Fifth Amendment.

It was once possible to characterize the so-called *Miranda* rule as resting (however implausibly) upon the proposition that what the statute here before us permits—the admission at trial of un-*Mirandized* confessions—violates the Constitution. That is the fairest reading of the *Miranda* case itself. The Court began by announcing that the Fifth Amendment privilege against self-incrimination applied in the context of extrajudicial custodial interrogation, see 384 U.S., at 460–467–itself a doubtful proposition as a matter both of history and precedent, see *id.,* at, at 510–511 (Harlan, J., dissenting) (characterizing the Court's conclusion that the Fifth Amendment privilege, rather than the Due Process Clause, governed stationhouse confessions as a "*trompe l'oeil*"). Having extended the privilege into the confines of the station house, the Court liberally sprinkled throughout its sprawling 60-page opinion suggestions that, because of the compulsion inherent in custodial interrogation, the privilege was violated by any statement thus obtained that did not conform to the rules set forth in *Miranda,* or some functional equivalent. See *id.,* at 458 ("Unless adequate protective devices are employed to dispel the compulsion *inherent* in custodial surroundings, *no* statement obtained from the defendant can truly be the product of his free choice") (emphases added); *id.,* at 461 ("An individual swept from familiar surroundings into police custody, surrounded by antagonistic forces, and subjected to the techniques of persuasion described above cannot be otherwise than under compulsion to speak"); *id.,* at 467 ("We have concluded that without proper safeguards the process of in-custody interrogation . . . contains inherently compelling pressures which work to undermine the individual's will to resist and to compel him to speak where he would not otherwise do so freely"); *id.,* 457, n. 26 (noting the "absurdity of denying that a confession obtained under these circumstances is compelled").

The dissenters, for their part, also understood *Miranda*'s holding to be based on the "premise . . . that pressure on the suspect must be eliminated though it be only the subtle influence of the atmosphere and surroundings." *Id.,* at 512 (Harlan, J., dissenting). See also *id.,* at 535 (White, J., dissenting) ("[I]t has never been suggested, until today, that such questioning was so coercive and accused persons so lacking in hardihood that the very first response to the very first question following the commencement of custody must be conclusively presumed to be the product of an overborne will"). And at least one case decided shortly after *Miranda* explicitly confirmed the view. See *Orozco* v. *Texas,* 394 U.S. 324, 326 (1969) ("[T]he use of these admissions obtained in the absence of the required warnings was a flat violation of the Self-Incrimination Clause of the Fifth Amendment as construed in *Miranda*").

So understood, *Miranda* was objectionable for innumerable reasons, not least the fact that cases spanning more than 70 years had rejected its core premise that, absent the warnings and an effective waiver of the right to remain silent and of the (thitherto unknown) right to have an attorney present, a statement obtained pursuant to custodial interrogation was necessarily the product of compulsion. See *Crooker* v. *California,* 357 U.S. 433 (1958) (confession not involuntary despite denial of access to counsel); *Cicenia* v. *Lagay,* 357 U.S. 504 (1958) (same); *Powers* v. *United States,* 223 U.S. 303 (1912) (lack of warnings and counsel did not render statement before United States Commisioner involuntary); *Wilson* v. *United States,* 162 U.S. 613 (1896) (same). Moreover, history and precedent aside, the decision in *Miranda,* if read as an explication of what the Constitution *requires,* is preposterous. There is, for example, simply no basis in reason for concluding that a response to the very first question asked, by a suspect who already *knows* all of the rights described in the *Miranda* warning, is anything other than a volitional act. See *Miranda, supra,* at 533–534 (White, J., dissenting). And even if one assumes that the elimination of compulsion absolutely requires informing even the most knowledgeable suspect of his right to remain silent, it cannot conceivably require the right to have *counsel* present. There is a world of difference, which the Court recognized under the traditional voluntariness test but ignored in *Miranda,* between compelling a suspect to incriminate himself and preventing him from foolishly doing so of his own accord. Only the latter (which is *not* required by the Constitution) could explain the Court's inclusion of a right to counsel and the requirement that it, too, be knowingly and intelligently waived. Counsel's presence is not required to tell the suspect that he *need* not speak; the interrogators can do that. The only good reason for having counsel there is that he can be counted on to advise the suspect that he *should* not speak. See *Watts* v. *Indiana,* 338 U.S. 49, 59 (1949) (Jackson, J., concurring in result in part and dissenting in part) ("[A]ny lawyer worth his salt will tell the suspect in no uncertain terms to make no statement to police under any circumstances").

Preventing foolish (rather than compelled) confessions is likewise the only conceivable basis for the rules (suggested in *Miranda,* see 384 U.S., at 444–445, 473–474), that courts must exclude any confession elicited by questioning conducted, without interruption, after the suspect has indicated a desire to stand on his right to remain silent, see *Michigan* v. *Mosley,* 423 U.S. 96, 105–106 (1975), or initiated by police after the suspect has expressed a desire to have counsel present, see *Edwards* v. *Arizona,* 451 U.S. 477, 484–485 (1981). Nonthreatening attempts to persuade the suspect to reconsider that initial decision are not, without more, enough to render a change of heart the product of anything other than the suspect's free will. Thus, what is most remarkable about the *Miranda* decision—and what made it unacceptable as a matter of straightforward constitutional interpretation in the *Marbury* tradition—is its palpable hostility toward the act of confession *per se,* rather than toward what the Constitution abhors, *compelled* confession. See *United States* v. *Washington,* 431 U.S. 181, 187 (1977) ("[F]ar from being prohibited by the Constitution, admissions of guilt by wrongdoers, if not coerced, are inherently desirable"). The Constitution is not, unlike the *Miranda* majority, offended by a criminal's commendable qualm of conscience or fortunate fit of stupidity. Cf. *Minnick* v. *Mississippi,* 498 U.S. 146, 166–167 (1990) (SCALIA, J., dissenting).

For these reasons, and others more than adequately developed in the *Miranda* dissents and in the subsequent works of the decision's many critics, any conclusion that a violation of the *Miranda* rules *necessarily* amounts to a violation of the privilege against compelled self-incrimination can claim no support in history, precedent, or common sense, and as a result would at least presumptively be worth reconsidering even at this late date. But that is unnecessary, since the Court has (thankfully) long since abandoned the notion that failure to comply with *Miranda*'s rules is itself a violation of the Constitution.

II.

As the Court today acknowledges, since *Miranda* we have explicitly, and repeatedly, interpreted that decision as having announced, not the circumstances in which custodial interrogation runs afoul of the Fifth or Fourteenth Amendment, but rather only "prophylactic" rules that go beyond the right against compelled self-incrimination. Of course the seeds of this "prophylactic" interpretation of *Miranda* were present in the decision itself. See *Miranda, supra,* at 439 (discussing the "necessity for procedures which assure that the [suspect] is accorded his privilege"); *id.,* at 447 ("[u]nless a proper limitation upon custodial interrogation is achieved—such as these decisions will advance—there can be no assurance that practices of this nature will be eradicated"); *id.,* at 457 ("[i]n these cases, we might not find the defendants' statements to have been involuntary in traditional terms"); *ibid.* (noting "concern for adequate safeguards to protect precious Fifth Amendment rights" and the "potentiality for compulsion" in Ernesto Miranda's interrogation). In subsequent cases, the seeds have sprouted and borne fruit: The Court has squarely concluded that it is possible—indeed not uncommon—for the police to violate *Miranda* without also violating the Constitution.

Michigan v. *Tucker,* 417 U.S. 433 (1974), an opinion for the Court written by then-JUSTICE REHNQUIST, rejected the true-to-*Marbury,* failure-to-warn-as-constitutional-violation interpretation of *Miranda.* It held that exclusion of the "fruits" of a *Miranda* violation—the statement of a witness whose identity the defendant had revealed while in custody—was not required. The opinion explained that the question whether the "police conduct complained of directly infringed upon respondent's right against compulsory self-incrimination" was a "separate question" from "whether it instead violated only the prophylactic rules developed to protect that right." *Id.,* at 439. The "procedural safeguards" adopted in *Miranda,* the Court said, "were not themselves rights protected by the Constitution but were instead measures to insure that the right against compulsory self-incrimination was protected," and to "provide practical reinforcement for the right," *id.,* at 444. Comparing the particular facts of the custodial interrogation with the "historical circumstances underlying the privilege," *ibid.,* the Court concluded, unequivocally, that the defendant's statement could not be termed "involuntary as that term has been defined in the decisions of this Court," *id.,* at 445, and thus that there had been no constitutional violation, notwithstanding the clear violation of the "procedural rules later established in *Miranda,*" *ibid.* Lest there be any confusion on the point, the Court reiterated that the "police conduct at issue here did not abridge respondent's constitutional privilege against compulsory self-incrimination, but departed only from the prophylactic standards later laid down by this Court in *Miranda* to safeguard that privilege." *Id.,* at 446. It is clear from our cases, of course, that if the statement in *Tucker* had been obtained in violation of the Fifth Amendment, the statement and its fruits would have been excluded. See *Nix* v. *Williams,* 467 U.S. 431, 442 (1984).

The next year, in *Oregon* v. *Hass,* 420 U.S. 714 (1975), the Court held that a defendant's statement taken in violation of *Miranda* that was nonetheless *voluntary* could be used at trial for impeachment purposes. This holding turned upon the recognition that violation of *Miranda* is not unconstitutional compulsion, since statements obtained in actual violation of the privilege against compelled self-incrimination, "as opposed to . . . taken in violation of *Miranda,*" quite simply "may not be put to any testimonial use whatever against [the defendant] in a criminal trial," including as impeachment evidence. *New Jersey* v. *Portash,* 440 U.S. 450, 459 (1979). See also *Mincey* v. *Arizona,* 437 U.S. 385, 397–398 (1978) (holding that while statements obtained in violation of *Miranda* may be used for impeachment if otherwise trustworthy, the Constitution prohibits "*any* criminal trial use against a defendant of his *involuntary* statement").

Nearly a decade later, in *New York* v. *Quarles,* 467 U.S. 649 (1984), the Court relied upon the fact that "[t]he prophylactic *Miranda* warnings . . . are 'not themselves rights protected by the Constitution,' " *id.,* at 654 (quoting *Tucker, supra,* at 444), to create a "public safety" exception. In that case, police apprehended, after a chase in a grocery store, a rape suspect known to be carrying a gun. After handcuffing and searching him (and finding no gun)—but before reading him his *Miranda* warnings—the police demanded to know where the gun was. The defendant nodded in the direction of some empty cartons and responded that "the gun is over there." The Court held that both the unwarned statement—"the gun is over there"—and the recovered weapon were admissible in the prosecution's case in chief under a "public safety exception" to the "prophylactic rules enunciated in *Miranda.*" 467 U.S., at 653. It explicitly acknowledged that if the *Miranda* warnings were an imperative of the Fifth Amendment itself, such an exigency exception would be impossible, since the Fifth Amendment's bar on compelled self-incrimination is absolute, and its " 'strictures, unlike the Fourth's are not removed by showing reasonableness,' " 467 U.S., at 653, n. 3. (For the latter reason, the Court found it necessary to note that respondent did not "claim that [his] statements were actually compelled by police conduct which overcame his will to resist," *id.,* at 654.)

The next year, the Court again declined to apply the "fruit of the poisonous tree" doctrine to a *Miranda* violation, this time allowing the admission of a suspect's properly warned statement even though it had been preceded (and, arguably, induced) by an earlier inculpatory statement taken in violation of *Miranda. Oregon* v. *Elstad,* 470 U.S. 298 (1985). As in *Tucker,* the Court distinguished the case from those holding that a confession obtained as a result of an unconstitutional search is inadmissible, on the ground that the violation of *Miranda* does not involve an "actual infringement of the suspect's constitutional rights," 470 U.S., at 308. *Miranda,* the Court explained, "sweeps more broadly than the Fifth Amendment itself," and "*Miranda*'s preventive medicine provides a remedy even to the defendant who has suffered no identifiable constitutional harm." 470 U.S., at 307. "[E]rrors [that] are made by law enforcement officers in administering the prophylactic *Miranda* procedures . . . should not breed the same irremediable consequences as police infringement of the Fifth Amendment itself." *Id.,* at 308–309.

In light of these cases, and our statements to the same effect in others, see, *e.g., Davis* v. *United States,* 512 U.S., at 457–458; *Withrow* v. *Williams,* 507 U.S. 680, 690–691 (1993); *Eagan,* 492 U.S., at 203, it is simply no longer possible for the Court to conclude, even if it wanted to, that a violation of *Miranda*'s rules is a violation of the Constitution. But as I explained at the outset, that is what is required before the Court may disregard a law of Congress governing the admissibility of evidence in federal court. The Court today insists that the *decision* in *Miranda* is a "constitutional" one, *ante,* at 1, 8; that it has "constitutional underpinnings", *ante,* at 10, n. 5; a "constitutional basis" and a "constitutional origin", *ante,* at 9, n. 3; that it was "constitutionally based", *ante,* at 10; and that it announced a "constitutional rule," *ante,* at 7, 9, 11, 14. It is fine to play these word games; but what makes a decision "constitutional" in the only sense relevant here—in the sense that renders it impervious to supersession by congressional legislation such as §3501—is the determination that the Constitution *requires* the result that the decision announces and the statute ignores. By disregarding congressional action that concededly does not violate the Constitution, the Court flagrantly offends fundamental principles of separation of powers, and arrogates to itself prerogatives reserved to the representatives of the people.

The Court seeks to avoid this conclusion in two ways: First, by misdescribing these post-*Miranda* cases as mere dicta. The Court concedes only "that there is language in some of our opinions that supports the view" that *Miranda*'s protections are not "constitutionally required." *Ante,* at 8. It is not a matter of *language;* it is a matter of *holdings.* The proposition that failure to comply with *Miranda*'s rules does not establish a constitutional violation was central to the holdings of *Tucker, Hass, Quarles,* and *Elstad.*

The second way the Court seeks to avoid the impact of these cases is simply to disclaim responsibility for reasoned decisionmaking. It says:

> "These decisions illustrate the principle—not that *Miranda* is not a constitutional rule—but that no constitutional rule is immutable. No court laying down a general rule can possibly foresee the various circumstances in which counsel will seek to apply it, and the sort of modifications represented by these cases are as much a normal part of constitutional law as the original decision." *Ante,* at 11.

The issue, however, is not whether court rules are "mutable"; they assuredly are. It is not whether, in the light of "various circumstances," they can be "modifi[ed]"; they assuredly can. The issue is whether, *as mutated and modified,* they must *make sense.* The requirement that they do so is the only thing that prevents this Court from being some sort of nine-headed Caesar, giving thumbs-up or thumbs-down to whatever outcome, case by case, suits or offends its collective fancy. And if confessions procured in violation of *Miranda* are confessions "compelled" in violation of the Constitution, the post-*Miranda* decisions I have discussed do not make sense. The only reasoned basis for their outcome was that a violation of *Miranda* is *not* a violation of the Constitution. If, for example, as the Court acknowledges was the holding of *Elstad,* "the traditional 'fruits' doctrine developed in Fourth Amendment cases" (that the fruits of evidence obtained unconstitutionally must be excluded from trial) does *not* apply to the fruits of *Miranda* violations, *ante,* at 11; and if the reason for the difference is *not* that *Miranda* violations are not constitutional violations (which is plainly and flatly what *Elstad* said); then the Court must come up with some *other* explanation for the difference. (That will take quite a bit of doing, by the way, since it is *not* clear on the face of the Fourth Amendment that evidence obtained in violation of that guarantee must be excluded from trial, whereas it *is* clear on the face of the Fifth Amendment that unconstitutionally compelled confessions cannot be used.) To say simply that "unreasonable searches under the Fourth Amendment are different from unwarned interrogation under the Fifth Amendment," *ante,* at 11–12, is true but supremely unhelpful.

Finally, the Court asserts that *Miranda* must be a "constitutional decision" announcing a "constitutional rule," and thus immune to congressional modification, because we have since its inception applied it to the States. If this argument is meant as an invocation of *stare decisis,* it fails because, though it is true that our cases applying *Miranda* against the States must be reconsidered if *Miranda* is not required by the Constitution, it is likewise true that our cases (discussed above) based on the principle that *Miranda* is *not* required by the Constitution will have to be reconsidered if it *is.* So the *stare decisis* argument is a wash. If, on the other hand, the argument is meant as an appeal to logic rather than *stare decisis,* it is a classic example of begging the question: Congress's attempt to set aside *Miranda,* since it represents an assertion that violation of *Miranda* is not a violation of the Constitution, *also* represents an assertion that the Court has no power to impose *Miranda* on the States. To answer this assertion—not by showing why violation of *Miranda is* a violation of the Constitution—but by asserting that *Miranda does* apply against the States, is to assume precisely the point at issue. In my view, our continued application of the *Miranda* code to the States despite our consistent statements that running afoul of its dictates does not necessarily—or even usually—result in an actual constitutional violation, represents not the source of *Miranda*'s salvation but rather evidence of its ultimate illegitimacy. See generally J. Grano, Confessions, Truth, and the Law 173–198 (1993); Grano, Prophylactic Rules in Criminal Procedure: A Question of Article III Legitimacy, 80 Nw. U. L. Rev. 100 (1985). As JUSTICE STEVENS has elsewhere explained, "[t]his Court's power to require state courts to exclude probative self-incriminatory statements rests entirely on the premise that the use of such evidence violates the Federal Constitution. . . . If the Court does not accept that premise, it must regard the holding in the *Miranda* case itself, as well as all of the federal jurisprudence that has evolved from that decision, as nothing more than an illegitimate exercise of raw judicial power." *Elstad,* 470 U.S., at 370 (dissenting opinion). Quite so.

III.

There was available to the Court a means of reconciling the established proposition that a violation of *Miranda* does not itself offend the Fifth Amendment with the Court's assertion of a right to ignore the present statute. That means of reconciliation was argued strenuously by both petitioner and the United States, who were evidently more concerned than the Court is with maintaining the coherence of our jurisprudence. It is not mentioned in the Court's opinion because, I assume, a majority of the Justices intent on reversing believes that incoherence is the lesser evil. They may be right.

Petitioner and the United States contend that there is nothing at all exceptional, much less unconstitutional, about the Court's adopting prophylactic rules to buttress constitutional rights, and enforcing them against Congress and the States. Indeed, the United States argues that "[p]rophylactic rules are now and have been for many years a feature of this Court's constitutional adjudication." Brief for United States 47. That statement is not wholly inaccurate, if by "many years" one means since the mid-1960's. However, in their zeal to validate what is in my view a lawless practice, the United States and petitioner greatly overstate the frequency with which we have engaged in it. For instance, petitioner cites several cases in which the Court quite simply exercised its traditional judicial power to define the scope of constitutional protections and, relatedly, the circumstances in which they are violated. See *Loretto* v. *Teleprompter Manhattan CATV Corp.,* 458 U.S. 419, 436–437 (1982) (holding that a permanent physical occupation constitutes a *per se* taking); *Maine* v. *Moulton,* 474 U.S. 159, 176 (1985) (holding that the Sixth Amendment right to the assistance of counsel is *actually* "violated when the State obtains incriminating statements by knowingly circumventing the accused's right to have counsel present in a confrontation between the accused and a state agent").

Similarly unsupportive of the supposed practice is *Bruton* v. *United States,* 391 U.S. 123 (1968), where we concluded that the Confrontation Clause of the Sixth Amendment forbids the admission of a nontestifying co-defendant's facially incriminating confession in a joint trial, even where the jury has been given a limiting instruction. That decision was based, not upon the theory that this was desirable protection "beyond" what the Confrontation Clause technically required; but rather upon the self-evident proposition that the inability to cross-examine an available witness whose damaging out-of-court testimony is introduced violates the Confrontation Clause, combined with the conclusion that in these circumstances a mere jury instruction can never be relied upon to prevent the testimony from being damaging, see *Richardson* v. *Marsh,* 481 U.S. 200, 207–208 (1987).

The United States also relies on our cases involving the question whether a State's procedure for appointed counsel's withdrawal of representation on appeal satisfies the State's constitutional obligation to " 'affor[d] adequate and effective appellate review to indigent defendants.' " *Smith v. Robbins*, 528 U.S. ___, ___ (2000) (slip op., at 14) (quoting *Griffin v. Illinois*, 351 U.S. 12, 20 (1956). In *Anders v. California*, 386 U.S. 738 (1967), we concluded that California's procedure governing withdrawal fell short of the constitutional minimum, and we outlined a procedure that *would* meet that standard. But as we made clear earlier this Term in *Smith*, which upheld a procedure *different* from the one *Anders* suggested, the benchmark of constitutionality is the constitutional requirement of adequate representation, and not some excrescence upon that requirement decreed, for safety's sake, by this Court.

In a footnote, the United States directs our attention to certain overprotective First Amendment rules that we have adopted to ensure "breathing space" for expression. See *Gertz v. Robert Welch, Inc.*, 418 U.S. 323, 340, 342 (1974) (recognizing that in *New York Times Co. v. Sullivan*, 376 U.S. 254 (1964), we "extended a measure of strategic protection to defamatory falsehood" of public officials); *Freedman v. Maryland*, 380 U.S. 51, 58 (1965) (setting forth "procedural safeguards designed to obviate the dangers of a censorship system" with respect to motion picture obscenity). In these cases, and others involving the First Amendment, the Court has acknowledged that in order to guarantee that protected speech is not "chilled" and thus forgone, it is in some instances necessary to incorporate in our substantive rules a "measure of strategic protection." But that is because the Court has viewed the importation of "chill" as *itself* a violation of the First Amendment—not because the Court thought it could go beyond what the First Amendment *demanded* in order to provide some prophylaxis.

Petitioner and the United States are right on target, however, in characterizing the Court's actions in a case decided within a few years of *Miranda, North Carolina v. Pearce*, 395 U.S. 711 (1969). There, the Court concluded that due process would be offended were a judge vindictively to resentence with added severity a defendant who had successfully appealed his original conviction. Rather than simply announce that vindictive sentencing violates the Due Process Clause, the Court went on to hold that "[i]n order to assure the absence of such a [vindictive] motivation, . . . the reasons for [imposing the increased sentence] must affirmatively appear" and must "be based upon objective information concerning identifiable conduct on the part of the defendant occurring after the time of the original sentencing proceeding." *Id.*, at 726. The Court later explicitly acknowledged *Pearce*'s prophylactic character, see *Michigan v. Payne*, 412 U.S. 47, 53 (1973). It is true, therefore, that the case exhibits the same fundamental flaw as does *Miranda* when deprived (as it has been) of its original (implausible) pretension to announcement of what the Constitution itself required. That is, although the Due Process Clause may well prohibit punishment based on judicial vindictiveness, the Constitution by no means vests in the courts "any general power to prescribe particular devices 'in order to assure the absence of such a motivation,' " 395 U.S., at 741 (Black, J., dissenting). Justice Black surely had the right idea when he derided the Court's requirement as "pure legislation if there ever was legislation," *ibid.*, although in truth *Pearce*'s rule pales as a legislative achievement when compared to the detailed code promulgated in *Miranda*. [footnote 1]

The foregoing demonstrates that, petitioner's and the United States' suggestions to the contrary notwithstanding, what the Court did in *Miranda* (assuming, as later cases hold, that *Miranda* went beyond what the Constitution actually requires) is in

---

[1]As for *Michigan v. Jackson*, 475 U.S. 625 (1986), upon which petitioner and the United States also rely, in that case we extended to the Sixth Amendment, postindictment, context the *Miranda*-based prophylactic rule of *Edwards v. Arizona*, 451 U.S. 477 (1981), that the police cannot initiate interrogation after counsel has been requested. I think it less a separate instance of claimed judicial power to impose constitutional prophylaxis than a direct, logic-driven consequence of *Miranda* itself.

fact extraordinary. That the Court has, on rare and recent occasion, repeated the mistake does not transform error into truth, but illustrates the potential for future mischief that the error entails. Where the Constitution has wished to lodge in one of the branches of the Federal Government some limited power to supplement its guarantees, it has said so. See Amdt. 14, §5 ("The Congress shall have power to enforce, by appropriate legislation, the provisions of this article"). The power with which the Court would endow itself under a "prophylactic" justification for *Miranda* goes far beyond what it has permitted Congress to do under authority of that text. Whereas we have insisted that congressional action under §5 of the Fourteenth Amendment must be "congruent" with, and "proportional" to, a *constitutional violation,* see *City of Boerne* v. *Flores,* 521 U.S. 507, 520 (1997), the *Miranda* nontextual power to embellish confers authority to prescribe preventive measures against not only constitutionally prohibited compelled confessions, but also (as discussed earlier) foolhardy ones.

I applaud, therefore, the refusal of the Justices in the majority to enunciate this boundless doctrine of judicial empowerment as a means of rendering today's decision rational. In nonetheless joining the Court's judgment, however, they overlook two truisms: that actions speak louder than silence, and that (in judge-made law at least) logic will out. Since there is in fact no other principle that can reconcile today's judgment with the post-*Miranda* cases that the Court refuses to abandon, what today's decision will stand for, whether the Justices can bring themselves to say it or not, is the power of the Supreme Court to write a prophylactic, extraconstitutional Constitution, binding on Congress and the States.

IV.

Thus, while I agree with the Court that §3501 cannot be upheld without also concluding that *Miranda* represents an illegitimate exercise of our authority to review state-court judgments, I do not share the Court's hesitation in reaching that conclusion. For while the Court is also correct that the doctrine of *stare decisis* demands some "special justification" for a departure from longstanding precedent—even precedent of the constitutional variety—that criterion is more than met here. To repeat JUSTICE STEVENS' cogent observation, it is "[o]bviou[s]" that "the Court's power to reverse Miranda's conviction rested *entirely* on the determination that a violation of the Federal Constitution had occurred." *Elstad,* 470 U.S., at 367, n. 9 (dissenting opinion) (emphasis added). Despite the Court's Orwellian assertion to the contrary, it is undeniable that later cases (discussed above) have "undermined [*Miranda*'s] doctrinal underpinnings," *ante,* at 14, denying constitutional violation and thus stripping the holding of its only constitutionally legitimate support. *Miranda*'s critics and supporters alike have long made this point. See Office of Legal Policy, U.S. Dept. of Justice, Report to Attorney General on Law of Pre-Trial Interrogation 97 (Feb. 12, 1986) ("The current Court has repudiated the premises on which *Miranda* was based, but has drawn back from recognizing the full implications of its decisions"); *id.,* at 78 ("*Michigan* v. *Tucker* accordingly repudiated the doctrinal basis of the *Miranda* decision"); Sonenshein, *Miranda* and the Burger Court: Trends and Countertrends, 13 Loyola U. Chi. L. J. 405, 407–408 (1982) ("Although the Burger Court has not overruled *Miranda,* the Court has consistently undermined the rationales, assumptions, and values which gave *Miranda* life"); *id.,* at 425–426 ("Seemingly, the Court [in *Michigan* v. *Tucker*] utterly destroyed both *Miranda*'s rationale and its holding"); Stone, The Miranda Doctrine in the Burger Court, 1977 S. Ct. Rev. 99, 118 ("Mr. Justice Rehnquist's conclusion that there is a violation of the Self-Incrimination Clause only if a confession is involuntary . . . is an outright rejection of the core premises of *Miranda*").

The Court cites *Patterson* v. *McLean Credit Union,* 491 U.S. 164, 173 (1989), as accurately reflecting our standard for overruling, see *ante,* at 14—which I am pleased to accept, even though *Patterson* was speaking of overruling statutory cases and the standard for constitutional decisions is somewhat more lenient. What is set forth there reads as though it was written precisely with the current status of *Miranda* in mind:

> "In cases where statutory precedents have been overruled, the primary reason for the Court's shift in position has been the intervening development of the law, through either the growth of judicial doctrine or further action taken by Congress. Where such changes have removed or weakened the conceptual underpinnings from the prior decision, . . . or where the later law has rendered the decision irreconcilable with competing legal doctrines or policies, . . . the Court has not hesitated to overrule an earlier decision." 491 U.S., at 173.

Neither am I persuaded by the argument for retaining *Miranda* that touts its supposed workability as compared with the totality-of-the-circumstances test it purported to replace. *Miranda*'s proponents cite *ad nauseam* the fact that the Court was called upon to make difficult and subtle distinctions in applying the "voluntariness" test in some 30-odd due process "coerced confessions" cases in the 30 years between *Brown* v. *Mississippi,* 297 U.S. 278 (1936), and *Miranda.* It is not immediately apparent, however, that the judicial burden has been eased by the "bright-line" rules adopted in *Miranda.* In fact, in the 34 years since *Miranda* was decided, this Court has been called upon to decide nearly *60* cases involving a host of *Miranda* issues, most of them predicted with remarkable prescience by Justice White in his *Miranda* dissent. 384 U.S., at 545.

Moreover, it is not clear why the Court thinks that the "totality-of-the-circumstances test . . . is more difficult than *Miranda* for law enforcement officers to conform to, and for courts to apply in a consistent manner." *Ante,* at 14. Indeed, I find myself persuaded by JUSTICE O'CONNOR'S rejection of this same argument in her opinion in *Williams,* 507 U.S., at 711–712 (O'CONNOR, J., joined by REHNQUIST, C. J., concurring in part and dissenting in part):

> "*Miranda,* for all its alleged brightness, is not without its difficulties; and voluntariness is not without its strengths" . . . *Miranda* creates as many close questions as it resolves. The task of determining whether a defendant is in 'custody' has proved to be 'a slippery one.' And the supposedly 'bright' lines that separate interrogation from spontaneous declaration, the exercise of a right from waiver, and the adequate warning from the inadequate, likewise have turned out to be rather dim and ill defined. The totality-of-the-circumstances approach, on the other hand, permits each fact to be taken into account without resort to formal and dispositive labels. By dispensing with the difficulty of producing a yes-or-no answer to questions that are often better answered in shades and degrees, *the voluntariness inquiry often can make judicial decisionmaking easier rather than more onerous.*" (Emphasis added; citations omitted.)

But even were I to agree that the old totality-of-the-circumstances test was more cumbersome, it is simply not true that *Miranda* has banished it from the law and replaced it with a new test. Under the current regime, which the Court today retains in its entirety, courts are frequently called upon to undertake *both* inquiries. That is because, as explained earlier, voluntariness remains the *constitutional* standard, and as such continues to govern the admissibility for impeachment purposes of statements taken in violation of *Miranda,* the admissibility of the "fruits" of such statements, and the admissibility of statements challenged as unconstitutionally obtained *despite* the interrogator's compliance with *Miranda,* see, *e.g., Colorado* v. *Connelly,* 479 U.S. 157 (1986).

Finally, I am not convinced by petitioner's argument that *Miranda* should be preserved because the decision occupies a special place in the "public's consciousness." Brief for Petitioner 44. As far as I am aware, the public is not under the illusion that we are infallible. I see little harm in admitting that we made a mistake in taking away from the people the ability to decide for themselves what protections (beyond those required by the Constitution) are reasonably affordable in the criminal investigatory process. And I see much to be gained by reaffirming for the people the wonderful reality that they govern themselves—which means that "[t]he powers not delegated to the United States by the Constitution" that the people adopted, "nor prohibited . . . to the States" by that Constitution, "are reserved to the States respectively, or to the people," U.S. Const., Amdt. 10. [footnote 2]

* * *

Today's judgment converts *Miranda* from a milestone of judicial overreaching into the very Cheops' Pyramid (or perhaps the Sphinx would be a better analogue) of judicial arrogance. In imposing its Court-made code upon the States, the original opinion at least *asserted* that it was demanded by the Constitution. Today's decision does not pretend that it is—and yet *still* asserts the right to impose it against the will of the people's representatives in Congress. Far from believing that *stare decisis* compels this result, I believe we cannot allow to remain on the books even a celebrated decision—*especially* a celebrated decision—that has come to stand for the proposition that the Supreme Court has power to impose extraconstitutional constraints upon Congress and the States. This is not the system that was established by the Framers, or that would be established by any sane supporter of government by the people.

I dissent from today's decision, and, until §3501 is repealed, will continue to apply it in all cases where there has been a sustainable finding that the defendant's confession was voluntary.

---

[2]The Court cites my dissenting opinion in *Mitchell* v. *United States,* 526 U.S. 314, 331–332 (1999), for the proposition that "the fact that a rule has found 'wide acceptance in the legal culture' is 'adequate reason not to overrule' it." *Ante,* at 13. But the legal culture is not the same as the "public's consciousness"; and unlike the rule at issue in *Mitchell* (prohibiting comment on a defendant's refusal to testify) *Miranda* has been continually criticized by lawyers, law enforcement officials, and scholars since its pronouncement (not to mention by Congress, as §3501 shows). In *Mitchell,* moreover, the constitutional underpinnings of the earlier rule had not been demolished by subsequent cases.